The Development of Sport in Donegal, 1880–1935

The Development of Sport in Donegal, 1880–1935

Conor Curran

CORK UNIVERSITY PRESS

First published in 2015 by
Cork University Press
Youngline Industrial Estate
Pouladuff Road, Togher
Cork, Ireland

British Library Cataloguing in Publication Data
A CIP catalogue record for this book is available from the British Library.

ISBN 978-1-78205-120-6

Typeset by Tower Books, Ballincollig, County Cork
Printed in Poland by Hussar Books

www.corkuniversitypress.com

Contents

Acknowledgements

As a young goalkeeper at the Ian Rush International soccer tournament in Wales in 1991, I was particularly aware of the fact that I came from a strong Gaelic football area and that there was only one other player from the south/south-west of the county in the Donegal under-fourteen and under-sixteen squads. In writing this book I hope that I have, in some way, managed to explain the reasons for this cultural diversity.

This book would not have been written without the assistance of my two PhD supervisors, Professor Mike Cronin and Professor Matthew Taylor. Professor Cronin's assistance and knowledge has transformed the way I think about history, society and sport, while Professor Taylor's expertise has also made me look at the writing of sports history and the development of society in a different way.

Professor Richard Holt, Professor Dilwyn Porter and Dr Neil Carter also provided much advice during my trips to England and deserve thanks for their friendliness and encouragement. I would also like to thank Dr Dónal McAnallen and Dr Richard McElligott for their thoughts on the GAA in Ulster and Kerry respectively. The encouragement and friendship of Dr Tom Hunt, Dr Patrick Bracken and Dr David Toms was also a great help at various stages throughout the writing of this book. I am also grateful to the staff of the National Library of Ireland in Kildare Street and those working at the National Archives in Bishop Street for their help in retrieving source material. The staff of the Cardinal O'Fiaich Library in Armagh also deserve thanks for their assistance during my visit there, while I am also indebted to the staff of the Grand Lodge of the Freemasons Library in Molesworth Street for their help. I am also thankful to the staff of PRONI in Belfast for their help in locating, and gaining permission to examine, the papers of the Irish Football Association, and Sarah O'Shea of the Football Association of Ireland for granting me access to their archives. I am also grateful to the staff of the GAA's archive in Croke Park for their assistance in viewing the organisation's records. Those working in the Folklore Commission Archives and in the Research Department at University College Dublin also gave significant archival assistance while in Donegal, the staff of the County Archives at Lifford and the Central Library, Letterkenny, were very helpful. I would also like to thank Edward Molloy for providing me with a number of books on the GAA in Donegal which otherwise would not have been accessible, and John McConnell for providing me with the photograph which appears on the cover of this book.

I would like to express my gratitude to Lee-Ann Anderson, Permissions and Licensing Administrator of Taylor and Francis, for allowing me to republish parts of my article 'The Development of Gaelic football and Soccer Zones in County Donegal, 1884–1934', first published in *Sport in History*, volume 32, number 3. In addition, I am thankful to Professor James S. Donnelly Jr., the co-editor of the journal *Éire-Ireland*, for granting me permission to publish parts of my article, 'Sport and Cultural Nationalism: the Conflict between Association and Gaelic football in Donegal, 1905–1934', first published in volume 48, 1 and 2, which forms the basis for chapter seven of this book. I would also like to thank Maria O'Donovan and the staff of Cork University Press for their commitment and effort shown in bringing this book into publication.

I am also grateful to the staff of the History Department of St Patrick's College in Drumcondra, in particular to Professor James Kelly who initially suggested I take up the study of sports history and culture, and to Dr Matthew Stout who drew the maps for this book. I would also like to thank Dr Dáire Keogh, Dr Daithí Ó Corráin, Dr Juliana Adelman and Dr Carla King for their advice during my time in the college as a student and employee, while Professor Diarmaid Ferriter was also very helpful to me during his time there. Finally I would like to thank my family for their never-ending support and encouragement, and my girlfriend Joanne O'Keeffe for her kindness and understanding of my passion for sport and history.

Abbreviations

AGM	Annual General Meeting
AOH	Ancient Order of Hibernians
AC	*Anglo-Celt*
BH and NWA	*Ballyshannon Herald and North-Western Advertiser*
CC	Cricket Club
CE	Civil Engineer
DJ	*Derry Journal*
DP and DN	*Derry People and Donegal News*
DP and TN	*Derry People and Tír Conaill News*
DS	*Derry Standard*
DC	District Clerk
DI	District Inspector
DL	Deputy Lieutenant
DD	*Donegal Democrat*
DI	*Donegal Independent*
DPP	*Donegal People's Press*
DV	*Donegal Vindicator*
FH	*Fermanagh Herald*
FSW	*Football and Sports Weekly*
FA	Football Association
FAI	Football Association of Ireland
FC	Football Club
GA	*Gaelic Athlete*
GAA	Gaelic Athletic Association
GFC	Gaelic Football Club
HMS	His Majesty's Ship
IR	*Impartial Reporter*
IAAA	Irish Amateur Athletic Association
IPP	Irish Parliamentary Party
IRB	Irish Republican Brotherhood

ABBREVIATIONS

JP	Justice of the Peace
LS	*Londonderry Sentinel*
NACA	National Athletic and Cycling Association
NS	National School
PRONI	Public Records Office of Northern Ireland
RC	Rugby Club
RIC	Royal Irish Constabulary
TD	Teachta Dála
UH	*Ulster Herald*
YMCA	Young Men's Christian Association

INTRODUCTION

During the nineteenth century, sport underwent a revolution that was heavily influenced by the social and economic changes brought about by the Industrial Revolution in England. Traditional games became modernised and codified, while commercialised matches and events were staged in newly-built stadia in cities before huge crowds, as well as in the less developed venues of suburban areas.[1] How this sporting 'revolution' affected the development of sport at a micro level, in a peripheral Irish setting, has received only limited attention. The growth of sport in Donegal, a rather isolated county lying in the north-west of Ireland, but at the time part of the United Kingdom and the British Empire, has thus far received little analysis. Many regions where sport developed into a major commercial enterprise in England and Scotland in the late nineteenth century had decisive factors which, as will be seen, were lacking or poorly developed in Donegal. Some areas of these two countries, in particular, can be defined as having had a central role within the sporting 'revolution' and the development of modern sport. For example, John Bale has shown how areas associated with the growth of professional soccer in Britain are heavily linked with England's industrial core, which stretched from Merseyside and Lancashire to Greater London, with Central Scotland also noted for its importance, but being seen as less influential.[2] The organisation of governing bodies for codification and competitions was a feature of sport's development at a macro level and in particular, competitive structures for association football were the earliest to be developed and extended furthest.[3] Competitions such as the English FA Cup, first staged in 1871, the Scottish FA Cup (1873), the Welsh FA Cup (1877) and a number of national and regional leagues added greatly to the spread of interest in association football in Britain, while the latter years of the nineteenth century saw significant growth in competitive structures for cricket teams in the midlands and north of England.[4]

Neil Tranter is, however, careful to point out that the growth of sport in the late Victorian/Edwardian era was not a uniform development throughout Britain and that regional variations were commonplace. He highlights the case of East Northumberland and Stirling where the fragile existence of clubs in a number of sports was caused mainly by financial problems.[5] Therefore, while at a macro level there were clear patterns and trends in the rates at which sport developed, some regional areas experienced discontinuity and a failure to develop permanent structures for the spread of sport. Tranter's assertion, made in 1998, that 'beneath the level of the grand and the famous there is a history of the more mundane and obscure still waiting to be satisfactorily uncovered', still rings true.[6]

Many of the problems behind the slow development of sport in Donegal stemmed from the county's failure to industrialise and develop second- and third-level education at this time, while the slow evolution of transport and communications networks were also a major hindrance. As Mike Cronin has stated, in the late nineteenth century, 'the absence of modernising forces across most of Ireland meant that many of the social and economic changes, which would empower the sporting "revolution" in Britain, were absent'.[7] It was in Belfast and Dublin that patterns of sporting development in Ireland most resembled those of England's industrialised cities.[8] The case of County Donegal provides a clear example of how sport functioned at a micro level in a peripheral Irish county and how events in parts of late nineteenth-century England – which saw a transformation in levels of codification, the institutionalisation of leagues and cups and the development of professional structures, with the mass support they drew – failed to have a serious effect on the county's sporting infrastructure. By the end of the second decade of the twentieth century, Donegal's competitive sporting calendar was still relatively empty and the majority of its sporting teams remained confined to playing friendly matches. By 1920 team sports were limited to Gaelic games and soccer and, even then, not every village or town could boast of these clubs, with local enthusiasm and patronage usually the determining factor in a club's existence. With the exception of the administrative structures of the GAA, competitive sport generally remained localised and attempts to bring in or unite a wider sporting community throughout the county were generally unsuccessful. At times links with sporting bodies in bordering counties were more prominent.[9] Most of Donegal's soccer and GAA clubs did not own their own grounds and the county lacked a centralised sports arena for Gaelic games or association football. In addition, cricket, hockey and rugby failed to attract a significant following throughout the county.

This book is the first comprehensive study of sport in Donegal, focusing on the period from 1880 until 1935. In assessing developments at a local and national level, it examines how structures for competitions and teams underwent significant change within the county and throughout Ireland from the late Victorian period until the early years of the Irish Free State. Donegal was a peripheral area and was not affected by the sporting 'revolution' to the same extent as most parts of Britain, with the growth of sport in the county taking place at much slower rates of development. However, this does not mean that sport was not able to develop there. This book will illustrate the incomplete nature of the Irish sporting 'revolution' and how the growth of sport in Donegal relied mainly on local individuals' enthusiasms rather than on national, or even provincial, administrative agencies. Of particular importance in the decision to undertake an examination of sport is the diversity of the county – socially, culturally and physically – which means that it differed from a number of other Irish counties and many sports lacked a particular unity in their administration to work effectively. How the growth of sport in Donegal contrasted with wider developments will be examined as, despite these failures, by the end of 1934 there were at least sixty-seven Gaelic football teams in operation and 103 soccer teams.[10] Zones where these codes were most popular were clearly evident. Competitive structures, organised by the GAA's County Board, were in place for both Gaelic football and hurling at various levels and public support, although varying throughout the county, was sufficient to give the GAA a firm footing within society.

The development of Gaelic and association football will be given particular emphasis as these were the most popular team sports within the county by the middle of the 1930s. However, the GAA and soccer in Donegal did not develop in isolation from other sports. Cricket, hockey and rugby were all being organised in the latter decades of the nineteenth century, but were generally seen as 'minority' sports by the early part of the twentieth century and continued to have less prominent roles within Donegal society for the rest of the period covered here. These codes will also be explored in detail as they attracted strong interest from the county's Protestant population, although Roman Catholics were by no means excluded from participation in them. Significantly, the role of sport within Protestant culture in rural Ireland has received scarce academic attention. (It is important to note here that the term 'Protestant' will be used to cover all strands of Protestantism while acknowledging the different denominations within this religious category such as Protestant Episcopalians, Presbyterians and Methodists.) The GAA has mainly been viewed by historians as a nationalist, Roman Catholic organisation, but not every Catholic was an active 'nationalist' and, as David Fitzpatrick has stated, 'the geographer's definition of "nationalists" must embrace not only heroes but opportunists, not only dreamers but incurious followers' and there have been 'nationalists of distinguishable categories'.[11] Similarly, not every Protestant who played sports such as hockey, cricket or rugby was a unionist, but the terms 'unionist' and 'nationalist' will be used throughout to denote general allegiances, despite variations in the levels of enthusiasm afforded to wider politics by those in Donegal's sporting communities.

This book will examine the role of sport within the county, and a number of players, officials, supporters and patrons of sporting clubs and committees within Donegal society will be identified. Why some sports clubs developed in certain areas as opposed to others within the county will also be examined. In addition, this study of sport in Donegal is located within the wider context of sports history and Irish social, economic, cultural and political history and will add to the historiography and understanding of sports in both Ireland and Britain and to the historiography of Donegal generally. The lack of research undertaken on sport in Donegal is of particular significance here. The twenty-first century has seen an increase in the volume of work on sport's relationship with society in Ireland undertaken at doctoral level, reflecting its growing acceptance as a topic for study in universities. The publication of Tom Hunt's ground-breaking examination of sport in Westmeath (2007), which set the standard for the study of local sport in Ireland, has been followed by other doctoral works including Liam O'Callaghan's analysis of rugby in Munster (2011) and specific studies of the GAA undertaken by Dónal McAnallen in 2010 and Richard McElligott in 2011.[12] Lengthy examinations of the GAA in Dublin and cricket in County Tipperary have also added greatly to our understanding of sport at county level and illustrate the importance of empirical research in studies of this type.[13]

Despite this progress, the majority of Irish historians have largely ignored sport in their assessments of how the country developed. Gaelic games have received some attention, although generally only the political aspects of the GAA, and initial specialist literature on that organisation's history focuses particularly on this.[14] Diarmaid Ferriter's assertion – 'in truth the evolution of the GAA was not a narrow pursuit in sporting Anglophobia but Irish sport embracing the British model of sport codification and mirroring the European, African and Asian trend of ball games becoming an important part of the social fabric' – is a more suitable reflection of trends of development within the GAA.[15] Until recently, an overemphasis on the role played by the Irish Republican Brotherhood and the 'Ban' overshadowed many of the sporting and other social activities which took place.[16] As late as 1998, Mike Cronin was able to correctly state that the involvement of the Irish Republican Brotherhood in the early GAA has been a key theme in the writing of GAA history in his analysis of these works.[17] More recent work by Cronin and Paul Rouse and a number of other academics has done much to place the organisation in the context of the sporting 'revolution'. In assessing the Association's contribution to Irish society and its people, these thematic publications, featuring a range of authors, have done much to shed light on the role of the GAA.[18] Therefore, an alternative, less political version of early events within the Association is now being established.

In illustrating the way the GAA developed in Donegal, this book challenges the macro-argument of W.F. Mandle that the early GAA was an overtly political organisation and contends that national politics were not at the root of the growth of the GAA in Donegal. His statement that 'until 1905 the GAA was principally a nationalist, indeed an extreme nationalist, organisation that played its games and ran its meetings largely as a nationalist exercise' cannot be applied to Donegal.[19] In this county it was a slow development and a much more laboured one than has been acknowledged throughout the GAA's historiography. The work of 'Carbery' has offered little on the early GAA in Donegal and, while briefly addressing the 1905–07 County Board, he makes the assertion that this development continued 'with tenacious earnestness' while failing to recognise its subsequent decline.[20] When the Association did finally become established in Donegal in the 1920s, it was more to do with the enthusiasm of individuals and an absence of existing consistent structures for team sports for young men than with any strong political identity. The power of agency in the spread of sport is shown as the GAA in Donegal relied primarily on individuals' enthusiasm. Academic work on the history of Donegal, with the exception of a handful of articles and recent publications, has neglected the place of sport within Donegal society.[21] A small number of Donegal's GAA clubs have published interesting accounts of their involvement in the early GAA, based mainly on oral and newspaper sources.[22] While all noteworthy, these were generally written in isolation from national and international sporting trends and shed little light on how their development fitted into, or was influenced by, these macro level developments.

This book will explore the development of sport in Donegal and its clubs and competitions in greater detail than my 2007 Master's thesis, 'The Social Importance of Gaelic Games and Association Football, 1884 to 1914' and it provides a much more comprehensive analysis of the rivalry between Gaelic football and soccer in the county.[23] It will also cover a longer timespan than the earlier thesis, incorporating the period from 1880 until 1935. This is important as the GAA in Donegal did not begin to develop until the 1920s and did not become firmly established until the following decade. It also allows for an assessment of the GAA in Donegal's role in Ireland's struggle for independence and for an examination of why the GAA failed to spread throughout the county.

Major studies of Irish soccer by Neal Garnham, Alan Bairner and John Sugden have failed to address the development of the game in Donegal to any great extent, although a small number of clubs have published their own histories.[24] Therefore, its early growth throughout Donegal and how this fitted into developments throughout Ireland, will be explored further here. The conflict between Gaelic games and soccer in Donegal has attracted little interest from historians and is examined in full in this book. While Dónal McAnallen has looked at this theme in an overview of the difficulties the GAA faced in Ulster in the period from 1884 to 1945, he focuses largely on events outside Donegal.[25] Neal Garnham also addressed the core conflict in *Association Football and Society in Pre-partition Ireland* but with little reflection on what was happening in the north-west.[26] Outside Ulster, there have been only a few attempts to address this topic. Those playing and organising cricket and soccer at the turn of the nineteenth century in County Westmeath were targeted in the local press.[27] Unlike Donegal, not every county in Ireland suffered from this conflict of interests. A study of the GAA in Dublin has illustrated that no rivalry existed between the administrative bodies of Gaelic games and soccer.[28] In Cork and Limerick, it was rugby which came into conflict with the GAA.[29]

As shown by Michael Oriard in his study of press coverage of college football in America, newspapers heightened public awareness of sport and helped the spread of the game.[30] Andrew Walker has argued that association football in Lincolnshire was primarily experienced through the contemporary press.[31] In an Irish setting, Eoghan Corry has stated that at the beginning of the 1900s, as the GAA grew in confidence, its members were eager to gain attention in the media and has discussed the relationship between the GAA and the press in a recently published book.[32] Cronin, Duncan and Rouse have also examined the relationship between the media and the GAA. Donegal, however, has received little attention in this regard but this relationship will be fully discussed for the first time here.[33] In Donegal, the GAA–soccer conflict was facilitated and debated through the local press and, given the lack of remaining club records and other archival sources, most of what was written on this is preserved through these newspapers.

According to David Russell, 'there is often a tendency to talk in generalizations, to speak of certain sports as "national" or concentrated in the "north" or "industrial regions"'.[34] The geography and regional variations of sports in Britain has been well investigated by historians such as Russell, John Bale, Mike Huggins, Alan Metcalfe and Tony Collins and an attempt will be made to build on this work within an Irish setting.[35] In examining this competition between sports and the geography of a variety of codes, this book takes a unique look at how sport developed in a peripheral Irish county.

Although research of sporting patterns throughout Ireland is therefore still in its infancy, two counties in particular, which both received significant academic attention at doctoral level, were chosen for the purpose of providing a comparison with Donegal. A number of aspects of the development of the GAA in Donegal will therefore be contrasted with that of another peripheral county, Kerry, located in the south-west of Ireland and with a similar geographical structure, an emphasis on agriculture and also a lack of major industries, and in many ways similar to Donegal in its rural location. A comparison of sporting activity with that in Westmeath will also be provided. Westmeath, lying in the centre of Ireland, was 'a very untypical county', had good transport links with Dublin and the Land War had little effect there. It was also politically stable and prosperous in the late nineteenth century.[36]

Women generally remained on the periphery of sport in Donegal in the period covered here and for this reason this book will focus mainly on male team sports, although an interesting theme for future research would be the failure to develop camogie throughout the county despite the formation of an association for this sport in Letterkenny in February of 1934.[37]

Chapter breakdown

A thematic approach is generally used throughout. Chapter 1 outlines the social, economic and political state of Donegal in the late nineteenth century; it illustrates how society was developing in the opening decades of the twentieth century and attempts to set the scene for the spread of sport in the county. It addresses the factors which, while benefiting the growth of sport in England at this time, hindered its progress in Donegal. However, of great importance to the development of sport in the north-east of the county was its close location to Derry city. A number of political changes towards the end of the nineteenth century also paved the way for Catholics to gain a greater say within society, and in turn, later raise the profile of Gaelic games in the county. Chapter 2 provides an assessment of the state of sport in Donegal in the late nineteenth and early twentieth centuries, with particular emphasis on the role played by pre-codified hurling within society. The place of regattas and annual athletic sports within the county is discussed while an examination of cricket, hockey and rugby clubs allows for an assessment of the religious composition of those playing and organising these sports, with particular attention being paid to cricket. The role of sport in Ballyshannon is examined in detail, as the publication of two newspapers there in the late nineteenth century allows for a comprehensive analysis of associational culture within the town.

Chapter 3 examines the reasons for the weak state of the GAA in Donegal between 1884 and 1905. It illustrates how there was only isolated interest shown in Gaelic games in the county in this period and that early attempts to get the Association up and running generally took place in the north-east, with the help of the GAA in Derry city. In Chapter 4, the reasons for the successes and failures of Donegal's first GAA County Board will be considered. Similarly, the development of the GAA after the re-founding of the County Board in 1919 will be assessed in Chapter 5, along with the political background to this organisation. It will show that the 1920s witnessed a tough struggle to get the Association on a firm footing. While the effects of the War of Independence and the Civil War were not as severe on the GAA in Donegal as in other counties, a number of other factors threatened the development of clubs. In Chapter 6, the development of association football in Donegal will be examined and it will show why, by the early 1930s, Inishowen, along with a concentrated area west of Lough Swilly, was primarily a soccer zone, while the game continued to be played in areas such as the west coast and the north-east. The final chapter examines the conflict between organisers of Gaelic football and soccer in the period from 1905 until 1934 and assesses the role played by newspapers and the presence of the GAA's 'Ban' on foreign games in fostering this competition between sports. In its entirety, this book will demonstrate how and why a delayed sporting revolution functioned in a peripheral Irish region.

1

DONEGAL: THE SOCIAL CONTEXT

Introduction

The case of Donegal provides strong evidence that the sporting 'revolution', which took place in parts of Britain in the late nineteenth century, was difficult to replicate without sufficient industry, transport and financial backing to support the development of clubs and governing bodies.[1] The sparse population and physical geography of the county was also a hindrance. Comprising 1,197,154 acres and lying in the north-west of the province of Ulster, Donegal is, by area, the fourth largest county in Ireland but by the 1880s its infrastructure was still quite underdeveloped.[2] It had been organised into a coherent structure in 1585 when it was formally recognised as a 'shire' and its boundaries slowly took shape in the decades following this.[3] Despite this, whether or not the county of Donegal was ever truly united, with its marked regional differences, is debatable. Patrick Fitzgerald has stated that 'all counties, of course, exhibit local variation but Donegal, not least in terms of its social and economic history, seemed unusually hard to represent as having had a particular "county" experience'.[4] The ways in which Donegal differed as a county from two other peripheral Irish counties, Mayo and Kerry, and the geographical and economic variations which existed within the county, will be examined here. Most sports in Donegal in the late nineteenth century lacked a uniting administrative board and activity was often restricted to local initiations, often depending on the enthusiasm of individual clubs and the number of nearby teams to interact with; the social conditions that were a significant factor in this situation are addressed here.

The nineteenth-century demography and geography of Donegal

Like much of Ireland, Donegal was affected by the mid-nineteenth-century famine that afflicted the country. The Great Famine, which took place between 1846 and 1851, had a devastating effect on Irish society. It caused the deaths of one million people out of a population of 8.25 million at its peak, and the migration of 1.5 million over a ten-year period from 1845 to 1855.[5] While the province of Ulster was not as badly affected as the west and south of the country, it was Leinster which suffered the least.[6] Donegal, with an average annual rate of excess deaths (or 'the number over and above those who would have died from the usual causes') of 10.7 per thousand between 1846 and 1851, fell below the national average and did not fare as badly as other areas, such as Cavan, where the rate was 42.7.[7] This was because seasonal migration and emigration were firmly established and this gave many people a chance to escape while the famine was still in its early stages.[8] Donegal, at the time of the Great Famine, had been divided into a number of Poor Law Unions which, in 1838, had been organised throughout Ireland to relieve the hardship of the poor who could be admitted to workhouses, based within the area covered by these unions. These were located in Ballyshannon (which also covered parts of Fermanagh and Leitrim), Donegal town, Dunfanaghy, Glenties, Carndonagh, Letterkenny, Milford and Stranorlar. These towns had their own workhouses where the destitute poor, including 'widows with two or more children' and people of an old age or those suffering from illness or disabilities were admitted and were entitled to meals and beds although they also had to work.[9] The mixed nature of the famine's impact on Donegal, and the organisational spread of the Poor Law Unions, are illustrative of the geography of the county.

While sporting events such as athletic meetings and regattas had already taken place as well as the traditional game of camán in many areas in Donegal, it was in the late nineteenth century that the development of clubs in codified sports began to increase. By the end of the 1880s codified matches had been played within the county in rugby, association and Gaelic football, hurling and cricket, although linking clubs for games was not easy as Donegal contained a number of geographical and economic variations. One reporter summarised these when he stated in 1883 that

> The county of Donegal may be roughly regarded as being divided into three parts. A wild stretch of barren waste and mountain runs through the middle of the county from north to south, and is practically uninhabited; the eastern portion of Donegal is well settled, and the people comfortable; but the western portions of the county are congested in some parts and waste in others.[10]

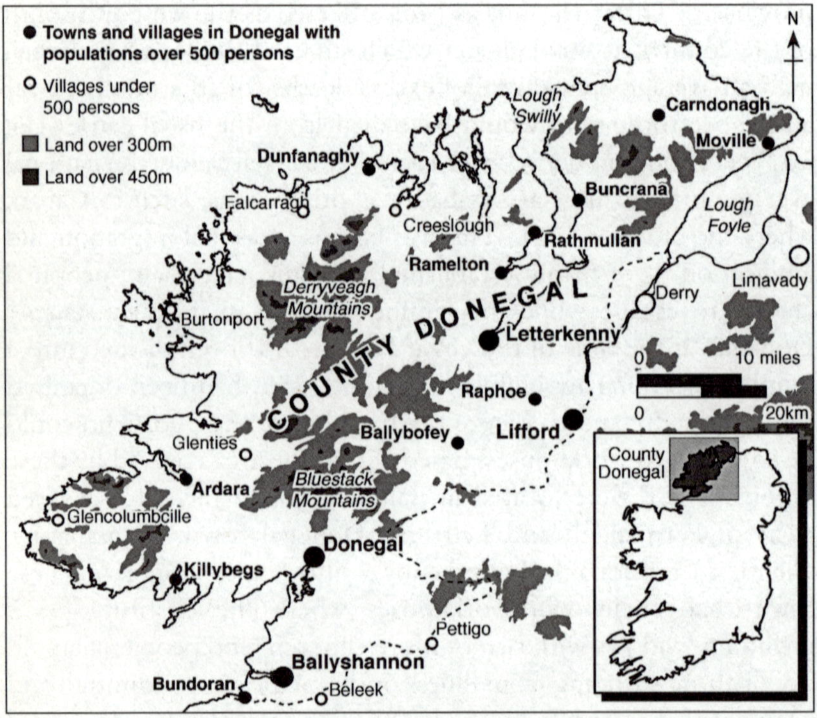

Fig. 1.1: Towns and villages of County Donegal with populations over 500 persons, 1881
SOURCE: *Thom's Official Directory 1884*, p. 1057

Figure 1.1 highlights the geography of Donegal, which is divided by the Derryveagh mountains in the north-west and the Blue Stack mountains further south. This rugged landscape meant that the west and east of the county remained divided, physically, culturally and economically. While Dublin's population was 348,525 and Belfast had a population of 208,122 in 1881, Donegal had only two towns with populations of over 2,000, Ballyshannon and Letterkenny.[11]

Not all towns and villages in Donegal were sufficiently developed to earn a mention in *Thom's Official Directory for the Kingdom of Great Britain and Ireland* in the early 1880s and only those with over 500 inhabitants were noted. As can be seen in Table 1.1 only four other towns, Ramelton, Moville, Ballybofey and Donegal town, were inhabited by over 1,000 people, while there were only nine other villages with populations of over 500 persons. These were Raphoe, Buncrana, Killybegs, Carndonagh, Bundoran, Dunfanaghy, Ardara, Rathmullan and Lifford.[12] Significantly, there were only three villages to the west of the Derryveagh and the Blue Stack mountains with populations of over 500 people. One of these was Dunfanaghy in the north-west while Ardara and Killybegs in the south-west were also more densely populated than other areas around the coast. The majority of County Donegal's more urban areas were located in the north, north-east and south of the county.

TABLE 1.1
Towns and villages of County Donegal inhabited by over 500 persons, 1881

Town/village	*Population in 1881*
Ballyshannon	2,840
Letterkenny	2,188
Donegal	1,416
Ramelton	1,406
Moville	1,129
Ballybofey	1,009
Raphoe	986
Buncrana	764
Killybegs	764
Carndonagh	726
Bundoran	703
Dunfanaghy	598
Ardara	552
Rathmullan	515
Lifford	511

SOURCE: *Thom's Official Directory, 1884*, p.1057

David Russell has noted the influence of 'cultural boundaries' on the development of sporting patterns in his study of rugby and soccer zones in Lancashire and Yorkshire. He states that 'it is obvious that certain areas, whether because of topography, urban structure, economic base or more likely a marriage of all three, enjoyed clearly defined cultural patterns and identities'.[13] In particular, 'the spread of soccer from East Lancashire in the early 1880s stopped virtually at the Yorkshire boundary not because of some mystical force exerted by the boundary line, but because that line runs through the Pennines.'[14] The influence of the geology of a region should also be taken into consideration in accounting for the divergence in interest levels in soccer and Gaelic football throughout Donegal. Certainly the geography of the county meant that some areas, and communities, remained isolated from each other.

As will be shown later, religious denomination played a significant part in the decision to play certain sports available within the county. There were a number of religious denominations to be found in Donegal in 1881. Roman Catholics made up 76.5 per cent of the total population of 206,035; 12 per cent belonged to the Church of Ireland while just over 10 per cent were Presbyterians. Methodists made up just 1 per cent of the population.[15] The West Donegal region was mainly inhabited by Roman Catholics and was badly affected by seasonal migration to Scotland and the Laggan. It contains the Rosses, which is made up of the parishes of Templecrone and Lettermacaward, with Dungloe the only present-day town located in this area.[16] The Rosses was largely isolated from the more commercialised trading centres of Derry, Letterkenny and Strabane in the late nineteenth century as the area had no railway and piers while the road network was also inadequate.[17] Further north, the parishes of Gweedore and Cloughaneely make up the rest of the north-west coastal area and like the Rosses, agriculturally this is a poor region.

It is also important to distinguish how some parts of East Donegal differed culturally from other areas in the county as this had significance in the development of sport. As shown in Figure 1.2 and in Appendix 1, there were only seven, out of Donegal's fifty-two parishes, which had a majority Protestant population in 1881. These were all located in the east of the county and can be identified on the map as 1. the parish of Aghanunshin (58 per cent Protestant), 2. All

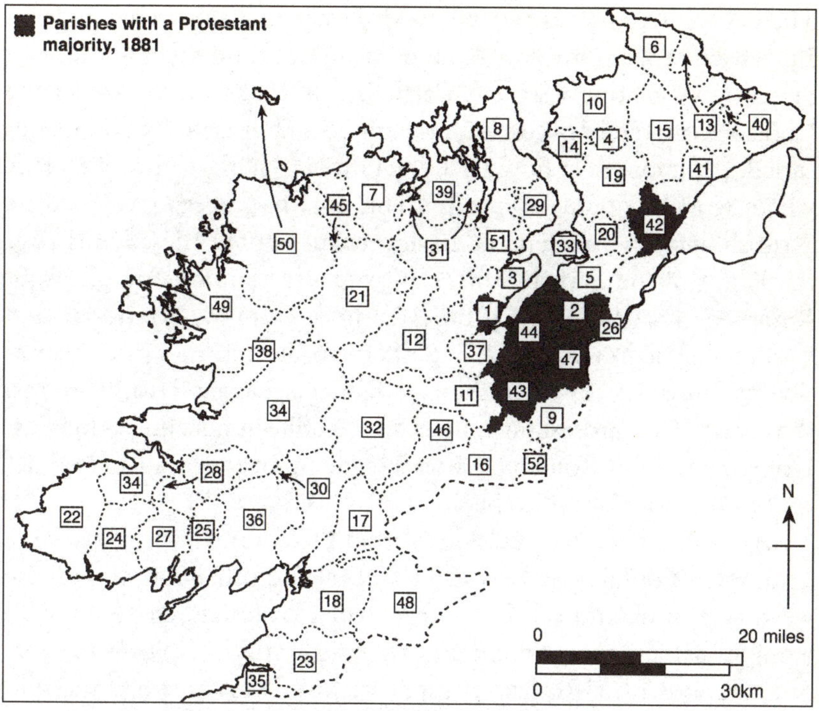

Fig. 1.2: Parishes of Donegal with a majority Protestant population, 1881. For a breakdown of these areas and figures see Appendix 1

SOURCE: 'Census of Ireland for the year 1881. Religious professions of the people. Table XXVIII. Religious professions and sexes of the inhabitants, and number of families, in each parish in the county of Donegal', pp. 451–52.
Retrieved from http://parlipapers.chadwyck.co.uk.jproxy.nuim.ie/fulltext/read-view.do?area=hcpp&id=1882-058905&source=&pagenum=452&resultNum=34&entries=187&queryId=..%2Fsession%2F1406552477_8061&backto=FULLREC&fromSearchHistory=&searchWithin=county+of+donegal&showall=&enlarge=Y [Accessed 28 July 2014].
Map adapted from 'Ulster Historical Foundation: Civil parishes of Donegal', retrieved from http://www.ancestryireland.com/civil-parish-maps-for-ulster/civil-parishes-of-county-donegal/ [Accessed 3 August 2014]

Saints (56 per cent), 26. Killea (64 per cent), 42. Muff (52 per cent), 43. Raphoe (58 per cent), 44. Raymoghy (55 per cent) and 47. Taughboyne (60 per cent).[18] As Lecky stated in 1908, the East Donegal Laggan Valley area was 'largely Protestant' and a more affluent region than the west of the county where the land was mountainous and poorer. This latter area was mostly populated by Roman Catholics and his assertion that 'there are two Donegals – an outer and an inner' summed up the divides between these areas.[19]

The Laggan region was generally a fertile area of land stretching from Inishowen at the bottom of Lough Swilly and running in a southerly direction past Stranorlar and Castlefin, although the centre of the Laggan is located between Letterkenny and Derry and its boundaries varied, depending on how far farmers were willing to travel to fairs where workers could be hired.[20] This area had been developed by Scottish and English settlers, having been granted these lands after the Flight of the Earls in 1607.[21] Carrigans, Manorcunningham, St Johnston, Letterkenny, Lifford, Raphoe, Convoy, Stranorlar and Castlefin all lie in this region.[22] Settlement during the Ulster plantation was most successful in the East Donegal Laggan area.[23] Prior to the Great War, Protestant influence was still significant in this East Donegal area and Roman Catholics made up between 50 and 65 per cent of the population in the Laggan Valley.[24]

As well as regional variations within the county itself, there were a number of differences between Donegal and other counties on the west coast of Ireland.[25] East Donegal had a Protestant character, with a unionist political sentiment and planter origins. Despite being part of a county with a Roman Catholic majority, this area had more in common ethnically and politically with what Jim MacLaughlin terms the 'predominantly Presbyterian and prosperous heartland of eastern Ulster', than with the economics and politics of the other Irish provinces. In this way Donegal differed significantly from 'impoverished western counties like Cork, Kerry, Galway and Mayo'.[26] Added to this, these Protestant settlers helped transform Donegal's economy and strengthened links with this unionist East Ulster area through their industrial enterprise. The Protestant population of the county was therefore 'a distinct Donegal community' with 'its own schools, newspapers, churches, marriage patterns, social networks and class structure'.[27]

The arrival of the aforementioned Scottish settlers in the seventeenth century and migration to England and Scotland from the following century onwards also meant that the structure of the county was altered, economically, politically and socially.[28] As MacLaughlin has noted, contrasting forms of worship, business practices and new methods of farming were all introduced by the Scots and Donegal was transformed from 'a bastion of Gaeldom into an ethnically-mixed enclave that was part of a much wider world'.[29] Differing attitudes to business and general progress shown by the descendants of these settlers, in contrast to those in the poor western region, added to greater opportunities, meant that by the late nineteenth century, the East Donegal area was more amenable to the development of sports such as cricket and hockey than areas along the west coast of Donegal, while a more efficient transport infrastructure was also in place there. In addition to these social factors, cultural differences between this area and predominantly Roman Catholic parts of Donegal influenced the decision to take up these sports. Although Jonathan Bardon has stated that 'there is growing scholarly evidence that seventeenth-century planters and their descendants did not separate themselves from the native Irish population as much as was formerly believed', he also notes that 'the vast majority of Ulster Catholics thought of themselves as part of an Irish nation, worthy of self-government; and Ulster Protestants, with a few notable exceptions drawn largely from the intelligentsia, saw themselves as Britons (though, perhaps with their own regional characteristics) who should not be cut loose from the United Kingdom'.[30]

The plantation was less significant outside of East Donegal.[31] While there was also a significant settlement in the south around Donegal town and Ballyshannon and on the western side of Lough Swilly, the area along the west coast was less densely settled.[32] In the south-west of the county, the landscape has more in common with the Rosses than the Laggan area, and Killybegs, Ardara, Glenties, Kilcar and Glencolumbkille are all located in this region. The land is better in the southern area of the county, which begins at the Eany river in Inver and stretches to the Drowes river in Bundoran, the most southern town in the county, covering the villages of Mountcharles, Laghey and Ballintra. Donegal is the central town of this area although Ballyshannon, along with Lifford, was an important military base in the late nineteenth century.[33] Ballyshannon, which had a population of 2,840 people in 1881, was the largest town in the county and home to a variety of sporting clubs and other voluntary organisations in the late nineteenth and early twentieth centuries and will later be assessed for its cross-community sporting activities. While 2,218 of these persons (78 per cent) were Roman Catholic, there were 481 Protestant Episcopalians living there while 100 Presbyterians and forty Methodists also resided within the township.[34] Many of these non-Roman Catholics were, as businessmen within the town, prominent members of Ballyshannon (and

Donegal) society and were heavily involved in its development as a thriving provincial town at the time. Writing in 1882, one reporter felt that 'with sea facilities, and a large contributory district from Donegal and Sligo, Ballyshannon ought to occupy a more commanding position. Some of her merchants are most intelligent men, with keen and shrewd ideas of business and push.'[35]

Gaelic games, along with politics, have played an important part in forging county identity and rivalries.[36] As will be seen later, the development of the GAA was a tough, slow struggle in Donegal, with Gaelic football not becoming firmly established until the 1920s. In particular, in this way Donegal differed from two other peripheral counties, Mayo and Kerry. These counties had larger Roman Catholic populations than Donegal and while emigration affected all three counties, this may partially help explain why the GAA was initiated earlier in these two counties, and was more sustainable, despite the general decline of the organisation in the 1890s. Mayo's overall population in 1881 was 245,212, of which Roman Catholics made up 238,262 or 97 per cent of this figure.[37] This was a much larger percentage of Roman Catholics than in Donegal where just over three quarters of the population belonged to this religious denomination. The remainder of those participating in sport in Donegal mainly became involved in other sports such as soccer, rugby, hockey and cricket.[38] Although Kerry had a smaller population (201,039) than Donegal, like Mayo, its population was overwhelmingly Roman Catholic. There were 194,283 Catholics living in Kerry and this was also 97 per cent of the overall total.[39] As the GAA was mainly a nationalist, Roman Catholic organisation, it is perhaps less surprising that it struggled to get up and running in Donegal. Cronin, Duncan and Rouse have stated that 'the reality is that Protestants have been greatly underrepresented in the Association', despite the involvement of some 'high profile members', with nationalist linkage and the education system amongst the factors which have curtailed this participation.[40] Ida Milne's study has illustrated how more Protestants took an active part in the GAA at grassroots level than has previously been acknowledged, although more work needs to be undertaken on this throughout the country.[41] While not all Catholics were interested in Gaelic games, it was this religious denomination that mainly played these sports.

Inishowen, a peninsula lying in the north-east between Lough Swilly to the west and Lough Foyle to the east, stretches to the most northerly point in Ireland, Malin Head, and was somewhat isolated from the rest of Donegal. Although Buncrana and Carndonagh are the biggest towns in this area, villages of note include Burt, Newtowncunningham, Killea, Portlough, Culdaff and Moville. Lough Swilly was an important British military base and until 1938, there were artillery stations in Rathmullan, Knockalla, Muckamish, Dunree, Inch and Ned's Point.[42] To the west of Lough Swilly lie the towns of Rathmullan, Ramelton, Milford and Kilmacrennan with Creeslough and Dunfanaghy situated further north-west.

Significantly for the development of sport in the north-east of Donegal, the close location of these northern areas to Derry city was a major factor in the spread of sport there and provides some indication of the overall weakness of the county as a social and economic unit. North Donegal shared a number of connections with Derry city including shipping and trade, with yarn exports from areas such as Dunfanaghy passing through its port in the latter part of the eighteenth century. Eggs were an important export from east and south Donegal in the 1830s and in the following decade, while the expansion of Derry's shirt-making industry to include products completed in St Johnston, Inishowen and parts of West Tyrone helped restrengthen the Donegal economy after the decline of the linen industry. By 1832 almost half of the emigrants boarding in Derry were said to have come from Donegal, while Derry city's population was thought to contain 3,000 migrants from its neighbouring western county in the early 1830s.[43] By the late nineteenth century, Derry was the main port in the north-west for emigrants and seasonal workers and the exportation of agricultural goods.[44] As Bardon has noted, the city had become a flourishing industrial and commercial hub by the early twentieth century and although its economy then experienced a decline, it was 'at the very edge of Ulster's industrial region centred on Belfast'.[45] Sporting events in the city of Derry had a strong attraction for those in the north-east as Inishowen 'was Derry's natural hinterland'.[46] This meant that relationships with GAA and soccer clubs in Derry city were often stronger than with those lying further south in Donegal, and organisers of all codes constantly struggled to develop structures which would see all areas in the county come together.

County Donegal's infrastructure: industry, education, transport and communications

The economy of the county and levels of industry were poor and this is significant as high levels of industry and commerce have been strongly linked to the early initiation and sustainability of sports clubs and governing bodies in some parts of England and Scotland.[47] Despite the relative prosperity of the Laggan area, other areas in Donegal were not as well developed and famine continued to be a problem for many along the coast. As late as 1879 it was reported that almost 66,000 people were affected and distress was commonplace.[48] Most of the land in Ireland was owned by landlords with one estimate putting this figure of ownership at 97 per cent in 1870.[49] In the 1880s County Donegal suffered from a general lack of industry and many people along the south-west coast in areas such as Kilcar, Killybegs and Glencolumbkille struggled to make ends meet. The failure of the potato crop in the late 1870s and a lack of available work in Scotland and the Laggan meant that many families in the west of the county were in debt. Inadequate assistance given by the Poor Law Union, combined with unreasonable demands by landlords, did little to alleviate their distress.[50] Living conditions in Gweedore were poor, with small homes built from turf; most had only a hole in the roof as a chimney, and a low entrance acting as a doorway. Many had no windows and little space for habitation.[51] The threat of eviction loomed over many peasants and in July 1884 it was reported following the removal of a number of people from their homes in the north-west that 'Gweedore has a sad notoriety. Poverty and privation have been the portion of its peasantry. Their lot is cast in circumstances in which comfort or any approach to competence is not in human power to maintain.'[52]

While the development of sport in England in the nineteenth century had been helped by a series of Acts which restricted working hours, these made little difference to those in Donegal and although their significance has been noted for allowing workers more free time for sport, particularly at weekends, it was in industrial centres such as Belfast and Dublin where the greatest changes occurred. The introduction of the 1874 Factory Act in Belfast meant that Saturday afternoons became free for many workmen.[53] However, in most parts of Ireland, these acts made little difference to the majority of

Irish workers as most of these people were only involved in subsistence agriculture.[54] For many Donegal people, Sunday remained the only day to participate in sport, and as late as 1906, there were calls in the local press for a reduction in working hours in Donegal town and Letterkenny. 'A Donegal counter-hopper', in a response to local criticism that camán was taking place in Donegal town on Sundays and that those involved were desecrating the Sabbath, stated that 'when shop assistants have to stand behind the counter from seven am till ten pm with merely time to swallow their meals, is it to be wondered at that when Sunday comes they want a bit of recreation?'[55] He also felt that 'a half-holiday once a week, or early closing every evening, would have more effect in remedying this evil than all the sermons that could be preached on the subject'.[56] A public meeting in regard to shorter working hours in Letterkenny was called for around this time after a petition for the compulsory closing of shops at seven (except on Saturdays) was presented by local traders to the town's Urban Council.[57] This lack of freedom undoubtedly impacted on the development of sport in the county. In the majority of cases in the 1890s, soccer and cricket matches were organised for Saturdays and this probably deterred those with less flexible working hours from taking part.[58]

One way in which the Industrial Revolution did have a big impact on Donegal was in the numbers who left the county to seek work in Britain and further afield. Emigration and seasonal migration were the only choices for many young people. The number of people living in the county had decreased from 296,448 in 1861 to 206,035 twenty years later.[59] Between 1851 and 1881, approximately 80,000 people left Donegal and many of these were young men and women.[60] In the late nineteenth century eighty-nine out of 149 electoral divisions in the county were said to be 'congested'.[61] These congested districts were areas where the standard of living was very low.[62] While social conditions had still not improved in areas along the coast such as Inver, Carrick and Kilcar as late as 1894, the setting up of the Congested Districts Board in 1891 helped relaunch the fishing industry in Donegal by early 1895 and this helped alleviate the famine which was prevalent in the county at the time.[63] In particular, Seán Beattie's study of this organisation has illustrated the mixed success of the Board, with a rise in living standards particularly notable over the period of its existence until 1923.[64]

Donegal in the 1880s was one of the most underdeveloped counties in Ireland and was primarily an agrarian society with 80 per cent of the male population working on the land in 1881.[65] In the late nineteenth century visitors to the west coast of the county noted how social and economic development lessened as they neared the coastline.[66] Although agriculture was said to be the main occupation in 1881, home industries such as knitting, tweed making and embroidery were commonplace in the agriculturally poor western area of Donegal. Fishing was also carried out along the coast, while the manufacture of kelp from seaweed for exportation to Glasgow was also a common activity in that area.[67] Donegal's primary fishing ports in the 1880s were located in Buncrana, Rathmullan, Donegal town and Killybegs.[68] Of more significance to the people of west and north-west Donegal was the reliance on seasonal migration to Scotland and the Laggan with Donegal natives making up 47 per cent of the Ulster total in 1880.[69] For many families in the west and north-west, sending their children to the hiring fairs for agricultural labour in the Laggan was not only necessary but the time spent there also served as work experience for future migration to Scotland.[70] Throughout the eighteenth century, there was a considerable presence of temporary Irish migrants seeking agricultural work in Britain.[71] By the end of the following century, annual migration to Scotland from West Donegal was the region's most prominent feature.[72] This part of life in Donegal had increased throughout the nineteenth century and by 1895 there were agricultural workers leaving the area in the springtime to return only after Christmas.[73] This migration in search of work was not unique to Donegal with natives of Roscommon and Mayo travelling to Kildare in search of seasonal jobs.[74]

By the 1890s the Poor Law Union of Dunfanaghy had a migration rate of 45.6 per 1,000 while the Glenties area's rate was 35.8 and Milford's was 12.9, although this had dropped substantially by the 1900s.[75] This seasonal migration also had, as Desmond Murphy has stated, a detrimental effect on education and literacy in the county and 'although the [illiteracy] rate fell from 52.1 per cent in 1861 to 20.6 in 1911, that figure was then the highest in Ireland and within Donegal there were three times as many illiterate Catholics as Protestants'.[76] West Donegal had the highest rate of any district.[77] This low level of literacy was also significant for the dissemination of sport as daily newspapers began to expand their coverage in the late nineteenth and early twentieth centuries.[78] While the National School system had been in operation since 1831 and Donegal had 410 primary schools by 1881, many parents in West Donegal placed a strong emphasis on preparing their children for the hiring fairs at market towns such as Strabane and Letterkenny, staged twice a year, where they were rented out for farm labour on the Laggan, usually for a six-month period.[79] Educational problems were exacerbated in the Gaeltacht due to language and teaching difficulties while superstitions and traditional customs were still prevalent by the late nineteenth century in the Rosses area.[80] While the rates of illiteracy were much higher than in other districts, at the beginning of the twentieth century the standard of living in West Donegal was improving and the acceptance of emigration to North America, instead of Scotland, made many families more aware of the financial advantages of staying in education.[81] By the latter decade of the nineteenth century, the reading of newspapers had become more common throughout Ireland and this skill was highly significant in preventing people from turning to alcohol as well as providing a foundation for modern life.[82]

The role of education establishments in the spread of sport in England and Ireland has been well documented.[83] In Donegal in 1881, fewer than a quarter of children over five years old were going to school and there were fewer than 2,400 post-primary scholars throughout the county.[84] Generally speaking, the education system in Donegal in the nineteenth century was poor and not conducive to the development of sport as the number of Donegal people who received post-primary education at the time was quite low.[85] These factors may have hindered the diffusion of sport as structures for its spread through Donegal's schools were weak, with little evidence that there were any prominent school teams or competitive structures for schools' sport in operation in the county by the 1880s. There were only a small number of second-level education establishments functioning in Donegal in the late nineteenth century.[86] These included the Royal School in Raphoe which had been founded in 1608, the Literary Institute in Letterkenny where young men were prepared for the priesthood and the Prior Endowed School in Lifford, which later became amalgamated with the Royal School in Raphoe. St Columba's Industrial School in Killybegs, which catered for those interested in technical education, was opened in 1896.[87] A polytechnic school was also in operation in Ramelton by that year.[88]

There is little to suggest that opportunities for Donegal people to receive third-level education were much better. Donegal had no colleges until the twentieth century and Trinity College, Dublin, founded in 1592, was Ireland's first university but catered mainly for Protestants.[89] Maynooth College was founded in 1795 but after 1817, only those wishing to become priests could enrol. In 1849 the Queen's colleges at Belfast, Cork and Galway were opened, but Catholic clergy were banned by the Synod of Thurles from working in these three education establishments. The Catholic University of Ireland was founded in 1854 but Pádraig Ó Baoighill has stated that 'the progress of the university was hampered by a number of factors – the smallness of the Catholic middle class, the scarcity of educational opportunities, and the lack of a system of secondary schools'.[90] The failure of the government to publicly acknowledge its importance through the awarding of a charter also hindered its development.[91] Given that the majority of Donegal's population was Roman Catholic, these factors did not help their chances of gaining third-level education. The introduction of the Royal University of Ireland in 1879 did however allow Catholics to attain degrees.[92] In any case, it is difficult to establish exactly how many Donegal students attended these institutions. There is clear evidence that former university students participated in the organisation of rugby and soccer in County Westmeath but given the lack of references to this type of dissemination of sport in the local press in Donegal, similar involvement in the formation of Donegal's sporting clubs in the nineteenth century is harder to prove.[93] Given Donegal's isolation from these education centres in the nineteenth century, those wishing to attend third-level education establishments would have been hindered by the lack of transport infrastructure and the limited education opportunities available for the majority of its population.

In general, the transport and communications network in Donegal in the 1880s was poor. In 1884 the county was described as 'mountainous and boggy' while lakes and rivers were said to be 'numerous, but small'.[94] In the north-west, the nearest telegraph station to Dunfanaghy around that time was situated eighteen miles away in Gweedore.[95] In addition to complaints in October 1886 in the *Derry Journal* about the absence of a telegraph station along the coast from Dunfanaghy in the north-west to Glenties in the south-west, a correspondent in Letterkenny commented that more inland rural areas such as Fintown, Churchill and Glenswilly were also hampered by the same problem and that the railway network also needed much development.[96] The fact that almost half of the landscape was agriculturally poor and the provision of roads in Donegal was still inadequate meant that travel at this time was time-consuming and difficult. West Donegal did not get its first surfaced road until 1834 and maintenance of these roads was at times inadequate.[97] In a letter to the *Derry Standard* in 1893, a Letterkenny resident complained about the 'impassable' road between his home town and Stranorlar and felt that this was due to the fact that as 'none of the Grand Jury reside in this district, there is no one to see that the work is right done [sic]'.[98]

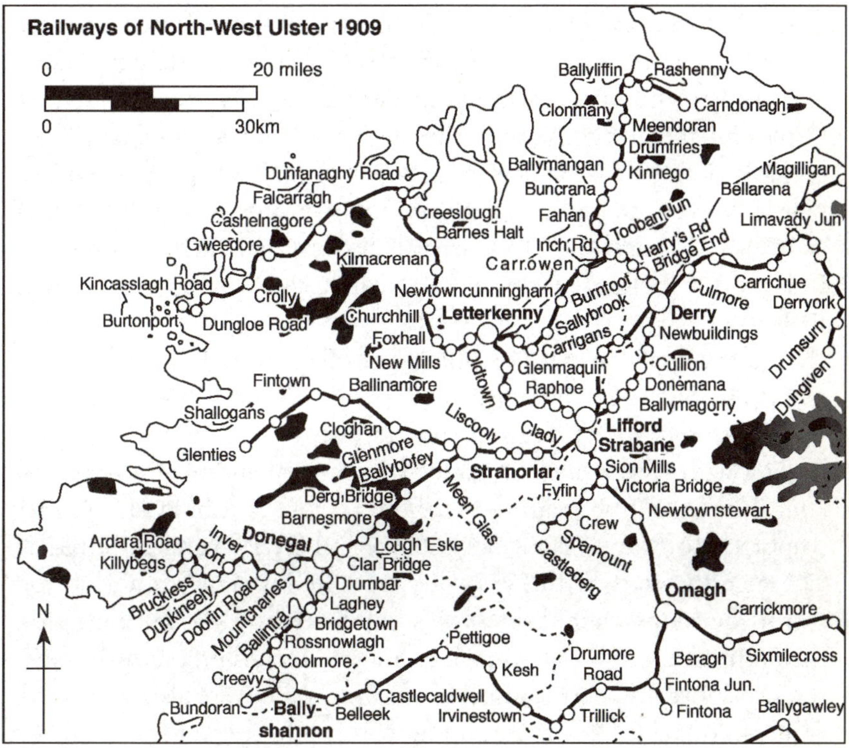

Fig. 1.3: Railways of North-West Ulster, 1909

SOURCE: Dave Bell and Steve Flanders, *The Londonderry and Lough Swilly Railway: A Visitor's Guide* (Donegal, 1995), p. 4

Ireland's first railway line was opened between Dublin and Kingstown, nowadays known as Dún Laoghaire, on the south side of the country's capital city in 1834.[99] The spread of the railway throughout the country, and throughout the world, was significant for sport, as players, administrators and supporters could then travel further to participate in sport and at cheaper rates.[100] By 1860, Donegal was the only county in Ulster which 'lacked a through main line'.[101] The development of sport in more southern counties such as Westmeath and Tipperary was helped by railway links between the major cities running through these counties.[102] Westmeath, for example, had a railway line east to Dublin by 1848 and west to Galway by 1851.[103] As can be seen in Figure 1.3, Donegal's coastal location meant that the railway stopped short of a number of more rural villages as there were no bordering western or northern counties. The first railway line did not open until 1863 and was built to expand trading links in the east of the county. Strabane, County Tyrone, was already connected to Omagh, twenty miles east, and to the principal town in Fermanagh, Enniskillen. It was from Strabane, lying on the border with the County Donegal village of Lifford and situated across the river Finn, that the Finn Valley railway line began and this followed the river in a western direction via Clady through the Donegal villages of Castlefin, Liscooly and Killygordon before reaching the 'twin towns' of Stranorlar and Ballybofey.[104]

On the final day of 1863, a line from Farland Point, on the edge of Lough Swilly in the Inishowen peninsula, was opened by the Londonderry and Lough Swilly railway company to improve trading with Derry city.[105] Although this was abandoned three years later, Buncrana, the main town of the region, 'a fishing village and seaport of some importance', was linked to Derry by rail in 1864.[106] These connections with Derry city were highly significant as, prior to this development, business was conducted by sea and on roads through the use of horse-drawn carriages. The fishing industry and the transport of whale blubber from the Arctic were also improved as a result of this.[107] A line running south through Inishowen from Tooban Junction to Letterkenny was opened in 1883, further improving transport links.[108]

Development of the railway in the south and west of the county was a lot slower, although by 1867, Bundoran was connected, through Ballyshannon, with Enniskillen in County Fermanagh by the Great Northern Railway.[109] The county initially lacked a singular railway company to cover all areas, and problems with funding made development difficult. It was not until 1882 that a line from Stranorlar/Ballybofey, courtesy of the West Donegal Railway, was put in place to improve transport through Barnesmore Gap and the Blue Stack mountains to Donegal town in the south of the county.[110] However, this line stopped two miles short due to financial problems and was not completed until 1889 with the help of the Donegal Railway Station Company. Up until then, the remainder of the trip had to be completed by horse and carriage.[111] The County Donegal Railway line south to Ballyshannon was not finished until 1905.[112] Transport in the south-west was improved with financial assistance from the Congested Districts Board as the County Donegal Railway line into the fishing village of Killybegs was completed in 1893 and a line into Glenties from Ballybofey was finished in 1895.[113] In Inishowen, the Londonderry and Lough Swilly Railway Company had extended the line from Buncrana further north through to Carndonagh by 1901.[114] The north-west of Donegal was, by 1903, served by the Letterkenny and Lough Swilly Railway which began in Letterkenny and wended towards the coast at Dunfanaghy Road before heading south-west with Burtonport its last stop.[115] Letterkenny and Strabane were linked by 1909 which meant that villages with stations such as Convoy, Raphoe and Lifford could benefit from this.[116]

The spread of the railway network in the county was a slow process, mainly due to lack of finance, the physical nature of the county and priorities being given to what were deemed as more significant trading links. Therefore, not every area could benefit from its presence. Proposals for the extension of lines to Ardara, Maas and Teelin in the south-west were unsuccessful while further north, attempts to have the railway reach Bunbeg and Carrigart came to nothing. The east coast of Inishowen was not served by the railway either.[117] The development of sport in many areas in the county was hampered by these delays and a number of areas remained isolated from important urban centres such as Buncrana, Letterkenny and Ballyshannon. It was the north-east, where the rail network was initially put in place, that was the heart of Donegal's sporting activity in the nineteenth century and, as will be demonstrated later, the speed with which sporting clubs and associations developed was generally quicker there than in more isolated areas such as the south-west or west.

Political changes in Donegal society

Despite its decline, the Ascendancy still controlled many aspects of community life in Donegal for most of the nineteenth century.[118] This position of power was to change, however, in the later decades of the century and this allowed Catholics to have a greater say in the running of society. The power enjoyed by the Tories and Liberals in Donegal politics had decreased in the 1880s and their grip on society was therefore weakened.[119] Popular nationalism in Donegal had been increasing since the middle of the 1870s and the militant effects of the Land War in 1884 encouraged Catholics to insist that their demands be met by those truly interested in solving their problems.[120] Clerical influence in Donegal society was illustrated in their organisation of the registration of voters in the 1885 elections. Desmond Murphy believes that 'although the nationalists captured all four Donegal seats, real political influence now lay with a hard core of politically active clergy'.[121] He has also stated that 'the Land War was the major determinant of political change in Donegal' as 'it shattered the already declining influence of the landlord class on political life and substituted instead a popular democracy whose centre of authority was the Catholic clergy'.[122] Given the social dislocation experienced within the county in the late 1880s with the introduction of the Plan of Campaign (whereby tenants would pay their rent into an estate fund if the level of rent they decided on was rejected by the landlord) and the jailing of the socially influential Fr McFadden, it is perhaps unsurprising that the development of sport there was a slow process, as energy was directed elsewhere.[123] With Fr McFadden's help, the plan was being implemented on ten estates in Donegal by 1888.[124]

Despite the rejection of Gladstone's Home Rule Bills in 1886 by the House of Commons and by the House of Lords in 1893, national administrative changes gave Catholics a greater say in organising their affairs.[125] A series of land acts such as those introduced by Gladstone in 1870 and 1881, the Ashbourne Land Act of 1885 and Balfour's Land Act of 1896 were passed to give tenants improved rights, although it must be noted that landlordism in the Free State was not finally removed until 1923.[126] The Local Government of Ireland Act of 1898 was intended to increase the level of democracy in local administration and by the end of 1918 the strong influence that Protestants had exerted politically in local and parliamentary affairs had ended.[127] Before 1898, the Protestant elite dominated local government in Ireland and the elections of the following year presented the opportunity for increased nationalist influence and a greater level of democracy.[128] Society in Donegal was transformed in the years between the Great Famine and World War I and Protestant dominance was slowly replaced by that of Roman Catholics.[129] By 1911, Protestants were in a minority in Donegal's four parliamentary constituencies and had only a slight majority in six of the county's parishes.[130] This meant that those interested in the Gaelic revival and promoting Gaelic games were beginning to come to the fore as Catholic farmers, professionals and businessmen were gaining more power in the county's local politics.[131]

This change in the governing of Ireland in 1898 also had an effect on the identity of the county within Irish society as counties became 'the major unit for local government', with elected county councils, urban district councils and rural district councils being created.[132] The Poor Law Unions had given scant regard to county boundaries and this reformation signalled the end of the political power of the landlords, while many nationalists took over from unionists in local government throughout Ireland, with the exception of Ulster.[133] Prior to this, grand juries, mainly consisting of unelected landlords, had been in charge of infrastructure at a local level, while Poor Law boards had looked after sanitation and welfare.[134] The survival of 'the county' as a structure was also aided by Irish legislation which took on a similar outlook to an Act passed in 1888 to form elected county councils in England and Wales.[135] While the All-Ireland Gaelic football and hurling championships had been contested on an intercounty basis since the 1880s, it was not common practice to field selections from all over the county until the 1920s.[136] Until then, in many cases, county selections were made up of the club which had won the county championship. As will be seen later, not everybody was interested in supporting the GAA in Donegal and a number of areas in the county remained disunited in their sporting choices.

The impact of the Great War (1914–18), and the Irish Revolution – the latter comprising the Easter Rising (1916), the War of Independence (1919–21) and the Civil War (1922–23) – on the development of the GAA and other sports in Donegal, will be discussed in depth later in this book. Despite the formation of the Irish Free State in 1922, Donegal continued to remain on the outside of more national affairs throughout this decade and into the 1930s. As Bardon has stated, 'Donegal, Cavan and Monaghan became peripheral counties of a state which, after a ruinous Civil War, steadily loosened its last ties with the British Empire.'[137]

There were some important national changes which aided the growth of Gaelic games in the 1920s and had a significant impact on the growth of the GAA in Donegal at this time. The arrival of the new Garda Síochána force in Donegal town on 18 October 1922 was greeted by 'a large number of townspeople who were on the platform when the train steamed in' and the following day at mass, the Reverend P.J. Kelly 'extended a welcome to the detachment of the Civic Guard, and said the people should assist them in the performance of their duties'.[138] These men were, according to Reverend Kelly, 'policemen in the real sense of the word, not like the police under the old regime – a semi-military force'.[139] Already a sharp contrast was being drawn between the Royal Irish Constabulary and the Garda Síochána, and public approval from those with social influence, like the Reverend Kelly, meant that the law was beginning to be recognised in a positive manner. In addition to this, RIC members had been banned from participating in Gaelic games and the GAA was now able to receive the input of a large body of men with significant social standing.

Another important development in the 1920s was that transport improved. The number of private cars on Donegal roads rose from 9,246 in 1923 to 32,632 in 1930, increasing access to GAA matches and other sporting events.[140] While there was a general failure to extend the railway network to more rural areas within Donegal, the development of sport in the 1920s and early 1930s also benefited from the provision of buses to matches.[141] The impact of these changes on the development of a sporting infrastructure in the county will also be discussed later. Economic developments were slow, however. According to Bardon, as late as the 1950s, a lack of economic and social development was especially obvious in Donegal,

Cavan and Monaghan, with the impact of the wartime policy of neutrality still hindering general progress within the twenty-six counties by this decade.[142] The continuous policy of neutrality, high tariffs and censorship were key factors in this failure to improve.[143] In addition, MacLaughlin has stated that 'from the 1920s to the 1950s, many of Donegal's towns and villages were extremely dilapidated places'.[144] Beattie has noted how the formation of the Department of the Gaeltacht in 1956 benefited counties on the western seaboard while later developments such as the formation of Údarás na Gaeltachta also helped the economic, cultural and social state of County Donegal.[145]

Conclusion

Industrial, educational, economic and transport structures were not in place in Donegal society to accommodate a widespread growth of sport in the late nineteenth century, as happened in many parts of Britain. Jim MacLaughlin has stated that 'in Donegal, as in much of rural underdeveloped Ireland, schools and churches were agents for social and political change'.[146] There is little evidence that either of these establishments were interested in promoting sport in Donegal in the late nineteenth century. This was probably due to the poverty of the county and the fact that there were other social issues which warranted greater attention. The Land War and the Plan of Campaign also drew much energy away from the organisation of sport towards matters which were considered more important for basic survival in the 1880s. Because of the regional variations which existed throughout Donegal, it can be said that the county was divided, economically, physically and culturally, between east and west and, as a result of the geographical structure of the county and the Plantation of Ulster, there were vast discrepancies between the levels of prosperity in these areas, with East Donegal being more amenable to the development of sport. Allied to this, parts of the Laggan area (such as Letterkenny) were closely located to Derry city, which was on the edge of Ulster's industrial region.

The loss of manpower through seasonal migration and emigration, combined with a lack of emphasis on education, further delayed the impact of the sporting 'revolution' in Donegal. While the introduction of the Factory Acts had benefited the development of sport in England and in Belfast and Dublin, the effect of these in Donegal was minimal. Attitudes of local business people towards working hours also impeded the time available for leisure. Tranter has stated that improvements in transport in Britain meant that 'in most cases, the geographic and social range of participation (in sport) was extended'.[147] Donegal did not fall into this category as the levels of transport improvements in the late nineteenth century varied throughout the county. It was not until the latter decades of the nineteenth century that Catholics began to gain a greater say in society with nationalist successes in the 1885 elections, while the Local Government of Ireland Act of 1898 gave them greater opportunities to voice their opinions. With the coming of the Garda Síochána in 1922 and transport improvements in this decade, the organisation of Gaelic games in Donegal was also strengthened. It is against the background of the late nineteenth century that the beginning of codified sport in Donegal will be examined. The reasons why – despite the relatively backward state of development within Donegal society in comparison with more industrialised areas – the organisation of matches, clubs and competitions did manage to go ahead will be addressed in the next chapter.

2

Pre-codified and 'minority' sports in Donegal

Introduction

This chapter assesses the decline of pre-codified sports throughout the county and explores the part played in the local community by annual sporting events such as regattas and athletics. The importance of cricket, rugby and hockey within Donegal society in the late nineteenth and opening decades of the twentieth centuries is also examined as these three codes were essentially 'minority' sports in Donegal and failed to gain widespread support. The social background and religious diversity of those playing and administrating these sports is analysed and it will be shown that matches and related social events formed an important part of Protestant culture within the county, although participation was not restricted by religious denomination. The impact of partition on sport is assessed and it will be illustrated that some club organisers in areas with close ties to the newly formed Northern Ireland state in the 1920s continued to view governing bodies and clubs across the border as an essential part of their sporting networks for both competitive and friendly fixtures.

Pre-codified forms of hurling and folk-football

In common with many parts of Ireland, of particular importance to a number of areas in Donegal in the nineteenth century were pre-codified versions of hurling. Richard Holt has stated that, organised under GAA rules, hurling and Gaelic football have provided 'the single most dramatic example of the powers of survival and adaption of ancient sports'.[1] When exactly football or stick and ball games were first played in Donegal is unclear, although an engraving of a form of hurling on a fifteenth-century grave slab at Clonca in the north of the county has been preserved.[2] Although stick and ball games, known in different areas as iomáin, camán (commons) and hurling, have taken place in Ireland since the seventh century, Eoin Kinsella has stated that modern hurling's development cannot be properly traced up to the late nineteenth century.[3] Forms of folk football have been played in Ireland since at least the sixteenth century but tracing the growth of these up to the nineteenth century is also problematic, given the infrequent references which appear in law, poetry and contemporary publications.[4] In general, there is more evidence for the playing of pre-codified hurling in Donegal than for unregulated forms of football in the nineteenth century and little has been recorded about the latter in the county. This may be because, at least partially, as Kinsella has stated, early forms of football had an 'anarchic nature, along with the general perception that it was a less skilful or exciting game than hurling' which meant that the former code was less likely to be written about.[5] Along with camán, a type of football was played on the beach at Tremone Bay in Inishowen in the nineteenth century, particularly between townlands on Christmas Day.[6] This game was still being played in the late 1870s, although examples in other areas are difficult to find. What is clear is that Donegal had a rich history of these stick and ball games prior to, and for a number of decades after, the founding of the GAA.

According to oral sources, pre-codified forms of hurling were played along the west coast of Donegal in Gortahork, Ardara, Glencolumbkille, Kilcar, Inver, Donegal town, Ballyshannon and Bundoran while it was also noted on Inishbofin island, Fahan and at Burt in the years prior to 1884.[7] Newspaper references to the decline of camán in the parishes of Fanad, Newtowncunningham, Carrigart, Killybegs, Croagh and Glenties are generally non-descriptive but some do hint at an increased interest in more modern forms of sport at its expense.[8] There appears to be only a small amount of written evidence of pre-codified hurling in the county recorded in contemporary publications. An account by William Shaw Mason, recording events in Culdaff in 1816, highlighted, along with their raffling of mutton, the lower classes' playing of 'kamman' at Christmas, which, he stated, consisted of 'impelling a wooden ball with a crooked stick to a given point, while an adversary endeavours to drive it in a contrary direction'.[9]

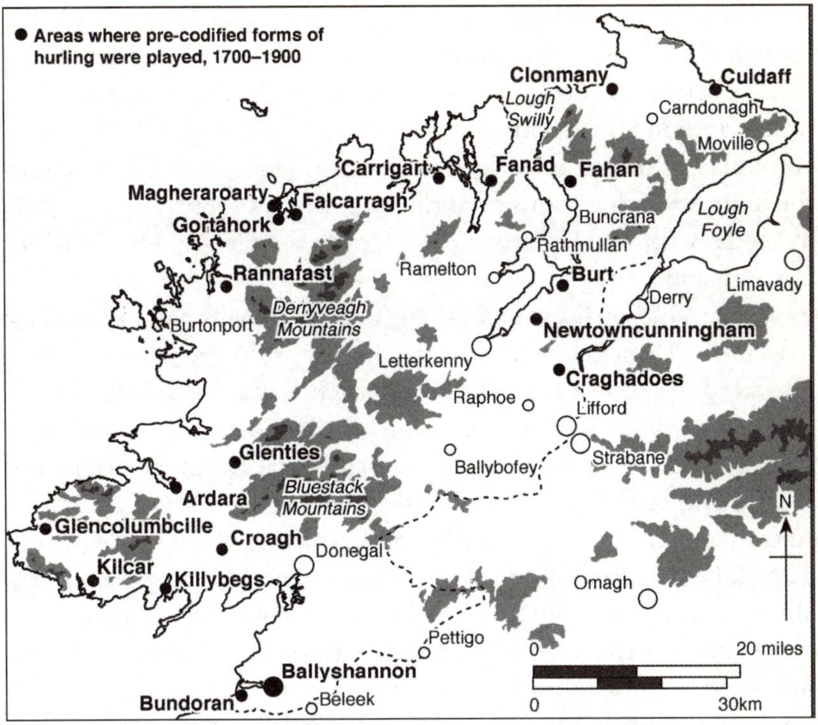

Fig. 2.1: Areas where pre-codified forms of hurling were played, 1700–1900

SOURCES: Ó Caithnia, *Scéal na hIomána,* p. 644; Campbell, Dowds, and Mullan, *Against the Grain,* pp. 73–6; Eoghan Corry, 'The Mass Media and the Popularisation of Gaelic games, 1884–1934' in Dónal McAnallen, David Hassan and Roddy Hegarty (eds), *The Evolution of the GAA: Ulaidh, Éire agus Eile* (Armagh, 2009), pp 100–11; Anthony Begley, 'The Liberator 1839: A Forgotten Ballyshannon Newspaper' in the *Donegal Annual 2003,* no. 55 (Letterkenny, 2003), pp. 54–69; Mac a' Ghoill, 'Cross-country Hurling in Ardara' in *CLCG Ard a' Ratha* (Ardara, 1980), pp 53–7; *DJ*, 1 January 1897 and 29 December 1899; *DV*, 14 February 1902; *DP and DN*, 23 May 1903, 8 July 1905 and 27 January 1906.

The Ordnance Survey Memoirs recorded in the 1830s to accompany a townland survey of maps of Ireland for tax purposes also unfortunately provide little evidence about forms of hurling or football in Donegal. A statistical report taken by Lieutenant W. Lancey in May 1834 in the Inishowen village of Clonmany illustrated that 'cock-fighting, hurling and dancing are declining. The game of common is still practised.'[10] Lancey also noted that in Killygarvan, 'the peasantry have no peculiar amusements or recreations' while he was particularly scathing of the public's lack of recreation in Mevagh. He stated that other than involvement in a horse-race on Rosapenna strands, 'they are, like the rest of the country, not addicted to public sports. They appear either to have lost or never possessed a taste for feats of activity or manly strength, and all their leisure time is taken up in moping over misfortunes, real or supposed.'[11] Lancey's accounts for the vast majority of parishes in Donegal at this time give the impression that forms of hurling were not widespread, but this is at odds with the information recorded later by the Folklore Commission.

According to this source, there were two main types of hurling played in Donegal. Camán, or 'commons', was played on a restricted field, with the ball being struck along the ground; cross-country hurling, which was more of a ball-carrying game, took place across townlands.[12] In some areas, such as Ardara, Burt and Gortahork, both types were played. This was also the case in Derry, Antrim and Down as well as the southern counties of Offaly, Cork, Tipperary, Limerick and Clare.[13] Cross-country hurling was generally played in the winter as crops would have been damaged at other times of the year, while beaches were often used as a substitute for fields for the other type of game, which could have been played on these at any time. This may partially explain the prominence of evidence for these games in more coastal areas in Donegal, although it was also played in inland counties.[14] Forms of hurling played an important part in the social life of a number of villagers around the coast of Donegal in the days before these games became codified. While it is difficult to establish who these individuals were or who exactly was responsible for initiating their games, there is plenty of oral evidence of the type of social conditions and the various types of hurling played at this time.

Niall Ó Dufaigh has recalled that in his youth there were not many Sundays when hurling was not played on the beach at Magheraroarty. This would date these games back to the 1870s at least. The locals availed of the strands from Gortahork to Magheraroarty, which stretched a distance of at least six or seven miles and were suitable even in times of snow and ice as the ground near the tide remained clear.[15] Both Ó Dufaigh and Seosamh MacGrianna, who described events in Fanad, recall that fighting between locals and their neighbours was commonplace but games still took place every Sunday. Fights would be worse when strangers participated, of course.[16] Games were also played in the evening after work at

Triagh a Locha and MacGrianna has noted the powerful striking ability of the bigger men who participated.[17] In Teelin, in the south-west of the county, games normally took place on level fields, and after the hay was gathered in the autumn, hurling would frequently be played there until St Patrick's Day in March.[18] Good playing fields were apparently difficult to obtain in Donegal. Whatever fields they could get were always small as the bigger ones were needed for crops and divided into strips and it was also therefore more difficult to gain permission to use these. This was a trend which was also common in the south of Ireland.[19]

There were a variety of balls used throughout the country. While the ball used in Donegal was generally known as a 'nagg' and made of wood, there were some differences further south as wood enclosed by leather was used in counties such as Clare and Limerick. The word 'sliotar', or 'hair ball', was also the name given to the ball in parts of Munster.[20] In Ardara, cross-country hurling was played with a 'bool' three inches in diameter, which had a lifespan of two months and weighed about half a pound; it was made of 'briar-root, rounded under the embers of the turf fire until it was round and hard on the outside'.[21] Cross-country hurling in Donegal was not dissimilar to 'hurling to the country' which was played with a silver ball in Cornwall at the end of the sixteenth century, although the ball was thrown here rather than being struck by sticks.[22] 'Hurling to goals' was also popular in this area at the time.[23] A form of one-handed hurling was said to be played in Rannafast on St Patrick's Day before the Great Famine and this was thought to resemble a game of the same type which was played in Cambridge until 1885.[24]

In the parish of Cloughaneely, it was traditional on Christmas Day for cross-country hurling to be played between townlands until darkness fell, with poitín drinking preceding the start of the day's sport. This tradition is believed to date back to the middle of the eighteenth century. The aim of this pastime was to keep the 'cnag' or ball in their own townland and bring it back from the place where they had originally met the opposition. The 'cnag' was about the size of a man's fist and normally made of wood.[25] These annual matches began after dinner with an elderly person from the locality throwing in the ball and were often rough with scarce attention being paid to weather conditions or the landscape. Games between local selections were also played on a restricted area with goal scoring deciding the winners.[26]

Ó Dufaigh also recalled a Christmas tradition of hurling in Gortahork, which is thought to date back to the 1740s.[27] Unsurprisingly these games contained elements of pre-codified ball games in Britain as examined by Hugh Hornby.[28] Sometimes held on traditional dates around festival times, these mass games were often violent and had no referee or rulebook and were played through neighbouring areas. They were eagerly awaited and provided much excitement for the locality, usually taking place over townlands such as those in Ashbourne, Derbyshire and on the Orkney islands at Kirkwall, with drinking commonplace.[29] While these are still carried on today in a number of areas in Britain as part of annual traditions, pre-codified hurling is no longer played in Donegal. A similar decline of traditional sports in England has been noted from the end of the eighteenth century, with key factors including industrialisation, urbanisation, a change in acceptable behaviour, improved law enforcement and the loss of patronage, from anxiety caused by the French Revolution, all influential.[30]

Céilís or traditional dances were held in barns after some games and Ó Dufaigh has stated that this continued until the Great Famine. With the social dislocation, death and emigration caused by the Famine, local interest in this form of hurling declined and former players and organisers lacked the motivation to continue their games.[31] However, Elizabeth Malcolm believes this decline was evident in Ireland prior to the Great Famine and that 'the change in the recreational pattern that occurred between the 1790s and the 1840s was drastic'.[32] She has also stated that before the Famine, seasonal and religious festivals were a highly significant part of recreation in Ireland.[33] The Famine was 'the final blow' to an already declining pastime. As Alvin Jackson has noted, 'it is clear that the Famine touched almost every aspect of Irish life in the mid- and late nineteenth century'.[34] Ó Caithnia has stated that the local priests and those involved in the Church were attempting to put a stop to the games as they felt the parishioners were becoming too heavily involved in them.[35] The clergy had also prevented the playing of commons in Cinn Mhuaighe in County Antrim around 1835 and prohibited the playing of football in Rostrevor in County Down at the same time. In the latter case it was claimed that football was polluting the minds of the people.[36] In looking at the decline of the pattern festivals in Westmeath in the second half of the nineteenth century, Tom Hunt believes that the Catholic Church's opposition to these stemmed from the view that these activities contained many 'non-Christian features'.[37] Fighting and drunkenness would certainly have been part of the Christmas Day hurling games in Cloughaneely. Hunt is also of the opinion that 'changes in the social structure of rural Ireland were accompanied by improved living standards and exposure to new cultural influences and new models of behaviour'.[38]

Ó Maolfabhail, Hegarty and McAnallen have noted that forms of traditional hurling continued to exist in Ulster 'up to the eve of the GAA's birth and later', particularly in Antrim and Down.[39] There was a similar trend in Donegal. Cross-country hurling did not go into decline everywhere and it was continued in the village of Ardara until 1906. The Glengesh pass was the setting for games between local farm workers between 1897 and 1906 which was an exceptionally late occurrence in terms of the survival of these pre-codified forms of hurling and illustrates that some areas were eager to carry on in the absence of a club structure.[40] The presence of traditional forms of hurling in an area did not necessarily lead to the formation of a club under GAA rules as these differed from camán and cross-country hurling and needed to be demonstrated. Of the first Donegal clubs affiliated to the Derry County Board in the period from 1888 until 1892, Burt was the only area mentioned by Ó Caithnia that went on to field a team in hurling competitions around this time.[41]

There is also strong evidence that the traditional game of camán continued to be played in Burt at least until the foundation of the GAA club there on 5 February 1888 with the visit of Derry club, St Patrick's.[42] A hurling match was played using, for the first period of play, Burt's traditional camán rules and those of the GAA in the second-half and the Burt Hibernians GAA branch was formed afterwards.[43] This switching of rules at the half-way point was not uncommon in football matches in London in 1863, prior to the standardisation of a set of rules for association football in 1882.[44] Undoubtedly the Burt village's camán tradition was a significant factor in the interest behind the organisation of a GAA club. It was noted that the Burt men played throughout with camáns instead of hurleys, were barefooted and used their preferred 'nag', a wooden ball, for the first half. The match was played without sidelines and it appears that the home team were victorious.[45] Most other areas where traditional forms of hurling had been played failed to organise GAA clubs at this time. There is evidence to suggest that camán had also been played in Newtowncunningham, where a club was founded in 1890, but both the Burt and Newtowncunningham clubs appear to have learned hurling under GAA rules with the help of Derry clubs.[46] This instruction seems to have been crucial in making the switch from traditional hurling to that under GAA rules, and in areas such as West Donegal where camán had been prominent, the game died away in Magheraroarty, Gortahork, Falcarragh and Rannafast without the help of those familiar with the new GAA rules or simply those with an enthusiasm for promoting Gaelic games. Seasonal migration to Scotland may also have reduced the manpower available for these teams, as it increased towards the end of the nineteenth century, as noted in Chapter 1.

In the early twentieth century, in some cases where instruction in the new rules could not be received, newly formed clubs simply continued with the traditional game. Ó Maolfabhail, Hegarty and McAnallen have stated that 'the rapid propagation and popularisation of Gaelic football under GAA auspices from the 1880s onwards probably cemented the displacement of surviving camán and shinny traditions in most of Ulster'.[47] Of the GAA clubs which were part of the Donegal County Board in 1905–07, only Brackey (Ardara), Burt, Croagh, Bundoran, Newtowncunningham and Fahan could be said to be areas where forms of hurling were recorded prior to the founding of the GAA in 1884. In fact, elements of the traditional game of camán survived until 1906, but with the decline of the County Board, they generally disappeared in Donegal.[48] However, this further illustrates the slow development of codified sport in the county. Seamus King believes camán mainly declined because the general set of rules created by Maurice Davin and advocated by him at the GAA's meeting on 18 January 1885 more closely resembled the southern game of iomáin or báire.[49] Iomáin or báire, a summer game, was played throughout a large area and with a stick resembling the modern version used in hurling with the ball being lifted by the hand for striking with the hurley.[50] As can be seen in the case of Donegal, the deterioration of camán was a gradual decline and the majority of the 1905–07 clubs failed to take up iomáin. Their disbandment meant that no form of hurling remained to be played in the majority of villages in the county.

Regattas and athletic events

Prior to the 1880s in Donegal, regattas and athletic events were quite popular amongst various communities in the county, and cricket had been played since the 1860s. However, efforts to regulate competitions under administrative bodies remained localised and lacked an overall county-based competitive structure. Regattas were an important social event around the coast and there are claims that these dated back as far as 1740 in Greencastle, when a regatta was staged in order to raise funds for the benefit of families who lost relatives at sea in a storm there the previous year.[51] Patrons played a crucial role in organising regattas and aquatic sports in most coastal areas. The Moville Regatta which took place in the autumn of 1862, with local fishermen as the main participants, had a distinguished committee of no less than sixteen patrons, including the Mayor of Derry 'and other leading men of this city and Moville'.[52] Friday 19 September was made into a general holiday by the local businessmen for the day and 'Moville presented a most animated appearance'.[53] The band of the Derry militia provided entertainment on the jetty while the flagship, *The Nelson*, 'was occupied by a select party, including the mayor and the judges of the racing'.[54] Sailing prizes included a suit of colours, a silver boat, a silver cup and a variety of new boats.[55] Events concluded with 'miscellaneous sports' being held on the green which included 'climbing a greasy pole for a leg of mutton'.[56] These general events seem to be quite common at other regattas throughout Donegal in the latter half of the nineteenth century.

Aquatic events were not restricted to annual regattas. A rowing match between the 'principal boat crews' belonging to Killybegs took place in late May of 1871. It was reported that 'the whole affair was got up by Joseph F. Sinnott, Esq., of Philadelphia, whose arrival in Killybegs lately was the subject of much rejoicing. He subscribed the money given in prizes, and supplied refreshments and drink very liberally to the boats' crews.'[57] Occasionally, events were staged to settle old scores, such as a sailing race, won by a boat owned by Mr McCandless of Moville and held in that village in July 1880:

> The challenge arose out of a difference of opinion as to the respective sailing qualities of a Greencastle boat, the property of Mr McCormick, and another boat of the same class (drontheim), belonging to Mr McCandless, of Moville. The reputation of the builders of the boats being involved, considerable excitement was created by the contest. Captain Crosby backed the Greencastle boat with a wager of £10, and Mr McCandless staked a like amount on his own craft.[58]

Patronage was also essential in building community spirit and improving the lives of locals who may not otherwise have had much leisure activity. These events were much anticipated by those in surrounding areas and provided a day's entertainment, and indeed competition, around the village, as a report on the Rosses Regatta in 1876 illustrates:

> A kind of rivalry was known to exist among the fishermen of adjacent localities, and the approaching regatta came to be looked upon as a suitable place for proving who were the champion seamen and whose were the best boats. This itself gave a large local importance to the proceedings and assisted in a great degree towards their success.[59]

The Burtonport Regatta in August 1878 also provided the local fishermen with something different to look forward to and it was claimed that prior to the event 'for the past week the numerous fishermen and other local mariners that inhabit the mainlands of the Rosses and Gweedore and the many islands that lie off their coasts were hard and fast at work preparing their little crafts for the contest'.[60] Less affluent individuals were heavily reliant on those with local influence for the organisation of events. The Teelin Regatta, held in July 1882, was 'organised and carried out with the most marvellous taste and magnificence' by 'the venerated priest of Carrick, Rev. F.W. Gallagher, and the estimable gentleman' John Doherty of Fahan, who was supervising the building of the pier in Teelin.[61] In addition, they were assisted by 'the much respected' Doctor Hallaghan and by 'the leading shopkeepers and literary men of the place'.[62]

Despite this interest, infrequency characterised the hosting of these events as noted in a report of the Killybegs Regatta in August 1878.[63] August was a popular month for regattas, with those in Downings, Lough Swilly, Movillle and Donegal Bay being held in that month in 1883.[64] They had many similarities with those noted by Hunt in Athlone and those held in other counties such as Fermanagh, Tyrone and Antrim.[65] Regattas continued to take place in Donegal into the twentieth century. The Lough Swilly Regatta, held in Rathmullan on the August Bank Holiday of 1922, was deemed to be 'the most successful fixture of the kind ever held at this beautiful resort', while the Lough Foyle Regatta was held at Moville the same day.[66] The Killybegs Regatta, held in August 1924, was said to be 'a great success' with cheap excursion fees attracting support from Strabane and Ballyshannon.[67] The Moville Sports of 1929 drew 'a large number of spectators', although the planned regatta was postponed due to the adverse weather.[68] However, these regattas failed to gain the more widespread support that soccer and Gaelic football attracted.

Trinity College was the venue for Ireland's first 'modern athletic meeting' in 1857 and these events were spreading throughout the county in the 1860s, but even by the early 1880s, athletics in Ireland was poorly organised. The Amateur Athletic Association, founded to govern British athletics in 1880, was beginning to gain control of athletics on the east coast and it was this that led Michael Cusack to motion for the founding of what would become the GAA in 1884, with the rival IAAA being set up the following year.[69] Like other sports in Donegal in the 1880s, the organisation of athletics under a national structure does not appear to have made any great administrative progress and there is little mention in the local press of any competitive structure for those with athletic aspirations. Athletic sports were held in many villages around the county and provided locals with a day out and the opportunity to watch and participate in competitive sport, as illustrated in a report of those held at Ramelton in May 1893 in a field lent by George B. White, JP.[70]

> The business people gave a half-holiday to their employees . . . from an early hour in the day pleasure-seekers kept pouring into the town, and at two o'clock, the hour appointed for the sports to commence, there was a regular 'rush' for the field, which certainly must have taxed the abilities of the gentlemen who 'kept the gate', as it was computed that over 1,200 people passed through to the grounds.[71]

The day's events consisted of athletic sports, novelty races and throwing the cricket ball and a football place kick competition. A number of prominent locals were heavily involved in the adjudication, with Dr Patterson acting as judge, John Mallins, solicitor, given the role of starter while James Coll, auctioneer, had taken on the position of secretary.[72] Walking matches were also held in Ramelton with Major W.G. Doyne and some local gentlemen involved in organising the 'first walking contest in the district' in January 1904. Coll was again involved as starter while judge, Dr Patterson, 'accompanied the competitors on his motor bicycle. He was followed by a large crowd on foot' throughout the five-mile course.[73] The following month, fifteen men competed in a seven-mile foot race between the post offices of Ramelton and Rathmullan and 'long before 2.30pm . . . large crowds from town and country had collected in the vicinity of the Ramelton Post Office'.[74] The event was organised by hotel keeper, Samuel Goodwin, and Major Doyne, and it was reported that 'the genial qualities of the major have made him a favourite with the people since he retired from his regiment, the 21st Lancers of Omdurman [Sudan] fame'.[75] There is little evidence that these competitions became a significant part of Donegal society at this time.

Unsurprisingly, members of other administrative sporting bodies were also keen to get involved in sporting events, with a number of the County Donegal Football Association committee involved in the 'inaugural' Rathmullan Athletic Sports of December 1895.[76] Although the weather could sometimes dampen spirits at these events with a general lack of enclosures for spectators, crowd safety was usually not a problem. An exception appears to have been an incident at the St Johnston and Carrigans Athletic Sports held in June 1893, where it was reported that a dancing competition had 'attracted more attention than any of the others' with the result that 'the judges' stand was invaded, and became so overburdened as to collapse, some fifty people falling in a heap'.[77] Fortunately, no one was injured.

Some of these events brought the opportunity to place a bet. These ranged from private competitions to those open to a wider range of contestants. A running match, 900 yards in length, was held in Carrigart between two members of the RIC, 'for a wager of £2 10 shillings' in September 1866.[78] At the Newtowncunningham Sports in September 1893, a bookmaker present 'found numerous ready backers of their several favourites'.[79] With the growth of sports clubs in the late nineteenth century, some of these were able to organise their own annual sports. The Letterkenny Cycling Club Sports, held in August 1895, was well attended while 'a number of book-makers were also present, having remained over from the Derry Races. This gave an additional interest and excitement to the sports'.[80] At this point soccer matches for medals were becoming an important part of the day's proceedings in areas such as Rathmullan.[81] This was a not uncommon fixture in other Irish villages at the time, such as in Fintona (Tyrone) where a match for a silver cup took place between the local club and Fermanagh side Lisbellaw at the Eskra sports committee's athletic meeting on St Stephen's Day 1896.[82] Some local organisations used these athletic meetings as a basis for excursions, with the Ballyshannon Temperance organisation, consisting of 'about 600 souls', travelling by train to Bundoran in July 1891 for the local Sports following mass in the morning at St Patrick's Church in Ballyshannon.[83]

These sporting events were also infrequent and were not held annually in every area. An exceptional case in Donegal was the Cranford Athletic Sports. By July 1909, this event, held with a strong emphasis on temperance, was said to be 'the premier sports in North-west Donegal – perhaps one of the best rural sports in Ulster', and the record crowd of 'over two thousand people' was the largest recorded in over twenty-five years of the event, placing its origins in the early 1880s.[84] This event had the value of a number of athletic attractions, novelty races, a football competition and a band.[85] By 1931 it was still in existence, and was apparently 'considered by many people to be the oldest meeting held annually without a break in the county' while it was also felt that 'the crowd of patrons is as big nowadays as it was in the past'.[86] While the importance of GAA-organised sports in popularising Gaelic football in the 1920s will be discussed in Chapter 5, more localised athletic events, such as those at the Mental Hospital grounds in Letterkenny in 1929 in aid of the Aonach Tír Conaill variety stall, continued to be held.[87] The emergence of association and Gaelic football as the dominant team sports in County Donegal in the opening decades of the twentieth century meant that many athletic sports events were hosted by GAA organisers, while soccer matches were often held as part of athletic sports in areas where the GAA had not managed to gain a foothold.[88]

State-sponsored athletic events had become more firmly established at this point with the transition from British rule in the twenty-six counties of the new Free State. The annually held Garda Síochána Sports (Donegal division) became popular in the 1920s with their fifth annual sports being held at Finner camp grounds in July 1930 as part of a 'Bundoran Gala', which included an 'open invitation golf tournament', mechanical hare dog racing and a dog show over the week of 29 June to 6 July.[89] The Garda Sports that year consisted of seventeen open events including the 600 yards flat championship of Ulster with a Garda band in attendance. In addition, 'excursions' by train and omnibus were organised while the day concluded with a Garda Dance in the local Palais De Dance with music from the Garda orchestra and Palanzo Band.[90] The sports, which were patronised by General O'Duffy and a number of TDs, were held under NACA rules and had an array of lap, gate, call, telegraph and megaphone stewards as well as judges, timekeepers and marksmen to ensure the smooth running of events. It was noted that 'a considerable number of the prizes went to Dublin, a large proportion came to Derry city and Donegal' and 'a large attendance' was present, although it is difficult to be precise about these figures.[91] The event is an example of a more formalised structure for sports meetings being in place within the county by the early 1930s.

Rugby

Early attempts to establish rugby in the county failed to have any major impact. Founded in 1854, Trinity College, Dublin was the first rugby club to be organised in Ireland. Students attending English public schools had helped establish the game there and by 1879 the Irish Rugby Football Union had been formed to govern the whole country's rugby affairs. Ten Ulster clubs were affiliated to this union in 1885 while the remainder were made up of clubs from Leinster (nine) and Munster (seven). A year later a Connacht branch was set up.[92] It is difficult to establish when the first rugby match was played in Donegal but a number of rugby clubs in the south of the county were up and running by the late 1880s. A rugby club was organised in Donegal town in 1887 under the captaincy of James Townsend Gahan.[93] Gahan was a civil engineer who was also a member of the Church of Ireland and a Freemason, and was later an inspector for the Congested Districts Board. Donegal's participation in matches appears to have been limited to friendly games against opposition such as local club Ballintra, although they did attract external opposition such as Foyle College from Derry in the spring of 1892.[94] The Ballintra club appears to have had a strong military influence. By 1889 the club was playing under the name of the Ballintra Fusiliers and they believed they owed their defeat in the 23 January match against Donegal to the absence of their captain and founder, Lieutenant John Thompson of the 59th Regiment.[95] Two months later they were in action again, against Big Park Blazers, in a match which 'lasted for nearly two hours' and 'much interest was shown in the game by the people of the neighbourhood'.[96] There is little evidence of any further growth and development of these three clubs, although in 1890 Donegal participated in friendlies against local teams Brownhall, Ballintra and Laghey.[97] The lack of a nearby competitive administration was no doubt detrimental to these clubs' development.

A rugby team did not exist in Ballyshannon until 1898, when it was organised by local hardware merchant and Derry rugby player James Sproule Myles, despite some efforts in October 1889 to initiate a club.[98] It was noted that 'one of the greatest difficulties in the way of carrying on rugby is the numbers of players required . . . in a town the size of Ballyshannon it is almost impossible to raise a sufficient number'.[99] An attempt was also made to disseminate the rules through the newspaper, but the game failed to develop at this time.

It appears that Myles had learned the game while attending Foyle College in Derry.[100] He was to become a leading figure within Ballyshannon and indeed County Donegal society. He was awarded the Military Cross for bravery during World War I and became a major and was elected to the fourth Dáil as an independent TD in 1923, where he remained until he lost his seat twenty years later.[101] He also presided over the Ballyshannon and Derry branches of the British Legion, had been part of the Ulster Volunteer Force prior to World War I and was described as 'a man who held the esteem of all creeds and all political parties'.[102] According to John Ward:

> As a young man he had excelled in sports, particularly rugby. He was quick footed, sure handed, and compensated with both for a lack in inches, he being of only medium height and weight. One of his fondest memories was of touring Canada with an Irish

> rugby side . . . The Major . . . was a man of many parts. In addition to his interest in the family business, his energy led him into captaining the local voluntary fire brigade, and he became an expert pilot for the coasters and tramp steamers that made the dangerous crossing of the bar and equally dangerous passage up the estuary to safe harbour below the Falls, carrying cargoes of coal, lumber, and other imports. This was a task he performed even at a late age. He was the last of his generation to do so.[103]

Writing in 2003, David Hassan stated that today 'rugby, with the exception of a small number of clubs in Donegal and Monaghan, has virtually no tradition in any of the three (Ulster) counties located south of the border'.[104] Rugby did not develop in Donegal as it did in other areas in Ulster, and Hassan believes that in the last quarter of the nineteenth century, 'in spite of its growing popularity, rugby continued to be seen as the almost exclusive preserve of one section of the Irish people'.[105] Hassan is in agreement with Sugden and Bairner who claim that 'some nationalists were attracted to the game, but the vast majority were not and the development of rugby depended to a huge extent on the participation of Protestants or, at the very least, those who identified with the Union'.[106] Certainly rugby in Donegal failed to challenge association football at the end of the 1800s and there was further competition from those interested in playing only Gaelic games in the twentieth century.

Despite the introduction of the game in County Westmeath by two graduates of Trinity College, it was never taken on by the civilian population and Hunt has identified a number of factors for this: an absence of opposition, a lack of a rugby-playing army regiment and the failure of the game to capture the public's imagination.[107] Some of these reasons were evident in Donegal too. Unfortunately for the diffusion of sport in Donegal, as previously noted, second-level educational establishments were sporadic in the nineteenth century, although there were some efforts to promote the sport of rugby by 1895 in the Royal School at Raphoe, which had been established as part of the five Royal schools.[108] This introduction of rugby was rather late in comparison with the Royal School in Dungannon, which attracted the Trinity Second XV in 1867.[109] Fixtures involving the Royal School, Raphoe, such as those against Derry Academy in 1895 and Foyle College the following year, seem to have been friendly matches.[110] They appear to have had little success in the Ulster Schools' Cup, which probably also hindered their development.[111] Given the importance of the education system in the spread of sport in Ireland, the failure of the Royal School, Raphoe, to establish a strong rugby tradition was not conducive to the growth of the sport in Donegal.[112] While Liam O'Callaghan has also noted the importance of those with education in disseminating the game, he believes that this sport was 'at a significant cultural distance from rural Ireland at this time'.[113] This was probably also the case in Donegal, where efforts to introduce rugby were generally limited to those in the south of the county and these failed to attract the interest of those outside a concentrated area close to Ballyshannon, until the 1930s.

Despite the official partition of Ireland in 1921, sports clubs in Donegal continued to participate in matches against teams in neighbouring counties that had become part of Northern Ireland as well as against those within the new Free State. Ballyshannon Rugby Club had been revived in the middle of the 1920s and it appears that James Sproule Myles was again heavily involved, although no great progress was made. Occasional newspaper references indicate the infrequent nature of matches, with a team containing local army men defeating 'the pick of Enniskillen' in October 1925, while the following month they faced Sligo Grammar School.[114] The club appears to have been preoccupied with association football in 1926, appearing as Ballyshannon Swifts in the local South Donegal league that year, while they also played Enniskillen in their favoured code.[115] Despite this, they were still able to attract those with local influence. At a club meeting held in September 1928 with bank accountant N.W. Hall in the chair, Myles was named president while vice-presidents included Dr Flood, Major Moore and R.J. Reynolds, a landowner and a former Justice of the Peace.[116] Reynolds was also president of the local horse racing committee and was later described as 'a popular and prominent figure in sporting circles, both in the hunting field and at local race meetings'.[117] He became a member of the District Council after the passing of the Local Government of Ireland Act and had also been president of the Ballyshannon Agricultural Society.[118]

With the lack of clubs in the south of the county, Ballyshannon continued to look to Sligo and Fermanagh for recreational fixtures.

In January 1933, they defeated Sligo RC, with James Sproule Myles returning to the field of play at the age of fifty-five.[119] Their team (which defeated a Sligo Second XV in April 1933) was said to contain a son of an Inver-based rector, Munro, who, it was reported, 'was considered a few years ago to be the fastest schoolboy playing the game in Ulster'.[120] However, there is no indication the club was a serious organisation, and it was reported that 'the Ballyshannon side was little more than a "scrap" one got together for the occasion'.[121]

Attempts to organise rugby were slow to develop in the north-east of the county. In March of 1930 a 'Free State selection' met a team made up of players from Northern Ireland at the Mental Hospital grounds in Letterkenny in what appears to be the first rugby match played in this town.[122] The match was described as 'a novelty' and was well attended.[123] There were few other attempts to spread the game until March 1932 when a club was set up in nearby Milford. It was reported that the newly established team had been loaned the grounds of local soccer club Milford Celtic, and 'team building' was 'going ahead rapidly'.[124] This seems to have coincided with the decline of the local GAA club at the time.[125] While local talent was said to be limited, the new club hoped to avail of those from adjoining areas. They were heavily defeated by a Letterkenny team in their first match but won the return game a few weeks later before a large crowd.[126]

The Milford club appears to have been well supported in the local community, with their dance in April 1932 also well attended.[127] Their committee for the 1932–33 season included patron, the Earl of Leitrim, while M. McCreadie, county councillor, was elected president. They were captained by Daniel Watters while P.A. McGeady, veterinary surgeon, was named vice-captain. P.P. MacEoin, CSE, was appointed treasurer while J.J. McAleese was named secretary.[128] Their team was temporarily 'strengthened by talent on holidays' but Letterkenny remained the only other nearby Donegal team at this time and no attempts were made to meet the Ballyshannon club.[129] Magee and Foyle colleges in Derry provided opposition for Milford in November and December 1932 respectively, while they also met Strabane on a number of occasions and played the City of Derry club at least once.[130] Other fixtures included those against the Milford soccer team and a selection named the 'Barbarians'.[131] Competitive matches appear to have been difficult to arrange. Hopes for a cup to be presented went unfulfilled, although they did manage to organise a seven-a-side competition in September 1933 in which they competed with selections from Letterkenny, Kerrykeel and Ramelton.[132] In 1932, Milford RC contemplated entering the McMillan Cup, a competition for clubs in Derry, Fermanagh and Tyrone, although it is unclear if they managed to take part.[133] By April 1933 they claimed to have 'done exceedingly well', considering they were 'labouring under great difficulties with players scattered over a wide area and the opportunities of having an occasional practice match out of the question'.[134] They were also said to have played 'the leading combinations of the north-west rugby circles'.[135]

Rugby struggled to form an identity for itself in Donegal, and opposition from other sporting organisers was evident. The playing of this code in St Eunan's College drew condemnation in the local press, while the Convoy GAA club passed a resolution against its presence there in April 1932.[136] The fact that some priests in Letterkenny were supporting rugby in the town by officiating at matches was a source of concern to GAA County Board officials, who at this point had their own administrative structure well established but were eager to prevent so-called 'foreign' games from weakening their support.[137] At a meeting of the County Board in March 1932, concerns were expressed about the playing of rugby at St Eunan's College and it was stated that nearby GAA clubs 'had done all they could to put down rugby in the town, but now it appeared that it required action by the County Board'.[138] Two members of a local GAA club visited the president of the college and the bishop, but 'got no satisfaction'.[139] Delegates felt that college students were being rendered illegal for Gaelic games due to their participation in rugby and that the former codes were not receiving enough attention from college staff.

The attitude to rugby in Letterkenny was exacerbated by the perception that those organising it were 'sons of Gaels, and people to whom they would naturally look for an ideal'.[140] TD and County Board delegate Brian Brady also expressed dissatisfaction on behalf of the GAA at a meeting of the Donegal Mental Hospital committee on 9 April 1933 that permission had been given by its chairman, Reverend John O'Doherty, for rugby to be played at the Mental Hospital grounds and that it was not discussed beforehand.[141] Brady got little support from those present, including a number of priests, and it was agreed that 'so long as there were no abuses, future similar games be allowed'.[142] Despite this religious backing, the game failed to attract much interest in Donegal outside the Milford, Letterkenny and Ballyshannon areas at this time.

Cricket

Neal Garnham has traced the first recorded cricket match in Ireland back to August 1792 between the Garrison and All Ireland selections in Phoenix Park.[143] Despite this, cricket was slow to spread to the rest of Ireland. The first Irish club, Phoenix CC in Dublin, was not founded until 1830.[144] There were clubs playing 'irregular matches' in Galway, Kilkenny, Wicklow and Dublin in that decade but it was not until the early 1870s that there were cricket clubs in every county in Ireland.[145] However, it took until the 1890s before the game took on a competitive structure in Donegal, which suggests an improvement in organisation and interest in this decade, but this establishment lacked any significant permanency.

Cricket in Donegal appears to have spread through the east of the county in the Laggan Valley. It is clear that a small number of Donegal clubs were involved in local competitions while some others were affiliated to cricket bodies based in Derry. The majority of clubs seem to have been mainly involved in friendly matches. Certainly the military in the county was involved, but the social background of club members varied and was not always of an elitist nature. Cricket was being played in Raphoe by 1864 and in 1892 this club was identified as the oldest established in the county.[146] Gerard Siggins has stated that there were clubs in counties Derry and Tyrone prior to this and the spread of the game was helped by the railway network.[147] As mentioned earlier, the Finn Valley Railway line had been established in 1863 and this seems to have helped the spread of cricket in this area. It was not long before the sport was beginning to develop, with teams recorded in Lifford, Finn Valley and Donaghmore and at the Royal School in Raphoe in 1865. There was also a club in the north of the county at Malin that year.[148]

Tranter has noted that cricket in Stirling suffered from poor organisation, 'a lack of explosive excitement and a refusal to make itself more attractive to spectators'.[149] While organisation was definitely a problem in Donegal, other challenges were more localised.

The physical divisions created by the Derryveagh and Blue Stack mountains undoubtedly hindered the spread of cricket to the west of the county. Difficulties with transport were illustrated in the reports of the Falcarragh, Swilly and County Donegal cricket clubs, who saw this as being detrimental to their development in the 1870s, while in 1890 the clubs of Ballybofey and Ballyshannon agreed to meet in Donegal town as the distance between these clubs was deemed to be too great to allow either to host the match.[150] South Donegal clubs such as Ballyshannon were therefore generally restricted to matches against more local opposition.[151] It was in the more prosperous East Donegal that the majority of the county's cricket clubs were formed and this introduction took place earlier than in the west.

Despite cricket being played in the Royal School in Raphoe the team would have had to look outside the county for schools' opposition due to a dearth of local secondary schools, which also hindered the spread of cricket in Donegal.[152] By 1870 there were four teams based in Letterkenny; Swilly, Letterkenny, the County Donegal CC and the Letterkenny military barracks all had practising elevens, while Castlefin, Finn Valley and Ballybofey were also participating in friendly matches.[153] The County Donegal XI was strong enough to defeat a Derry selection at Letterkenny in September of that year in a fixture reputed to be the first ever county match to be played within Donegal.[154] A year later the game had spread to the south of the county where it was being played by Donegal Town CC.[155] In the north-west there were two teams in the parish of Cloughaneely, with the Olphert family, the local landlords, prominent in the founding of the Falcarragh club in 1870.[156] Not every Donegal cricket club was listed in *John Lawrence's Handbook of Cricket in Ireland*, which is a useful guide to the game, but is considered incomplete as it relied on clubs sending their information to Lawrence.[157] These north-west Donegal clubs do not appear to have survived into the 1880s and exactly how much activity Donegal's other cricket clubs were involved in throughout the 1870s is difficult to establish.

Development of clubs in the west, south-west and south was slower than in the north-east and was characterised by a lack of permanency. This is unsurprising given their distance from the heart of cricket in the county. By May of 1881, a new club had been established in the south of the county at Mountcharles, numbering 'about forty members'.[158] Donegal Town CC defeated a team from Glenfin in September.[159] A club was set up in Ballyshannon in April 1882.[160] In West Donegal, there were three clubs in the Rosses area in 1885, and in the south-west there was a club in Ardara in 1891.[161] Cricket outside East Donegal failed to gain a competitive infrastructure and the contrasting economic and social conditions between the east and west of the county undoubtedly contributed to this. The lack of an organiser or committee to arrange competitive fixtures was also a major problem.

Lack of motivation, perhaps caused by a dearth of new opposition, was said to have been a problem for Falcarragh CC in 1874.[162] The club played only six matches in 1872 and again in 1873, against Letterkenny, Dunfanaghy and the County Donegal XI, and only seven members of the club put in an appearance for their away match against Letterkenny in 1873.[163] Given that they only had three clubs to play against, it must have been difficult for their forty members to maintain an interest throughout the season. With the wet weather, probably a major restriction in the growth of the game, some Donegal clubs were fortunate if they could participate in ten matches per season. The County Donegal CC played nine matches in 1877 and 'the wet summer' was reported to be a factor in this low number.[164] This is a small number of matches when compared to some of the more flourishing clubs, such as Belfast club North of Ireland which in 1878 could boast of playing thirty-one matches. This club had 380 members, while by the winter of 1884 the Enniskillen Cricket Club had almost one hundred people enrolled; Donegal membership figures are relatively low in comparison.[165] The securing of playing fields was also a factor in the development of some clubs. The Swilly club felt that their low number of three matches in 1871 was primarily due to 'not getting a proper ground early in the season'.[166] Difficulties in securing an adequate field were a recurring problem for the Ballybofey club and in 1892 they complained bitterly in the *Derry Standard* about the doubling of the rent by a local landowner and seem to have been relatively inactive that year, having passed a resolution repudiating 'the conditions as insulting'.[167] However, most clubs appear to have been able to obtain fields when necessary, despite having to cope with poor surfaces and uneven creases at times.[168]

By 1891 there were at least eleven cricket clubs in Donegal and the administrative structure of the game there appears to have differed from cricket in Westmeath and Tipperary in that it had, at least briefly, cup and league competitions in the late nineteenth century.[169] The East Donegal Cricket Cup competition, under the presidency of Dr William E. McFeeters, was first played for that year, being held on a knockout basis between the clubs of Convoy, St Johnston, Raphoe, Manorcunningham, Lifford and Ballybofey.[170] Lifford were awarded this trophy outright in 1893 having won three in a row and it appears there were no competitions held in 1894.[171] Despite the presence of this competitive structure, cricket's development in the area was hampered by a number of problems. The fielding of non-locals by clubs was said to be detrimental to the game. Of concern to 'the Gawk' in 1891 was that 'the union was established for the purpose of promoting cricket in East Donegal, and not [so] that a club might return the name of some "crack" who perchance might happen to be in the neighbourhood during the cricket season'.[172] Attendances at meetings were poor and not every club kept up to date with their arranged fixtures, while some teams suffered from a lack of members.[173] In 1895 it was replaced by the County Donegal Cricket League with Mr Alexander Weir, manager of the Convoy Woollen Factory, as secretary.[174] Thirty matches were organised for the six teams involved: Letterkenny, Manorcunningham, Raphoe, Clonleigh, Lifford and Convoy.[175] The league was not a very successful enterprise and appears to have disbanded after 1897, with Lifford struggling to field teams and scratching a number of fixtures that year.[176]

A number of clubs were very well patronised in their local communities. Subscriptions were crucial for the successful running of clubs such as Ballybofey CC, while concerts also formed a significant part of fundraising efforts.[177] 'The proceeds of a Christy Minstrel concert held during the winter', amounting to £4, was given to Raphoe CC in April 1890, while St Johnston's balance of £10 5 shillings in April 1901 was said to be thanks to their winter concert.[178] Lifford's concert in February 1895 brought together 'a select assembly' while at a concert held by the Ballybofey club in April 1892, 'the elite of the district was well represented'.[179] Cricket undoubtedly provided opportunities for social interaction. At the match between Lifford and the Royal School, Raphoe in 1865, 'the field presented an exceedingly gay appearance, owing to the presence of many of the fair ladies of Strabane and neighbourhood'.[180]

Teams were generally well treated after matches. After the above fixture, the players retired to the local Abercorn Arms Hotel for 'an excellent dinner', a central part of the cricket experience in a number of areas in Ireland at that time.[181] Some clubs organised excursions for the local community. In July 1890, Ballybofey clubman Patrick Roche organised a train which was said to have accommodated 'upwards of three hundred excursionists' for a match and overnight stay in Donegal town.[182]

Cup victories provided increased excitement and were well received by club supporters. After Lifford's East Donegal Cricket Union Cup success in August 1891, 'the victors on arriving in the historic little town were cheered along the street, and one enthusiastic supporter of the club went so far as to have a tar barrel [lit] in honour of the occasion'.[183] The deciding match in the 1895 County Donegal Cricket League, between Convoy and Raphoe, 'created a large amount of local interest, and at its conclusion the cricket field presented a scene of great enthusiasm and indication of deep interest by the sympathizers of the competing teams'.[184] Ballybofey's victory over Eglington from Derry in the 1910 North-west Junior League championship final at Strabane Park was another match which drew much attention from club supporters, and was a significant enough fixture to earn the accommodation of the local railway service.[185]

With military barracks at Lifford, Letterkenny, Ballyshannon and Dunfanaghy, local clubs availed of the participation of high-ranking army men and these barracks also fielded teams from time to time. In addition, regimental bands were at times present during cricket matches involving clubs in Ballyshannon and in County Fermanagh.[186] Military involvement in the form of the 'gallant Inniskillings' was crucial to the success of the Lifford club, the leading team in the East Donegal Cricket Union in the 1890s.[187] The involvement of the local regiment, in their red coats, could also be seen at the club's functions.[188] Along with military participation, much of the Lifford club's success at this time was due to Edward Fields, who emigrated to the United States of America in 1893, and there is some indication that a number of players learned the game from him at some point while schoolboys. On the eve of his departure, he was said to have 'neither spared time, trouble, nor expense' in making Lifford the champions of East Donegal and had taken the club's development into his own hands 'several years ago when most of all the members were little boys going to school, and on him they looked as their philosopher and guide'.[189]

Some individuals were eager to foster the game's growth through the workplace. John S. Weir, the managing director of the Convoy Woollen Mills Company, as well as being a magistrate, coroner, land agent and farmer, was a leading figure in Donegal cricket circles and put his own money into the sport. By the summer of 1892 he had taken the trouble of 'laying down a splendid crease and grand stand in a nice little holm attached to the mill'.[190] This company employed 'over forty workers in the mid-1880s, supported by a network of over one hundred agents'.[191] Although the mill's facilities lacked much in stature in comparison with that in the village of Sion Mills, County Tyrone, there are some similarities with its development, although the latter area was home to a model village, sporting facilities and a school; a cricket club, patronised by the mill owners, the Herdman family, was formed there much earlier, in 1864.[192]

TABLE 2.1

Cricket players in Donegal, 1880–1915

Category	*Number of players*	*% of total*
1: Professional	39	26
2: Domestic	2	1.33
3: Commercial	26	17.33
4: Agricultural	32	21.33
5: Industrial	46	30.66
6: Indefinite and non-productive	5	3.33
Total	150	100

SOURCES: *DJ, DP and DN, DV, DI* (1880–1915) and 'Census of Ireland 1901 and 1911'; retrieved from http://www.census.nationalarchives.ie/ [Accessed 28 September 2012]

Table 2.1, shown above, illustrates the socio-economic backgrounds of 150 Donegal cricketers who played the game between 1880 and 1915.[193] While military involvement was significant in the playing and organising of cricket matches, as shown above, Donegal's early cricket players who could be positively identified were primarily drawn from the industrial sector (31 per cent). Some clubs relied heavily on this class for player participation and the Convoy club's team which appeared in 1897 was made up of a number of those working in the local woollen mill, and contained a wool carder, an assistant loom tuner, a wool spinner, a blacksmith, a caretaker, a foreman tuner and a clerk. Those categorised as belonging to the professional class made up 26 per cent of the overall number while agriculturally based workers made up 21 per cent. The involvement of those defined as belonging to the commercial class was not as significant, with this figure constituting just 17 per cent. Only 3 per cent of the overall total were categorised as belonging to the indefinite and non-productive class while only two players or 1 per cent were employed in domestic services. Using a total of 273 players who participated in Westmeath between 1900 and 1902, Hunt has established that the majority of these were drawn from the semi-skilled classes (48 per cent) while the smallest number came from the gentry and aristocracy.[194]

Cricket in Donegal had a strong Protestant and unionist influence, although the sport was enjoyed by Roman Catholics as well. At dinner following the Donegal and Ballyshannon match in August 1882, 'the loyal toasts of the Queen and the Royal Family were given and honoured'.[195] The Convoy Cricket Club's annual concert and ball in November 1895 concluded with the singing of 'God Save the Queen', while in January 1901, St Johnston Cricket Club held a 'grand evening concert' in the local Orange Hall and these functions served as an important part of community life and were in many ways an expression of their identity.[196] Donegal's early cricket players were drawn largely from non-Roman Catholic denominations. Although Catholicism was the single most common religion of all players (36 per cent), over 30 per cent of players were identified as Presbyterians while almost 26 per cent of the overall total were members of the Church of Ireland. There was also a much smaller involvement of those in other denominations. This differed significantly from Westmeath where Hunt has identified a higher proportion of Roman Catholic players, with 90 per cent of those identified as belonging to this religious category. In contrast, members of the Church of Ireland made up only 9.7 per cent of the overall total there, although, like Kerry and Mayo, it must be noted that Westmeath had a higher proportion of Roman Catholics in the county.[197] The average age of a cricket player in Donegal between 1880 and 1915 was 26.64 years of age and this is quite similar to Hunt's figure of 24.63 years in Westmeath. The majority of Donegal's players were single (63 per cent) although a greater number were unmarried in Westmeath (90 per cent).[198]

TABLE 2.2

Places of birth of Donegal's cricket players, 1880–1915

Places of birth	*Number*	*% of total*
Donegal	113	75.33
Other Irish counties	17	11.33
Overseas	19	12.66
Unknown	1	0.66
Total	150	100

SOURCES: *DJ, DP and DN, DV, DI* (1880–1915) and 'Census of Ireland 1901 and 1911'; retrieved from http://www.census.nationalarchives.ie/ [Accessed 28 September 2012]

Wren, De Burca and Gorry have noted the impact of migration from the countryside on the development of Dublin's early GAA clubs.[199] While there is little indication that Donegal's early GAA clubs were greatly enhanced by migrant workers, the case of cricket differed slightly. Table 2.2 indicates the effects of migration into the county on cricket player participation in Donegal. Although Donegal was not highly populated by those born outside the county – the 1901 Census records that just over 94 per cent were born there with over 4 per cent born in Ireland's other counties and under 2 per cent born overseas – there is some evidence that migration into the county boosted cricket clubs.[200] While over three-quarters of all players were born within Donegal, over 12 per cent were born abroad. These birthplaces ranged from neighbouring countries (England and Scotland), to more outlying colonies of the British Empire at the time including India, Australia and Bermuda. Buncrana-based cricketer Alfred William Cuttriss was a civil engineer, draughtsman and a member of the Royal Engineers' staff and had been born in Boroda, India in 1872. His involvement is one example of the town's linkage with naval activity on Lough Swilly. In addition to this, six Convoy players had moved from Scotland and gained employment in the woollen mill there in the 1890s. Of the overall figure 11 per cent were born in other Irish counties, with a number of these men migrating to Donegal to take up positions such as solicitor, teacher, law agent and contractor's clerk. What is unclear is how many cricketers left the county in search of work, although emigration was a problem for Donegal Town CC in 1882.[201]

TABLE 2.3

Cricket administrators in Donegal, 1880–1915

Category	*Number of administrators*	*% of total*
1: Professional	26	38.80
2: Domestic	0	0
3: Commercial	20	29.85
4: Agricultural	8	11.94
5: Industrial	12	17.90
6: Indefinite and non-productive	1	1
Total	67	100

SOURCES: *DJ, DP and DN, DV, DI* 1880–1915 and 'Census of Ireland 1901 and 1911'; retrieved from http://www.census.nationalarchives.ie/ [Accessed 28 September 2012]

As shown in Table 2.3, the professional classes (39 per cent) were the most dominant category of sixty-seven officials identified as being involved in the administration of cricket in County Donegal. Although those belonging to the commercial sector were also heavily involved (30 per cent), the industrial and agricultural classes, which made up 18 per cent and 12 per cent respectively, had less influence in the organisation of club matters. Regarding religious denominations 40 per cent of these men were Roman Catholic while Church of Ireland members made up over a third (34 per cent) and Presbyterians comprised just over one-fifth of the overall figure (22 per cent). As will be seen later, this participation of non-Roman Catholics as players and administrators reached higher levels in cricket than in association and Gaelic football and hurling. The majority of cricket organisers in Donegal were married (55 per cent) and their average

age was 39.9 years of age, illustrating how this type of role was more suited to a perhaps less agile man than those playing the game. Cricket administration in Donegal, like player involvement, similarly benefited from the participation of those born outside the county, with just over 67 per cent born in Donegal while almost 30 per cent were born in other Irish counties. No fewer than seven of those involved in the running of the Ballyshannon Cricket Club at various stages in the period assessed here were born outside the club's home county, illustrating the attraction of Ballyshannon as a commercial hub in South Donegal at the time.

The case of Ballyshannon Cricket Club illustrates the difficulties in sustaining this sport in the county even with significant local patronage. The existence of the club in April 1882 was due to a number of leading members of local society.[202] These included Robert Sweeny, who was a woollen draper and chairman of the Town Commissioners, timber merchant Cecil Stephens and solicitors Robert McCredy (club treasurer), Alfred Stubbs, Robert Archer Ross Todd, R.F. Parker and F.M. Lowry.[203] Stubbs, 'a generous benefactor', and his brother Henry, who had become High Sheriff of County Fermanagh by 1901, were later said to be 'landmarks in Donegal'. Alfred was educated at Portora Royal School in Enniskillen and Trinity College, Dublin and became 'head of one of the leading firms of solicitors in the county'.[204] The club played at least seven matches in 1882 but was restricted to ties against clubs in Enniskillen, Donegal town, Mountcharles and North Leitrim due to transport difficulties.[205] Solicitors appear to have been particularly prominent in the club and in July 1889, a match dubbed 'legals versus illegals' was played.[206] Meetings were at times held in the offices of these men, while the local bathing and lawn tennis clubs also staged their administrative discussions in these offices and in those of the Town Commissioners.[207] The influence of the local military was prominent in the cricket club and their line-out often included Sergeant Major Evans, Sergeants Connors and Dale and Lieutenant MacKenzie.[208] Matches were at times played in the morning and on weekdays, thereby isolating those with less flexible working hours and free time.[209]

Like other cricket clubs, matches attracted the support of the local elite and at the match against North Leitrim CC in August 1882, 'the play was witnessed by a large company, including a number of ladies, whose summer toilettes of various colours, made a pleasing effect combined with the costumes of the players'.[210] Families in attendance included those of barrister R.L. Moore, DL, Belleek; Dr Simon Shiel, chairman of the Ballyshannon Union; bank manager Andrew H. Reid, JP; the family of prominent engineer Robert Crawford, and the Coanes, who ran a local hotel.[211]

The infrequent nature of annual organisation illustrates the reliance on local enthusiasm for the survival of sports clubs in Donegal society at this time. Like athletic events and regattas throughout the county, the playing of cricket was not always maintained in Ballyshannon on a yearly basis, and the club was revived in March 1889 having played no matches since 1885.[212] There is evidence to suggest that they struggled financially in 1889 while a call for new members was issued the following year.[213] A revival, initiated by Dr Condon, was staged in 1896 'after years of collapse'.[214] Problems continued into the new century with the Boer War (1899–1902) impacting on the local manpower available. In April 1900, it was reported that 'about 60 youths belonging to Ballyshannon and district . . . are going to the front next week'.[215] Two years later the local press noted that 'the suggested cricket club in Ballyshannon is now not likely to materialise owing to the departure of the staff to various parts of the country. There are several good players in town, but unfortunately not in sufficient numbers to keep a club going.'[216] It was again in operation in 1903 but was hampered by the failure of players to turn up for practice, and this appears to be the last year this club was in operation.[217]

Despite the lack of development made by cricket's administrative bodies, the number of teams playing in Donegal was not diminished by 1900, as there were at least thirteen cricket teams in the county that year.[218] Significantly, twelve of these were located in the north and east of the county. Like soccer and GAA teams, a small number of clubs were eager to affiliate to external committees. In 1903 Buncrana was registered with the County Derry Cricket Union.[219] Other clubs such as Ballybofey and Clonleigh became affiliated with the North-west Cricket Union in this decade but a gradual decrease in overall numbers meant that in 1914 Buncrana was the only Donegal club noted as competing in the North-west Senior League, along with clubs from Derry and Tyrone.[220]

In an interview published in 1895, prominent Donegal-born Irish international cricketer, L.H. Gwynn, identified a number of problems faced by those hoping to develop the sport in Ireland. As well as the unsuitable climate, he felt that cricket was being kept alive mainly by military regiments and that 'the lower order do not take to it'.[221] He believed that the game had no popular support and that it was not suited to 'the Celtic temperament'. There was no professional structure throughout the country and it was an expensive game to play with no real 'gates'. A lack of interest was also said to be a problem in country areas where there were 'not enough men who care to form a team' and he believed that the game was dying out in Ulster and Munster, although he noted a revival taking place in the West and in some counties around Dublin.[222]

As shown above and as has been proven in Westmeath, cricket was not simply an elitist pastime, but perceptions of the sport amongst cultural nationalists certainly hindered its development in the early twentieth century. By 1908, those playing cricket in Donegal were facing criticism from nationalistic journalists in the local press.[223] According to Cronin and Higgins, the Land War and the coming of the GAA had a detrimental effect on cricket and 'many culturally minded Catholics abandoned the game. Cricket retreated into an even smaller number of social settings where the game's imperial ties were not seen as problematic.'[224] The lack of a county-based structure was detrimental to its overall development while the Great War also had a serious effect on the progress of the game.[225] At the annual meeting of the Derry-based North-west Cricket Union in late January 1915, it was stated that there had been a 'serious effect on the game in the district in the early part of the season', caused by the political crisis and later on, the war. Interest in the matches practically ceased, and at the end of the season it was impossible for some clubs to carry out their fixtures. The financial situation of the cricket governing body had become their worst recorded and this was thought to have been as a result of a decline in donations, with the decision being taken to suspend all competitions also based on patriotic fervour.[226] Cricket in Donegal failed to develop any widespread support throughout the county in the twentieth century and its popularity remained largely restricted to the Laggan Valley area. Like cricket in Westmeath, it continued to exist and in 1927 the East Donegal Cricket league was revived.[227]

Members of this organisation met in the Ashe Rialto Hall in Convoy in April 1928. The meeting was chaired by Mr Sheskin of Ballybofey, with vice-chairman Mr Holmes of Convoy, treasurer W. Harris of Letterkenny and secretary J.G. Chambers of Raphoe taking up key roles.[228] Five East Donegal clubs were affiliated, with Urney of West Tyrone also involved, although they were suspended in the second round and St Johnston won the cup. Similarly Ballybofey did not complete all fixtures, scratching to Convoy, Letterkenny and Raphoe.[229] Like those playing rugby, Donegal's cricket clubs were keen to maintain links with those in other counties, given the lack of local opposition available. In September 1928 a Baronscourt team featuring the Marquis of Hamilton travelled to Convoy from Tyrone and the following year Burt participated in the Derry Mid-week Cricket League, although no other Donegal club registered for this competition.[230] St Johnston had become involved in the North-west Cricket Union by May 1930, but the revived East Donegal League again failed to branch deeper into Donegal.[231]

Hockey

By 1898 there were a small number of hockey teams located mainly in urban areas around the south and north-east of the county. This appears to have been part of a wider development within the north-west of Ireland, with the *Londonderry Sentinel* reporting that hockey 'has taken a hold in the district, and quite a number of clubs have been formed, the game continuing to make strides as a popular outdoor pastime'. The Northern Hockey Union was established by the end of 1896.[232] Like cricket and rugby, hockey remained a minority sport in Donegal, and participation in competitive matches generally meant affiliation with governing bodies based outside the county. County Donegal had no founding members in this Union and no attempt was made by its clubs to form their own administrative structure. However, by the early twentieth century, Raphoe Royal School, Letterkenny, Buncrana and the Raphoe Town club had become affiliated to what had by then become the North-west Hockey Union.

In April 1898, Raphoe Town, a 'newly instituted' hockey club, fielded a mixed team against a female selection from the local Royal School club.[233] The town club entertained their opponents afterwards in the Orange Hall, where tea and refreshments were provided, illustrating the strong Protestant ethos within this sport in the area.[234] Some local hockey clubs illustrated their support for Britain's war involvement in the south of Africa. Letterkenny took on Derry Lacrosse on 18 November 1899 at the Brandywell in a match before a small attendance, the proceeds from which went towards the Mayor's Fund for soldiers' widows of the Boer War.[235]

Despite winning the North-west Hockey Union's league in 1908, the Letterkenny Hockey club did not build on this progress and it was Raphoe which emerged as Donegal's leading hockey club.[236] They won the North-west Cup in 1913 and, although the North-west Hockey Union was also suspended during the Great War, Raphoe re-affiliated with this administrative body for the 1924–25 season and the following season won the Senior League, Charity Cup and Junior Cup.[237] Over the course of the next decade they won the league a further three times although they did not participate every year.[238] Ballybofey Hockey Club also competed successfully in leagues run by the North-west Hockey Union, winning their Intermediate League in 1930. Participation in this competition and the sport's strong links with British culture meant that at times they competed against teams representing the security forces of Northern Ireland, such as a Sergeants' XI, a Royal Ulster Constabulary team and the Royal Artillery. Entertainment at cup finals was also sometimes provided by these bodies, with the (Derry) City B Special Constabulary band performing prior to the 1931 North-west Senior Cup Final between YMCA and Raphoe.[239]

In the south of the county, clubs emerged in Donegal town and Ballyshannon but generally remained isolated from competitions in the north-east. On New Year's Day 1898, Donegal Town Hockey club defeated Stranorlar in an away friendly and it was reported that 'in Mr Gahan, Mr Bevan, Mr Townsend and Captain Hamilton, Donegal have a quartette that any team might be proud of', while Dr Johnstone was said to be the home team's best player.[240] Evelyn Barclay Bevan was a member of the Church of Ireland and a landed proprietor, while Gahan, as noted above, was instrumental in the setting up of a rugby club in Donegal town in 1887. F.G. Townsend was also a member of that denomination and a civil engineer, while Dublin-born Captain Hamilton was a Church of Ireland landowner who resided at Brownhall Demesne. By February 1898 the Donegal club had extended their range of fixtures to include the Sligo Hockey Club but do not appear to have increased their seasonal structure beyond the playing of occasional friendly matches at this time.[241]

In March 1901 a club containing ladies and gentlemen was said to be 'practicing [sic] steadily' in Ballyshannon and played Tyrone clubs Fintona and Strabane that month.[242] For their initial match against Fintona, six men and five ladies were on the team. The involvement of Protestants based in the town was significant for the Ballyshannon Hockey Club. Along with Dr Condon, a Roman Catholic and local JP, their side contained Church of Ireland members Robert Neely, a merchant, and bank clerk Donald McNair, the team's captain. William Coleman and Henry Madden, who were both Presbyterians, were also bank clerks while Arthur H. Lipsett was an auctioneer and belonged to the Church of Ireland.[243] In addition, two Reid ladies, and the misses Lipsett, Hamilton and Biggar also took part. Some of these players were boarders born outside Donegal, with McNair born in Java, while Coleman had migrated from Antrim and Madden from Clonmel.

There were also a number of Protestants heavily involved in the running of the club in the early twentieth century. Presbyterian Robert Myles, a merchant and clerk of the petty sessions, was named as president in 1901 while Robert's brother, James Sproule, was selected as honorary secretary. The committee included Church of Ireland members Matthew Charles Ambrose, an Inland Revenue officer, and Dr Creighton, a noted tennis player who had won the local championship the previous year.[244] By 1903, Presbyterian bank clerk William N. Neilson was also involved on the hockey club's committee along with several members of the military.[245]

As Jennifer Kelly and R.V. Comerford have noted, 'one way to explore social networks is to trace them through the structures of a developing associational culture, or in other words, formal voluntary activity, such as participation in clubs, societies and voluntary organisations'.[246] Pádraig Deignan has shown that the presence of 'Protestant fraternal associations such as the YMCA, Sligo Constitutional Club and the Freemasons was crucial in preserving a sense of common Protestant culture and social activity and in providing a setting to ease the transition from union to Free State' in Sligo.[247] Some comparisons with activity in Ballyshannon can be made, although there is no evidence a constitutional club was in operation there. The Myles brothers had been part of the local YMCA in the late nineteenth century while a number of other members who also participated in local sport included hockey club vice-president Robert Lipsett, a Church of Ireland grocer and auctioneer; treasurer Finlay Nelson McCready, a Presbyterian who worked in the hardware and ironmongery businesses; and secretary M.B. Deacon.[248] Some of these men were also involved in the Ballyshannon Agricultural Association with James Sproule Myles acting as secretary in 1897, and all were Freemasons.[249]

In 1757 Ballyshannon was the first Donegal town to gain a warrant for a Masonic lodge, although the Masonic Hall was not built there until 1906, with the financial assistance of James Sproule Myles. Deacon, an Episcopalian law clerk, was master of the Ballyshannon Masonic Lodge in 1899.[250] The foundation of these lodges in Donegal was a slower development than in other counties and the county had the lowest membership figures in Ulster in the eighteenth century. With the condemnation of secret societies in 1814 by Pope Pius VII, the number of Roman Catholic Freemasons lessened significantly and this further decreased with Pius IX's denunciation of the organisation in 1864.[251] Although it is difficult to be precise about annual membership figures, in the period from 1882 until 1935 there were at least 221 men enrolled as members of the Ballyshannon Lodge, but the majority do not appear to have been directly involved in local sports clubs.[252] In 1908 James Sproule Myles was master of the lodge and after a ladies' and gentlemen's hockey match at home to Leitrim club Manorhamilton in February 1908, the visitors received dinner in the Masonic Hall, and an 'impromptu dance' was then held.[253] Another dance, said to be 'a brilliant social event', had taken place after a match versus the same opposition in Manorhamilton the previous week.[254] Myles had been named Sovereign of Prince Masons and Provincial Senior Grand Warden by the time he died in February 1956 and as Seán Beattie has noted, 'his charity work among people of all denominations represented the visible expression of his deeply held Masonic beliefs'.[255] Along with those named above, some other prominent Ballyshannon businessmen who took up positions in local sports committees and who were also members of the Freemasons included Robert Archer Ross Todd, Ralph Hall Reid, William Coleman and N.W. Hall.[256]

These links to elements of Protestant culture within the town did not disappear with the formation of the Irish Free State. Deignan has also shown that in Sligo, 'the British Legion provided a sense of community for all ex-servicemen'.[257] By 1925, it was said that there were 130 ex-servicemen residing in Ballyshannon, although at a British Legion reorganisation meeting in the Market Hall in 1927 it was noted that a clubhouse was needed along with financial assistance.[258] An analysis of its committee that year illustrates that a number of Catholics were also involved, further underlining the cross-community representation within local organisations in the town.[259] In June 1928 a tennis tournament in aid of this organisation was held there, while a Poppy Day collection for disabled ex-servicemen later that year gathered over £59.[260] Despite difficulties in fielding teams at times, hockey continued to be played in Ballyshannon.

Ballintra was another area where there was a sufficient Protestant contingent with an interest in hockey to organise a club, but this appears to have been a later development than that in Ballyshannon. After they defeated Ballyshannon in August 1933 the club held a dance in Rossnowlagh, and another one was arranged for the following month.[261] It was noted that 'these dances are now the chief events in the district', illustrating the social value of the sport for some members of the community.[262] By February 1934 Ballintra was the only Donegal club competing in the North-west Intermediate League and Cup despite the heavy travelling expenses required.[263] This league contained a number of clubs with strong religious backgrounds including two YMCA selections along with Methody and Christ Church.[264] Donegal Town Hockey Club, while not affiliated to this league, also met religious selections around this time and participated in matches against the Church of Ireland Derry Cathedral XI on a number of occasions in the early 1930s, with social functions being held afterwards.[265] A few schools, such as the Prior School of Lifford, that were involved in the North-west Boys Hockey League by the winter of 1930, were keen to encourage the sport but the game failed to develop significantly outside Raphoe.[266]

Conclusion

The survival of pre-codified hurling into the early twentieth century in Donegal has illustrated the failure to react to more mainstream changes in the organisation of sport in some areas. While the more industrialised nature of many parts of Britain must be noted, the inability to replicate some English and Scottish patterns of sporting development associated with the sporting 'revolution' is clearly evident. In particular, the failure of the East Donegal Cricket Union and the County Donegal Cricket League to develop throughout the county, or even to be maintained for a period longer than half a decade in the 1890s, highlights the contrast between a sustained sporting revolution and an incomplete one. The acknowledgement of the work of individuals in the spread of sport, rather than any central administrative agency, is fundamental to understanding how sport spread in Donegal. Tranter's assertion that 'at the macro level the organisational "revolution" in sport was reflected in the widespread establishment of governing bodies to oversee the rules and organise and run competitions' may be successfully applied to some parts of Britain, but at a micro level, in the case of Donegal, this was not how sport developed.[267]

While County Donegal in the late nineteenth century lacked many of the factors associated with the growth of sport in some parts of Britain, its population was able to take pride in and initially organise localised, sometimes annually held, events. In a number of villages, teams and clubs were developed, although the majority of these had to do without a competitive structure for their games. Crucial factors in the lack of sustainability in Donegal appear to have been the scattered population, the level of patronage, the physical nature of the county with its poor transport network and the difficulty in getting groups of people together as a result of this.

Of major significance to the spread of cricket and hockey in north-east Donegal was the area's close location to Derry city and Tyrone. This illustrates the influence of external agents in the dissemination of these codes within the county and is a key factor in the development of sport in Donegal. The influence of sports clubs and governing bodies from Derry on the development of sport in north-east Donegal is of major significance to the theme of this book. In this way, the development of sport in Donegal was perhaps unique in an Irish setting in that it benefited from this proximity. Until more research is undertaken on the influence of bordering cities on other Irish counties, it is difficult to draw an accurate comparison here. Another key finding is that these two codes developed quicker in the north-east area than in more isolated regions and the physical nature of the county hampered their spread to other more isolated areas. The impact of large towns in counties located close to South Donegal, such as Enniskillen and Sligo, was insufficient to quicken the development of sport there, although those in Ballyshannon undoubtedly benefited from sporting networks in the former urban setting.

The failure of cricket, hockey and rugby clubs to form substantial networks outside their local areas in Donegal in the opening decades of the twentieth century is reflective of the problem of uniting the county. Protestant involvement, particularly in the East Donegal and Ballyshannon areas, was strong within clubs in these codes and the majority of teams interested in playing these sports in Free State Donegal were forced to look to those in bordering counties for competition. This illustrates the failure of partition to have any significant effect on links with sporting bodies in Northern Ireland after its formation, and also highlights the cultural and religious divisions within Donegal society.

In addition, more work is needed on the development of sporting patterns throughout Ireland and it is therefore difficult to establish how Donegal fitted into national patterns in the development of each of these sports, although a comparison with Hunt's work on Westmeath has shown a number of similarities. However, it must be noted that a wider variety of sports were available in Westmeath but there is little evidence that archery, polo, croquet and badminton were formally organised in Donegal in the nineteenth century. This may reflect Westmeath's more prosperous state at the time and the significant influence of its gentry and 'big house' residents on the organisation of sports such as tennis and croquet.[268]

3

The early GAA in Donegal, 1884–1905

Introduction

Although a talented cricketer and someone who was also interested in rugby, Michael Cusack was eager to reform Irish athletics, which was dominated by elitism and was poorly governed in the early 1880s. He was also keen to revive traditional Irish football and hurling for workers excluded from athletics. It was this desire that was fundamental to his and Maurice Davin's organisation of the Gaelic Athletic Association for the Preservation and Cultivation of National Pastimes, at a meeting on 1 November 1884 in Thurles, County Tipperary.[1] According to Richard Holt, the foundation of 'the GAA was also part of a much wider international phenomenon: the creation of modern sport'.[2] It also had a significant role in the Gaelic Revival, which was taking place in Ireland at the time, and Roy Foster has stated that it was 'the first landmark, emphasising physical training in the manner of contemporary Czech gymnastic clubs, and constructing a powerful rural network'.[3] Donegal's isolated, peripheral geographical position was not conducive to the spread of the GAA in the early years of the Association. The development of the early GAA failed to make any substantial difference to the lives of most people in Donegal. The majority of Donegal's early GAA clubs, mainly located in the Inishowen peninsula, were operational only because of their proximity to Derry city, where the GAA was already in existence and their activities generally took place in isolation from the rest of the county.

The slow development of the GAA in Donegal

There was no recorded involvement by anyone from Donegal at the founding meeting of the Gaelic Athletic Association.[4] No doubt distance would have proved a hindrance to people wishing to travel from Donegal and it is unknown if there were any messages of support sent from the county.[5] Irish Republican Brotherhood interference in the Association's affairs led to Maurice Davin's resignation in April of 1887, but they in turn faced strong opposition from the Catholic Church. By 1889, the clergy actively discouraged involvement in the GAA after failing to prevent the IRB from taking over the organisation.[6] Financial problems and the Parnell 'Split' of 1890–91, when the GAA became divided over support for the disgraced leader of the Irish Parliamentary Party, meant that by the early 1890s the Association was practically defunct.[7] The number of GAA clubs nationwide dropped from over 1,000 in 1888 to 557 by 1890 and after the Parnell affair, this further declined as the 1893 National Convention attracted only fourteen men, while only three teams entered that year's hurling championship.[8]

It is clear that Donegal's peripheral geographical position was not conducive to the spread of the GAA there in the early years of the Association. Given its lack of urbanisation and distance from the heart of GAA activity at the time, perhaps it is natural that, with its rather isolated north-western position, it was one of the last counties in Ulster to organise clubs. The direction in which the GAA spread illustrates this. As a number of historians have stated, the Association was slow to get up and running in the province of Ulster and its strength was mainly in the south of the country. Indeed Michael Cusack, in a letter written to Maurice Davin prior to the founding of the GAA, was adamant that 'the business must be worked from Munster' as he felt that the organisation would not be well received in Dublin. Cusack also believed that much of the manpower would come from provincial Ireland.[9] The early GAA was generally restricted to Munster and Leinster and, while attracting 'much of the old secret society and factional tradition', saw little participation from those involved in Ribbonism in the north of the country.[10]

Despite the slow level of GAA development in Donegal there is evidence that a number of GAA clubs were operating in Ulster in these early years of the organisation. By 1888, out of nine counties, there were five GAA County Boards in the province and over a hundred clubs.[11] This early growth began initially in County Cavan and later spread through Fermanagh and South Ulster.[12] The first official GAA club in Ulster was the J.G. Biggar club in Ballyconnell,

County Cavan, which was founded in 1885; the following year the same club was involved in the first GAA match to be held in the province.[13] GAA clubs were also being organised in Derry in 1885 and two years later there were branches in Armagh, Fermanagh and Monaghan.[14] Significantly for those interested in Gaelic games in Donegal's north-eastern area, a GAA county committee was organised in Derry in 1888.[15] A few weeks prior to Christmas 1889, the number of GAA clubs there was said to have doubled from the previous year to fourteen.[16] One Ulster GAA writer has stated that 1888 was a year of 'phenomenal growth and development' for the GAA.[17] This was not the case in Donegal. GAA activity in the 1880s in County Donegal was restricted to the north-east of the county. Outside of a small area close to Derry city, the organisation of Gaelic games attracted little interest in other villages in Donegal in the nineteenth century. Speaking in 1930, B.C. Fay, the secretary of the Ulster GAA Council, stated that one of the difficulties in the development of the GAA in the county was that it had an 'unwieldy nature' and this was a fair summary of attempts to spread its codes there.[18]

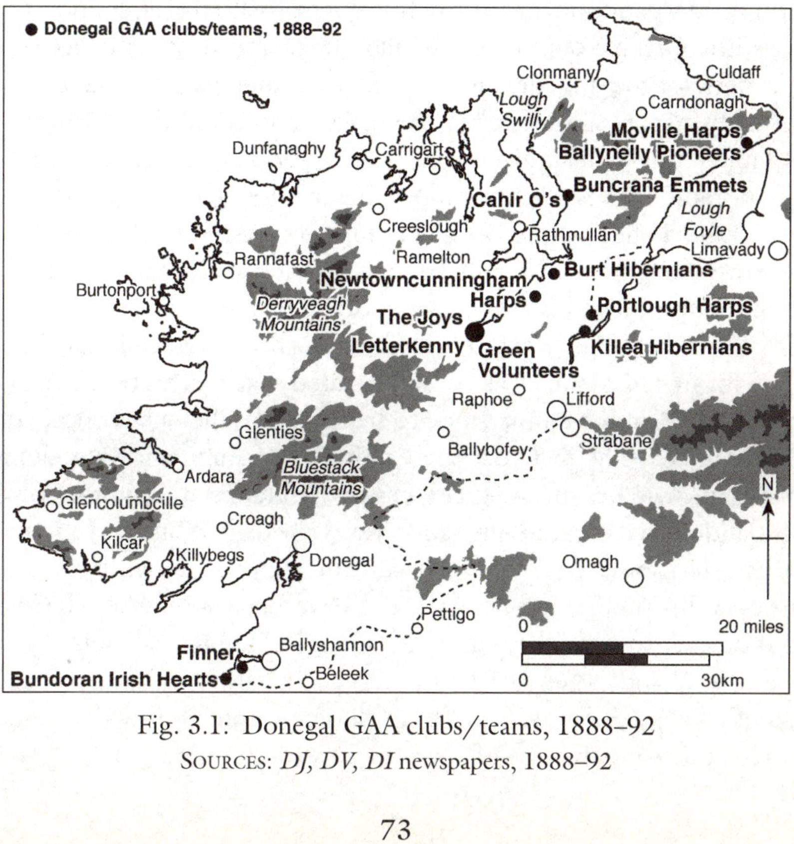

Fig. 3.1: Donegal GAA clubs/teams, 1888–92
SOURCES: *DJ, DV, DI* newspapers, 1888–92

According to Tom Hunt, 'early club units formed specifically to play Gaelic games were transient structures whose lifespan was often very short'.[19] This was generally the case in Donegal. Figure 3.1, shown above, illustrates the location of the county's first GAA clubs and teams. The north-east Donegal based branches of Burt Hibernians, Buncrana clubs Cahir O's and Emmets, Portlough Harps, Killea Hibernians and Newtowncunningham Harps were all in operation between 1888 and 1892. Significantly these clubs were all based in the Inishowen peninsula and were all located in a concentrated region which was relatively near to Derry city, where a GAA county committee that encouraged participation from Donegal clubs was present. Cultural boundaries and distance from 'the place of innovation' have been cited as reasons for variations in the geographical diffusion of association football in Britain.[20] Inishowen, where the majority of GAA action took place between 1888 and 1892, was an area which remained somewhat isolated from other parts of the county, geographically and culturally, and this no doubt hindered the spread of the GAA in Donegal. Other teams in operation in this period included the Bundoran Irish Hearts, Finner, the Joys, the Green Volunteers, Moville Harps and Ballynelly Pioneers but none of these made any attempt to arrange fixtures against the six clubs named above. It may be inaccurate to call these other six combinations 'clubs'; given their scarcity of matches the possibility of sporadic arrangements cannot be overlooked. Hunt has also noted the ad hoc nature of the organisation of early GAA matches, where young men living in an area would challenge those from neighbouring districts to a Gaelic football match.[21]

While the frequency with which the north-eastern clubs used the train for matches is unclear, it can be stated that they were all, unlike many others in the county, able to benefit from the railway network in the area.[22] The fact that the Cahir O's of Buncrana sometimes played its matches on the green beside the train station in the town also added to its accessibility and drew crowds.[23] While there is evidence that some Derry clubs used 'outside cars' drawn by horses around this time, it probably would have been somewhat cheaper and quicker to travel by train.[24] Burt was located just six miles from Derry city and, after 1883, was served by the Londonderry and Lough Swilly Railway. Buncrana, 'a small market town' located twelve miles north-west of the city, was the terminal point of this train system, while eight miles to the west of Derry lay Newtowncunningham, also served by the rail network.[25] Killea, located less than five miles south-east of Derry, was also relatively close to the city and Carrigans village in this parish was also served by the Great Northern Railway system at the time.[26] Nearby Portlough village was also within walking distance of the train network and also quite close to Derry. The GAA clubs of these areas were therefore able to benefit from this transport network and the link with Derry in their participation in Gaelic football and hurling matches. A number of towns where the railway network was slow to develop, such as Killybegs, Glenties and Ballyshannon, failed to organise any GAA clubs in the county at this time.[27]

Other areas in Donegal lacked the enthusiasm, support or simply the competitive structure for GAA clubs to develop. There were no attempts to establish GAA clubs in the north-west, west or south-west of the county until 1905 as soccer gained popularity in these areas in the 1890s. In the south of the county, the Bundoran Irish Hearts GAA club was founded in 1889 but later switched to association football having played only one match against Finner.[28] The lack of activity in nearby Ballyshannon did not help the GAA team's development there. In April 1893, Derry soccer team Collon Rovers defeated 'Caheroes' of Buncrana and this indicates the GAA club may have taken up soccer after their decline.[29] Transfer from Gaelic football to soccer was not uncommon around this time in other counties, such as Westmeath, while other early Irish clubs switched between rugby, soccer and Gaelic football on a regular basis.[30] Soccer in Donegal at this point did not attract the type of negative attention which came with the cultural revival at the beginning of the twentieth century. One study of events in County Galway has shown how soccer clubs in Tuam and Dunmore came under pressure to switch to Gaelic football in the late 1880s, although how exceptional this was at the time is unclear.[31] It is clear, however, that in Donegal, players and administrators were not, at least in this decade, subject to the press condemnation or monitoring later experienced. As a result, crossover between codes and amongst players was not uncommon.

The GAA struggled to make any impact in the larger urban areas in the county. Donegal's largest towns, Letterkenny and Ballyshannon, suffered from a general apathy towards the organisation of

Gaelic games. Despite the town of Letterkenny being described in December 1889 as having the potential for 'finding the necessary fibre' for the hosting of exhibition matches with a view to promoting Gaelic games, it was not until November 1891 that any of these sports were recorded as being played there.[32] This occurred when a Gaelic football match between the Joys and the Green Volunteers was played.[33] However, it appears that the Green Volunteers were not a fully committed GAA team as later in that month they played Derry club Ivy in an association football match.[34]

According to RIC reports a Gaelic football club was in existence in Letterkenny during 1892 and 1893 but few details were given as to the extent of its activities other than to say that it was a Gaelic football club and was established only for athletic purposes.[35] The popularity of cricket and association football in Letterkenny no doubt curtailed interest in Gaelic games there.[36] The failure of those in the southern town of Ballyshannon to show sufficient interest in Gaelic games at this time undoubtedly led to a lack of organisation of the GAA in this area. Members of the community with social influence who had organised local sporting events showed no interest in promoting Gaelic games. This was not always the case in Westmeath; in Mullingar the men organising their Gaelic football club in the early 1890s were 'leaders of their particular community'.[37] Needless to say these areas in South Donegal were too far from Inishowen to have any involvement with the north-eastern clubs, given the state of transport and communications at the time.

The difficulties in initiating the GAA into Donegal society were illustrated in Rathmullan at Christmas 1886. The organisation of a fourteen-a-side hurling match by Rathmullan native and Metropolitan hurling club member Cathal MacGarvey appears to have been an exceptional attempt to encourage Gaelic games prior to 1888.[38] Plans were made for another match to be held on New Year's Day but this received no further attention in the local newspapers.[39] Whether or not MacGarvey hoped to set up a club is also unrecorded. Hurling did not gain a foothold in Rathmullan without his leadership as he returned to Dublin after his Christmas holidays. Someone new or returning to a community, with a strong passion for the game and knowledge of the playing rules, was often a significant factor in the spread of sport within an area.[40] Clearly there was not enough enthusiasm shown after MacGarvey's departure, but in any case a lack of organisation and equipment, the failure to obtain their own pitch, an absence of local opposition and sufficient financial aid were other reasons why this did not succeed. At the beginning of the 1890s association football was the most popular sport in this village with a number of prominent Rathmullan-based men becoming heavily involved in the County Donegal Football Association by 1896.[41]

RIC reports provide some explanation as to why the GAA did not flourish in Donegal in the late 1880s. The strength of the National League was deemed to be a hindrance to the spread of the GAA there and the GAA lacked the cultural space necessary to develop because of this. In March 1889, one District Inspector remarked that 'it is curious that the GAA has not spread to County Donegal, if it had, probably the National League would not be so powerful there, as it is at present'.[42] This organisation was the successor to the Land League, was 'firmly under Parnell's control, and combined a moderate agrarianism, a Home Rule programme and electoral functions'.[43] In 1888 there were at least thirty-seven Irish National League clubs in Donegal.[44] Given the social dislocation in the county with the Land War, evictions and widespread poverty in areas such as Gweedore around this time, the organisation of the GAA in the county was probably not high on the agenda of those involved. It appears that, given the RIC's view of the GAA as a nationalist organisation, they saw little need for the GAA in Donegal, with the prominence of the National League there. In any case, National League branches in Donegal do not appear to have made the same effort or had the same interest in promoting the GAA as those in other areas in Ulster, such as South Derry.[45]

The lack of Fenianism in County Donegal was a problem for the spread of the GAA in the nineteenth century given the amount of influence the Irish Republican Brotherhood held in the Central Council of the GAA by 1887.[46] The RIC do not appear to have been overly concerned with the state of nationalist organisations in Donegal in the late 1880s. Writing in November 1887, District Inspector Reeves illustrated his views on the state of secret societies in Donegal:

> We have had very little information from the Co. Donegal latterly but except in a few places where the population is pretty thick. I do not think that secret society work is carried out to any great

> extent. The physical condition of the county and its population thinly scattered over a wide area prevents I think as a rule the formation of secret societies.[47]

He also felt that there were no travelling members of secret societies from outside the county visiting Donegal and this was significant, as it went 'far to show that secret organisation is not kept up from a distance'.[48] The isolated, rural nature of the county, which was not conducive to a strong communications network, is also apparent in his comments; this lack of urbanisation, and lack of IRB involvement in Donegal, was undoubtedly a problem for the spread of the GAA there. Desmond Murphy has highlighted a number of reasons why the IRB did not develop in Donegal after its formation in 1858. He states that 'agrarian tension probably hindered the spread of Fenianism in Co. Donegal in the 1860s' and that Donegal at that time 'represented a mosaic of political culture'. The isolated position and poor communications system of West Donegal, the failure of those in North Donegal to embrace national emancipation, the weakness of agricultural labourers and emigration in the east of the county have all been identified as reasons why the Fenian movement did not gain sufficient support.[49]

Significantly for the failure of the development of the GAA in Donegal in the late nineteenth century, the county was located further away from the early centres of the GAA in South Leinster and Munster than were Kerry or Mayo. GAA events were being organised in Tralee in 1885 and in November 1888 the first county convention was held there.[50] The early development of sport in Kerry was helped by a more centralised railway line, which connected the urban centres of Listowel and Tralee, having been put in place in 1880.[51] The GAA chose to hold its most significant athletic meetings in 1885 in towns which had major rail connections, as Clonmel (Tipperary) and New Ross (Wexford) were also selected.[52] Political involvement in the GAA in Kerry was also closely linked to more national trends, as a number of members of the Irish Republican Brotherhood were involved in the initial GAA sports held in Tralee in June 1885 and later became involved in the GAA's executive.[53] In 1891 the county claimed its first All-Ireland hurling title and while activity ceased temporarily, in line with the national decline of the GAA in the early 1890s, the GAA in Kerry was revived in the early 1900s.[54] Therefore, while Kerry may appear as peripheral as Donegal in a geographical sense, there were a number of subtle differences which meant Donegal remained isolated from more centralised GAA affairs.

Similarly, the GAA got off to an early start in Mayo, with clubs in operation by 1885. Twelve teams had affiliated to the Central Council of the GAA by the end of 1886 and the county's first championship final for Gaelic football took place in 1888.[55] After a decline in the 1890s, Mayo re-affiliated to the Central Council of the GAA in 1902.[56] Ballina was the early centre of the GAA there, and a railway network was in place in this town since 1873, easing sporting transport difficulties.[57]

Matches, rules and competitions

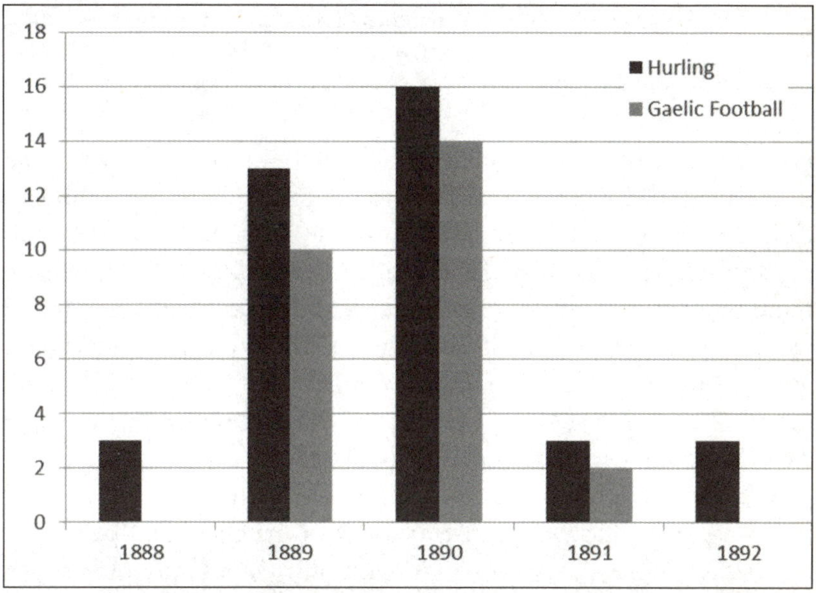

Fig. 3.2: Hurling and Gaelic Football matches involving Donegal club teams, 1888–92

SOURCES: *DJ*, *DV*, *DI* and *Sport* newspapers, 1888–92

The following section demonstrates that Donegal's GAA teams and clubs relied heavily on those in Derry for matches and struggled with the rules while failing to establish their own competitive structure. In the period from February 1888 until Christmas 1892 Donegal's GAA selections took part in a combined total of sixty-four matches, as illustrated in Figure 3.2.[58] Thirty-eight hurling matches were

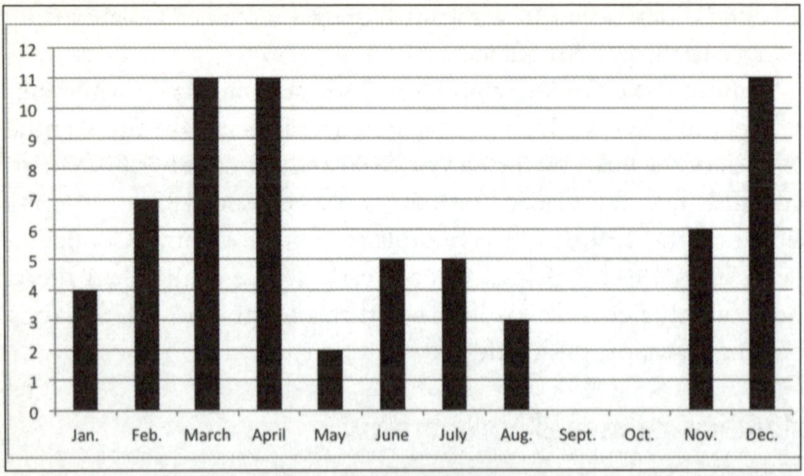

Fig. 3.3: Number of GAA matches played on a monthly basis involving Donegal clubs, 1888–92
SOURCES: *DJ, DV, DI* and *Sport* newspapers, 1888–92

played and twenty-six Gaelic football matches took place, with one unspecified match being held prior to the founding of the Cahir O's club. Twenty-one of these fixtures were back-to-back matches with hurling taking place first, followed by Gaelic football. This made more sense for reasons of organisation. Fifty-seven of these matches were 'challenge' or friendly matches, with Donegal teams being involved in only eight competitive fixtures in these years. Fifty-one matches were against Derry opposition while the remaining fourteen were between Donegal clubs. This illustrates the Donegal clubs' general lack of interest in competition and their reliance on Derry teams for opposition. The vast majority of matches were played by north-east Donegal combinations, with only Bundoran in the south hosting a Gaelic football match in 1889. The early years of Donegal GAA thus existed as part of the Derry hinterland rather than as a countywide phenomenon.

Figure 3.3 shows when these games were played. Matches generally took place in the spring and winter. Twenty-nine matches were played in the spring months. Seven were held in February with twenty-two taking place in March and April while twenty-one were held in the winter months of November, December and January. Twelve matches were held in the summer and only three were held in the autumn. No matches were held in September or October and this can be explained by the fact that the harvest was usually gathered in these months. As Hunt has noted in his study of Gaelic football in Westmeath from 1890 to 1893, teams lacked their own grounds and usually had to make do with the loan of farmers' fields. Winter and spring provided the best opportunities, when crops would not be damaged by players and spectators.[59] There was a similar pattern in Donegal, although the higher number of matches played in March, April and December can also be explained by the fact that tournaments were held in Derry on St Patrick's Day, Easter and at Christmas. Interestingly, the Cahir O's played continuously through the summer of 1889 while the majority of other GAA clubs in Donegal appear to have been inactive throughout the summer, with fields being used for farming. The club had secured a pitch from local butcher William Longwill, thus explaining their exceptionally prolonged period of activity.[60]

Under GAA rules at the time, hurling games were supposed to last for eighty minutes and Gaelic football was to have an hour's play, with teams changing over at half-time. A number of rules, generally regarded to have been drawn up by Maurice Davin, had been adopted for the playing of Gaelic football and hurling by the GAA by early 1885.[61] Hurling was initially given twelve rules while ten were devised for Gaelic football. The latter code's regulations were drawn mainly from football rules in England while some traditions of rural Ireland were also included in that wrestling, away from the play, was also permitted.[62] Hurling under GAA rules differed in a number of ways from earlier versions of stick and ball games in Ireland. The rules of these new codes limited the number of players on each team to between twenty-one and fourteen, although this number was reduced to seventeen in 1896.[63] The referee had the power to send players off for foul play and he was assisted by two umpires. The width between the goalposts in hurling was bigger than in Gaelic football (twenty feet as opposed to fifteen with crossbars ten feet from the ground) and the length and width of hurling pitches were also greater. The goal frame was originally the same shape as that of soccer but this was adapted in 1886 with point posts being introduced to both sides of the goalposts and the crossbar set at eight feet off the ground in 1896. The H-shape goal frame was not adopted until 1910. The playing area of a hurling field was set at 200 yards long and 150 yards wide, while a Gaelic football pitch was a lot smaller, measuring 120 yards in length by 80 yards wide. Again these figures were later reduced towards the end of the nineteenth century and by 1910 both fields had the same measurements, 140 to 170 yards long by 84 to 100 yards wide. Forfeit points were initially awarded against teams who put the ball out over their own end-line but this rule was changed in 1896. Initially a goal was worth more than any number of points but this was later reduced to equal five points and finally three.[64]

The initial rules of the GAA were often open to interpretation and unclear to players and spectators at times.[65] Gaelic games in Donegal were no different in this respect. Implementation of these rules was not always straightforward. Matches were sometimes cut short due to poor timekeeping and lateness in arrival. Generally the captains came to an agreement. In January 1890, hurling and Gaelic football matches between Newtowncunningham Harps and McCarthy's were reduced to fifteen minutes each, 'owing to the lateness of the evening'.[66] The early sunset in winter matches sometimes put fixtures under pressure. Burt Hibernians' hurling match against St Columb's at the Derry County Board's Christmas tournament in 1890 had to be scrapped as it was deemed too dark to start.[67] Referees were generally from a neutral club with umpires being from opposing clubs, but this did not prevent disputes and it is clear that the referees did not, or could not, always keep up with the play. A goal scored by Lambhill Harps of Glasgow against Cahir O's in July 1890 was hotly disputed and the fact that the Harps' umpire said nothing and the referee was in the middle of the field when the goal was scored did nothing to help matters.[68]

Sunday was the nationwide day for Gaelic games with tournaments also being held at Christmas, Easter and on St Patrick's Day in Derry.[69] This was in accordance with the beliefs of the Catholic Church and it was also a continuation of previous sporting traditions in Ireland. As noted earlier, Ireland, significantly, did not benefit hugely from the nineteenth-century development of regulated working hours that had been highly significant to the growth of modern sport in England.[70] Therefore Sunday was the only day of rest for those involved primarily in agriculture and services such as retailing, and the GAA provided an outlet for many of these workers. Tournaments enabled the Derry GAA to bring together their affiliated clubs for a series of matches throughout the day and draw bigger crowds than one-off matches would attract. They consisted of hurling and Gaelic football matches, with athletic events such as races and jumping competitions adding to the day's entertainment. Gold and silver medals were sometimes provided as an incentive while individual skills competitions such as the long puck and football place-kicking gave players an increased chance to demonstrate their talents.[71] These additional events gave spectators better value for money than what was available at rugby and soccer matches.[72]

However, not every Donegal club was interested in participating in these tournaments. While Burt Hibernians took part in the Christmas tournament at Pennyburn in 1888, they did not enter the following year, having decided not to affiliate as was required to enter the Derry County Committee's competitions.[73] Buncrana Emmets showed no interest in tournaments and preferred to play challenge matches. This lack of ambition is also illustrated in the fact that only Burt Hibernians took part in the Derry hurling championship of 1889 and again in 1891, while Newtowncunningham Harps, in entering both the Gaelic football and hurling championships in the latter year, were the only other Donegal club to experience championship action. These championships would begin in the early months of the year and often had a number of months between each match due to the slowness of committee organisation and protests, but were usually finished in the summer. There were no championships held in 1888, with the Derry County Board only becoming organised late in the year, while administrative problems meant that 1890 also passed without matches of this type taking place. This lack of widespread participation by all the north-east Donegal clubs in the Derry championships and tournaments, while acknowledging organisational difficulties at the time, illustrates a failure of the majority of these clubs to commit to the Derry County Board and a general desire to stick to challenge matches.

Donegal teams struggled at times to adapt to the rules and skills required for Gaelic games. Their lack of experience and unwillingness to adapt were sometimes to blame for their poor performances. Burt Hibernians' failure to evolve was at times thought to be detrimental to their progress. After their defeat at the 1888 Christmas tournament in Derry, one local reporter felt that 'it was evident that on hard ground they would go a long way to defeat any of our local teams'.[74] This was a reference to their barefooted appearance despite the wet conditions. Their decision to stick with the traditional camán, which differed from more modern forms, attracted attention in the local press and its perceived awkwardness was blamed for their defeat in the Derry hurling championship semi-final of 1889.[75] Other clubs suffered from similar problems. After Portlough Harps were defeated by Young Irelands in April 1890, one reporter advised them to replace their camáns with hurleys, to keep their positions on the field and to 'pass the ball more instead of driving her by random'.[76] Clearly positioning on the field and distribution of the ball also proved difficult for a number of Donegal teams. Killea Hibernians were also advised in March of 1890 'to pay more attention to their places' and the following month the Buncrana Emmets players' style of play was also questioned in the local press.[77] Largely defensive but practical tactics were evident, as their hurling victory over Cahir O's was said to be partly due to their tactic of 'beating the ball over the lines' and it was reported that 'their whole team playing full-backs made it very hard for the Cahirs to score'.[78]

1889 and 1890 were actually the years in which the early North-east Donegal GAA clubs partook in the majority of their matches.[79] An examination of the Donegal clubs' involvement between 1888 and 1892 illustrates that a significant growth took place, from four matches being played in 1888 to twenty-three in 1889. This was because the number of clubs increased from two in 1888 to four at the end of 1889 and activity became more frequent. 1890 was the peak year of activity, with thirty Gaelic football and hurling matches played.[80] Seventeen of these were hurling and thirteen were Gaelic football. It was during this year that all six of the north-east clubs were active. However, in 1891 only five matches were played, while the following year only three were recorded.

A number of clubs tried their hand at Gaelic football as well as hurling in 1889 and 1890. This was despite problems within the sport in Derry at the time. A number of Derry GAA clubs were fielding soccer players and the Derry county committee, in banning handling of the ball in Gaelic football, did not understand, or want to rigidly enforce, the rules of the Central Council at that time.[81] In addition, the catching of the ball in the air did not become popular with Ulster Gaelic football teams until 1910.[82] Given these problems, it must have been difficult for Gaelic football teams in

Donegal to develop the standard of their play and attract interest. In tracing the development of this sport, W.F. Mandle has claimed that in the latter decades of the nineteenth century Gaelic football was 'to the modern eye, an unstructured shambles' and despite attempts to improve the scoring system and tactics, it was not until 1914 that it became 'an attractive open game'.[83]

The socio-economic background of Donegal's early GAA clubs

There were a variety of factors involved in the founding of early GAA clubs. These included the coming together of those involved in farming, industry, education and the retail trade to form GAA branches. Members of pre-existing sports clubs, such as soccer, also contributed to the formation of GAA clubs.[84] There is less evidence for this in Donegal although given the rural nature of a number of clubs it is not unlikely that members were drawn from farming networks. Two of the first Donegal clubs were formed after visits from Derry GAA branches in the late 1880s. Burt Hibernians were the first GAA club to be formed in the county, with the help of St Patrick's GAA club of Derry, on 5 February 1888.[85] This club also helped to set up the Derry clubs, Emeralds and John Mitchel's, in September 1888.[86] The initial staging of a friendly match and close cooperation were the methods by which the Cahir O's GAA club in Buncrana was formed on Sunday 18 November 1888, with the help of Derry GAA club St Columb's, who played an exhibition match there.[87] By November 1889, Killea Hibernians were affiliated to the Derry county committee, while Portlough Harps joined this organisation the following month.[88] Those wishing to participate in Gaelic games in North-east Donegal benefited from the encouragement of those in the GAA in Derry in the way that soccer clubs in the area were also encouraged to participate in the North-west Football Association in the city in the early 1890s. By January of 1890, Newtowncunningham Harps had made contact with Derry club McCarthy's and hosted this club for Gaelic football and hurling matches that month.[89] In April 1890, Buncrana Emmets were welcomed into the Derry GAA.[90] While the development of the GAA in Ulster was generally slow at this time in comparison with nationwide trends, Donegal's number of six clubs ranked quite low amongst national figures, with only Tyrone having a lower number, which illustrates the lack of development of the Association in these counties.[91] Tyrone's lack of growth may also have hindered the spread of the GAA in the bordering East Donegal area.

Donegal's first GAA teams were keen to show a strong national allegiance through their names and colours worn. The fact that two clubs were named Hibernians, and three others were named Harps, is evidence that these organisations were keen to display their Irish identity without explicit national or political identities, not unlike a number of those in Westmeath around this time.[92] The names of Buncrana's GAA clubs differed in that their founders chose to honour deceased Irish leaders. The Cahir O's club was named after Sir Cahir O'Doherty and the town's other club, Buncrana Emmets, took their name in memory of Robert Emmet.[93] The choosing of patriotic colours was also evident in their kit. Green and yellow were the colours chosen by Killea Hibernians at the 1889 Christmas tournament in Derry, while Portlough took to the field in green and red.[94] This wearing of green illustrates an expression of these clubs' nationalist identity, a practice not uncommon amongst other GAA clubs at the time.[95] Burt Hibernians wore orange and green in their Derry hurling championship victory over St Columb's (green and white) in January 1889 and a brief examination of some other Derry clubs also shows an eagerness to display their political allegiances. Clubs such as St Patrick's, Hibernians, Emeralds, John Mitchel's and William O'Brien's all featured in 1890 and this political naming of GAA clubs at the time in other counties, such as Meath, highlights their desire to build a nationalist identity and a rejection of British culture.[96] Dublin's early GAA clubs, of which there were 114 by 1888, generally took their names from 'either individuals or incidents in Irish history'.[97] However, there were some exceptions, such as those called after sea locations and poetic names. The titles of the Donegal clubs lacked this diversity.

Despite this need to show their Irish identity, there is no evidence that any of these Donegal clubs were founded, or infiltrated, by the Irish Republican Brotherhood. The political allegiances of the organisers of the clubs of Burt Hibernians, Cahir O's and Newtowncunningham Harps were clearly established in an RIC Northern division report of February 1891 and District Inspector A. Gambell stated that 'the leaders are not secret society men: but some of the members may belong to the AOH'.[98] The Ancient Order of Hibernians was opposed to the IRB's ideologies and distanced themselves from the unlawful activities of their predecessors, the Ribbonmen.[99] Gambell's account establishes that these three Donegal clubs were not involved in the IRB and that the IRB in Derry failed to infiltrate them. Given that there was little connection with the IRB, one must assume that the clubs, while eager to display their nationalism through naming policies and colours worn, were participating mainly for recreational reasons and in some areas such as Burt, desired to carry on local traditions.

RIC reports provide some indication of the membership of Burt Hibernians, Cahir O's and Newtowncunningham Harps in 1890. These clubs had between them approximately sixty-eight members. The fact that they did not all have enough members to each field the maximum numbers of players allowed on a team also shows that membership was not huge. Burt Hibernians had twenty members while Newtowncunningham Harps and Cahir O's were both said to have twenty-four registered on their books. The rural nature of these clubs, with their lower population base, can be compared with five clubs in Derry city, which had altogether an estimated 252 members. The 1889 Derry hurling and Gaelic football champions Hibernians were said to have seventy-four members, which illustrates the gulf in strength and support between a city club and one in rural Donegal.[100] While these figures may not have been totally accurate, they do provide a rough guide to the numbers in each club and are generally the only record available of membership taken. Marcus De Burca has calculated in conjunction with Michael Cusack's estimates for 1888 (which stated that the GAA had 'about 1,250 clubs' nationwide with 50,000 members) that there would have been about forty persons per club.[101] Therefore, the three Donegal clubs' membership figures estimated by the RIC in 1890 were well below average countrywide figures around that time.

Unfortunately, the lack of remaining census records from 1891 and sufficient biographical data in the press prevents a detailed analysis of the socio-occupational status of a large number of players. However, it is possible to examine a small number of players from the Burt Hibernians and Cahir O's clubs, using the 1901 census, newspaper sources and the Burt club's official history book. Out of forty-four players used by these teams in the 1888–92 period, twenty were positively identified. Unsurprisingly, given the rural nature of these clubs, eleven players were employed in agriculture. Seven players were involved in industrial work while two others were employed in the commercial sector. Players ranged in age from fifteen to forty-eight and the majority were Roman Catholics. The ratio of married to single men was almost equal.[102]

Donegal's early GAA clubs appear to have struggled to attract the patronage of those with social status in the county at the time. As Neil Tranter has noted in his study of organised sport in central Scotland in the nineteenth century, financial assistance was a regular element of sports patronage.[103] Certainly, the earliest Donegal GAA clubs generally were able to raise subscriptions and travel to away matches, but there is little mention in the local press that they attracted the interest, involvement or financial backing of the more prominent members of society. This was in contrast to soccer clubs, such as Letterkenny FC, which in October 1891 received a subscription of £5 from County Tyrone linen manufacturer E.T. Herdman, and Ramelton Sunbursts, which received £2 from the same man the following February.[104] In March 1892, Ramelton FC received a 'liberal' subscription from gentleman and farmer James W. Fullerton, and by the beginning of the 1892–93 season, both Buncrana FC and Moville FC were each able to report that they had the sum of £20 on their hands.[105] Cricket clubs also received the support of prominent locals, such as doctors and the military, while there is little evidence that the early GAA clubs did likewise or managed to form significant social networks.[106]

While in their early days the Burt Hibernians benefited from the donation of £5 given by Matthew McCay, a farmer and director of a nearby building company, it is difficult to establish exactly how much financial aid, if any, the other Donegal GAA clubs received from external sources.[107] The lack of finance available to the Burt club is also illustrated in the fact that they played barefooted at the Christmas tournament in 1888.[108] Other clubs were quick to raise funds for their equipment. Only a few months after their formation, Newtowncunningham Harps appear to have been in a sound financial position. By April 1890 it was being claimed that they were in a position to purchase 'twenty-one suits of uniform' and it was noted that 'besides a splendid stock of hurleys, the treasurer still has a surplus of £10 in his till'.[109] One can only assume that this was raised through subscriptions and local patronage given that the source of the financial aid went unrecorded.[110]

As Hunt has noted, drawing up a socio-occupational account of spectators is difficult without casualty lists, such as those used by Garnham, Mason and Tranter in their work on crowds.[111] As in Westmeath, there were no major casualties at Donegal sporting events in the period covered here and emphasis will instead be placed in this section on the behaviour of crowds. Tranter has shown that in Stirling crowd disturbances actually decreased in the last decade of the nineteenth century and this supports the views of Mason and Crump that the problem was smaller and less common in Britain than Dunning, Hutchinson and Vamplew have claimed.[112] In comparison with incidents in Glasgow, Cappielow and Belfast, GAA matches provided little evidence of crowd disorder leading to major casualties.[113] The sectarian nature of crowds has been identified by Garnham as a cause of disruption at soccer matches in Belfast. GAA matches, with their nationalist links, were generally free from attracting support divided along religious or political lines. However, this does not mean that behaviour at GAA matches was always exemplary.

Drunkenness at matches was commonplace in the early GAA and this aroused clerical anger.[114] There are a number of references in the local press which indicate that GAA administrators were also anxious to show that they could host a sports event without any trouble. The *Derry Journal* GAA correspondents were eager to portray a peaceful atmosphere at their matches, to show that these men were capable of organising Gaelic games in a civilised manner.[115] Negative constructions of the Irish race were widespread during the Victorian era in British journals, with *The London Illustrated News* and *Punch* eager to portray the Irish as showing an unruly and lazy nature with a fondness for alcohol.[116] After Burt Hibernians' defeat of St Columb's in the Derry hurling championship in January 1889, it was noted that 'not a hitch of any description took place to mar the day's proceedings. Shortly after four o'clock, the games being over, the large concourse of people quietly dispersed, and in a few minutes Springtown resumed its normal quietness.'[117] Two months later, when the clubs of Young Ireland, St Columb's and Bright Stars came to Buncrana on St Patrick's Day, similar sentiments were expressed by the reporter.[118]

However, not every event went according to plan and at times spectators proved difficult to manage. After the Derry Christmas tournament in 1889 the failure of supporters and players to control themselves was noted. It was claimed that 'there were two great drawbacks to the tournament, viz, the rough play indulged in by one or two teams, and the manner in which the spectators crowded in on the field in spite of the energetic and hard-working committee'.[119] The interventions of supporters could sometimes interfere with the standard of play. After Buncrana Emmets had defeated Cahir O's in April 1890, it was claimed that 'the Cahirs' difficulties were augmented by the conduct of the spectators, who in their anxiety to witness the game, mingled freely with the players'.[120] Without proper enclosures crowd control was obviously difficult for these clubs. After the Derry GAA tournament on 1 November 1890, club members were thanked 'for assisting to keep the spectators outside the touchlines, which task was no easy one'.[121] The county committee was also advised to have a perimeter of wire placed around the field to prevent this occurring again.[122] It is clear that organising tournaments and matches at this time was not always an easy task and the impatience and excitement of spectators added to this.

Musical entertainment also provided an important part of the match day's activities and was normally an anticipated part of proceedings. At the Derry GAA Christmas tournament in 1888, 'several bands marched to the grounds, bringing contingents' but it was noted that no musical performance took place at the match, much to the disappointment of the reporter.[123] The Fahan flute band entertained spectators during a match in December 1892[124] and on Easter Monday 1893, the teams of Burt Hibernians and St Patrick's 'marched to the Waterside, accompanied by the St Patrick's Flute Band, where the Burt team were hospitably entertained' by the home team.[125] This marching and musical performance was an exhibition of their nationalist identity while the post-match entertainment illustrates the friendly relations between most Derry and Donegal GAA clubs. While the excursions of a number of Derry and Dublin teams have been well documented, there is no evidence that Donegal clubs travelled to other counties outside of Derry for matches, perhaps due to the financial costs involved.[126] Cahir O's were the hosts for an enjoyable trip for the Derry clubs of Young Ireland, St Columb's and Bright Stars on St Patrick's Day 1889. Having left early in the morning, these clubs were able to avail of ten o'clock mass in Cockhill, illustrating the strong Catholic ethos of the GAA.[127]

Outside of a small number of areas, the GAA at this time was not held in any great regard by the people of Donegal. Gaelic games in Donegal undoubtedly provided opportunities for social interaction for a small minority of people but without any major celebrations within the community these players do not appear to have gained the recognition of the county's social, economic or political elites. In the late nineteenth century, GAA matches throughout Ireland provided more opportunities for entertainment than simply playing in or watching a match.[128] Unfortunately, the extent of the match-day activities involving Donegal clubs received little notice in the local press other than the occasional reference to 'refreshments' being provided.[129] It appears that it was the duty of the home team to supply these after the match. One can assume that this tradition usually took place in a local pub and it can also be presumed that it involved plenty of alcohol being consumed. St Patrick's trip to Burt in February 1888 was rewarded 'with true Donegal hospitability', while after Newtowncunningham Harps' hurling victory over Hibernians of Derry in December 1892, the visitors were entertained in Mr Patton's public house.[130] Garnham has stated that claims that the GAA was 'a bastion of healthy exercise . . . had little basis in fact', despite efforts to propagate a puritan image at the time.[131] Some efforts were also made by the Derry County Committee to provide food for visiting teams and supporters at their tournaments, such as the hiring of a caterer from a local bakery and the provision of tickets for 'county clubs' at a tournament held on the anniversary of the founding of the GAA in 1890.[132] Unlike the case of the secretary of the Dublin Wolfe Tones club, who gave the Kickhams no. 2 team a history of Drimnagh Castle before a match in 1898, there is no evidence that Donegal's early clubs were similarly entertained by GAA administrators within Derry city during their visits there.[133]

The decline of the early GAA in Derry and Donegal

The deterioration of the GAA in Derry in the early 1890s meant that Donegal clubs lacked the inspiration and, given their reliance on those in Derry for challenge matches in the period from 1888 to 1892, the opposition needed to sustain their clubs. By 1892 the

Derry GAA had severely declined and no championships or tournaments were held in the city. As the fate of the GAA in Donegal had become so entwined with that of Derry, weakness there had a heavy impact on Donegal. The role of the clergy in the GAA has been discussed in a number of works. Despite initial support in the 1880s, this had declined, perhaps most notably in parts of Ulster, by the end of the decade, with clerical condemnation of the GAA evident in Armagh, Monaghan and Fermanagh as accusations of IRB involvement became commonplace.[134] Marcus De Burca has noted the support given to the GAA by Bishop Patrick O'Donnell of the Raphoe diocese in Donegal as being an exception, along with that of Archbishop Croke's successor, Fennelly, in the early 1900s.[135] Simon Gillespie and Roddy Hegarty have stated that between the years 1884 and 1902, the attitude of the Catholic Church to the GAA varied between individual members and dioceses and the influence of local bishops.[136] In the years prior to the establishment of the Irish Free State in 1922, relations between the two organisations had been strained, due to the involvement of high-ranking Republicans within the GAA.[137]

The overall spread of the GAA was therefore not helped by clerical opposition and it has been suggested that 1889 and 1890 were not good years for the GAA in Ulster.[138] A number of reasons have been given for the deterioration of the Association there in 1889. Marcus De Burca, David Hassan and Dónal McAnallen have all noted opposition to the playing of Gaelic games on Sundays from Sabbatarians, and it is evident that in 1889 the GAA in Ulster faced strong opposition from the clergy of the Catholic Church, including Donegal-born Archbishop Logue of Armagh.[139] This was because he and a number of other clerics disapproved of the strong IRB connections within the Association, although this clerical pressure appears to have taken place mainly in the east and south of the province.[140] Clerical opposition was also evident in counties such as Meath, Westmeath and Kerry around this time.[141] While there appears to be scarce evidence that attempts to play Gaelic games in Donegal suffered directly from either of these problems, in broader terms these did not help matters, as the clergy impacted on the development of the GAA in Derry to which the majority of Donegal GAA clubs were connected. Certainly this was evident in 1890, as it was not uncommon for a number of Derry clubs, such as Young Irelands and St Patrick's, to travel as far afield as Dundalk and Dublin because of clerical condemnation.[142] It was not until September of that year that the Derry County Committee agreed to continue with 'Sunday playing' and this must have had a disruptive influence on fixtures involving Donegal clubs wishing to travel to Derry for matches.[143]

Despite appointing officers in May 1890, the Cahir O's participated in only eight matches that year and in August were said to have been inactive.[144] This appears to have been due to the disarray of the Derry County Committee at this time. In July 1890 a letter from the secretary of the GAA in Derry, Patrick Campbell, to the Central Council of the GAA requested that they send a representative to sort out the Association in the city.[145] The Derry clubs Young Emeralds, McCarthy's and Young Irelands had switched to association football by August of that year, while there is evidence that transferring of players was also a problem and that the Derry committee 'encountered opposition to their rules' from the beginning of the season.[146] This county committee had changed personnel on a number of occasions between 1888 and 1890 and RIC reports have chronicled the presence and decline of the IRB in this Association.[147] After a visit from future president of the GAA Frank Dineen, a new county committee was formed in September 1890, but Cahir O's did not affiliate.[148] In fact, there were only eight clubs represented at this meeting, with Burt Hibernians, Newtowncunningham Harps and Buncrana Emmets the only Donegal clubs to send representatives, illustrating the damage done by IRB involvement and clerical condemnation.[149] Desmond Murphy has stated that the position of the clergy in Derry towards Gaelic games changed with the IRB's takeover of the GAA at the 1887 convention in Thurles, where the IRB were confronted by clerics in an attempt to gain control.[150] This loss of enthusiasm was also quickened by the support shown for Parnell by many GAA members during 1890–91. This led to the clergy within Derry City then beginning to encourage the growth of association football within the Catholic working class and by 1895 this game had become the dominant sport there.[151]

There were only four matches played by Donegal clubs from the end of July to December 1890 and a total of only eight matches played during 1891 and 1892. This was a dramatic decrease in matches after the summer of 1890.[152] Neither Portlough Harps nor Killea

Hibernians rejoined the new Derry GAA committee, disillusioned perhaps with the state of the GAA in Derry that summer. There is little other evidence of why they would have folded.[153] The number of matches played by these clubs was quite low in comparison with other counties, such as Down, where clubs like Leitrim Fontenoy's, powered by 'a strong neighbourhood network', played twenty-one hurling matches between 1888 and 1892.[154] The irregularity in the staging of matches made it difficult for teams to improve and the aforementioned problems in Derry were detrimental to teams' morale.

Burt Hibernians were content to focus on hurling. In the period from 1888 until 1893 they are recorded as having played thirteen hurling matches and only three Gaelic football games.[155] Perhaps this was crucial to their later strength in this sport and was in many ways a continuation of the strong tradition of playing forms of hurling in the area. The lifespan of these Donegal clubs varied but this club differed in that it continued, at some level, to organise matches in the years after 1892. Despite the decline of the majority of Donegal GAA clubs in the early 1890s the Burt club managed to organise a number of matches in 1892 and 1893 and appeared occasionally at Christmas time in the latter half of this decade. The club participated in a camán match against City of Derry on St Stephen's Day 1895 and four years later against Fahan on the same day.[156] Campbell, Dowds and Mullan believe that the future success of the club in the early 1900s was a result of their 'regular practice and occasional challenge games' in the last decade of the nineteenth century.[157] In maintaining their tradition, these authors believe that the club was exceptional within Donegal.[158]

By July 1892, Derry club Hibernians were publicly requesting opponents such as Burt Hibernians to participate in friendly matches, which illustrates that some clubs there were still in operation but struggling to find opposition.[159] This request was granted by Burt the following month and significantly admission was free, which perhaps shows that support was limited at this time.[160] A meeting of the Derry GAA County Committee was held the same month but it was adjourned as there were only three clubs in attendance and, significantly, none of these were from Donegal.[161] In addition, none of the GAA clubs noted by the RIC during 1892 were involved in this meeting, indicating a lack of desire for competition. In September there were calls for a revival of Derry GAA competitions in the

Derry Journal, with news that the hurling championship trophy won by St Patrick's the previous year had been secured by the county committee.[162] A meeting was held by this committee the following month, but there were no further competitions held until the early 1900s.[163]

Although Dónal McAnallen believes that there was no split in the GAA in Ulster over the Parnell affair, he is of the opinion that it broke the spirit of the GAA nationally and many people withdrew from national organisations after this.[164] While the opinions of the Donegal clubs on the Parnell 'Split' are unrecorded, other problems around this time did little to help their survival. Lack of communication between the Central Council of the GAA and those in the GAA in Donegal was also noted by the RIC. Although a number of Donegal GAA clubs were said to be affiliated to the Central Council, the fact that a Donegal man, James Martin, who had formerly been involved in the GAA, had been elected as 'Donegal GAA representative at Thurles' for 1890 without his consent and by virtue of his name still appearing on the administrative books illustrates the poor communications that Donegal had with those running the national body for Gaelic games at this stage.[165] The continued problem of distance from Munster was also noted in *Sport* at the beginning of 1891. The writer felt that 'it is too inconvenient and expensive for the representatives of Leinster and Ulster to attend meetings of the Central Council held at Limerick Junction'.[166] Limerick Junction in Tipperary was deemed to be an inconvenient venue for Ulster and Leinster delegates and it was claimed that 'Ulster is falling asunder for the want of being looked after by someone in authority, and parts of Leinster are nearly as bad'.[167] McAnallen has also stated that in the years between 1892 and 1898 the GAA was in a state of disarray in Ulster and a revival did not begin until November 1898 in Belfast, with an athletics tournament being hosted by the Red Branch hurling club.[168] This revival did not take place until the early twentieth century in Donegal.

Elsewhere, there were also a number of changes within the GAA's Central Council which made the organisation and its games more attractive, with the GAA reorganising and attempting to attract new members during 1893–94.[169] With a policy of 'de-politicisation', the GAA and its secretary, Richard Blake, brought in a number of administrative changes that stressed a move away from the IRB and political matters during this decade, while the playing rules were also improved.[170] These overall changes may not have had any great influence in a county like Donegal at this time, where the GAA was ineffective for most of the 1890s, but did help the progress of Gaelic games there in later years.

In the period from 1902 until 1905 a small number of references to hurling matches involving Donegal clubs appeared sporadically in the local press. With no public interest expressed in the forming of a GAA committee in Donegal at this point, a number of Donegal clubs had to make do with occasional competitions and tournaments, such as the hurling match played at the Moville Sports during Easter 1902. Burt Hibernians took part in the Gaelic Athletic Sports in Derry city in aid of St Eugene's Cathedral bazaar and the North-west Hurling League in 1903, along with St Mura's of Fahan, but both clubs failed to fulfil their fixtures in this league.[171] Teams also were organised by Gaelic League branches in the south of the county at Ballyshannon, Bundoran and in the east at Doneyloop but, like Raphoe Rangers who also appeared briefly, they did not prosper.[172] Without a county committee to organise competitive fixtures, it was difficult for these teams to make any progress, and they themselves could not bring about the administrative momentum required.

Conclusion

Neal Garnham, in assessing the GAA's advantages over rugby and soccer in the late nineteenth century, has emphasised the GAA's nationalist appeal, the opportunities it offered those excluded from sport due to social standing and work commitments, its wider range of events and the availability of alcohol for patrons,[173] but despite this, the GAA failed to have an impact in County Donegal. In addition to poor organisation, it was the failure to gain sufficient popular support and, in turn, adequate financing that hindered its early development. As can be seen in the evidence for crossover from GAA to soccer, Gaelic games did not provide any major threat to soccer in the county at this point and a lack of familiarity with Gaelic football, and an absence of nearby opposition, may also have influenced sporting choices. Added to this, the lack of evidence for IRB involvement in Donegal's clubs suggests that these GAA clubs were not overtly nationalist, and soccer was not seen as a 'foreign game' at this stage. Having illustrated the slow evolution of sport in a peripheral Irish area, the danger of placing too much emphasis on the linkage between the growth of the GAA and nationalist politics is obvious.

The rural nature of the Inishowen clubs hints at an agriculturally based membership and as those employed in agriculture generally worked on Saturdays, Gaelic games may have been the only sports available to these players. What is clear is that a number of difficulties such as transport, lack of competitive structure and the sparsely populated, rural nature of the county (which also impeded the spread of team sports such as cricket and rugby) also affected the GAA's development. Huggins and Tolson have argued that the positive effect of the railways on the development of sport in Victorian Britain has been overstated, but the case of Donegal suggests that the incompleteness of the railway network in this period was certainly a hindrance to the development of sport. The presence of the rail network in a concentrated area in Inishowen appears to have, at least briefly, benefited local GAA clubs' activities.[174] Once again we find that early sports clubs in Donegal relied heavily on those in external areas for instruction, particularly Derry, and, when left on their own to organise competitions, were unable or lacked the motivation to arrange significant structures for the development of team sports throughout the county. Of key significance in this chapter is the impact of the Parnell Split and, while clerical condemnation did not directly lead to the collapse of Donegal's GAA clubs, it was Donegal clubs' over-reliance on the GAA in Derry, as seen in the number of matches against Derry clubs, that led to their demise with the collapse of the GAA in that city.

4

THE FAILURE OF THE GAA IN DONEGAL, 1905–1919

Introduction

In looking at the development of soccer in north-east England between 1876 and 1890, Mike Huggins has summed up what he considers to be 'key issues' in its establishment. These include its acceptance within society, the involvement of those who helped disseminate the game and their networks, the structure of the economy and society and the evolution of values within this sport.[1] In Donegal, efforts to establish the GAA were characterised by a transition from the initial prominence of hurling to the dominance of Gaelic football and this took place under the shadow of association football, which retained its popularity in a number of areas around the county. Despite the foundation of the first County Board in Donegal in 1905 and the subsequent organisation of competitions until 1907, attempts to permanently establish GAA clubs and competitions continued to be a failure until 1919, and efforts to tie its sports with cultural nationalism were insufficient to give the games a permanent foothold within Donegal society in the opening decade of the twentieth century. The efforts of Seumas MacManus and the clergy of the Roman Catholic church were of much importance to the new board's development, and when this input declined, the GAA in Donegal could not be sustained.

The advance of the GAA in Donegal, 1905–1907

The nationwide revival of the GAA in the late 1890s continued into the opening decade of the twentieth century.[2] By the early 1900s the organisation's national and regional administrative structures were being transformed, and the development of both Gaelic football and hurling into more exciting spectator sports saw attendances increase, while clerical support was again forthcoming.[3] Although this change was slower to take hold in Ulster, the Ulster GAA Council was founded in 1903 and by 1905, Donegal was the only Ulster county in which a County Board was not in operation.[4] It was in this year that the first proper attempt was made to give the GAA a formal, organisational foothold within Donegal society through the foundation of the inaugural Donegal County Board on 23 October 1905, at a meeting held in Mountcharles.[5] This was organised by IRB suspect and writer Seumas MacManus, one of the leading activists in the Gaelic Revival in the county and chief Cumann na nGaedheal organiser in South Donegal. The County Board was presided over by the Very Reverend Dr Edward Maguire and it was decided at this initial meeting that two sub-committees were to be formed for the western and eastern areas, as the size of the whole county was deemed to be too big to have only one County Board to administer all the clubs. In fact, it would have made more sense to have organised the divisions into north and south. The presence of the Very Reverend Maguire, and other key figures in the Catholic Church, indicates a significant level of support from the clergy in the Donegal GAA for the first time.

The area covered was more extensive than where the first GAA clubs were organised and the new organisation's competitions were exclusive to Donegal clubs, thereby attempting to loosen the affiliation to Derry. It was the Western Board who were first to organise fixtures for their six camán clubs. Camán was the first sport to be played, although matches did not get underway until December.[6] Attracting interest was difficult from the beginning. A number of the teams represented at the Grand Camán Parade, a demonstration to promote Gaelic games and the Irish language held in Mountcharles on 8 October 1905, did not affiliate. Despite messages of support from throughout the county, not every area was keen to provide more tangible support to the GAA.[7] A Gaelic football league was set up in the West Division in May 1906 but only five clubs affiliated. In the eastern section there were six clubs registered for Gaelic football purposes and four of these also took part in hurling in this division.[8]

The number of GAA clubs in Donegal increased gradually in 1906 although not every GAA club in Donegal managed to officially register.[9] In May 1906, Seumas MacManus stated that there were thirty clubs in the county, with twenty of these affiliated with the GAA.[10] This appears to be fairly accurate, as in the period between February 1905 and the end of 1906, there were twenty-nine Donegal GAA clubs mentioned in the local press. Eighteen of these were involved in competitions run by the Donegal GAA County Board, while eleven did not take part in these leagues and appeared only occasionally.[11] The organisation of clubs was stronger in the south, with sixteen of the total number founded in this area, and this is a reflection of MacManus' local influence.

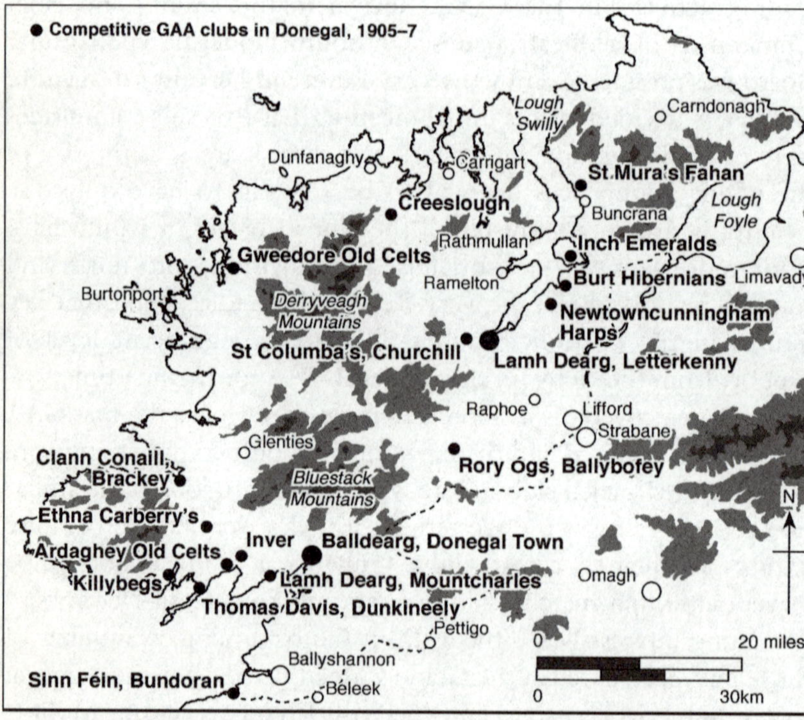

Fig. 4.1: Competitive GAA clubs in Donegal, 1905–07
SOURCES: *DJ, DI, DV* and *DP and DN*, 1905–07

Figures 4.1 and 4.2 illustrate Donegal's competitive and non-competitive clubs during the years of the first County Board. As can be seen in Appendices 3 and 4, GAA clubs founded in 1905 were certainly of a more politicised nature than the nineteenth-century clubs in Donegal, which had been created primarily for recreational and social purposes. A major factor in the organisation of the GAA in

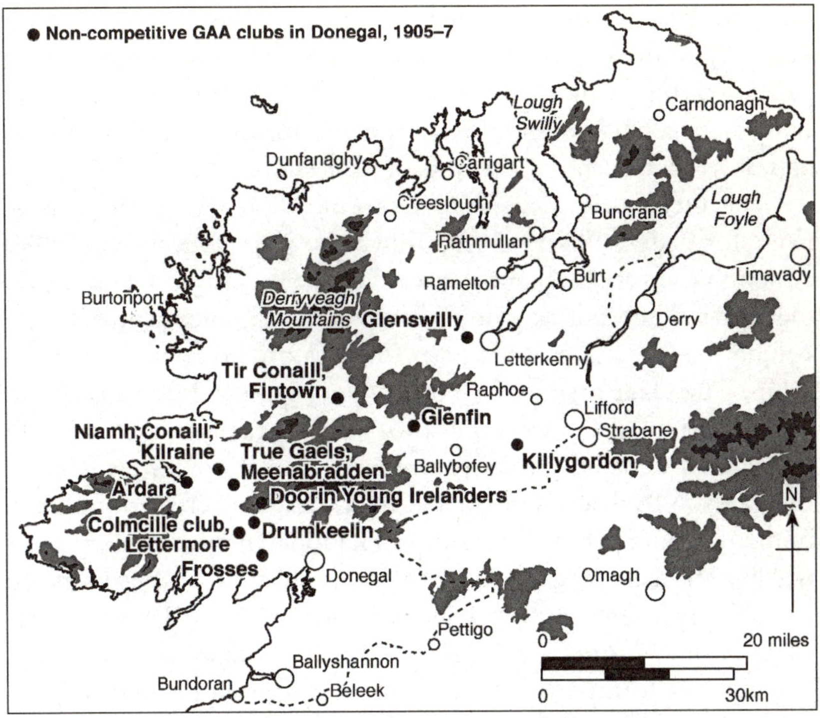

Fig. 4.2: Non-competitive GAA clubs in Donegal, 1905–07
SOURCES: *DJ, DI, DV* and *DP and DN*, 1905–07

Donegal in the early 1900s was the spread of cultural nationalism. The latter years of the 1890s saw a rise in political nationalism, which re-emerged with the Local Government of Ireland Act, the centenary of the 1798 Rebellion, the Boer War, the foundation of the United Irish League and increased voting opportunities.[12] By the beginning of the 1900s the rhetoric of journalists D.P. Moran and Arthur Griffith, who both advocated the rejection of West Britonism and encouraged the promotion of a more distinct Irish identity, was taking affect within Irish society.[13] Two cultural groups that were involved in the organisation of Gaelic games and the rejection of British culture in South Donegal in 1905 were the Gaelic League and Cumann na nGaedheal, although this interest was mainly generated by Seumas MacManus. The Gaelic League, founded in 1893 by Eoin MacNeill and Douglas Hyde, was devoted to reviving and fostering the Irish language and traditions and was initially intended to be non-sectarian.[14] Tom Garvin has stated that it 'never became a political society formally, nor did it ever become a mass organisation like the

GAA or the post-1916 Sinn Féin'.[15] He has also stated that it was generally an urban movement consisting of young, studious men. It expanded during the years of the Boer War, with membership trebling between 1898 and 1901, and the majority of its members appear to have been civil servants or professionals.[16]

The first Gaelic League branches in Donegal appear to have been formed in Barnesmore, Killybegs and Donegal by 1896, although the very first meeting was held at Brockagh.[17] This movement was significant as a number of Gaelic League members were behind the formation of the first GAA County Board in Donegal in 1905. The chief organiser of this board, Seumas MacManus, had been secretary of the Donegal town Gaelic League branch in 1896 and gained valuable administrative experience through his work in this body.[18] Both the GAA and Gaelic League were significant in bringing young people into the Irish national movement and membership of these organisations was thought to be necessary to enhance their cultural and political fulfilment.[19] On 19 September 1903 a new *Coiste Ceanntair* or district council of the Gaelic League was formed in Donegal town to go along with that in Inishowen and a number of those who were involved in the founding of the 1905 GAA County Board were in attendance.[20] Seumas MacManus, the Very Reverend Edward Maguire and solicitor P.M. Gallagher were all heavily involved in both organisations.[21] By 1903, there were at least twelve Gaelic League branches in South Donegal.[22] Of more importance to the organisation of GAA clubs in Donegal in 1905 was Cumann na nGaedheal, which encouraged economic and cultural nationalism along with pacifism and feminism.[23] Founded by Arthur Griffith in 1900, it quickly became a cover for the Irish Republican Brotherhood.[24]

The first GAA club organised in 1905 was the Lámh Dearg club in Mountcharles, which grew out of Seumas MacManus' branch of Cumann na nGaedheal. Significantly, MacManus was at the forefront of this Cumann na nGaedheal branch's activities throughout the year. Founded in February and named after his deceased wife, Ethna Carbery, this group were the main advocates of the playing of Gaelic games in County Donegal at this time.[25] Five GAA clubs organised that year in the south of the county developed out of branches of this political organisation.[26] Both the Croagh and Dunkineely GAA clubs had been organised in May by local men, Seamus McHugh

(Dunkineely) and farmer John McGrath (Croagh), in conjunction with a visit to Bruckless Hall from Seumas MacManus and Patrick Healy, who gave an address on 'the revival of the old games'.[27]

The Cumann na nGaedheal movement in the north of the county appears to have been weaker and there is no evidence that any GAA clubs were founded in this area because of that organisation.[28] Cumann na nGaedheal attracted little interest outside South Donegal and MacManus' militant, anti-British approach was perhaps too radical for the majority of those in the county at this time. It was the Irish Parliamentary Party, which advocated a policy of Home Rule for Ireland, which received the support of Bishop O'Donnell and the majority of voters.[29] Irish Parliamentary Party candidates won all the seats in the Donegal constituencies in the 1906 election.[30] In any case, after the foundation of the County Board, Cumann na nGaedheal rallies seem to have declined while by 1906 MacManus' preoccupation with a career in America also impacted significantly on their organisation as well as on that of the GAA. Desmond Murphy has also stated that 'the intense nationalism of the Bishop made it impossible to criticize the [Irish Parliamentary] Party without seeming to personally insult him'.[31] Nationally, it is difficult to establish the exact extent of Cumann na nGaedheal involvement in GAA clubs around this time, although there is evidence that the Rathmines Hurling club, which was in operation in Dublin in 1902, had its origins in this political movement.[32] Clubs in Mountcharles, Meenabradden, Ardaghey, Burt, Newtowncunningham, Gweedore and Inch displayed their Irish allegiance by taking on titles associated with an Irish identification. Croagh and Dunkineely took on the names of deceased Irish nationalist activists while Irish saints were remembered through the naming of clubs in Fahan, Churchill, Lettermore and Kilraine in their honour. The club names of those in Fintown, Donegal town, Letterkenny, Ballybofey and Brackey contained references to local clans, high kings and kingdoms.

Gaelic League branches were involved in the founding of GAA clubs in Longford, Westmeath, Dublin, Derry and Fermanagh at the beginning of the twentieth century and there is also evidence to suggest that a number of West Tyrone GAA clubs, founded prior to 1900, had their origins in the movement.[33] The Gaelic League fostered the development of Gaelic football and hurling through the inclusion of matches in their festivals.[34] While there is no doubt many GAA members were also involved in the Gaelic League, there is only minimal evidence that Gaelic League branches actually organised GAA teams during 1905 in Donegal. The Balldearg GAA club had been formed on 20 October at a meeting which brought together a large number of young men from Donegal town.[35] A Gaelic League branch was re-established there around this time and the GAA club was started in conjunction with this.[36] While all enrolled at the formation of Gweedore Old Celts in November 1905 were Irish speakers, it is unclear if there was any connection to this organisation. They did, however, state that their club 'promises to be the most Irish club in Co. Donegal, or perhaps all Ireland'.[37] It appears that Gaelic League clubs were not of sufficient strength in the county to make any huge impact on the GAA at this time. One nationwide problem the Gaelic League experienced was that it was primarily an urban organisation and never managed to gain sufficient interest in Irish-speaking areas where it should have been more prominent.[38] In 1934 it was stated by Peadar McGinley, a man heavily involved in the Gaelic League in Donegal in the 1905–07 period, that League organisers had fallen out with Bishop O'Donnell after they had declined to register the Feis Tír Chonaill as a Gaelic League function in 1906, in fear of non-Catholics being isolated. A disagreement over the necessity of a test in Irish for admittance to the National University was said to have worsened this relationship with the result that 'from then on the League was not welcome in Tír Chonaill'.[39] While this may be an oversimplification of the state of the Gaelic League in the county, certainly co-operation between this Association and GAA branches in Donegal was minimal during the years covered in this book, although there were some exceptions.

Members of other political organisations were eager to get involved in the GAA in the autumn of 1905. In Letterkenny, those present at the formation of the Lámh Dearg GAA club on 18 September included a number of members of the Irish National Federation and the United Irish League.[40] The Bundoran hurling club took on the name of Sinn Féin, which suggests a strong loyalty to this movement, while the GAA club in Creeslough was founded at a meeting of the village's Ancient Order of Hibernians branch.[41] The Glenfin club was also said to have been linked to this body but, overall, the fact that only two Gaelic League clubs and one AOH branch formed GAA clubs in Donegal throughout 1905 and 1906 does not suggest any major involvement from these political branches.[42] Seumas MacManus' claim in September 1905 that the AOH in his own division had done 'remarkable work' in the development of the GAA, while criticising heavily the north-west branches of the AOH which he felt had done little to promote Gaelic games, was somewhat vague.[43] Some clubs, such as Killygordon, were evidently organised after contact from Seumas MacManus, while others, such as Ballybofey, were helped by visiting clubs who introduced them to the rules through friendly matches.[44] There is no indication that any new clubs were formed in 1907 and this can be explained by the overall decline of GAA activity in the county that year.

As well as playing matches, a number of Donegal's GAA clubs were heavily involved in nationalist activities in South Donegal in 1905, where an emphasis was placed on eradicating elements of British culture from Irish society. Cumann na nGaedheal outings also served as anti-recruitment drives. Having travelled to Glenties by brake and car in June, the thirty-five members of the Mountcharles Cumann na nGaedheal branch present listened to their president, Seumas MacManus, continue what he had been advocating in the local press. He called for 'the revival of the old Irish game of camán, and the substitution of Gaelic football for the football which the Saxon had introduced'.[45] MacManus also discouraged the youths present from joining the British army. Camán matches quickly became a vehicle for the promotion of Irish culture at these outings. On their trip to nearby Croagh in mid-July, 'March of the Camán Man' was sung during the large marching procession.[46] Following the scoreless draw between Inver and Croagh, there followed nationalist speeches, recitations and singing, with Padraig MacGiolla Iosa leading renditions of 'Clann na nGaedhael go deo' (Clann na nGaedheal forever). This was a reference to an Irish-American organisation which recognised the IRB's Supreme Council as the true government of Ireland.[47] He then delivered an address upon 'The Duty of Ireland' and the Mountcharles choir sang 'O'Donnell Abú' (O'Donnell forever), as the large crowd listened on a height above the playing field. Events concluded with MacGiolla Iosa being presented with a camán dating back to 1875 which was to be displayed at the Oireachtas Exhibition in Dublin. This was an exhibition which had been established in 1897 to promote Irish culture.[48] Anti-English rhetoric and nationalist songs and speeches were common at Cumann na nGaedheal branch events in South Donegal.[49]

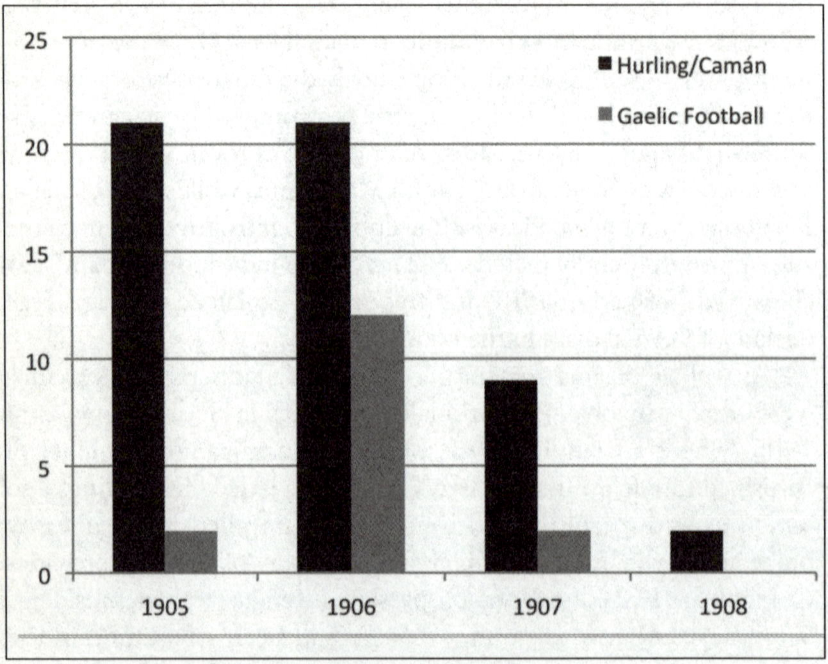

Fig. 4.3: Gaelic football and hurling club matches in Donegal, 1905–08

SOURCES: *DJ, DI, DV* and *DP and DN*, 1905–08

As can be seen in Figure 4.3, in the period from July 1905 until August 1908 Donegal GAA clubs were involved in at least sixty-nine matches. Two additional hurling exhibition matches were played in Donegal by Derry and Tyrone teams. Fifty-three of these Donegal games were camán or hurling and sixteen were Gaelic football. The peak year of activity, with thirty-three GAA matches played, was 1906. Donegal's southern clubs normally played camán or commons. This was noted after Burt Hibernians' defeat of Ardaghey Old Celts in the county final of 1906 when it was recorded that the latter team had struggled to adapt to the grass field in Letterkenny.[50] This also suggests a difficulty in securing playing fields in the southern region. The Burt team were clearly used to a faster type of game as indicated in a later interview with one of their players.[51] Certainly prior to the founding of the West County Board in October 1905 there is evidence that the scoring system was still measured by the number of hails scored rather than goals and points, and traditional equipment such as camáns and a bool were used, which again illustrates the slow evolution of hurling in Donegal.[52]

Thirty-five of the camán/hurling games were of a competitive nature while seventeen were challenge matches and one was unspecified. This indicates a shift in the nature of matches from those preferred by the early Donegal GAA clubs, where the number of challenge matches played outweighed the number of competitive fixtures in the late 1880s and early 1890s. At least sixteen Gaelic football matches were played between 1905 and 1908 with eleven of these competitive, while five friendlies were recorded. Although actual figures were probably higher due to underreporting, they do illustrate the greater popularity of hurling and camán over Gaelic football in Donegal at the time, and most notably, they indicate the problems with the dissemination of the latter sport in the county. As noted in Chapter 2, pre-codified forms of hurling had been in existence in Donegal since the eighteenth century while association football was firmly established in many areas by 1905. This helps explain the popularity of hurling over Gaelic football. The predominance of forms of hurling over Gaelic football is also a reflection of the 1888–92 figures, where hurling was the preferred code, although it must also be noted that back-to-back fixtures in both codes between two clubs had lessened greatly since the earlier period. This was probably due to the leagues not being run simultaneously and only a small number of clubs fielding both Gaelic football and hurling teams.

The availability of 1901 and 1911 census returns meant that a more detailed analysis could be made of the occupations of those who participated in these GAA matches.[53] A total of 254 camán and Gaelic football players were named in the local press in the period from 1905–07; it was possible to identify 195 of these players and their occupational categories are shown in Table 4.1. Tom Hunt has established that those identified in his study of 500 Gaelic football and hurling players came primarily from the agricultural class (62 per cent); with the commercial class (21 per cent), industrial class (15 per cent) and professional class (2 per cent) following behind. There were no players from the domestic class participating in these GAA clubs.

TABLE 4.1

Occupational categories of GAA players in Donegal, 1905–07

Category	*Number of players*	*% of total*
1: Professional	13	6.66
2: Domestic	4	2.05
3: Commercial	20	10.25
4: Agricultural	80	41.02
5: Industrial	63	32.30
6: Indefinite and non-productive	15	7.69
Total	195	100

SOURCES: *DJ, DP and DN, DV, DI* (1905–07) and 'Census of Ireland 1901 and 1911'; retrieved from http://www.census.nationalarchives.ie/ [Accessed 28 September 2012].

Richard McElligott has also produced an extensive study of Kerry GAA players and has noted that of 910 players active there between 1888 and 1916, it was the agricultural sector in which the greatest number were employed (38 per cent). This was followed by 33 per cent in the industrial sector while 19 per cent were involved in commercial work. Professionals made up 5 per cent of the overall figure. Students and unknowns comprised 3 per cent while only 2 per cent of players were employed domestically.[54] Like those analysed by Hunt and McElligott, the majority of recorded participants in Gaelic games in County Donegal from 1905 until 1907, 41 per cent, came from the agricultural class. The industrial sector accounted for 32 per cent of the total number of players identified, while those in the commercial class made up 10 per cent of the total number. Those described as professionals made up 7 per cent while the domestic class and the unclassified category together accounted for only 10 per cent of the overall figure. A number of rural clubs certainly were made up primarily of those involved in agriculture, most notably Newtowncunningham Harps, St Columba's of Churchill and St Mura's of Fahan. Generally, clubs seemed to attract players mainly from the agricultural and industrial areas. Unsurprisingly, there was less involvement from the agricultural sector in more urban areas, such as Bundoran.

Of the 195 players 82 per cent were single and this meant that they had more free time to devote to their clubs. The figure for married players was higher than that found elsewhere. Although the marital status of every player identified could not be found, 16 per cent of Donegal's players were married and this was a higher percentage than that found by McElligott and Hunt. In Kerry, 6 per cent of the players were married, while the players analysed by Hunt were nearly all single.[55] Hunt has also stated that 'marriage brought responsibilities and new financial obligations to a group with limited social income, and lifestyle decisions were made that excluded physical recreation'.[56] The fact that most of the players in Donegal were Roman Catholic (97 per cent) illustrates that Gaelic games were predominantly seen as a nationalist pastime. This was similar to the findings of Hunt and McElligott, although the ratio was slightly higher in Kerry than in Donegal, as 98 per cent of the players there were Catholics.[57] The largest number of players in Donegal were aged between 21 and 25 years (31 per cent) with the smallest number (2 per cent) being aged 15 or under. The majority of players identified by Hunt (45 per cent) and McElligott (38 per cent) also came from the 21–25 age bracket.[58] Of the 195 Donegal players identified, there was only one whose age was unrecorded. The average age of a GAA player in Donegal was calculated to be 24.29 years old. This was marginally older than the average age in Kerry which was 23.67 years and that of Hunt's survey, which was an average age of 23.2 years.[59]

Using information gathered in newspapers it was possible to trace the social background of ninety-one Donegal GAA administrators from 129 of those named for the period from 1905 until 1907. These included County Board and club presidents, vice-presidents, secretaries, treasurers, captains, vice-captains and delegates from fifteen clubs.[60] What is notable about Table 4.2 is that the professional class was more involved as administrators than as players, with 32 per cent of the total coming from this sector. This was the highest percentage of any class. This can be explained by the presence of the clergy and national school teachers who, in their role as pillars of society, were eager to organise Gaelic games for those in their localities. They also probably had more experience of organisation and the paperwork necessary for this task. The clergy of the Roman Catholic Church were heavily involved in the 1905 County Board while the involvement of national school teachers can be seen in the example of the

Gweedore Old Celts. This club benefited from the presence of no less than six national school teachers on its committee.[61] The involvement of the industrial class was also significant, with 25 per cent coming from this sector. The shift from the strength of the agricultural sector as players to a more secondary role in administration is also evident; only 22 per cent of this category were involved as administrators. Involvement of the domestic classes was non-existent while just 1 per cent of administrators came from the indefinite and non-descriptive category. Richard McElligott has noted that in Kerry it was the commercial class (41 per cent) which had the greatest involvement as officials. This differs from Donegal. There was also more involvement of the industrial (22 per cent) and agricultural (21 per cent) classes than professionals in Kerry, who made up just 15 per cent.[62] The oldest administrator in County Donegal was sixty-four years of age while the youngest was just seventeen. Again, the majority of those identified were Roman Catholics (96 per cent) while Presbyterians (2 per cent) and Church of Ireland (2 per cent) made up the rest. Most administrators were single (65 per cent) which, as previously noted, meant more time for recreational activities.

TABLE 4.2
Occupational categories of Donegal GAA administrators, 1905–07

Category	*Number of administrators*	*% of total*
1: Professional	29	31.86
2: Domestic	0	0
3: Commercial	18	19.78
4: Agricultural	20	21.97
5: Industrial	23	25.27
6: Indefinite and non-productive	1	1.09
Total	91	100

SOURCES: *DJ, DP and DN, DV, DI* (1905–07) and 'Census of Ireland 1901 and 1911'; retrieved from http://www.census.nationalarchives.ie/ [Accessed 10 December 2011]

With the rise of cultural nationalism, Donegal's GAA clubs began to attract more interest than those in the 1888–92 period had managed and a number of those with social influence were willing to act as patrons. Most notable of these were the clergy of the Roman Catholic Church. A number of Donegal's clergy offered financial support in the 1905–07 period but perhaps most significantly, both Canon McFadden and the Very Reverend Dr Edward Maguire gave Gaelic games their public backing while criticising 'foreign' games at Cumann na nGaedheal rallies.[63] A number of priests were so disillusioned with society in Donegal at this time that they briefly supported local branches of Cumann na nGaedheal around Donegal town.[64] There is little evidence that there was any major clerical involvement within the GAA in Donegal prior to this. Jim MacLaughlin claims that 'as leaders of "their people" priests in particular were responsible for instilling a deeply conservative sense of patriotism in Donegal'.[65] Seumas MacManus was probably aware of this and used his considerable organising skills to try to win over the support of the common people and advance the Gaelic Revival through the clergy of the Roman Catholic Church.

The Grand Camán parade of October 1905 was organised with the help of a number of those involved in the GAA in Derry. Advertisements were placed in the local press and excursion trains were organised from Derry, Ballyshannon and Killybegs.[66] 'Almost two thousand people were present' on the strand for a camán competition between local clubs and a camán exhibition match which was played between players representing Derry and Tyrone, despite the wet conditions.[67] This event gained the notice of the RIC and 'a large force of police was in Mountcharles for the occasion, and in addition plain-clothes men accompanied the contingents from Derry, Strabane, Donegal and Ballyshannon'.[68] It was also held with the co-operation of those in the local Catholic Church. The day began with a march to the Mountcharles Catholic church, where mass was celebrated by the Very Reverend Edward Maguire. Afterwards the congregation moved on to Inver strand where the Very Reverend Maguire took the chair on the motion of *Donegal Independent* editor P.A. Mooney and Dunkineely draper and publican, Peter Ward.[69] Letters from Bishop Patrick O'Donnell and the Reverend James C. Cannon supporting the movement and native pastimes were then read aloud.[70] Bishop O'Donnell saw abstinence from alcohol as being fundamental to the growth of Gaelic games. This view was echoed by MacManus in his own speech, and he encouraged the promotion of the Irish Ireland movement which called for the use of the Irish language, playing of Gaelic games and purchasing of Irish-manufactured goods. The Reverend James C. Cannon claimed that 'the whole movement will give renewed spirit to the fine old social spirit of Tír Conaill which is now, as it has been in the stories past, the spirit of a true Irish Ireland'. The meeting concluded after a number of nationalist speeches and the singing of 'God Save Ireland'.[71]

At the foundation meeting of the County Board, Bishop O'Donnell, the Very Reverend Dr Maguire and Reverend James C. Cannon were all given significant roles. Bishop O'Donnell was appointed patron and gave his promise that he would donate a cup for camán purposes, to be competed for between the east and west champions.[72] This final was scheduled to take place at a festival organised by the Bishop to promote Irish culture and to raise funds for the building of St Eunan's College, this no doubt adding to the prestige of the competition.[73] The administrative skills of the clergy were not overlooked. Vice-Presidents appointed included the Reverend James C. Cannon (east) with the Reverend C. Boyce being appointed to look after the Western Division's financial matters.[74]

President, the Very Reverend Dr Maguire, was initially keen to organise clubs as well as offer financial support and he stated that he would write to his friends throughout Donegal to ask them to set up clubs.[75] The following month a manifesto written by himself and the two divisional secretaries was published in the local press and an appeal was made 'to the youth of the county in general, and in particular to leading men (both young and old) in each district in the county where a Gaelic athletic club is not already formed, to found such at once'.[76] This was critical, they believed, 'so that no district in Donegal may any longer lie under the reproach of lagging in shame when Ireland has arisen up and is casting from her the tokens of littleness and slavery'.[77] There is no evidence that Bishop O'Donnell made any attempts to organise clubs and his role appears to have been primarily as patron, although he was known to attend matches and present prizes after tournaments.[78] After 1906, however, both Bishop O'Donnell and the Very Reverend Dr Maguire's interest in the promotion of the GAA seems to have fallen dramatically.

Given their influence on society, this decline of clerical support was a significant blow to the GAA in Donegal in 1907. While

Bishop O'Donnell was noted by one contemporary as 'doing wonders in the way of encouraging the promotion of Irish games in his diocese', there is little evidence that he gave much support to the promotion of Gaelic games in Donegal after the Aonach an Dúin festival in July 1906 and, as noted earlier, had sought to isolate the Gaelic League in the county.[79] The West County Board also lost the influence of the Very Reverend Dr Maguire, who transferred to Letterkenny in 1906 to take up a new post as president of St Eunan's College. Members of the clergy such as the Very Reverend Dr Maguire and Canon McFadden were not as vocal in their promotion of Gaelic games as they had been in 1905 and this may have reduced public awareness of the GAA in Donegal, given the significance of the clergy within the Catholic community. The Very Reverend Dr Maguire's replacement as president of the West County Board, the Reverend Hugh Gallagher, appears to have been more interested in athletic meetings and encouraged these at a meeting of the board in April 1907.[80]

Patronage was also received from those with less influence in society. Financial donations from administrators P.M. Gallagher and Peter Ward and the Mountcharles branch of Cumann na nGaedheal, who donated £3 towards the purchase of a trophy for Gaelic football, benefited the 1905 West County Board.[81] Internal subscriptions were evidently necessary for the existence of a number of the 1905–07 clubs. It was decided in January 1906 that the Mountcharles Cumann na nGaedheal branch members would each contribute one shilling to their camán team's travelling expenses on a monthly basis.[82] The Ballybofey club noted the necessity of fees for the purchase of team kits at their founding meeting in May 1906.[83] Help also came from those sympathetic to clubs' ideals. Killygordon received a 'substantial subscription' from local bank official Patrick Paul McConnell, while subscriptions to the value of £4 were also gathered by the club in January 1906.[84] Having a regular field was important as it meant the club had a base for practice and matches and most clubs in Donegal relied on local landowners to lend their property for the game.[85] An exception was the Tír Conaill GAA club, Fintown, which by 25 November 1905 had held its second practice in a field it bought from James Quinn of Meenmore.[86]

Attendance fees were evidently in use and the Sinn Féin, Bundoran club felt that admission fees were of a critical nature, as 'expenses come rather heavily on a club, yet limited in numbers, so it is absolutely necessary that a nominal charge for admission should be made'.[87] Not everyone could be made to pay to watch, however, and the club complained after a match in December 1906 that 'the gate results were not at all in comparison with the huge crowd which assembled to witness the game'.[88] This had not improved by the following spring, when one reporter commented in a match preview that 'it is sad to see men going half a mile round looking for a chance to get in without paying' and readers were reminded that 'such a day's sport cannot be provided for nothing'.[89] The level of funding available to individual clubs from the county board seems to have been minimal and Balldearg were grateful to receive support from the local drama club.[90] Affiliation fees were, of course, necessary, with the entrance fee for clubs for the 1906 West Gaelic football league fixed at two shillings and six pence.[91] However, by June of the following year, it was decided that no entry fee would be necessary for this competition, reflecting the weak financial state of many clubs and the difficulty in attracting enough teams.[92]

The decline of the GAA in Donegal, 1907–19

GAA activity in Donegal had lessened significantly by 1907.[93] Newspaper reports indicate a serious decline at this point. During 1907 there were sporadic references to GAA clubs in Burt, Newtowncunningham, Bundoran (two), Ardaghey, Croagh, Dunkineely and Donegal town.[94] This total of eight clubs was a severe drop from the twenty-nine the previous year and De Burca's figure of five in Donegal for 1907–08 is lower, although not all of the above clubs may have been registered with the Central Council and therefore may have gone unnoticed.[95] More significantly, Donegal shared with Derry the lowest number of affiliated clubs in Ulster at this time and this highlights the disbandment of the majority of the clubs founded in 1905 and 1906 at this stage. Out of a provincial total of 105, Antrim had the highest number with eighteen. By comparison, there were 124 in Connaught, 222 in Munster and 337 in Leinster. Cork had the highest number of clubs with seventy-seven while Dublin, with sixty-eight, had the highest number in Leinster and the second highest overall.[96]

Dónal McAnallen has noted a number of problems the GAA in Ulster faced in this decade. These included opposition to Sunday games from the clergy of the Catholic Church and Sabbatarians, the refusal of the Great Northern Railway to facilitate the GAA, and competition with soccer. Problems gaining access to pitches and facilities also affected some counties.[97] While there is only minimal evidence of attempts to prevent Sunday matches in Donegal and none of any conflict with the train company, this overall state of affairs did little to help the growth of the GAA in Donegal as the Ulster GAA Council was not in a very prosperous state and was poorly organised at the time.[98]

There were also a number of more localised problems with fixtures. The organisation of matches and competitions proved difficult in both divisions. Matches were not played on a weekly basis and this undoubtedly hampered progress. Initial fixtures organised by the Eastern Division were staggered with gaps over a five-week period.[99] By February 1906 one reporter claimed that in the West Division 'the hurling competitions in this division are going on slowly. It will be a long time before the final match is played.'[100] Some clubs had difficulties fielding teams. The Lámh Dearg camán team of Mountcharles had only played one match by April 1906 and this was said to have been due to a scarcity of players.[101] The following month the Eastern Division delegates passed a motion to decrease the number of players from seventeen to fifteen in matches where clubs were in short supply.[102] Getting enough men together on a regular basis for matches proved problematic for a number of clubs within the county and may have led to their decline and inactivity.

The Eastern Division chose to play their Gaelic football and hurling leagues simultaneously and began in December 1905.[103] Not every club played both codes and this difference in organisation caused some problems in the selection of the County Donegal Gaelic football team to play Derry in the Ulster Gaelic football championship on St Patrick's Day 1906.[104] Details regarding the Eastern Gaelic football final are unclear while the Western final does not appear to have been decided until 1907, with Balldearg noted as the winners in the press.[105] The final was abandoned twice in 1906 due to the incursions of the tide on the strand when the initial match, held in October, and the replay, staged much later in December, were in progress, indicating difficulty in securing a proper venue and poor timekeeping.[106] While delays between matches were quite common in those days within the GAA in other counties such as

Dublin, these factors were not beneficial to development as interest would have waned without weekly matches.[107]

Clearly it was difficult to bring all areas of the county together and there is some evidence to suggest a lack of co-operation, possibly resulting from the distance between towns where meetings were being held, such as Letterkenny (Eastern Board) and those in the south of the county such as Mountcharles (Western Board), and differing attitudes to how Gaelic games should be administered in each area.[108] The issue of poor communications between the two divisions was highlighted at the Western Board's meeting in October 1906. Concerns were expressed by national school teacher and chairman Edward Daly regarding the lack of communication between the eastern committee and their own board. It was stated that 'on every occasion when a move was made by this side to fraternise with the eastern section their advances were either treated with contempt or totally disregarded'.[109] There is some evidence to back up his view. In May 1906 the clubs of Burt Hibernians, Newtowncunningham Hibernians, St Mura's and Lámh Dearg agreed to pay their affiliation fees to the Eastern Board, 'but to recognise no other authority in the county'.[110] There appears to have been some controversy over who should receive the affiliation fees with the Western Board secretary Alex McDyer later stating that he would let the Eastern Board control this as 'an arrangement where the responsibility was divided would be liable to lead to disagreement'.[111] The six members present at the October meeting agreed unanimously to separate from the Eastern Division as they believed that 'the present arrangement interfered more or less with freedom of movement'.[112] There is no evidence that plans illustrated by the Western Board to hold a general meeting for all GAA delegates in the county at the Aonach an Dúin festival in Letterkenny in July bore any fruit.[113]

As McAnallen has noted, at a higher level, support from the Ulster Council in developing the games appears to have been poor.[114] In Donegal, the relationship between those involved in positions of office in the Eastern and Western boards and those in the Ulster GAA Council is hard to establish, given the lack of evidence in the archives of either organisation for this early period. It is clear that a number of delegates were appointed for each division and efforts were made to attend these provincial meetings.[115] However, one problem was the failure of the Ulster board to hold any of their monthly meetings in Donegal. This was highlighted at the Eastern Board's meeting in April 1906 when secretary Johnnie Dowds was instructed to write to the secretary of the Ulster Council, George Martin, in the hope that the next meeting would be held in Letterkenny as the committee thought it was unfair that none of their meetings were held in Donegal.[116] Two years later this request still had not been granted.[117] Funding does not appear to have been forthcoming to the Donegal organisation. At their meeting in April 1907, the Fermanagh County Board was critical of the lack of finance given to them by the Ulster Council and claimed that Donegal had also suffered a loss.[118] Given the importance of finance in the running of sporting clubs, the level of finance available to the GAA clubs in Donegal did little to maintain them or the divisional boards to which they were affiliated. There is certainly evidence that this provincial council was experiencing financial difficulty around this time and that county boards in Derry and Tyrone also struggled to maintain their status in the early decades of the twentieth century.[119]

Other more localised problems with administration were also apparent. The absence of 'delegates from the country' was noted at the Western Board's October 1906 meeting but it was hoped that this was simply due to difficulties in attending Saturday meetings.[120] A re-organisation letter circulated by the Western Board secretary, Alex McDyer, in November 1906 illustrated the problems in gathering attendees at meetings and dealing with protests.[121] A camán league did take place in 1907 with Sinn Féin, Bundoran, defeating Ardaghey in the Western final in July but little has been recorded about the other clubs' matches that season.[122] Evidence of club activities in the Eastern Division around this time is also scarce.[123] The camán league recommenced for the 1906–07 season on December 9 when Lámh Dearg defeated newly affiliated Inch Emeralds in a well-attended match.[124] It appears that Burt won the East Donegal hurling championship for 1907 as they went on to play against Bundoran Sinn Féin for the county championship. This match was won by the latter team but they received little attention in the local press at the time.[125] This decline was mirrored in the Western Division. A Gaelic football match organised by the Western Board was held between Balldearg and Dunkineely in November 1907 and a small number of camán matches took place in Bundoran in 1908 but it is clear at this stage that both divisions had collapsed.[126] Of critical importance to the decline of the GAA in Donegal at this point was the loss of organisers.

The lack of instruction from central sporting agencies regarding the development of sport in Donegal is a key element of this book. The man responsible for organising the initial County Board meeting, and chief organiser of the GAA in the county, Seumas MacManus, was not involved by 1907 and was showing more interest in his literary career in the United States.[127] Significantly, no new clubs appear to have been affiliated after 1906 and without MacManus' influence in organising them, this is perhaps unsurprising. The number of GAA clubs did not grow sufficiently for the Association to gain a proper foothold as not every parish was able to or eager to organise their own GAA club. The Western Board also lost vice-president P.A. Mooney, who passed away in June 1907.[128] This loss and the withdrawal of initial officers and supporters no doubt contributed to the decline of the playing of Gaelic games in the county. The GAA, after MacManus' departure, certainly lacked any public figures with social influence and affluence to promote the games in the way that he had attempted. This can be compared to events in County Kerry. The GAA in Kerry enjoyed a revival in the early 1900s, largely due to the organisational and propagandist efforts of T.F. O'Sullivan. Although he was transferred to Dublin in 1907, his role as chief organiser was taken over by Austin Stack, who proved a more than effective replacement.[129] In contrast, with the loss of MacManus, Donegal had nobody with the drive and personality to promote Gaelic games and this continued to be the case until 1919.

Problems continued within the Ulster GAA Council into the second decade of the twentieth century. Disputes regarding the hosting of meetings and match results were commonplace and the fact that Ulster Council meetings were mainly held in the counties of Antrim, Monaghan and Cavan continued to be a cause of concern to other Ulster counties.[130] Donegal remained isolated from these activities for much of this decade. One Derry GAA official claimed in 1915 that a lack of trophies and insufficient popular support were responsible for the lack of success of the GAA in his county.[131] In Donegal, it was the latter which proved most problematic. While this period was generally one of great inactivity in the formation of clubs and organising committees in Donegal, there were a small number of localised attempts to reorganise Gaelic games on a competitive basis in the years from 1910 until 1914. Despite the donation of a number of trophies, these attracted little interest, mainly due to a dearth of clubs. The Assaroe Cup was initially donated by Henry J. Toal, an Inland Revenue Officer, to the Aodh Ruadh club of Ballyshannon in March 1910 for Gaelic football purposes.[132] However, this competition had not been organised by the following October as there were no clubs located within close proximity of the host club.[133] Another difficulty was the prominence of the Woods soccer cup in the Ballyshannon area at the time and the greater popularity of association football over the Gaelic code throughout the county.

With this lack of interest, it was then decided to contact a number of hurling teams. A hurling competition finally began in June 1911 but with only three Donegal teams taking part, Ardaghey, Tír Conaill (Letterkenny) and Aodh Ruadh (Ballyshannon).[134] In fact, outside of these teams, the Aodh Ruadh club had to be content with friendly hurling matches against only four other clubs, three of these being based in Leitrim and the other in Fermanagh, while Gaelic football in the Ballyshannon area also suffered from an absence of teams.[135] There is no evidence that the Assaroe Cup was held again in 1912 and Aodh Ruadh claimed at their AGM held in October 1911 that they found away games difficult as travelling was awkward for some players.[136] Other cups offered for competition in 1911, 1913 and 1914 attracted little interest.[137] Clearly soccer was the preferred choice of sport at this point, and easier to organise given the fact that it was quite well established in Donegal since the 1880s and its rules were well known, while it also required fewer players. Given the lack of nearby Donegal clubs and Ballyshannon's geographical position, with a close proximity to the Leitrim border, it was at times easier to travel to play Leitrim clubs and the Aodh Ruadh club did this in 1915 with a small number of hurling and Gaelic football matches against Leitrim clubs.[138] Relations between these clubs were positive, with the Ballyshannon (and later the Bundoran branch) joining the Leitrim County Board in May 1917.[139]

The precise scale of Donegal GAA involvement in the First World War is difficult to establish given the lack of contemporary accounts of GAA recruitment. At least 8,000 Donegal men are said to have been actively involved so it is also likely that some GAA members participated.[140] Cronin, Duncan and Rouse have stated that 'thousands of GAA members' followed the call of John Redmond to enlist in the British Army and have noted the collapse of clubs such as Killaloe in County Clare as a result of this.[141] In 1916, a pivotal year in Ireland's fight for independence, the Easter Rising saw Patrick Pearse lead a rebellion of around 1,200 members of the Volunteers, Irish Citizen Army and Irish Republican Brotherhood against the British forces.[142] While this uprising was generally centred in Dublin and lasted only a week, a republic was declared by Pearse and public opinion swayed against the British with his execution and that of thirteen others. Added to this, the arrests of 3,419 people around the country and their treatment ensured 'a scale of resentment against British rule in Ireland which was unprecedented'.[143]

One GAA writer, in a review of the Donegal County Board, claimed in 1923 that 'the year 1916, with its strong Irish spirit, was responsible for the growth of Gaelic football' in Donegal.[144] While there may have been a rise in the number of Gaelic football selections appearing in 1916, by the following year the figure had decreased. In 1915 there were four of these operating in the county. This had risen to ten in 1916 but in 1917 the figure had dropped to seven.[145] This does not suggest any significant overall growth at this time. William Murphy has concluded that 'the overwhelming majority of those who fought in 1916 were not members of the GAA'.[146] Cronin, Duncan and Rouse have estimated the number of GAA members who participated in the fighting to be around 350 although Wren, De Burca and Gorry have shown that Gaelic League membership was a more significant motivating factor in taking up the fight rather than GAA involvement.[147] Certainly Donegal's involvement at Easter 1916 was minimal. While this can be explained by the fact that most of the fighting took place in Dublin, the IRB movement in the county was weak and Ernest Blythe has provided an account of the difficulties he encountered in his recruitment efforts at the end of 1914. He struggled to find sufficient numbers interested and has stated that he only managed to persuade about twenty men to join.[148] Blythe has also noted that Bishop O'Donnell's support for the Irish Parliamentary Party 'may have given public opinion a special slant' and he felt that 'economics may have been a factor' in the lack of support he encountered.[149] Donegal's involvement was therefore restricted to a handful of men in Dublin, including Joe Sweeney, who would go on to help organise the County Board in 1919. A mix-up in communications meant that thirty-three Volunteers who had mobilised at Creeslough took no part in the Rising.[150] It is not unreasonable to suggest that there was no involvement of any Donegal GAA clubs in the fighting and there is little evidence that any were formed as a direct result of nationalist fervour created by events in Dublin at this time.

In July 1918 GAA matches, still seen by the RIC as prospective political gatherings rather than sporting events, came under increasing pressure from the government when it was announced that public meetings would require permits. However, the GAA chose to defy this and ordered its clubs not to apply for these or its members to play in matches where permits had been granted.[151] Evidence of trouble arising from this in Donegal is minimal. That same month there were claims that a Ballyshannon-Kinlough hurling match had gone ahead in Bundoran after the venue had been switched to confuse the RIC, who had stated that it would be stopped by force; there is little evidence of interference in other matches held during July.[152] A sports day, consisting of 'Gaelic football, dancing and foot races' organised by the Seán McDermott Sinn Féin club, Frosses, was held on 7 July after suggestions by a police sergeant and two constables that it be postponed and a permit obtained were ignored.[153] Despite calls from the Central Council for mass participation in Gaelic games on Sunday, 4 August 1918, there are no press reports of Donegal GAA clubs' involvement in Gaelic Sunday.[154] De Burca has stated that this event was 'the greatest single act of defiance outside the purely political sphere between 1916 and 1922' with almost 100,000 taking part.[155] This event allowed matches to again go ahead without restrictions and Cronin, Duncan and Rouse have stated that it 'linked the GAA to the gathering momentum of radical nationalism which led to the election victory of Sinn Féin in 1918'.[156]

Given the small number of clubs operating in the county at the time, it is unsurprising that there was no wide-scale organisation in Donegal. It also highlights how the GAA in Donegal was not operating in ways envisaged by the Central Council. However, this government prohibition of Gaelic games may have brought about a slight rise in nationalist feeling in South Donegal GAA circles. A Gaelic football tournament involving teams from Donegal town,

Ballyshannon, Bundoran, Mountcharles, Frosses, Ballintra and Killybegs was held in Donegal town on 25 August 1918 and drew no interference from the authorities despite the decent attendance present.[157] The Aodh Ruadh club hosted another of these gatherings at the end of October and again there were no attempts to prevent this despite a police patrol being present nearby.[158] Donegal remained on the periphery of these more centralised GAA trends and external intervention was required in order to spark the GAA into action on a wider scale within the county.

Conclusion

The cultural revival struggled to gain significant impetus within Donegal society and attempts to promote the Irish language through the GAA were largely ignored. The loss of key administrators had a critical effect on the first County Board in 1907. The difficulties experienced by the Ulster Council did little to help the GAA in Donegal while internal problems, and in particular the failure of the first County Board's administrators to work together throughout the county, had a severe effect on efforts to implement competitive Gaelic games on a permanent basis there. A widespread failure of those with the energy, enthusiasm and knowledge of Gaelic games to come forward and arrange GAA competitions in the years after this until 1919 was also highly significant. In areas where this interest was present, a lack of available nearby clubs to link up with was problematic.

Despite this decline, some promise had been shown. However, given the voluntary nature of sports administration in the county at the time, a scarcity of sustained assistance from those with social influence and financial backing was detrimental to the GAA's progress. The problem of transport and getting sufficient numbers together is again apparent, as was the tendency to stick with the more traditional game of camán by a number of clubs. The rural nature of the early GAA in Donegal is also illustrated in the agricultural background of the majority of players, while national school teachers were also beginning to take an interest in the organisation of the GAA within the county. However, unlike in Dublin, where the Christian Brothers were heavily involved in teams registered with a Schools Board in 1904, they failed to introduce a system for schools Gaelic football and hurling, something which might have helped spread interest in the GAA within the county.[159] The lack of impact of the 1916 Rising on the formation of GAA clubs is also apparent and IRB recruitment from the county remained low in the build-up to the rebellion against British rule. Despite this, there is some indication that the rise of nationalism was beginning to have an effect on the organisation of Gaelic football at local sports and this will be addressed in Chapter 5.

5

The growth of the GAA in Donegal, 1919–1935

Introduction

It was during the period from 1919 to 1935 that the GAA in Donegal finally was established on a permanent basis. In 1919 County Board meetings and competitive matches were again organised and from this time they were continued annually. The development of the GAA in this period was reliant on the dedication of a small number of enthusiastic administrators and their ability to integrate the GAA into local society, initially by the organisation of Gaelic football at local sports days. The provision of annual competitive fixtures for young men interested in team sports was a key factor and improvements in transport and press coverage also meant that Gaelic football began to attract the public's attention. However, as will be seen, this was a slow, mundane development and an analysis of club figures reveals the existence of teams in the 1920s was characterised by instability and lack of development. Factors such as emigration, finance, disputes with the County Board, a lack of support in some areas and competition with soccer all affected the survival of clubs. It was not until the 1930s that Gaelic games were more firmly established in the county and this was helped by improvements at administrative level and the organisation of district committees. Although political involvement in the new County Board and its clubs was initially strong, participation of Donegal's GAA members in the War of Independence and Civil War was minimal and there was no major disruption to fixtures. Hurling generally failed to develop, partially because it was neglected by the County Board but also as a result of difficulties in its dissemination. It remained restricted to Inishowen and outside of this concentrated area, to Ballyshannon and Letterkenny, where Garda Síochána involvement boosted its development.

The revival of the GAA in Donegal

Efforts to redevelop an administrative structure for Gaelic football and hurling in Donegal were begun at the Ulster GAA convention in Derry on 16 March 1919. Secretary Eoin O'Duffy, a native of Monaghan, was instructed to take the necessary steps to form a County Board for Donegal and after the convention, Donegal representatives Curran, Rodden, Fullerton and McGovern met and decided to hold this foundation meeting in Strabane, County Tyrone early the following month.[1] This was the first time any significant decisive action had been taken since the 1905–07 period and prior to this meeting O'Duffy noted the failure of those interested in forming a County Board to maintain enthusiasm for this despite his encouragement.[2] Other areas in Ulster, such as Tyrone and Down, were also in need of reorganisation around this time.[3]

Initially there was strong political backing for the new Donegal County Board, with Sinn Féin members heavily involved in the meeting, which took place at the Barrack Street Hall, Strabane on 3 April 1919.[4] This was chaired by O'Duffy with Sam O'Flaherty appointed president. Members of the Dáil, P.J. Ward and Joseph Sweeney, were named vice-presidents along with Dr J.P. McGinley. John Curran of Letterkenny was named county secretary while Patrick McCartan, Donegal town, became treasurer.[5] However, McGinley's influence in the GAA in the following years seemed to dwindle in comparison his political and professional career, while O'Flaherty was later sacked from his position as president after it was stated in 1923 that he had taken no part in the County Board 'for a considerable time'.[6] Given that O'Duffy later became Garda Commissioner, his involvement in the GAA in Donegal seemed to have been limited to official duties such as throwing in the ball at Ulster championship matches, but it was he, as secretary of the Ulster Council, who was largely responsible for the revival of the GAA in Ulster at this time.[7] His early influence in the GAA in Donegal can also be seen in that at a County Board meeting on Sunday, 4 May 1919, the bye-laws of the Monaghan County Board were adopted provisionally as a model.[8] Ward was president for a number of years, but like McGinley, by the middle of the 1920s was no longer involved in the County Board. Both these men seem more interested in their professional careers at this point.

The Donegal County Board began to meet on a regular basis after it was re-founded. At first, its delegates appeared preoccupied with the selection of a county team for competition in the Ulster Gaelic football championship of 1919.[9] There was no major interest shown by the public and initial numbers of delegates present at meetings were low.[10] At a meeting on 4 May 1919 in Donegal town, a decision was taken that, it was hoped, would help the overall structure of the GAA in the county: district leagues were to be established. It was decided that six districts would be formed.[11] It was intended that the winners of each division, played on a league basis, would meet in the latter stages of the county championship on a knockout basis.

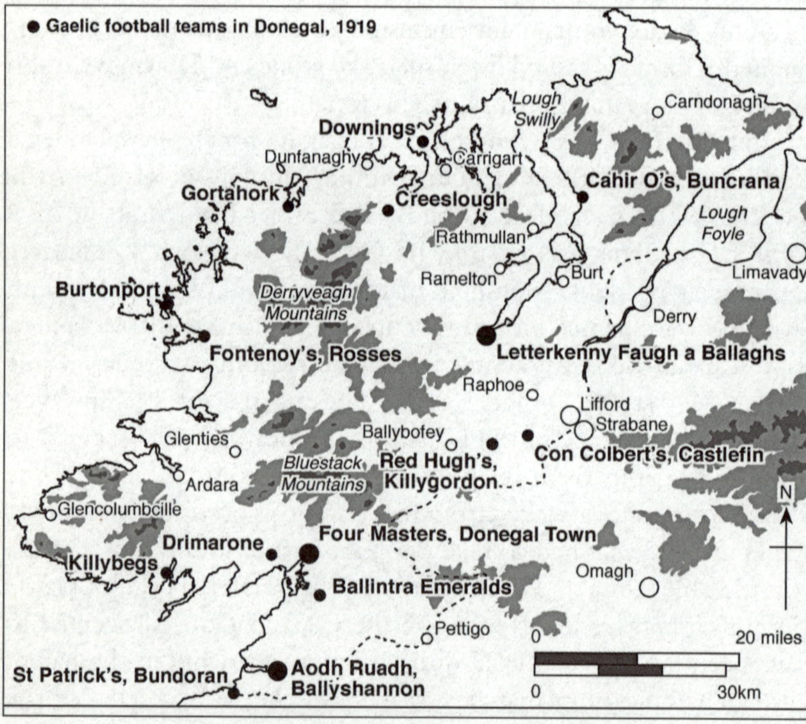

Fig. 5.1: Gaelic football teams in Donegal, 1919

SOURCES: *DD, DP and DN, DV, DJ, DI*, 1919. The teams of William Pearse's, Rabstown (Tyrone) and Kinlough (Leitrim) are excluded from the map but included in the overall tables as they participated in the Donegal county championship that year.

Figure 5.1 illustrates the Gaelic football clubs in operation in Donegal in 1919. In the south, the teams of Aodh Ruadh and St Patrick's of Bundoran were in action by May 1919 and were joined in their district league by Four Masters of Donegal town, Drimarone, and Kinlough from County Leitrim.[12] The Eastern Division was also operational by June with three Donegal clubs from Letterkenny, Castlefin, Killygordon and two Tyrone clubs, Clady and Rabstown, all participating on a league basis.[13] A number of these were formed from a sense of patriotism. The 1919–20 Gaelic football county champions, St Patrick's, was established on 2 March 1919.[14] H.J. Kelly, who presided over the meeting, illustrated his nationalist views on why Gaelic games should be played and this type of ideology seems to have been the reason why many Donegal GAA clubs were formed around this time. Kelly had also presided at a Sinn Féin demonstration in Bundoran in January 1918 in which Edward Daly, future vice-chairman of the GAA club, had also participated.[15] Aodh Ruadh, Ballyshannon was exceptional amongst clubs in the county at the time in that it was in operation since 1909, having been founded through the local branch of the Gaelic League.[16]

Nationalist involvement initially boosted the development of clubs in the east of the county in the early years of the new County Board. It is likely that two branches organised in 1919, Letterkenny and Castlefin, were organised by Sinn Féin members, as Letterkenny GAA members John Curran and Michael Dawson were heavily involved in that political party, while Castlefin GAA member and County Board president Sam O'Flaherty was later elected as Sinn Féin representative to the Dáil. The naming of the Castlefin club as Con Colbert's suggests the presence of Sinn Féin men, as a branch there bearing that name was in operation by 1916 and O'Flaherty had recruited over twenty members as Volunteers the following year.[17] GAA clubs had appeared infrequently in Letterkenny throughout this decade with lack of regular opposition and competitions a major factor in this disruption. The 1919 club, which seems to have been named the Faugh a Ballaghs, may have simply been a continuation of those previously organised, especially given the involvement of Curran and Dawson.[18] Curran, as referee, was said to have been responsible for outlining the rules to the Killygordon Red Hugh's team before one of their first matches, a friendly against Letterkenny, around this time. The Killygordon club had apparently been formed by a group of former soccer players, although the exact date of this is unclear, as is the amount of political involvement.[19]

William Murphy has noted that 'recent historians have recognised an important overlap between membership of the post-Rising party and the GAA' and cites the work of David Fitzpatrick on County Clare as an example of how they supported Sinn Féin activity in that county.[20] However, he also feels that the GAA were eager to keep an identifiable distance from Sinn Féin.[21] Apart from the involvement of the aforementioned men, the organisation of GAA clubs in Donegal by Sinn Féin members seems inconsistent around the county. Desmond Murphy has noted a decline in enthusiasm for this political party in Donegal by 1919. This, he believes, was because 'many people, while privately sympathetic, had no wish to antagonise the economic or political patronage of the AOH'.[22] He also feels that 'the quality of leadership offered by Sinn Féin at local level was sporadic' and states that the founding of a large number of branches was only due to individual enthusiasm.[23] RIC reports do not suggest any major correlation between the number of Sinn Féin clubs and those of the GAA in Donegal by the autumn of 1919. In September they estimated that there were fifty-eight Sinn Féin clubs in the county with 5,488 members, while noting the presence of only seven GAA clubs and 189 members.[24] While GAA activity would suggest that this number was fairly accurate, with affiliated clubs recorded in Letterkenny, Castlefin, Killygordon, Drimarone, Donegal, Ballyshannon and Bundoran by the beginning of August, this number is quite low in comparison with branches and membership of Sinn Féin throughout the county.[25] References to Gaelic football at Sinn Féin sports are scarce, although, as noted, it was exhibited at the Frosses branch sports in July 1918 and 'football', presumably Gaelic, was also played at Fanad Sinn Féin club's sports in June 1919.[26] These two references do not suggest any great attempt to promote the game throughout the county by other Sinn Féin clubs.

The period between January 1917 and June 1923 in Ireland was marked by violence, with more than 7,500 people killed or injured.[27] The GAA in Donegal was not greatly affected by the War of Independence fought between the Irish Republican Army and the British forces. While GAA activity was restricted to some extent, matches continued in 1919, 1920 and 1921, with county championships and leagues being organised in the South and East in each of these years and intercounty fixtures taking place. Admittedly, the social dislocation in the west may have had a delaying effect on the organisation of a league there. Despite the war breaking out in January 1919, it was not until December that any action was recorded in the county, and this attack at Dungloe was not a success.[28] Desmond Murphy believes that Sinn Féin struggled to keep its momentum going in 1919 in Donegal and as a result the growth of the IRA was much slower there than in other areas of the country. The general peacefulness of the county remained until late in the summer of 1920 and this change only came about as a result of the withdrawal of the police from a large part of West Donegal. The north and east of the county remained quiet, while civil disorder was more common than armed violence amongst Republicans in South Donegal. Murphy has also identified a number of problems faced by the IRA in West Donegal and these included a lack of well-trained men, a poor supply of arms, the failure of Volunteers to obey orders and a lack of co-operation between units and their leaders. In other parts of the county, which were relatively quiet, a scarcity of weapons and weak leadership hindered the development of units.[29] While dismissing the theory that a lack of arms was a significant factor, Peter Hart has suggested that in areas where Protestants 'formed a large minority in conjunction with strong anti-republicans – as in Donegal or counties Dublin and Wicklow – IRA activity might well be smothered'.[30]

As Tom Garvin has noted, while organisational problems were not uncommon in other areas such as Mayo and Roscommon, it was in Cork and Waterford where organisation was said to be best.[31] The most active counties were in Munster, and Cavan was also said to be heavily involved. Donegal was said to be one of the most inactive, along with Kilkenny, Kildare, Mayo and Wicklow.[32] It is perhaps no surprise then that the GAA was able to continue relatively unhindered in Donegal in these years. Although from the summer of 1920 until the Truce on 11 July 1921 there were twelve deaths recorded in the county, Murphy believes that 'the sporadic military campaign and the failure to win over already ambiguous support to the Republican cause meant that a low degree of political consciousness continued to exist in Co. Donegal right up until the Truce'.[33]

An Ulster GAA Council reorganisation meeting was held on 22 October 1921.[34] This was the first meeting since May of 1920 and this in itself illustrates the level of disruption at provincial level.

However, at this meeting Donegal delegates Denis Gallagher and Joe Murray were able to report on the presence of fourteen clubs in the county and that leagues were being run.[35] Disruption in the GAA at this time varied from moderate inconvenience in Dublin to severe restriction in Kilkenny and Tipperary.[36] It is difficult to establish the exact amount of involvement of Donegal GAA members in the war and the length of disruption caused by IRA activities, but neither seems to have been substantial.

A number of County Board officials were involved in the war. High-ranking IRA men such as 1919 County Board officers Joe Sweeney and P.J. Ward were arrested early in 1920, but it appears that Sweeney's involvement in the Board had decreased at that stage.[37] Secretary John Curran was apparently 'being hunted by the British Government from post to pillar' in April 1920.[38] Others who later became involved in the GAA such as Joe McDevitt, who was heavily committed to the Kilcar club in 1925, and Michael Callaghan, a man fundamental to the organisation of the GAA in 1930 in Killybegs, have been identified for their participation.[39] However, the County Board was able to continue, as evidenced by their condemnation of the imprisonment of Ward and Sweeney and that of a number of others at a meeting in May 1920 in Ballybofey.[40] The board later expressed satisfaction with the involvement of the Falcarragh GAA club in the White Cross Fund in November 1921 and had sanctioned the visit of the Letterkenny team to play a fundraising match for this organisation in September.[41] A match was also held in Ballybofey in November 1921 for the Prisoners' Dependants' Fund between Donegal and Derry selections.[42] This type of contribution to fundraising for prisoners and their dependants was common amongst the GAA during the revolutionary period.[43]

Newspaper reports indicate some instances of disruption to GAA fixtures in Donegal in 1921 caused by social dislocation but these were relatively infrequent. After the first match of the 1921–22 season played in the East Donegal league in June 1921 between Killygordon and Tyrone club Clady, it was stated that both were not at their previous standard but were still able to field good teams, which suggests some inactivity.[44] The imprisonment of a number of Donegal town and Killygordon players led to a decision being taken by the County Board in September 1921 that these clubs' county final fixture for 1920–21 would be postponed until their players' return.[45] League fixtures did not recommence outside of the East division until later in that year but clubs, such as St Patrick's, Bundoran in the south (who organised a number of challenge matches against clubs further afield from July to September), did manage to persevere.[46]

At the end of the war there was an increase in club formation and organised competitions, indicating a rise in support for Gaelic games and a move towards national pastimes. Tom Hunt has noted that a number of Westmeath's initial hurling clubs were formed through 'contiguous diffusion', whereby the formation of clubs in an area near Castlepollard was a result of contact between those interested in organising the GAA in these closely located districts.[47] Contiguous diffusion and nationalist fervour may well have been the reasons why a number of East and South-west Donegal GAA clubs were formed in the aftermath of the War of Independence. In the winter of 1921–22 there were two clubs in Castlefin, while others were organised in Ballybofey, Stranorlar, Raphoe and Murlog and competed in a Tyrone and Tyrconnell Gaelic football league with seven Tyrone clubs lying in a similar location relatively near the Donegal-Tyrone border. There is also evidence that the O'Toole's club of Raphoe had a strong nationalist backing.[48] With the deterioration of this league in May 1922, the existence of the majority of these clubs unsurprisingly came to a halt.[49]

In the south-west, it was not until 1921 that the Glenties and Ardara clubs were up and running and it seems that these were also formed out of a sense of nationalist duty. Both were organised in the months following the Truce. The Glenties club came into existence on 24 July after a Gaelic football match was organised in the village and a week later they played Tyrone club Clady to help their players with the rules and skills required.[50] Ardara was formed on 21 October in a local store, with nationalist fervour the reason given by local historians as to why both the Ardara and Glenties clubs came into existence.[51] The game appears to have been spread through challenge matches. At the end of that month they met and Glenties' short experience of Gaelic football was probably a help to Ardara's early development, while both teams also had former soccer players in their ranks.[52] There is some evidence to suggest Sinn Féin involvement in the early Ardara club. In an interview given much later, a member of the Ardara team of 1923, Charlie Gallagher, stated that nearly all of the players were members of the political organisation and that was what brought them together.[53] While GAA clubs in Bundoran, Donegal and Ballyshannon again returned to activity in November 1921, leagues were also organised in the west and south-west that winter as more rural clubs became involved in the Donegal GAA.[54] Four teams were affiliated to play in the West Tír Conaill league, these being Falcarragh, Gweedore, Kincasslagh and Derrybeg, while in the south-west, a league comprising the clubs of Killybegs, Glenties and Ardara began in December.[55]

The GAA in Donegal also seems not to have been severely disrupted by the Civil War, which began in June 1922 and ended in May of the following year and was fought between the pro-Treaty Free State Army and the anti-Treaty Irish Republican Army.[56] The 1922–23 county championship was again played on a league basis with divisional winners meeting in the final and there is no evidence of any matches being disrupted because of GAA members' involvement.[57] Again it is difficult to state exactly how many players and officials were involved but there is no evidence to suggest any problems like those experienced in Kerry and Cork, where intercounty teams refused to play while leading members were imprisoned.[58] Throughout 1922 and 1923 GAA activities were seriously disrupted at a national level. This was clearly the case in a number of counties, but in Donegal matches appear to have gone ahead relatively unhindered and reports of County Board meetings register little discussion of any related problems in the county.[59] A reference was made in the press to the possibility that players in the east were in jail in June 1923 but little else was stated on the matter.[60]

While Liam Ó Duibhir has noted some important aspects of Donegal's role in the Civil War, there is little to suggest that any GAA members or officials were heavily involved. Donegal's elected Dáil representatives were generally in favour of the Treaty, having debated this at meetings of Sinn Féin branches and area councils at the end of 1921.[61] There is little evidence to suggest that activity within the county greatly affected the GAA there, although in the build-up to the war in April 1922 it was reported that the Bundoran team could not travel to play their county championship semi-final against Glenties as their cars had been 'commandeered'.[62] This match was not played until 20 May.[63] Cronin, Duncan and Rouse have stated that 'it seems clear that by offering a neutral space for its members to play the games that they loved, irrespective of their political loyalties, the GAA played some part in fostering national reconciliation'.[64] There is scarce evidence that the Association in Donegal acted in any major way to heal differences between those with diverging views on the conflict, and given the lack of activity throughout the county, this is perhaps unsurprising.

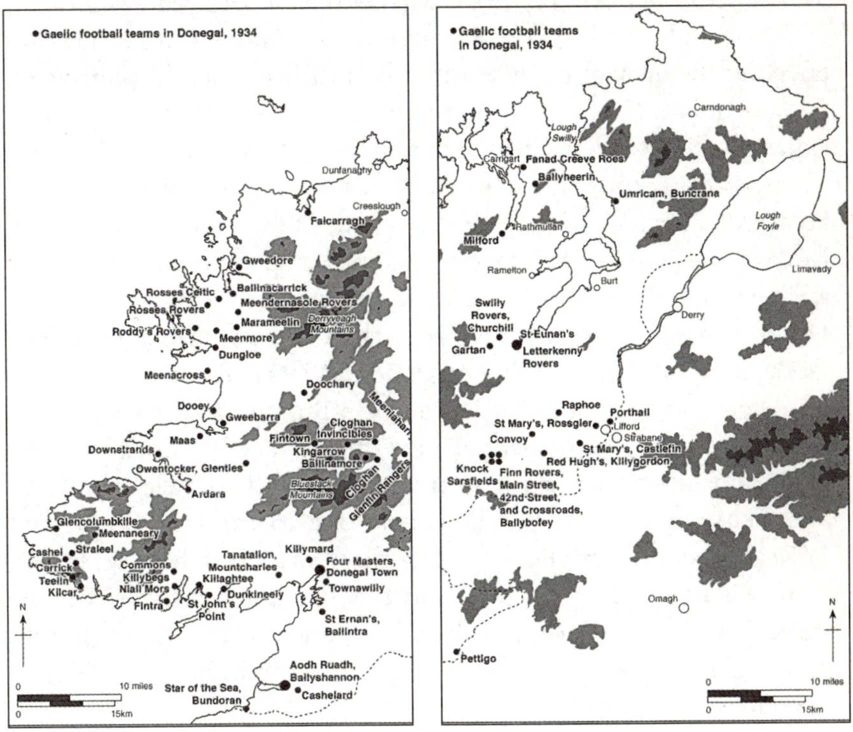

Fig. 5.2 (a) (*left*) and (b) (*right*): Gaelic football teams in Donegal, 1934
SOURCES: *DD, DP and TN, DPP, DJ, DV* 1934

As can be seen in Figure 5.2 (a) and (b), there was a remarkable change in the number of Gaelic football teams in operation by 1934, particularly in the western half of the county. The areas where Gaelic football had become established by then can be assessed through an examination of the number of clubs involved and their levels of permanency. For this purpose, the county has been divided into five areas: south, east, west, south-west and Inishowen. As can be seen in the overall tables in Appendix 5, the number of Gaelic football teams participating in Donegal rose and fell throughout the 1920s, beginning with eighteen in 1919 and reaching a peak of thirty in 1924.[65] The latter figure may be partially explained by a rise in numbers in Inishowen and in the south of the county that year. It was not until the 1930s that these figures really began to grow annually with a rise from thirty-nine in 1930 to forty-eight teams noted in 1931. Despite a drop to forty-five in 1932, in 1934 there were at least sixty-seven teams playing Gaelic football in Donegal.

At an individual club level, there were a number of key factors affecting the growth of clubs throughout the county. As illustrated in Appendices 6–10, many clubs founded in the 1919–34 period experienced decline and revival in a similar way to that described by Tranter in his study of soccer clubs in nineteenth-century Central Scotland, where he stated that they came and went with the 'regularity of a yo-yo'.[66] Even county championship-winning clubs were affected in Donegal, with a decline experienced in Bundoran and Donegal town, despite clubs from these towns having won the Gaelic football championship of 1919 and 1924 respectively. A loss of players and interest in Gaelic games in Bundoran, along with the failure to secure a permanent ground, meant that St Patrick's struggled to maintain their club throughout the 1920s. Their revival, as Star of the Sea in 1930, was largely due to the efforts of H.J. O'Kelly and Edward Daly.[67] Both these men had been founder members of the club in 1919 and this illustrates the reliance on those with previous organisational experience and a significant standing in the town, and the importance of the work of individuals in establishing the GAA in Donegal.[68]

Both the Donegal town and Bundoran clubs returned to strength in the early 1930s with Bundoran victorious in the 1934 county championship final.[69] Local interest in Gaelic football in Donegal town was spread through the organisation of the Four Masters Cup in November 1932.[70] By the end of 1933 the South Donegal District League was said to have 700 members and by 1934 there were ten clubs in the area, as shown in Appendix 6. While not a massive increase from early 1920s figures, it did highlight a transition from soccer to Gaelic football in the majority of these villages and towns and a commitment to furthering the latter code, which had not always been apparent prior to these decades.[71]

An example of the inconsistent nature of GAA clubs in Donegal can also be seen in the table for the eastern area, which is detailed in

Appendix 7. In 1934 there were twenty-five in the area, but this was by no means a steady growth. Some clubs such as those in Castlefin undoubtedly were unhappy with treatment received from the County Board and this led to their withdrawal on a number of occasions.[72] The coming and going of Castlefin teams was not an exception by any means; competition with soccer and a lack of finance and fields affected Letterkenny clubs throughout the 1920s.[73] There was no club in the eastern area that managed to appear every year in this decade.

Transport difficulties for those in the west of Donegal continued to be a problem. As late as February 1934, local county councillor K.J. Brennan claimed that 'the roads in the Upper and Lower Rosses were the worst in the county, incapable of bearing heavy traffic'.[74] As shown in Appendix 8, the number of clubs appearing annually in this area was low for much of the 1920s and after reaching a total of four in 1921–22, did not begin to increase or reach double figures until the early 1930s. During the period from 1881 until 1926, Donegal's population was reduced by 26 per cent and emigration had a considerable impact on its sports clubs.[75] This was noted in the West Division in May 1926, where only one GAA club was competing in the county championship that year.[76] Emigration also seriously affected the number of players available in other areas such as Ardara, Glenties and Letterkenny. The loss of players was not unique to Donegal, however, with the *Gaelic Athlete* noting the problem in Kerry in 1926.[77] Along with Gweedore, a handful of junior clubs also became organised in the early 1930s and this undoubtedly boosted the spread of the game in the west of Donegal.[78] Not all became affiliated and some had disbanded by the following year. This, however, reflects the increased interest in Gaelic football in villages where it may not have previously been played and, while junior competitions had been held regularly in the county since 1928, increased levels of formation of junior teams appears to have been a feature of the GAA there in the early 1930s.[79] By 1934 there were fourteen clubs in the west of the county and Gaelic football was finally beginning to gain a foothold along the west coast.

It was not until the 1930s that areas in the south-west such as Kilcar, Carrick, Glencolumbkille, Dunkineely and Killybegs began to play a more permanent role in the GAA, as Gaelic football spread from larger villages to the more rural outlying townlands in a number of parishes, as can be seen in Appendix 9. District and parish leagues were formed to help the spread of Gaelic football in a number of villages in the latter months of 1930.[80] The organisation of a Gaelic football league for teams representing townlands in Kilcar and Glencolumbkille was said to be due to the efforts of the Reverend T.R. Griffith of Carrick in October of that year, a man who had previous experience of GAA administration in Ballyshannon.[81] It was he who donated the Slieve League cup for competition between six local areas.[82] By 1933 there were enough local teams for parish leagues in both Kilcar and Glencolumbkille.[83] A GAA club was revived in the neighbouring area of Killybegs in November 1930, with a practice match helping introduce the sport to a number of players.[84] This revival had a knock-on effect in other nearby areas. The St Catherine's Cup, donated by the Killybegs Niall Mór club, was organised in November 1931 and plans were drawn up for games between the other local teams with a 'Central Council' formed to administer affairs.[85] This increased activity eventually led to involvement at county championship level and by March 1933 there were seven clubs from the division involved. While not every one of the seventeen clubs noted in the area that year took part, it marked a shift in activity from the three core areas of Ardara, Glenties and Killybegs in the 1920s to more rural, outlying parishes.[86] By the end of 1934, Gaelic football was becoming firmly established in the South-west Division.

It was in the Inishowen divisional area that Gaelic football made the least impact. Despite the existence of five teams there in 1920, the number of GAA clubs in Inishowen remained low for much of the 1920s and until 1934. As can be seen in Appendix 10, 1924 was the peak year for clubs, with six in existence, and the short lifespan of the Inishowen Gaelic football league explains this number of clubs. The spread of Gaelic football was difficult and reports indicate that these teams had no great tradition of this code. After St Mary's (Clonmany) were defeated by Cahir O's in the opening league match, an absence of training and experience was noted.[87] A week later, a lack of combination was a problem for both the Cahir O's and Burt Hibernians.[88] This brief structure was the only real attempt in this decade to organise a Gaelic football league there. It must also be stated that a number of Inishowen GAA clubs placed more emphasis on hurling and the formation of Gaelic football teams attracted little interest. In the years from 1925 to 1928 there were no Gaelic football teams organised there and the development of soccer was clearly given more importance by a number of those with social influence in the area. By 1934 there were at least thirty-two soccer teams in Inishowen, while only one Gaelic football team was recorded in the area that year.[89]

Not all of the sixty-seven Gaelic football clubs noted throughout the county in 1934 became registered and Donegal's figure of affiliated clubs remained low nationally. Marcus De Burca's account of these, taken from the Annual Congress reports for 1935, indicates that Donegal had thirty-three GAA clubs affiliated with the Central Council. Antrim had the highest number of clubs in Ulster with fifty-seven and of the others, only Cavan (forty) and Tyrone (thirty-nine) had more clubs in the province, which had an overall total of 287. Both Derry and Fermanagh, with sixteen each, had the lowest number in Ulster.[90] The majority of clubs lay in Leinster (679) and Dublin, with 100 clubs, had the highest number in this province. However, it was Cork that had the highest number of clubs (147), out of Munster's total of 427.[91]

The failure of hurling in Donegal

There are a number of widely accepted reasons for the failure of hurling to develop in Donegal. Writing in 1993, Kevin Whelan outlined the areas located in what he called 'hurling's core region' and accounted for this distribution. He has noted the dominance of the game in Cork, Tipperary and Kilkenny, with a lesser role being played by counties Clare, Limerick, Laois, Offaly, Galway, Wexford and Waterford.[92] Whelan stated that these areas illustrated 'striking continuity with the earlier "iomáin" region' while strong cultural boundaries, allied with regional pride, were also prominent factors in its development. The prominence of hurling in the south of the country was also connected with Norman influence in the late medieval period, suitable terrain and a plentiful supply of ash for the manufacture of hurleys. 'Popular Irish nationalist politics' associated with the spread of the GAA also thrived in these areas of the country in the nineteenth century.[93] Hurling continued to be played in small pockets in countries Antrim and Down and in Inishowen after 1907. While camán was more frequently played in the 1905–07 period in Donegal, it was in the 1920s that the organisation of Gaelic football gained more significance and, as shown in Appendix 11, hurling struggled to gain the recognition previously afforded to it within the county. The number of teams and clubs playing hurling in the 1919–34 period peaked in 1925–26, reaching a figure of thirteen, but by 1934 this figure had dropped to ten and the sport was struggling.

Other more localised reasons can be said to have hindered the spread of hurling in the county in the 1920s. While nationally many counties have struggled to devote equal attention to both Gaelic football and hurling, in Donegal efforts to promote hurling fluctuated after the re-founding of the County Board. Although hopes were expressed at the initial County Board meeting in April 1919 that hurling would prosper in Donegal, it was stated that 'the board are not in a position this year to embark on any competitions' and it was also hoped that clubs would be ready to field hurling teams the following year.[94] Already priority was being given to the organisation of Gaelic football and the arranging of these teams, delegates and leagues dominated initial County Board meetings. In fact the Board did not manage to organise a county championship final in hurling until November 1924 and Inishowen's hurling clubs were excluded from this as they had not affiliated.[95]

Throughout this decade and into the 1930s, the Donegal County Board continuously placed Gaelic football in a pre-eminent position, while the organisation and selection of the county hurling team seems to have had priority over activities at club level. In many areas where Gaelic football was beginning to replace soccer, such as in the south-west and south, there were no hurling clubs and the majority of the clubs in the 1905–07 West Division were no longer in existence. It was, therefore, harder to start anew and hurling teams were much more difficult to set up than those of Gaelic football, which was in some ways similar to soccer. Hunt has noted the difficulties in organising hurling in comparison with football or cricket as each player needed 'specialist equipment'. He has also stated that 'it required that each player develop a great range of skills under the pressure of the attention of a direct opponent' and also 'the knowledge and experience of a practitioner of the game' from an area where hurling thrived.[96]

While hurling in Donegal did benefit from the input of the Garda Síochána from southern counties in the years after 1922, this was not sufficient to give the game the same structure and footing that Gaelic football was to experience.[97] Certainly some outstanding hurlers came to the county, but this was not enough for the widespread organisation of clubs, as many were involved only as players and, while selection was gained at intercounty level, club hurling did not have enough native players instructed, or interested, in a game which generally requires tutelage from a young age. An example of this can be seen in the fact that in 1928, there were said to be two Killybegs-based guards selected on the county hurling team, although the nearest hurling club team was in Ballyshannon.[98]

Given the lack of interest shown in hurling by the new County Board in the initial years after its inception in 1919, clubs such as Carndonagh, Inch, Moville and Newtowncunningham attempted to remain involved with the GAA in Derry city, which was more conveniently located for them than such areas in County Donegal as Letterkenny and Ballybofey where County Board meetings were held. However, this was not an entirely satisfactory arrangement as organisation in Derry was also problematic and interest levels varied; by 1923 some Inishowen clubs were growing increasingly dissatisfied with the treatment received from the Derry Board.[99] On 24 August 1923 the Inishowen GAA District League was formed at a convention organised by the Ulster Council secretary, B.C. Fay and held in St Mary's Hall, Buncrana.[100] Despite the initial involvement of seven clubs in this league, this structure was allowed to disband and it is unclear if the 1924 hurling league was completed.[101]

Relations between the Donegal GAA and Inishowen were discussed at a meeting of the Donegal County Board in September 1923. Problems paying affiliation fees were evident and it was claimed that 'the Inishowen league were not in any way amenable to the Donegal County Board' and as a result, would not be allowed to participate in the county championship or have their players selected for the county team until they had defined their status.[102] At the final County Board meeting of 1924 this had still not been resolved.[103] While the Donegal County Board remained in control of the organisation of hurling in the county, their efforts to organise clubs and competitions did not reflect their intentions stated at meetings. At the Annual County Convention in Mountcharles on 6 January

1925, a number of ways of promoting the game in the county were discussed. These included junior members of clubs being encouraged to take up the game and the writing to national schools to request assistance in promoting hurling.[104] A hurling league was organised for teams in the north-east in 1926 although it does not seem to have been completed.[105] In January 1927 the County Board managed to secure a trophy for hurling purposes, which took on the title of its patrons, the *Derry People* Cup. This came after much pressing from Ballyshannon delegates for a cup to be secured.[106]

Outside Inishowen, interest in hurling amongst clubs was minimal. Some of these isolated clubs attempted to keep it alive with the help of external influences. A hurling club was revived in Ballyshannon in April 1923 after almost four years of inactivity and this club was to become the most important hurling club outside of the north of the county in the period covered here. It was reported at the meeting that 'it was only among the juvenile section that interest in the game was retained. The coming of the guards to the town gave it the necessary impetus and it is remarkable how popular it has become during the last few months.'[107] This club was almost exceptional outside Inishowen in that its members agreed to start a hurling club first that year and later a Gaelic football one as it was felt that starting both together would lead to the failure of each.[108] This may have been one reason why the majority of Donegal clubs stuck to Gaelic football as the running of two teams involved in different codes may have been difficult from an organisational as well as financial point of view. Crossover of fixtures and players was a hindrance given that Sunday was the only day for Gaelic games at this point and that most Gaelic football clubs in Donegal did not field hurling teams.

The efforts of an 'energetic new committee and members of the present club – backed up by [a] dint of perseverance within – and by the generous financial support of the people of the town' were noted as factors in the Ballyshannon club's county final win in 1924.[109] This passion for hurling, allied with strong financial backing, was clearly lacking in the majority of other GAA clubs in Donegal at this time. The Ballyshannon club set up their parish league in April 1925 and were also instrumental in the organisation of the south-western league on 1 October 1925 at a meeting in the local Mall.[110] It seems however that this lasted only one season, but illustrates the club's eagerness to take the initiative and organise competitive matches almost independently of the County Board. They continued into the 1930s despite a lack of competition, with the decline of the south-western hurling league, which must have made it difficult for their players to stay motivated.

Things did not improve until the County Board decided to organise a separate committee for hurling at the Annual Convention in January 1933 after a proposal by Guard Michael Walsh, who had been heavily involved in the Letterkenny hurling club.[111] This was followed by a meeting held on 30 April 1933 in Carndonagh with national school teacher Michael Doherty presiding. A number of problems which had hampered the development of hurling in the county were outlined. Doherty felt that the lack of interest by the County Board and a scarcity of trophies were key factors.[112] A temporary committee was formed with Doherty appointed chairman and Walsh taking up the role of honorary secretary.[113] The location of participating clubs and venues for the hosting of meetings were generally centred in Inishowen and this reflects where interest was greatest in the game. At a meeting held in Buncrana on 14 May 1933 it was stated that four Inishowen clubs – Culdaff, Carndonagh, Buncrana and Burt – as well as eastern club Letterkenny and Ballyshannon in the south had entered the county championship. A league was to be run in the northern area for the Cardinal O'Donnell cup. Subscriptions were invited to improve funds and home clubs were deemed responsible for arranging meals for the visitors at matches. They were also asked to do their own advertising and away teams requested to pay their own travelling expenses.[114] There was strong participation by national school teachers, with three involved, while the movement also received the backing of Brother Albinus of St Eunan's College and Superintendent Burke. Significantly, it was announced that the County Board had given them permission to carry on alone, independent of their administration.

By the end of 1933 the state of hurling in Donegal had improved significantly with an increase in the number of affiliated clubs, competitions and matches that year. At the first annual convention of the Donegal hurling board on 16 December 1933 in Derry, secretary Michael Walsh was able to report on 'a very successful season'.[115] He stated that seven senior teams had affiliated, with another Inishowen club, Inch Emeralds, joining the above teams. Six of these clubs were involved in the county championship and Cardinal O'Donnell Cup competition. It was also noted that fifty-eight matches had been played since 28 May and games were said to be of a high standard, while a juvenile competition – involving clubs from Letterkenny, Burt and Carndonagh – was played in conjunction with the championship. The financial state of the board was said to be positive and officers were re-elected and the good work of a number of officials praised.[116]

Progress was slow but steady in 1934. Eight clubs affiliated that year and a junior championship had also been run along with the senior championship; a number of underage competitions were organised and financially the board was in a healthy state. Unsurprisingly, there were some problems such as the number of matches not being as high, a single league system replaced the double league matches in operation the previous year. It was also noted by the chairman at the annual Convention that 'gate receipts at club and trial matches were very small' and punctuality could have been better.[117] He also felt that the Ulster Council could have given more support to promote the game, particularly in the GAA's Golden Jubilee year. This overall failure to develop weak hurling areas in the county continued to prevail, despite attempts by some clubs isolated from the heart of hurling in Inishowen.

It was an uphill battle to try to get hurling organised in areas such as the south-west. This was despite some exhibitions hosted by the Ardara GAA club at their annual sports in 1926 and 1931.[118] In a review of attempts to organise the sport in Ardara and Glencolumbkille at the divisional meeting of the South-west Committee in January 1934, it was stated that hurling there was being 'sadly neglected'.[119] This was said to be due to the fact that little help was given by the County Board and that the area was too far away from the county's most fertile hurling region, Inishowen. Other reasons were also offered:

> The greatest obstacle was finance, and only a few adults in each place purchased camáns. These were too old ever to become adept at the game, so not being satisfied with the progress they were making, they developed the inferiority complex mentally and gave it up.[120]

The writer hoped to see the game organised amongst youths as he felt that 'the only hope for the revival of hurling lies with the schoolboys'.[121] Hopes expressed at the Ulster GAA Convention in

March 1926 that County Boards would use their influence to procure suitable grounds for the promotion of hurling in schools were not fulfilled in Donegal.[122] It was in Inishowen that the game continued to survive, whereas most GAA clubs in the county were content to focus primarily on Gaelic football, with a small number of hurling teams and clubs located in larger urban centres such as Letterkenny and Ballyshannon.

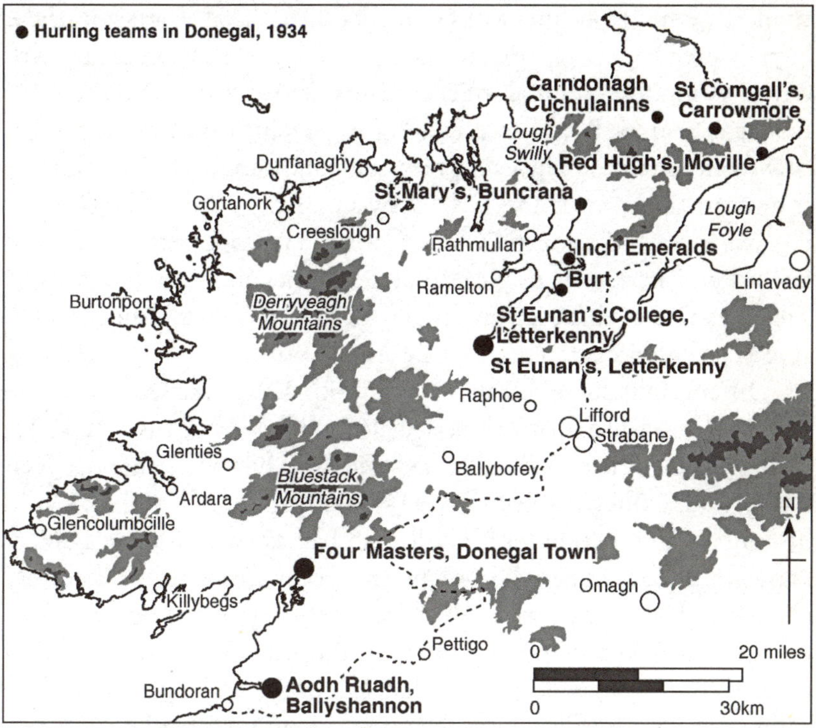

Fig. 5.3: Hurling teams in Donegal, 1934
SOURCES: *DD, DV, DJ, DP and TN, DPP*, 1934

The success of the GAA in Donegal

Along with club matches and intercounty competitions, interest in Gaelic football in the 1920s was spread by the organisation of 'GAA Sports' throughout the county and the hosting of matches at athletic sports under GAA rules, all of which helped boost levels of finance. As mentioned, Gaelic football had been played at tournaments in Donegal town in August 1918 and March 1919 while Ballyshannon hosted a Gaelic football tournament in September 1918.[123] It was also played at the Mountcharles Gaelic Sports in July 1920 and at the Donegal town Aeridheacht in August of that year.[124] The first annual Tír Conaill GAA Sports were held at the Mental Hospital grounds in Letterkenny on 28 August 1921 and drew a gate of more than £70.[125] The high point of the day's events was a match between Derry and an East Donegal selection. These sports generally included athletics and novelty races and excluded 'foreign' games. This seems to indicate an increase in involvement of GAA officials in local sports and these men were eager to make sure their interests were served. Organisation for a number of events was helped by the dedication of Donegal County Board secretary John Curran, who travelled regularly from Letterkenny to act as official handicapper throughout the county in the early years of the new County Board, although not every area visited adopted Gaelic games. He appeared at sports in Lifford and Rathmullan in 1923 and Glenties the following year.[126] This meant that through his encouragement, Gaelic football could, at least, be demonstrated at these parish events.[127]

Other events such as athletics and football place-kicking were also held at the County GAA Sports, held under NACA rules in 1922, with 'valuable prizes' for each event and an exhibition game between Derry and Donegal selections also taking place.[128] The GAA, in hosting athletics along with Gaelic football as part of a day's entertainment and, through the organisation of a Gaelic football county championship, offered a variety of competitions at the beginning of the 1920s. This differed greatly from the way in which association football, which had no widespread league or cup, was organised. While progress continued to be slow, a number of administrative decisions improved matters. The areas covering Gaelic football leagues did not always remain constant and divisions were forced to amalgamate on a number of occasions in this decade.[129] A number of rules were put in place in November 1924 to help ease organisational difficulties. These included the collection of five shillings from every home club and publication of lists of registered players. Of more importance was a new rule which meant that teams not on the field within ten minutes of the appointed time would lose the points.[130] In addition to the county championship, the organisation of secondary cup competitions such as the Dr McGinley Cup in 1925 and the *Democrat* Cup the following year, boosted the number of matches available and prolonged the GAA season.[131] A competition for junior teams was re-introduced in 1928 while the St Vincent de Paul Charity Cup also got underway for senior teams that year.[132] This organisation of competitions, generally on a divisional basis initially with each winner meeting in the latter stages, was beneficial as travelling expenses had to be carefully monitored.[133]

The decision to adhere to district leagues could be said to be one of the major successes of the GAA in Donegal in the 1920s as, despite the problems which existed, competitions were guaranteed annually. Knowledge of skills and tactics was also spread in the local press through the publishing of chapters from Dick Fitzgerald's *How to Play Gaelic Football*, on a weekly basis in 1933.[134] The inclusion in the local press of the County Board bye-laws also undoubtedly helped clarify matters at the same time.[135] At intercounty level, the decision allowing Donegal to play in the Junior Gaelic football championship in 1930 would later give a boost to the GAA in the county as, until then, they had little success in the Ulster Gaelic football championship and this enabled them to compete at a level more suited to their players' abilities and resources.[136] Although they returned to the senior championship in 1931 and 1932, in 1933 it was again decided to participate at junior level. Match organisation and problems getting players together and to venues on time had plagued the intercounty team for most of the 1920s, with little success achieved on the playing field.[137] The long journey to Clones in Monaghan was blamed for Donegal's McKenna Cup semi-final defeat in 1928 with claims that 'some of the Donegal players had to travel a distance of over 140 miles, and were on the road at 4am on Sunday morning'.[138] The lack of a tradition of Gaelic football was also said to be a problem.[139]

It was in the early 1920s that a small group of men based in the south and south-west of the county began to exert more control over the administration of the County Board and it was in these areas that the playing of Gaelic games grew in strength. In fact, in the period from 1925 until 1934, only one man from outside these areas, Michael Dawson from Letterkenny, was elected chairman, and his tenure lasted only briefly.[140] An analysis of the positions of secretary and treasurer also illustrates the dominance of officials from the south-west and south, with only four men from outside these regions taking up the position of secretary in this nine-year period, while Seán Conaghan from Glenties was elected treasurer for each of these years.[141] At a meeting of the County Board held in May 1923, it was agreed that three centres – Letterkenny, Ballybofey and Donegal town – would be used as venues for these meetings, with regular alteration between them.[142] This also undoubtedly isolated clubs outside these areas, while strengthening the influence of those based nearby.

As shown in the previous chapter, national school teachers played a significant role in the 1905–07 GAA, both as players and administrators, and were again heavily involved in the years from 1919–34. The transfer of gardaí from areas outside the county undoubtedly injected new life into the Donegal GAA in the 1920s and 1930s. As Marcus De Burca has stated, 'throughout the country Garda support provided a badly-needed stimulus in areas where native games had previously not gained wide local acceptance'.[143] The involvement of school teachers was also not unique to Donegal, although the study of schools' sport in Ireland also lacks a definitive history. One GAA writer stated in 1934 that 'you'll find a national school teacher in every club – because the colleges where these men are trained are truly Gaelic'.[144] He went on to state that in colleges such as St Patrick's, Drumcondra and De La Salle, Waterford, social conditions undoubtedly contributed to the development of a pro-GAA ideology. National school teachers certainly played a prominent role in developing the GAA in Donegal. Using biographical data from newspapers, an examination of the occupations of those involved in the Donegal County Board between 1919 and 1934 illustrates the significance of national school teachers in the highest administrative offices of the County Board as chairmen, secretaries and treasurers. As can be seen in Table 5.1 below, out of a total of forty-eight positions available in these years, national school teachers occupied at least 50 per cent of these. Admittedly, some officers retained their positions for long spells but there was an unquestionable influence of national school teachers within the County Board, particularly after 1924, with Seán Ó Caiside, Charles McDyer, Seán Ó Cinnéide, Joe Maguire, P.J. McGinn, Aidan Sweeney and Seán Conaghan all involved in various roles. There was also a notable involvement of members of Dáil Éireann but this had lessened significantly by the middle of the decade.

Table 5.1
Names and occupations of chairmen, secretaries and treasurers of the Donegal GAA County Board, 1919–34

Year	Chairman	Occupation	Secretary	Occupation	Treasurer	Occupation
1919	Sam O'Flaherty	Army commandant	John Curran	Foreman printers	Patrick McCartan	Unknown
1920	Sam O'Flaherty	Army commandant	John Curran	Foreman printers	John Curran	Foreman printers
1921	Sam O'Flaherty	TD	John Curran	Foreman printers	John Curran	Foreman printers
1922	Sam O'Flaherty	TD	John Curran	Foreman printers	John Curran	Foreman printers
1923	P.J. Ward	TD	John Curran	Foreman printers	John Curran	Foreman printers
1924	P.J. Ward	TD	John Curran	Foreman printers	John Curran	Foreman printers
1925	Seán Ó Caiside	NS Teacher	John Curran	Foreman printers	Seán Conaghan	NS Teacher
1926	Seán Ó Caiside	NS Teacher	Michael Dawson	Civil engineer	Seán Conaghan	NS Teacher
1927	Seán Ó Caiside	NS Teacher	Eunan Coyle	Unknown	Seán Conaghan	NS Teacher
1928	Seán Ó Caiside	NS Teacher	Charles McDyer	NS Teacher	Seán Conaghan	NS Teacher
1929	Seán Ó Caiside	NS Teacher	Charles McDyer	NS Teacher	Seán Conaghan	NS Teacher
1930	Michael Dawson	Civil engineer	P.J. McGinn	NS Teacher	Seán Conaghan	NS Teacher
1931	Brother Lucien	Cleric Catholic Church	Aidan Sweeney	NS Teacher	Seán Conaghan	NS Teacher
1932	Brian Brady	TD	Seán Conaghan	NS Teacher	Seán Conaghan	NS Teacher
1933	Seán Ó Caiside	NS Teacher	Joe Maguire	NS Teacher	Seán Conaghan	NS Teacher
1934	Charles McDyer	NS Teacher	Seán Kennedy	NS Teacher	Seán Conaghan	NS Teacher

SOURCES: *DJ, DP and DN, DV, DI* (1919–34) and An t-Ath Seán Ó Gallchóir, *The Raidió na Gaeltachta Book of Donegal GAA Facts*, p. 97

I am grateful to Dónal McAnallen for his assistance with a number of these occupations.

These teachers had probably been active in Gaelic games while at college and significantly had an almost missionary zeal in their drive to promote the GAA in Donegal. Added to this, they were able to benefit from shorter working hours and longer holidays than most other workers and could put their administrative skills to good use. In contrast, evidence in the local press that national school teachers were heavily involved in the promotion of soccer competitions at this time is less obvious.[145] The exact amount of involvement at GAA club level is perhaps more difficult to analyse but undoubtedly many clubs benefited from their input. The importance of teachers to the development of the GAA was encouraged by County Board delegate Joe McDevitt in February 1925 at a meeting of the South Donegal District League, when he stated that it was 'the duty of teachers, especially in County Donegal, to get [Gaelic] football and hurling into the schools and to encourage these games as much as it is in their power'.[146] This meant that, at least in theory, these men were able to encourage the playing of Gaelic football and hurling in their schools and get younger players involved at an early age.

Dónal McAnallen has noted the significance of army members and of the Garda Síochána in the development of the GAA in Monaghan, Cavan and Donegal in the years after 1922. Top-class players from Leinster and Munster boosted county teams, in particular the Gaelic football side of Monaghan and the hurling selections of Donegal and Cavan.[147] There were nearly 7,000 young gardaí active in the Free State's initial years, most of whom were 'in their early twenties'.[148] Many of these young men were therefore at a suitable age for participation in sport and Garda Commissioner Eoin O'Duffy was eager to avail of this. In 1923 he issued a circular 'urging the Civic Guards to join local hurling, [Gaelic] football and athletic clubs' and later that year stated that Garda members should not play soccer or rugby.[149]

Despite some criticisms of Garda involvement in GAA teams, there can be no doubt that some clubs were, at least initially, immensely strengthened by the participation of gardaí, both as players and administrators.[150] Glenties had the presence of 'four stalwarts of the Civic Guard' along with Captain Kavanagh of the National Army in a game against Ardara in December 1922, while the Donegal Young Tír Conaills team, which defeated Ardara in February 1924, also included four gardaí.[151] At a Donegal GAA County Board meeting in November 1923, Ulster Council president B.C. Fay praised the work of Chief Superintendent Seán B. MacManus and the gardaí, who were said to be 'great acquisitions to the local clubs'.[152] Members of the gardaí were also involved as referees and this no doubt helped the organisation of Gaelic football.[153] Administrative involvement at club level was also notable in some areas. The re-organisation of the GAA in Letterkenny in 1930 was said to have been largely due to the input of Superintendent Cronin, and there were no fewer than three other guards in attendance at this meeting with Chief Superintendent Leahy presiding.[154]

Transferral of gardaí was therefore a blow to the County Board and clubs, given that these men were frequently moved around the country. The County Board lost the input of Chief Superintendent MacManus when he was moved to Galway in June 1924.[155] Even temporary absence could damage a club. Milford GAA club lamented the loss through injury in October 1930 of Guard Neary, 'an energetic worker and a strong advocate of the national pastimes', as his absence was said to have been 'a severe loss to those who are carrying on against big odds'.[156] Garda transfer seriously impacted on the decline of this club and in March 1932 it was stated that it had been 'built up on members of the Gardaí' and 'there were vacancies left in the team which frequent transfers caused and at the same time failed to provide substitutes'.[157]

Liam McNiffe has stated that 'from about 1935 onwards there was a gradual but inexorable decline in active participation by Gardaí in sport', mainly due to the replacing of O'Duffy in 1933; his successor, Eamon Broy, was not as encouraging of sport.[158] It is difficult to establish when Garda participation in the GAA in Donegal was at its peak but in February 1928, county chairman Seán Ó Caiside complained at the Annual County Convention that the Gardaí 'as a body were not doing their duty towards the Gaelic games' and 'in their apathy . . . the Guards were not acting in accordance with the wishes of their Chief Commissioner'.[159] This appears to be a reference to problems experienced by the Ballybofey club the previous month as they failed to get their garda players released for a match in Letterkenny.[160] However, this seems to have been an isolated incident. The Garda Síochána had clearly helped put the GAA on a stronger footing in the county and without their influence, the development of Gaelic games in Donegal would have been further delayed.

Nationally, administration of GAA affairs improved under the secretary, Pádraig Ó Caoimh, who was appointed to this role in 1929.[161] Organisation of Gaelic games in Donegal undoubtedly improved in the early 1930s. The Gaelic football minor championship was inaugurated in the spring of 1931.[162] An insurance scheme for players became available in Donegal in October and by 1934, the financial situation of the County Board had improved.[163] This was a result of improved administration. At the 1933 Annual County Convention, it was decided to have four district committees organised, working subordinately to the County Board, and by the beginning of the following year a marked improvement was noticeable.[164] This was said to be due to better management of affairs at divisional level. It was noted that the number of affiliated clubs had risen from sixteen in 1932 to twenty-nine in 1933.[165]

Donegal's extended run in the 1933 All-Ireland Junior Championship undoubtedly increased enthusiasm for Gaelic football and this was noted after the county's victory over Cork in the semi-final in September. The result, it was claimed, had 'added a zest to the game' between Croagh and Tanatallon and 'on learning of Donegal's victory in Croke Park, great joy and enthusiasm was expressed by all in the town and district . . . the news being eagerly awaited at the houses where wireless sets were installed'.[166] This appearance in the final was also the result of improvements in organisation. They had won only one Ulster championship match in the 1920s but the following decade saw an improvement in organisation at intercounty level with the procuring of a trainer, the provision of adequate training facilities and accommodation and meals for players being arranged in 1933.[167] This was reflected in the build-up to the All-Ireland Junior Gaelic football final against Mayo. Players' fitness levels were carefully monitored and an examination of the letters of County Board chairman Seán Ó Caiside illustrate the lengths he went to in order to secure success and improve the status of Gaelic football in the county.[168] Preparation was improving vastly with Ó Caiside giving advice, via letters, to each team member on their Cork opponents and proper lifestyle choices in the run-up to the semi-final.[169] The hosting of intra-divisional matches with a view to selection for the county team was said to have been beneficial to the standard of play.[170] While Ó Caiside's relationship with a number of Eastern Board delegates, many of whom felt they were not getting fair treatment in the selection of their players for the county team, was poor, he can be seen as the man who carried the Donegal GAA through the difficult period of the 1920s and his passion for Gaelic football is evident in his writing.[171]

While the influence of the clergy was limited within the County Board in this decade, the involvement of Brother Cassin and Brother Lucien was particularly important to the Ballyshannon club in the 1920s, as they allowed matches to be played on the local Rock school field.[172] The absence of regular, club-owned playing fields must have been detrimental to those with aspirations of strengthening their clubs, given the importance of a fixed venue as a focal point for players, officials and supporters. Clubhouses also had to be obtained and at times improvisation was necessary. After the death of Aodh Ruadh club member Patrick Daly of Ballyshannon in February 1932, it was noted that his house had regularly been used 'as a club-room without ever a word of demur'.[173] The importance of those with social standing can be seen in the participation of local TDs Brian Brady and Micheál Óg McFadden in the Donegal GAA, as their influence in the government led to the securing of training grounds at Finner Camp prior to the 1933 All-Ireland Junior final.[174]

Like other sports, the development of the GAA in the 1920s also required financial assistance and many clubs experienced monetary problems. The weak financial state of clubs was not helped by the financial difficulties experienced by the Ulster Council, which was forced to pay an entertainment tax to the British government, whereas after 1927, GAA teams in the Free State were exempt from paying fees of this kind.[175] Dónal McAnallen believes that much of the poor financial state of the Ulster Council was down to the fact that Eoin O'Duffy, the honorary treasurer from 1925 until 1934, was residing in Dublin and too far away to organise accounts properly. While attendances were decreasing, the Council did not deal with business affairs carefully enough. It was not until 1934, with the election of Gerry Arthurs as secretary, that the Ulster Council began to manage these matters in a more efficient way.[176] Many Donegal GAA clubs in the period from 1919 until 1934 suffered from a failure to consistently organise and put these practices into place. A major exception was the Aodh Ruadh club in Ballyshannon which, with a strong infrastructure, was instrumental in keeping Gaelic games alive in this area. Its members were heavily involved, not only at club level but in the County Board and they benefited from the involvement of those who had previous experience of organising sport. Unlike the vast majority of GAA clubs in Donegal at the time, they offered both hurling and Gaelic football teams and an increase in club membership was noted from seventy-six in 1924 to 121 in 1926.[177] They were, for most of the decade, able to secure a playing field and ensured that their activities were well publicised in the local press with club official Brother Cassin providing a regular column in the *Donegal Democrat* prior to his transfer to Dundalk in 1928.[178]

The club was relatively stable financially and its officials' dedication meant that lulls in activity did not last for very long. They also attracted support from a wide section of the local nationalist community and in January 1930 could boast of the involvement of members of the local clergy, Garda Síochána, the National Bank and a number of national school teachers.[179] In 1931 it was stated that the club's annual Christmas social was 'one of the principal attractions' in the town's festive activities, having been organised consecutively for twenty years.[180] The club managed to come up with new ideas to keep things going and invited local businessmen and professionals to take up membership in May 1933.[181] They were also the only Donegal club to organise a celebratory event for the GAA's Golden Jubilee in 1934.[182] This perseverance and ability to consistently organise events in the community was in contrast to many clubs in Donegal.

Financial difficulty amongst GAA clubs was a recurring theme throughout the county and public appeals for financial support were crucial for the survival of many clubs in the 1920s and early 1930s. The Donegal County Board felt it necessary to appeal for financial assistance in March 1924. It was reported that

> As matters stand the local clubs are finding it hard to exist. Of the 21 clubs in the county the majority can only find financial assistance to keep them going in fits and starts. The cause of this

> is – each club draws its meagre support from its playing members only. The public up to the present has evinced no interest in the clubs' success or failure.[183]

It was also stated that clubs were unable to contribute to the County Board and delegates had to pay for their own transport to attend County Board meetings.[184] Even the purchasing of trophies required external patronage. In August 1926, the County Board launched what turned out to be a successful appeal for subscriptions to the Dr Maguire Cup fund in the local press while they also benefited from the donation of cups from local newspapers towards the end of the decade.[185]

This financial difficulty differed vastly from Cavan, where one writer illustrated the strength of the sport in this county in an article after they heavily defeated Donegal in 1926:

> Cavan is the home of Gaelic football. There the game has been reduced to a fine art as practically no other football has been known in the county for upwards of forty years. Cavan county people spare no expense in promoting the game and almost every small town in County Cavan sends an annual subscription to the Cavan County Board. Last season the small village of Bawnboy alone sent £25, and the same village boasts of a local team for the past 36 years . . . in Donegal it is quite different.[186]

Despite some early promise shown in Belturbet, soccer failed to gain enough popular support to compete with the GAA in the county in the early twentieth century.[187] Cavan was certainly in a different league to Donegal, not just from a Gaelic football standard but also financially. While the Donegal County Board continuously struggled with finance and organisation, at the beginning of 1929 Cavan was reported to be one of the strongest GAA counties in Ireland and had spent £140 in the previous year on developing their county ground, Breffni Park.[188] There is no evidence to suggest that the GAA in Donegal owned any playing fields at this point. Cavan was also located more centrally within Ireland, lying in the south of Ulster and nearer to the centre of the Ulster Council in Clones and the Central Council in Dublin, and transport to these areas was undoubtedly easier than from Donegal. The terrain also differed, with few mountains and little isolation from these centres of GAA activity.

The paying of admission fees continued to be a problem and could not, in many cases, be enforced without proper enclosures and the majority of Donegal's clubs were unable to erect these. There are numerous references in the local press to spectators not paying to watch matches in the 1920s.[189] Poor attendances were particularly evident in these early years of the new County Board. The crowd at the Bundoran–Donegal town match in November 1921 was said to be 'the smallest that had ever assembled to witness a league competition', while the attendance at the Killybegs–Glenties match a year later was also poor.[190] The reporter was at a loss to figure out why this was so, but recorded that 'possibly the game is not sufficiently varied or outstanding enough. Players should strive to combine hand and foot and otherwise show off the game to better advantage.'[191] A lack of new clubs in the area, 'with too much sameness in the recurring Killybegs–Ardara–Glenties' fixtures was also suggested as being detrimental to interest levels at this time.

Dances, with an Irish theme, were seen as a good way of raising money amongst Donegal's clubs in the 1920s and early 1930s. Many GAA clubs were eager to illustrate an allegiance to Irish music and dancing at these events and the organisation of 'foreign' dances was banned under the rules of the GAA, with County Boards asked to enforce this rule and check dance programmes in 1932.[192] After a dance in aid of the GAA was held in Donegal town in September 1921, it was reported that 'Irish dances were in the ascendant. No jazzing or one stepping. Any attempt to introduce these ugly, disgusting things would have been immediately frustrated and criticised.'[193] At the dance on the evening of the Ardara GAA Annual Sports in August 1926 'Irish dances were the rule'.[194] Those who did not stick to these ideals, such as an unnamed Gaeltacht club in 1931 and the Gweedore GAA club the following year, were heavily criticised in the local press.[195] Some clubs sporadically organised whist drives in the 1920s in order to boost their funds. By 1931, card drives were 'becoming very popular in the county', with GAA clubs in Ballybofey, Milford and Letterkenny all hosting card drives in the spring of that year.[196] Others were keen to help out with local charities. In August 1931, the Bundoran GAA club gave 'valuable assistance' in organising the athletic fixtures at a local dress parade and an athletic contests day in aid of the St Vincent de Paul association.[197] The frequency of these events varied, however, and they did not become weekly features of social life in Donegal.[198]

Tadhg Ó hAnnracháin has stated that 'as an institution, the GAA was no more successful than the state in inculcating usage of the Irish language'.[199] Donegal's GAA clubs certainly failed to show much interest in co-operation with local branches of the Gaelic League. At a County Board meeting in March 1925, proposals were made for collections for the Gaelic League to be made by the GAA in areas where no branches of the League existed. It was also hoped that more respect would be shown for the Irish language.[200] However, these ideals amounted to nothing more than rhetoric in most cases. Calls from Seán Ó Caiside for GAA clubs to form Irish language classes in October 1927 appear to have been largely ignored.[201] At the Ulster Gaelic League Convention in May 1928, it was hoped that co-operation between the GAA and Gaelic League would improve, while 'responsibility for calling conferences' was to be given to 'two of the Executive members of the county'. The use of propaganda was said to be encouraging as was the revival of Gaelic League feiseanna; it was hoped these would be held in counties where none existed.[202] A Gaelic rally to discuss the amalgamation of the GAA and the Gaelic League was held in Ballyshannon the following month with Seán Ó Caiside presiding.[203] At the Annual GAA Convention held in Glenties in January 1932, the chairman, Brother Lucien, stated that while much progress had been made with clubs and finance, 'it was sufficient to play Gaelic games alone, but they were asked to enter whole-heartedly into the spirit of supporting Irish industries, the language, dancing and everything which tended to the realisation of the dreams of our ancestors and our own – namely an Irish Ireland for the Irish'.[204] Clearly, organisation of clubs and competitions was difficult enough, and most players were happy just to play Gaelic games, without giving much thought to their background. In August 1934, a cup was presented by D.C. Mac Fhionnlaoich on behalf of the Donegal Gaelic League to Guard Walsh for a schools hurling league, but other than this, co-operation between these two bodies does not appear to have been very substantial.[205] As noted earlier, the failure of the Gaelic League to develop in Donegal may have hindered the development of the GAA at various stages, but it must be stated that once the latter organisation did begin to become established in the

1920s, little effort was made by the County Board and clubs to organise off-field activities associated with the promotion of Irish culture, other than GAA affairs.

Attendances improved in the late 1920s as the GAA became more widely recognised within society. The GAA was well publicised in the local press and the securing of trains for county finals and intercounty matches eased transport difficulties, with these games generally being held in centralised urban areas. The organisation of adequate transport was crucial to success, and when this was neglected attendances at matches such as the Antrim versus Donegal Ulster hurling championship fixture at Letterkenny in October 1928 suffered.[206] As the 1920s wore on, county finals became the showpiece of club Gaelic football and gate receipts were generally good for these fixtures. While a replay of the 1920 final attracted only 400 spectators, support increased throughout the decade.[207] By 1923 trains were being arranged, with a special train put on for the final in Glenties.[208] The following year, 'trains and motor cars must have brought at least a thousand people' to Letterkenny for the decider.[209] The 1928 county final held in Glenties drew a crowd that paid over £60 at the gate.[210] This was no doubt helped by the provision of 'special railway facilities on the Donegal line, while buses and motors brought in many from a distance'.[211] By the mid-1920s motor cars were becoming an important mode of transport to matches, with car ownership growing in the following decades; bicycles and trains also helped players, officials and supporters in their quest to attend matches.[212]

Popular support for Gaelic games in areas such as Ballyshannon meant that excursion trains were regularly put on for intercounty matches by the middle of the decade. Excitement was built up with sensationalist previews, such as the following for the Donegal–Cavan Ulster Gaelic football championship clash in 1926:

> The excursion to Cavan on Sunday next will be a large one. Ballyshannon and wife, Bundoran and wife and perhaps Belleek and wife are all going not to speak of all that will come from Donegal, Letterkenny and 'down the line'. The fare is low, 5s. – and the game promises to be so thrilling that everyone is interested. Anyhow, at the time, the Slashers' town is worth a visit.[213]

Crowd figures at McKenna Cup matches earlier that year illustrate the popular support intercounty matches were able to attract.

Approximately 8,000 attended the Donegal–Tyrone clash in February while around 6,000 spectators attended the replay.[214] The 1927 McKenna Cup final between Donegal and Monaghan at Clones drew receipts of £90.[215] These matches were a big day out for many supporters. The GAA's popular appeal grew in these decades and the National League, organised in 1926, added to the media profile of these games. By the end of this decade, the attendance at the All-Ireland Gaelic football final had reached over 30,000.[216] The hosting of matches also boosted revenue within local towns and after a Donegal versus Armagh Ulster championship match at Ballyshannon in June 1928, it was noted that 'it was really heartening to see the crowds, and it brought a little badly needed cash into the town'.[217]

However, it would be incorrect to assume that everything went smoothly. De Burca has stated that 'some of the crowds and gate money from 1925 onwards concealed a widespread tendency to endure mediocrity in the running of clubs, boards and councils'.[218] In Donegal things were no different. Despite the increase in the number of cups available towards the end of the decade and improvements in transport to finals and intercounty matches, problems remained. While the county championship final was developing as an important occasion within Donegal society, the 1925 final between Aodh Ruadh, Ballyshannon and Dunfanaghy did not take place, as the former club refused to travel, citing illness in their team. A scratch match was hastily arranged although Kilcar were later awarded the title.[219] In 1929, the refusal of the Killygordon captain and his team, a few moments prior to the final's throw-in, to play on the pitch in Glenties undoubtedly tarnished the image of the GAA in the county.[220] Chairman Seán Ó Caiside later spoke of his humiliation, having been forced to refund angry supporters the £39 gathered at the entrance.[221] This final was not resolved until the summer of 1930 after a number of protests resulted in Ballyshannon finally gaining victory.[222]

Lack of support particularly affected the development of GAA clubs in the east. A general lack of interest in Gaelic games in Letterkenny was certainly a problem. One GAA reporter was scathing in his criticism of the limited local support at the Donegal versus Tyrone Ulster championship match held there in 1924.[223] The following year a correspondent claimed that 'Letterkenny may excel in many of our county institutions, but for a goodly number of years back, its reputation as a GAA stronghold is not up to the mark', although he did think it was recovering.[224] However, this problem continued into the 1930s. At the club's AGM on 21 February 1934, it was noted that receipts for home matches were disappointing.[225] At the Eastern Board Convention early that year, outgoing secretary Leo McCarron gave a rather pessimistic account of the division's progress. He stated that while the other divisions were doing fine financially, he could not say the same about his own area. He felt that although they had nine senior teams, none of them were fully functioning clubs.[226] McCarron added that 'it was a matter of a few enthusiastic Gaels helping to carry on a team' and complained that there was basically too much talk and not enough action being taken. Many clubs were unable to pay gate levies to the County Board as at times gates did not match the amount of the levy requested. Other administrative problems included a failure of appointed referees to turn up for matches, with the result that spectators lost interest. Fixtures in the county championship for the area had not been completed and McCarron even went as far as to say that 'the people of the area have become absolutely de-nationalised'.[227] This, he felt, was centred in their location, claiming that 'they were in the middle of a planters' area' and he later went on to state that many people in Letterkenny would not take any part in matches on Sundays.[228] Certainly there may have been a larger non-Catholic population in the east than in areas such as the south-west, with the result that Gaelic games organisers did not have a monopoly on choices of sport such as they had in the south-west. Cricket, soccer and rugby clubs were in operation in the early 1930s in East Donegal and, added to this, attracting interest in the GAA appears to have been difficult for some clubs. One Ballybofey delegate complained at the Annual Convention in January 1934 that for five home matches in 1933 they had received an average of only five shillings at the gate per game which was said to be a poor return.[229]

An improvement in levels of commitment was noted at the Board's Annual Convention on 6 December 1934, where it was highlighted that matches were 'well played in a sporting spirit, the standard of competition improved, [and] all competitions were completed'.[230] This was, it was stated, because 'Gaels faced these difficulties with determination and very quickly it had become evident that a new era had been born ... enthusiasm was renewed'.[231] This may be an oversimplification of matters, as problems still dogged the organisation of clubs, but there was certainly an improvement. In 1933, gate receipts at club and intra-divisional matches in Donegal amounted to a record sum of £203 12 shillings and 2½d. A training grant was also received from the Ulster Council with the financial report 'very satisfactory'.[232] By January 1934 the Donegal County Board had managed to clear its debt and treasurer Seán Conaghan stated that 'gates were good, enthusiasm had never been so widespread, and support from the public had never been more generous'.[233] This credit balance of £93 18 shillings and 6d, including a debt of £45 16 shillings due from the Ulster Council, was helped by a successful public appeal prior to the All-Ireland Junior Gaelic football final, and despite Donegal's defeat, this run and appearance at Croke Park no doubt gave the GAA in the county a much-needed morale boost. More care also appears to have been taken in regard to financial matters, with itemised reports being submitted and an auditor used to clarify matters. Much of this changeover was said to be due to the work of chairman Seán Ó Caiside who was praised for his successful 'endeavour to clear up the financial mess they were in'.[234] Interestingly, it was also noted that the subscribers 'included the names of a number of Protestants and unionists from the county, and also the names of a number of former residents of Donegal, now in Dublin and elsewhere'.[235] This reflects an increase in popular support for Gaelic games in the county at this point, while political involvement had also improved with TD Brian Brady donating a record £8 1 shilling.[236] Funds were boosted by a number of those with Donegal links residing in Dublin prior to the 1933 All-Ireland Junior final through the organisation of a committee and appeal in support of Donegal and a reception for the team was arranged.[237] Clearly the GAA in Donegal was now attracting increased support from those with influence within and outside of the county and others sympathetic to the GAA there, something which had been lacking since the early 1920s after the decline of involvement of the 1919 County Board founders. This was crucial in putting the Association on a firm footing in the county.

Giving up Sundays, for many the only day of the week off work, in order to help with organisation of GAA matches and generally being unpaid for it except for limited travel expenses, required dedication. The Dungloe club, for example, benefited from a number of dedicated organisers who kept the club going in these years and, like Aodh Ruadh, were eager to find opposition outside their own area if necessary. One of these dedicated Dungloe officials was John Tuohy, a bank official said to be 'the life of the GAA movement there' before his departure in March 1925, while Packy Gallagher, a man who 'spent his time and cash freely for the welfare of the GAA' was also heavily involved in improving the Association in this area.[238] One Ballybofey County Board delegate expressed his own dedication in a letter to Seán Ó Caiside in July 1933:

> I'll try and lend a hand at Dungloe on Sunday myself but when a wife and four weans want to go to Bundoran it is not easy breaking down the opposition. It is a long time since I had a Sunday to myself now but what matter, if we can get the games of the Gael on a proper footing.[239]

It is also evident that in many areas, organisation was undertaken by a small number of men and help was difficult to attain. In January 1930 Ó Caiside complained that there were not enough newcomers in the GAA and that they were relying on 'old friends'.[240] F.J. Murphy illustrated that this was still the case in Ballybofey three years later when he stated that support 'for GAA matches is not big and the same few are saddled with all the work'.[241] The decision to become involved reflected a belief prevalent amongst many GAA members that there was a higher nationalist purpose involved rather than simply sport for recreational purposes. It was largely due to this dedication that the GAA was firmly established in Donegal by 1935. At this point, the structure of Gaelic games in Donegal, with its weekly matches and regular press coverage, far outweighed anything that any other sport in the county could offer and the GAA had made a substantial improvement since the early 1920s. More significantly, it was there to stay.

Conclusion

In 1934 the GAA celebrated its Golden Jubilee and the organisation's official historian, Marcus De Burca, has stated that by the end of these first fifty years 'it had manifestly achieved its twin objectives of 1884 of reviving the traditional field games of Ireland and erecting a barrier to the tide of Anglicisation periodically threatening to engulf the island'.[242] While this may have been the case elsewhere, in Donegal, and generally throughout Ulster, the development of Gaelic games had been a slow, tough struggle. This chapter has shown the importance of individuals in organising the GAA in Donegal. The organisation of competitive structures in the 1919–35 period was crucial to the spread and success of Gaelic football. However, this was dependent on a small group of enthusiasts who were dedicated to making it the most popular team game in the county. When this enthusiasm was absent locally, or, in the case of hurling, restricted to a handful of areas, the dissemination of these sports undoubtedly suffered.

The power of agency in the spread of sports is apparent, as without the external influence of provincial and national organisers, the spread of Gaelic games was a mundane, sometimes laboured, development. The rate at which this occurred in Donegal illustrates how the GAA there struggled to gain popular support and the survival of clubs was characterised by inconsistency. It has also been shown that political involvement within the organisation was sporadic and the success of the GAA in the county was not dependent on this. As Peter Hart has stated, there is only limited evidence to suggest 'a strong link' between GAA members and IRA activity.[243] This was generally the case in Donegal and, as seen in the movement for Ireland's independence, Donegal remained on the periphery of more regionally concentrated military events.

Despite organisational difficulties, the GAA's development of annual competitive structures provided young men with team sports. In contrast, by 1919, participation in soccer was limited to friendly games and this was not enough to maintain interest. As will be seen, the GAA benefited from a lack of direct competition from soccer until 1925 and its superior administrative structure meant that Gaelic football was, in some areas, the only code available. This was a feature of the south and south-west where GAA clubs became the focal point of a number of parishes and provided young men with a recreational and social outlet. GAA organisers showed an astute awareness of this and in initially arranging Gaelic football at local sports were able to demonstrate how the game should be played. The provision of regular County Board meetings, in larger, urban areas where club delegates could discuss matters and build social networks, was also crucial. Cronin, Duncan and Rouse have noted the GAA's expansion in the initial decades of the Free State.[244] This did not become particularly noticeable at club level in Donegal until the 1930s and this again highlights the slow evolution of sport within Donegal society. Improvements in administration at national level in the early 1930s were reflected there, and an improved knowledge of Gaelic football and organisational strategies saw the county compete at All-Ireland level for the first time. The challenge provided by association football, and its bearing on the geographical spread of Gaelic football, will be discussed in the next chapter.

6

The development of association football in Donegal, 1881–1935

Introduction

Although there are earlier recordings of a game like soccer in Ireland, the first association football match to be held on the island did not take place until October 1878, when the Scottish teams of Queen's Park and Caledonians met for an exhibition game in Belfast. The Irish Football Association was not formed until two years later, a development that came much later than the foundation of the English Football Association in 1863.[1] While the founding of the English FA was significant, there is strong evidence that other organised and structured forms of football that were played prior to this were also highly influential in the development of modern football.[2] Football clubs of various codes in England were in operation as early as 1855, but those in Donegal were not founded until the early 1880s and struggled to establish permanent league and cup structures.[3] The development of the County Donegal Football Association in 1894 occurred earlier than efforts to form governing bodies for soccer in many other Irish counties, although it lasted only briefly.[4] This chapter focuses on the early development of the game and will look at the reasons for its geographical spread throughout the county, as by the middle of the 1930s the popularity of soccer had declined in the south and south-west, while the game had become firmly established in the north-east of the county. It also assesses the social background of these players and administrators and illustrates how this differed from those involved in the Gaelic Athletic Association.

The growth of association football in Donegal in the nineteenth century

The reasons for the popularity of soccer have been advanced by Tony Mason and these included the simplicity of the rules and the lack of equipment, physical strength and little financial input needed by players, and the fact that any number of players could take part in a variety of places. In addition to this, he wrote that 'football has, and had, that combination of spontaneity and order which allowed scope for individuality and unpredictability within an organised, disciplined, context'.[5] Despite claims that the game of soccer was first played in the Rosses area of Donegal in the late 1880s, forms of this code were certainly being played in the county by the early part of that decade.[6] Football 'under the association rules' was played between selections representing the villages of Castlefin in East Donegal and Croaghan of West Tyrone in July 1881, although this match contained elements of folk-football.[7] These players paid little attention to the timeframe as the game began at four o'clock in a 'best of three' series and continued until it got dark, with gambling forming an important part of the day's proceedings.[8] Some of these early matches, such as the February 1885 game between the 'amateur clubs' of Doaghbeg and Rossnakill on the shores of Lough Swilly, varied in the playing time and the number of players used.[9] Soccer also formed part of athletic clubs' meetings and local annual competitions during this decade. Private patronage was a crucial element of these early matches.[10] In January 1882, the Letterkenny Athletic Club was given the use of a field belonging to the Hegarty ladies of the local hotel and 'a well-contested match' took place between two local selections.[11] In June 1885 at the annual Cranford Athletic Sports, Kerrykeel FC defeated Cranford FC in a football match played 'under association rules' in Cranford Park, which belonged to the Earl of Leitrim.[12] Despite this early promise, neither of these soccer clubs were ambitious enough to enter the IFA Cup that year, and no Donegal clubs took part in this competition that season, as none were amongst the thirty-one clubs noted as being affiliated to the national governing body for soccer at their AGM in May.[13]

Association football matches were also being played in the south of the county with teams representing Donegal Town and Mountcharles meeting in the spring of 1882.[14] James Walvin has noted the growth of English clubs such as Sheffield Wednesday and Preston North End from existing cricket clubs.[15] While crossover from cricket to soccer took place in Irish counties such as Westmeath, there is only limited evidence that this happened in Donegal: in Ballyshannon (1882) and Carrigans (1895).[16] The number of soccer teams in Donegal began to increase in the early 1890s; in 1891 there were at least seventeen in the county and this figure had more than doubled by the following year.[17] This illustrates a significant growth from the handful of teams in the middle of the previous decade.

Some early clubs in north-east Donegal benefited from their close location to Derry, where a Football Association had been founded in April 1886.[18] Donegal had no football association at this point and a number of its north-eastern clubs looked to Derry for assistance in the diffusion of soccer into their areas, again demonstrating the strong influence of the city, as a major conurbation, for many in rural Donegal. This help was at first given through the playing of exhibition matches. The spread of soccer in Buncrana, Letterkenny and Ramelton in the early 1890s was aided by teams from Derry.[19] Participation in leagues and cup competitions was also encouraged and this gave Donegal clubs their first experience of competitive matches. Buncrana took part in the County Derry Challenge Cup in October 1890 and by November 1891, both Ramelton FC and Letterkenny FC had affiliated to the County Derry FA and were in the draw for its junior cup.[20] In 1894, seven north-eastern Donegal clubs were affiliated with the Derry-based North-West FA.[21] The development of the game was also promoted by visiting ships' crews such as those of the HMS *Aurora* and HMS *Jason* and military teams such as the Royal Engineers who challenged local clubs in the Lough Swilly area in the 1890s.[22] Donegal clubs' lack of success in Derry competitions led to the formation of the County Donegal FA in Ramelton on 24 March 1894.[23] The north-east Donegal clubs of Cranford, Cratlagh, Ramelton Athletic, Kerrykeel, Buncrana, Letterkenny, Swilly Rangers and Milford Swifts were all in the draw for the Donegal Cup in September 1894 along with Derrybeg Celtic from Gweedore in the north-west, illustrating a desire for competitive matches under their own governing body.[24] At this point, part of the bedrock of soccer in the county had been laid down.

The Donegal FA relied heavily on the work of individuals. The main instigator was Daniel Deeney, a national school teacher and honorary secretary of Carradoan FC.[25] He was supported by other club secretaries, P.G. Green of Kerrykeel FC, a clerk, and Joseph Devenney of St Adaman's Swifts.[26] While this new football governing body was met initially with enthusiasm, the league and cup competitions did not receive enough public support and matches were poorly advertised. The physical barrier of the Blue Stack mountains also meant that those in the south of the county were somewhat isolated from this centre of soccer activity. Travel was difficult, as noted in a report of a friendly between Cranford and Derrybeg Celtic in May 1895.[27] The transport network meant that clubs from other areas outside the north-east, with the exception of Derrybeg Celtic, Kincasslagh Shamrocks, Ardara Emeralds and Donegal Celtic, failed to join up, and the resignation of Deeney, who moved to Galway in 1896, was also a blow.[28] Internal disputes and the failure of a number of prominent clubs to acknowledge the rules meant that the Donegal FA could not develop in a successful manner and was disbanded in 1898.[29] Financially the organisation struggled and failed to install a proper method of collecting admission fees at matches, something which Metcalfe has identified as being the determining factor in whether a soccer club would flourish or deteriorate.[30]

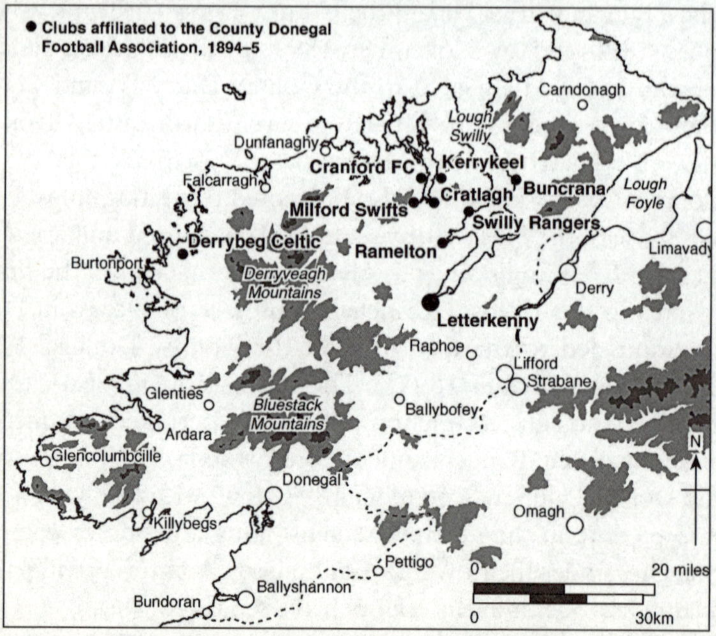

Fig. 6.1: Clubs affiliated to the County Donegal Football Association, 1894–5

SOURCE: *DJ*, 19 September 1894

The organisation of the Donegal FA was rather slow in comparison with the foundation of football associations in England. While the English and Sheffield football bodies were the first to be organised, the number of county and district associations was already increasing in the 1870s and early 1880s.[31] Ireland differed vastly from this; the development of similar bodies by 1890 was initially restricted to Belfast (IFA), Down, Antrim and Derry, while a Mid-Ulster Association was also in operation.[32] The Leinster FA was founded in 1892, the Munster FA was formed in 1901, and the County Monaghan FA was founded in 1904.[33] By the end of 1911 the Western Association Football League, which catered for clubs in Sligo, Roscommon and Leitrim, was in operation.[34] The growth of soccer in Donegal was certainly much faster than in Kerry, where soccer was not played until 1894 and remained a minority sport at this time.[35] Although the Donegal FA lasted for only four years, the county was therefore not as slow to develop a football association in comparison with other Irish counties and clearly benefited, at least initially, from this regional influence. However, it failed to build on this early promise, an indication of the difficulties in the spread of all sports throughout Donegal. By the middle of the opening decade of the twentieth century, the Leinster and Munster FAs, between them, could boast of having seventy clubs affiliated to the IFA, while Donegal's involvement in this national governing body was limited to fewer than a handful of clubs.[36] This contrasted greatly with the growth of soccer in many parts of England and Scotland, where regional bodies in Lancashire, Birmingham, Northumberland and Durham, Sheffield, Nottinghamshire and Stirlingshire all experienced significant rises in affiliated clubs and players in the late nineteenth century.[37] In Donegal, the number of soccer clubs and teams noted in the local press in 1905 (thirty-two) was actually less than the figure of thirty-five for 1892, which illustrates the slow development of this code after an initial spurt in the early 1890s.[38]

It appears that many Donegal soccer clubs were simply village or town combinations which got together, perhaps through social or work networks. Neal Garnham has stated that clubs had their origins in a range of existing sporting and social establishments.[39] However, unlike those in the east of Ulster and England, there is limited evidence that any teams were founded in Donegal from pubs or the church. Although it is difficult to identify Donegal soccer clubs which were formed with explicit religious connections – such as the club founded in 1889 in Newtownbutler, County Fermanagh by national school teacher H. Hobson for local Protestant youths – one example appears to be the Ballyshannon-based Protestant Young Men's Christian Association team, which appeared briefly in 1896.[40] There is some evidence that a number of Donegal clubs were organised to benefit young locals' development. South-west soccer clubs Ardara Emeralds and Killybegs Emeralds were formed in 1891 and 1896 respectively, specifically to provide a pastime for the youths of their towns.[41] It was stated in the local press that the youth of Ardara were in dire need of a sporting club, especially the apprentices and shop assistants who had 'to spend their leisure hours hanging around the corner'.[42] Similarly in Killybegs, a club was set up by local business men 'for the benefit of the youth of the town and parish'.[43] The setting up of a cricket and football club in Lifford in 1890 was said to have been arranged for militia men located there for training. The provision of equipment for cricket and football and the organisation of matches by permanent staff sergeants and officers had the result of 'keeping them from lounging about the streets of Strabane in anything like so large numbers as was the case in former years'.[44]

Political involvement led to the formation of the Boylagh Champion FC in Kilclooney on 1 February 1892, with a number of those prominent in the local branch of the Irish National League behind this foundation.[45] On St Patrick's Day that year they headed a large procession, which was well decked out in the national saint's colours.[46] A few Donegal soccer teams, such as those participating in the St Patrick's Temperance Guild Athletic Sports in August 1882, were teetotal, while it was not uncommon for players from clubs in Kerrykeel, Glenvar and Cranford to display their temperance badges during matches in the following decade.[47] Temperance was an important part of the ethos of some other Irish soccer clubs, including Manorhamilton Celtic of Leitrim, who held a dance in the local Temperance Hall on St Patrick's Day, 1908.[48] Some Donegal clubs were simply made up of local agricultural workers, such as the Straoughter Farmers' Sons, said to have been founded in Glenties in 1893. The local Sunlights club was organised in 1899 by shop assistant Willie O'Donnell, who had experience of the game in Letterkenny and was able to demonstrate the rules.[49] Evidence for those with their origins in educational establishments is also difficult to find but a team representing St Eunan's Seminary in Letterkenny was in existence in 1895 and Ramelton Polytechnic affiliated to the Donegal FA the following year.[50]

The level of industry in an area has also been noted as having a significant influence on the founding of sporting clubs.[51] Some early soccer clubs in County Fermanagh were associated with places of employment, such as the Lisbellaw club referred to as 'the weavers of cloth' in 1891 and a Post Office team in Enniskillen, which was founded in February 1892.[52] However, evidence of Donegal clubs formed in the workplace is difficult to find. This is probably due to the lack of industry in the county at the time, although a club representing Convoy Mills was affiliated to the County Donegal FA for the 1897–98 season.[53] In addition, evidence for clubs in Donegal which had their origins in organisations linked directly to cultural development are lacking, unlike in Armagh where Choir and Reading Room teams were present by the late 1880s.[54]

Seasonal migration from West Donegal contributed significantly to the popularity of soccer in this area, with returning locals instrumental in setting up teams at home, having had experience of the sport in Scotland.[55] Joseph M. Bradley has stated that 'in the second-half of the nineteenth century the growth of soccer was swift as it pervaded and was taken up by communities all over Britain including by the Irish who were firmly situated within the country's working class'.[56] Although there is evidence that a newly formed club was in existence in Dungloe by June 1892, it is unclear if there was any link to Scotland in this foundation.[57] Keadue Rovers was formed in April 1896 by brothers Maurice and Con Campbell, who had played for St John's of Perth.[58] Soccer became firmly established in the Rosses area in the 1890s.[59] While more research is needed on seasonal migration as a driver of the dissemination of soccer in Ireland, it appears West Donegal was not unique in this respect. Soccer in the Cavan villages of Bawnboy, Kilnavart and Ballyconnell was apparently initiated by returning seasonal migrants from Britain in the late nineteenth century.[60] The growth of this code in Achill Island, which lies off the coast of Mayo, can also be attributed to seasonal workers, although it seems this took place in the 1940s and 1950s and similarly, these young men worked in England as well as Scotland.[61]

Patrick Bracken has noted the presence of soldiers as being significant in the initiation of soccer in Tipperary in 1897.[62] Military involvement was also crucial to the game's development in Ballyshannon in South Donegal. A detachment of the 2nd Dorset Regiment provided the inspiration for the founding of a number of clubs in the area during 1896.[63] Erne FC were said to be the first of these, their players clearly coming from the local neighbourhood and composed 'mainly of young men on the port side of the water'.[64] As Mason has noted, 'many football teams in many places must just have been set up by groups of young men who just lived close to each other'.[65] In the period from March 1896 until May 1899, forty-seven Ballyshannon-based combinations were involved in at least seventy-two matches. The majority of these were friendly matches and clubs ranged from the most prominent – Erne FC and Ballyshannon Swifts, who appeared fairly regularly and used secretaries – to military detachments and local organisations such as the Young Men's Christian Association. Weaker, more rural combinations such as Abbey and Rock Wanderers appear to have been ad hoc arrangements, while youth teams such as the Young Bloods were also organised.[66] These early Donegal clubs do not appear to have engaged in any non-sporting cultural activities such as the trip organised by the Enniskillen Celtic club to entertain Leinster Senior League champions Tritonville in 1905, when the away team were brought to the Cinderella given by the Irish National Foresters.[67] Despite the initial progress made in Ballyshannon, by the early 1900s, the majority of these combinations were no longer in existence. Like the Bundoran soccer club, none of Ballyshannon's teams affiliated with the Fermanagh and Western District FA, which came into existence in 1906; difficulty in securing a playing ground proved a problem.[68] With the failure of the Donegal FA, the organisation of soccer in Donegal was restricted to inconsistently arranged, localised cup competitions until the 1930s.

The development of association football in Donegal in the early twentieth century

The main stronghold of soccer in Ireland in the early 1900s seems to have been County Antrim, particularly in regard to the number of clubs affiliated to the Irish Football Association, which had its headquarters in Belfast. By October 1906 there were six district areas in operation and the County Antrim FA had seventy-one clubs. There were sixty clubs affiliated in Leinster, while only ten were affiliated from Munster. The North-west FA, based in Derry city, had twenty-four clubs, while the Mid-Ulster area had forty-six clubs and the Fermanagh and Western District had only six.[69] There were at least nineteen soccer teams in Donegal and a lack of interest in joining the country's governing body was apparent rather than any major absence of clubs at this time.[70] An analysis of soccer clubs in Donegal in the period from 1905 until 1934, as shown in Appendices 12 to 14, illustrates the diversity between areas and changes in the popularity of soccer, through the organisation of teams, leagues and cup competitions across the county.[71] It also highlights the areas where the organisation of association football had almost completely fallen apart by the mid-1930s. As can be seen, it was in the east and north-east and Inishowen that the vast majority of soccer clubs were located by the 1930s, illustrating the game's popularity over Gaelic football in these areas. In particular, while there were only fourteen clubs recorded in the east and north-east in 1905, by 1934 there were sixty-six in these areas. Inishowen had also seen a growth from three in 1905 to thirty-two in 1934. By this time, the number of clubs in the south and south-west had failed to show any major growth. The number of South Donegal clubs reached a peak of seven in 1916 but by 1934 this was reduced to just two. Figures for the south-west were also poor and the 1905 figure of two had been halved by 1934. Soccer was almost totally wiped out in these two areas by 1934, despite the perseverance of clubs in Ballyshannon and Killybegs.

The theory that the War of Independence polarised public opinion against soccer has been mentioned in a number of club histories.[72] While it may have influenced a changeover in some areas, there was no widespread transfer of clubs from soccer to Gaelic football in Donegal. Examples of a direct switch from soccer to Gaelic football clubs are not very common, particularly outside the south and south-west. Both the Ardara and Glenties soccer clubs, said to have transferred to Gaelic football with the coming of the War of Independence, may well have been in decline prior to this. Newspaper reports indicate the presence of a soccer club in Ardara until at least December 1916 but it is difficult to establish, given a lack of subsequent coverage in the press, how much activity this club was involved in during the period from 1917 to 1921. Therefore, the soccer club in the parish may have already been in decline before the War of Independence.[73] Ardara Emeralds' last competitive action was the 1915 Britton Cup and this lack of regular competition may also have influenced the decision to get involved in Gaelic football.[74] By May 1917, Ardara soccer players were appearing for Dunkineely Pioneers, also indicating a decline in local soccer activity.[75] Unlike Killybegs Emeralds, a lack of success in other soccer competitions and the absence of a railway station may also have been detrimental to the club's development. Glenties' last soccer appearance also appears to have been much earlier than 1921, coming in a defeat against Donegal Celtic in 1917.[76]

Nationalism, local enthusiasm, personal preferences and the boredom of non-competitive soccer matches were all factors in the transfer from soccer to Gaelic football in Donegal. The movement of key organisers also led to a decline in soccer in some areas and may be a more satisfactory explanation than the anti-British theory. Switching of codes in sport was relatively common in Britain and France and this transfer of players has been well-documented.[77] Crossover of players and administrators was significant in the organisation of the GAA in Donegal in the 1920s as a number of those with experience of soccer later became involved as officials at GAA County Board level. This appears to have been down to the nationalist views of these men, some of whom were national school teachers and possibly learned Gaelic football at college and saw its organisation as a part of their nationalist duty. In Ardara, former soccer player and national school teacher Seán Ó Caiside was able to use his organisational and playing experience to ensure that Gaelic football became the most popular sport there, and indeed in the south and south-west of the county through his involvement at County Board level. Glenties man and national school teacher Seán Conaghan, who played a prominent role in his own club and in the County Board in the 1920s, had some experience as part of the Glenties United soccer team in 1917 and he and Ó Caiside were good friends.[78] This may have influenced his decision to become involved in Gaelic football. It is also clear that the spread of this code in Ardara, Glenties and Kilcar was helped by teachers who were dedicated to the promotion of the GAA, rather than soccer. Joe McDevitt, a nationalist who had been principal of Patrick Pearse's St Enda's school in Dublin, was also heavily involved in the organisation of the GAA in Kilcar.[79]

In the south of the county, Aodh Ruadh GAA club delegates Denis Nyhan and J.J. Woods had earlier been influential in the organisation of soccer in Ballyshannon.[80] Nyhan was also a national school teacher. The GAA also benefited from experienced soccer men such as former Killybegs Emeralds captain Tony Conwell, who became involved as a referee; another former soccer administrator, P.K. McDermott, of Donegal town, was a County Board delegate in 1925 and was also known to officiate at matches.[81] It is clear that given soccer's popularity over Gaelic football in the majority of areas in Donegal until the 1920s, many GAA men had been involved in soccer. Where these men were responsible for organising local sport, their previous organisation suffered if they decided to switch codes. Certainly if a small group of men known locally for the arranging of club activities decided to organise an alternative sports club, then local players would have no choice but to follow in order to continue as part of a team and as a social group. However, there was by no means a major transformation in codes all over the county.

While this changeover was particularly strong in the south and south-west, in the north-east the playing of soccer proved harder to curtail. Soccer continued to be played by many GAA players in this area and some of the difficulties experienced, in particular by the East Donegal GAA Board, will later be examined as this was a major problem for that body. The composition of a County Donegal soccer selection, which played a Sligo XI in 1928, highlights the majority of areas in which it could be said that GAA organisers had failed to make any great impact by this time. Players from Ballybofey, Lifford, Rathmullan, Kerrykeel, Buncrana, Ramelton, Carndonagh, Creeslough and Ballintra all participated and, with the exception of Ballybofey, these were areas which had been more or less unswayed by efforts to develop Gaelic football in the county.[82] Of these areas only Ballintra lies in the south, and the location of the other clubs, which are all in the north and east of Donegal, is perhaps a fair reflection of where soccer could be said to have succeeded.

Though the organisation of soccer had been slow up until the 1920s, an improvement in administration, particularly in the north-east and Inishowen, meant that by 1930 the game in these areas had become a significant threat for the development of the GAA. The presence or absence of competitions, as opposed to challenge matches, seems to be a key factor underpinning success. In the years after the collapse of the County Donegal FA in 1898 until the mid-1920s, soccer competitions in the north of the county were restricted to local sports events. The majority of clubs, with the exception of a small number who dared to challenge the more advanced clubs in Derry city by affiliating with their soccer organisations, appeared content to play friendlies.[83] One Falcarragh correspondent, writing in the *Derry Journal*, in calling for soccer 'to be established on a properly organised basis', recognised this problem in 1917:

> At present there are some good football teams in Donegal. Those in the same district may meet occasionally in a friendly encounter, but seldom or never are the 'crack' teams of the district brought together. This state of affairs tends to discourage the game, for it is impossible to sustain the interest and enthusiasm when there is no objective to strive for.[84]

This meant that the GAA was able to step into a vacuum that existed in Donegal by 1919 and provide organised leagues and cups for young men who may have previously been involved in soccer competitions but were by then restricted to participating in irregularly held friendlies. Certainly there was no guarantee that soccer competitions would be held annually and the short-lived nature of competitions illustrates this. Although the re-founding of the GAA County Board in 1919 came as part of Sinn Féin's nationalist mission, the development of Gaelic games in Donegal was undoubtedly helped by this lack of opposition in the form of a permanent, annual league or cup for all (or even some) of Donegal's soccer clubs. Cup competitions and an organised structure over a season provided additional interest for both players and spectators as enthusiasm would have waned without the challenge these provided. League matches gave clubs a guaranteed structure for most of the season while cup competitions also strengthened clubs' schedules.[85] Without this type of structure in Donegal, there was always the possibility that the organisation of soccer could be challenged by the GAA.

As shown below in Figure 6.2, the majority of league and cup competitions organised in County Donegal between 1906 and 1934 were held in the north-east of the county. Association football

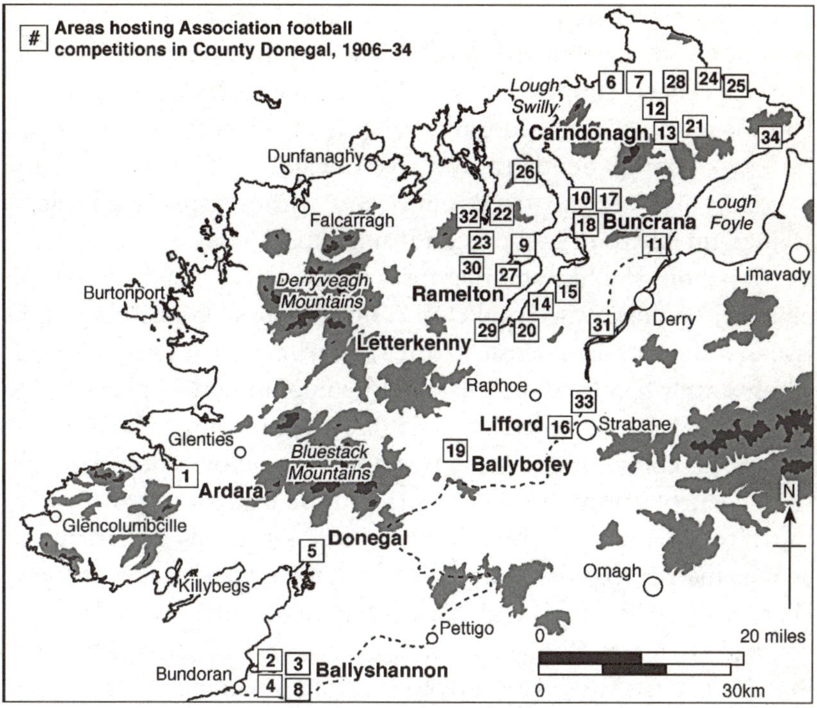

Fig. 6.2: Areas hosting Association football competitions in County Donegal, 1906–34

SOURCES: *DJ, DP and DN, DP and TN, DV, DI, DPP*, 1906–34. For a breakdown of these numbers and their competition names, patrons and years of existence, please see Appendix 15.

competitions were more prominent in the south and south-west of the county than in other areas in the opening two decades of the twentieth century. These were brief affairs, such as the Evans Cup (1906–07), the Woods Cup (1909–13) and the Britton Cup (1914–15), and were usually held over the winter and spring months and disbanded after a few years due to organisational difficulties or lack of interest.[86] This type of decline was not dissimilar to that experienced in competitions in other counties such as Tyrone, where the Clogher Valley Railway Cup was first organised in 1903 but appears to have lasted only until 1906.[87] These Donegal competitions attracted only a small number of clubs and external entries from Fermanagh in the Woods Cup illustrate the generally low level of clubs in the South Donegal area and the financial requirements for the successful running of a soccer club; these competitions were held in towns where patronage and facilities were easier to obtain.[88] Why none were organised in other areas in the county at this time may have been simply due to a lack of enthusiasm and patrons. Patronage, a key factor in the development of sport in many areas, such as Central Scotland and Westmeath, was crucial for the majority of Donegal soccer clubs and without this, many areas seemed unable to organise leagues and cups.[89]

Appendix 15 illustrates that these patrons were mainly local businessmen or those with local club connections, such as Robert E.L. Evans, a Birmingham bedstead fitter and wire mattress manufacturer whose family had lived in Ardara before migrating to England.[90] He was clearly quite comfortable by 1905, when he purchased a trophy for a local competition, as he was able to employ a domestic servant.[91] Patrons were, however, usually those living locally who were eager to encourage soccer in their areas, such as Ballyshannon cinema manager Frank Stewart; Donegal town watchmaker and jeweller William Britton; and Carol Mitchell, who ran a bottling company in the north-east. Other trophies were purchased by committees, such as those later involved in the Buncrana FA and Swilly Cup committee and descriptions of the cups were sometimes given in the local press as an incentive for clubs to register.[92]

Given that the Britton Cup was the only weekly competition in Donegal by 1915, it is difficult to establish the effect of the First World War on clubs in other areas, as the majority of these were involved only in friendlies. The exact degree of involvement by Donegal's soccer players in the war is difficult to trace, but some clubs did lose members at this time, which may have also harmed the development of the game.[93] Little mention, however, of the overall decline of clubs was made in the press. Sports clubs in Ireland did not enlist in the same numbers as those in England although there were some exceptions, such as some members of the Wanderers (Rugby) Football Club in Dublin, a club from which thirty-three members lost their lives in the war, and a rugby-playing company of the 7th Royal Dublin Fusiliers.[94] The involvement of soccer players was a personal choice not influenced by club membership. Neal Garnham has noted that initially on a national stage, '[association] football was maintained at such a level that it could divert men from less savoury pastimes, but would not prove an impediment to the war effort'. Leagues in Belfast and Dublin became more regionalised and finance was badly affected, with a reduction in manpower reflected in the levels of players and numbers of spectators involved, although by 1917 the numbers enlisting had 'slowed considerably'.[95] In 1919 an IFA commission on the reorganisation of soccer in the country concluded that 'the status of divisional associations and a number of the clubs of same had been seriously affected by the war'.[96] The amount of disruption caused by the War of Independence to soccer in Donegal is also difficult to establish clearly, but soccer continued to be played in 1919. Thirteen teams were involved in a five-a-side competition at the Cranford Sports in July of 1919 and twelve took part the following year, although it is unclear if this event was held in 1921.[97] At the Milford Sports in July 1921, fourteen teams took part.[98] No permanent district competitions were organised in the county from 1915 to 1925 and this allowed GAA organisers to get their games up and running relatively unopposed.

There was only one competition organised in the south of the county in the 1920s. The GAA was dominant in this area at this time, with a transformation in the organisation of soccer competitions to those in Gaelic football having taken place by the mid-1920s. This was crucial to the spread of Gaelic football, as GAA organisers faced scarce competition as no soccer league was formed until the middle of the decade. The South Donegal Football League, formed on 7 February 1926 in Donegal town, was the first attempt to hold a competition there since the Britton Cup.[99] The league had a relatively promising opening season, with six clubs taking part on a home and away basis. There were two clubs in Ballyshannon, Erne FC and Ballyshannon Swifts, a team said to be composed of players from the local rugby club. Others involved were Bundoran Celtic, Donegal Celtic, Ballintra and Belleek (Fermanagh). The league was not continued the following season. Efficient administration and the fostering of support within the community have been identified as being fundamental to clubs' survival in East Northumberland.[100] It appears that the development of soccer in South Donegal suffered greatly without these crucial factors. Along with an absence of ambitious, well-patronised clubs, the loss of three key organisers was a crucial blow to organisation.[101] The league's president, Commandant Cullen, a man who had shown 'tireless energy . . . in the promotion of soccer in the district and in the organisation of Bundoran United', left Finner Camp for the Curragh army base in May 1926 while Jim Harbison, who was said to be responsible for the organisation and running of the league, left to join Newry Town in October of that year.[102] The migration of leading official Mr Masterson was also detrimental to the league's continuation.[103] Both Bundoran United and Ballintra had struggled at times to field teams while, as noted earlier, the involvement of a rugby club suggests a lack of seriousness and perhaps more a means of keeping fit and socialising on their part.[104]

There is little to suggest that any of the Donegal teams, with the exception of Erne FC, were in a satisfactory financial state. At a meeting held at the beginning of the league, the ten shilling protest fee was halved, the chairman having stated that this 'was sufficient as none of the teams were wealthy'.[105] There is also evidence that the collecting of admission fees was difficult, with supporters watching from the railway line in Ballyshannon or sneaking in to view matches.[106] This came at a time when GAA clubs were being badly affected by emigration, so it is likely that this was also a problem for soccer organisers in the county. Given these difficult factors, it is unsurprising that soccer failed to seriously challenge the position of the GAA in the south and south-west of the county at this time. Erne FC was the only one of the competing teams still in operation by the end of 1927.[107]

Uniting the county for sporting purposes continued to be difficult. Attempts were made to encourage the spread of association football and bridge the gap between clubs in the north and south of the county, but these were also unsuccessful. Matches between South Donegal selections and teams representing Enniskillen and the Derry and District League, held in Ballyshannon and Derry city respectively in an attempt to raise funds and boost the profile of the game in South Donegal, had little long-term impact in the area despite local interest at the time.[108] These lacked the county-based appeal of Gaelic football with its provincial and All-Ireland championship structure and the rivalry this generated. In his assessment of the social impact of the GAA, Liam Ryan argued that the level of identification people in Ireland have had with parish and county teams surpassed that associated with religious, economic and political organisations.[109] Identification with a Gaelic football or hurling team representing the county was perhaps easier than a regional soccer selection whose players did not have a county championship in which to compete. Soccer clubs, often made up of players from other areas outside the club's own town, have sometimes lacked the parish identity that GAA teams could claim.[110] In any case, the hosting of once-off exhibition soccer matches in an urban setting may not have been the ideal means of generating interest and developing the game. Soccer clubs in South Donegal in 1926 were generally based in larger towns and the hosting of matches featuring district selections did not lead to the organisation of any clubs in more outlying, rural areas.

With the relatively successful organisation of GAA competitions in the south and south-west by the second half of the 1920s, there was only a handful of soccer teams located in these areas in this decade. Throughout Donegal, many clubs remained at a junior standard rather than making any great progress at provincial or national level in this period due to the casual nature of cup competitions and the failure to maintain a league structure for all of the county. Killybegs Emeralds' continued existence illustrates the peculiarities of the development of sport in a peripheral area and the importance of individuals in the growth of sports clubs in Donegal. Given their south-western location, their efforts to continue were all the more surprising. The perseverance of this soccer club may be partly due to their earlier tradition of success in soccer competitions and, perhaps crucially, the train line into the town meant that clubs could travel for friendly matches in periods when Killybegs was not involved in competition. It also gave them greater licence to travel further afield. They also arranged matches between club selections and were known to take on visiting ships' crews.[111] Ballybofey Wanderers, Killybegs and Ballyshannon met in challenge matches towards the end of the 1920s and early 1930s and were all involved in the 1930 Donegal Cup, won by Killybegs the following year.[112] The Killybegs club was also ambitious enough to enter the Connacht Cup, which they won in 1934.[113] Unlike many areas in the south-west of the county, the town's annual sports organisers were open to soccer and a match against non-Donegal based opposition, such as Strabane, was played annually as part of the Killybegs Regatta and Sports.[114] It is clear, therefore, that Killybegs Emeralds benefited from the input of local men who were eager to organise soccer rather than Gaelic football, and the tradition of soccer in this area was not forgotten.

The south and south-west contrasted greatly with the north of the county. Evidence of military involvement in the promotion of soccer in the Lough Swilly area does not appear to be a satisfactory explanation for the growth of soccer there.[115] While teams from the garrisons at Forts Leenan and Dunree did participate in matches against Donegal clubs in the 1920s and 1930s, they appear to have been the exception rather than the norm.[116] Certainly there is scarce evidence that any army officials were involved in the promotion of organised cup competitions in Inishowen. An increase in soccer competitions in that area from 1925 onwards undoubtedly hindered the spread of Gaelic football and in turn further boosted the development of soccer, but these were initiated by local men. In the period from 1925 until 1934, a total of seventeen separate competitions were organised in Inishowen and, while adding to popular support for soccer there, interest in Gaelic football was greatly diminished by this. Writing in December 1934, one GAA correspondent accurately admitted that 'while Inishowen has come to be recognised as the life spring of hurling in Donegal . . . soccer has stepped in to supply the people their football requirements, and is therefore the recognised football game of the area'.[117]

The Ballyliffin Cup, initially hosted in June 1925 to promote tourism, was the catalyst for a growth in interest in localised cup competitions.[118] This cup had been organised by the local development committee. They had initially arranged a challenge soccer match for medals between two Derry clubs, which attracted 1,500 spectators on 24 August 1924 in the village. This was said to be 'the forerunner to a series of matches' to be arranged 'with a view to popularising this splendid health resort in future'.[119] The following month they also organised a match in aid of the Nazareth Fête, with 'over 400 people' travelling from Derry as part of an excursion for the day. There were 'over a thousand' spectators present at the match.[120] Although a number of matches in the Inishowen Gaelic football league had been played there early in 1924, little interest was shown by local organisers in advancing this development.[121] It is likely that soccer was seen as being more attractive to spectators, with its rules more clearly understood in the Inishowen area. Encouragement to play soccer in this area was provided by the chairman of the Inishowen District Council in 1924, Patrick Quigley, who was also chairman of the Ballyliffin Development Committee. Another member of the Inishowen District Council, James P. McIvor, later donated a cup to the Burnfoot FA in 1927.[122] These men, who had significant local influence, certainly helped the progress of soccer there, as they showed little interest in promoting Gaelic football. Exceptions were rare. At the presentation of the Culdaff Cup in August 1934, County Councillor Pat Lynch advocated that clubs play Gaelic games instead, but in general soccer was the choice of code in these competitions without too much debate.[123]

The 1920s were perhaps a crucial time for the development of sport in the area, and it was soccer that received most support at that time. The poor relationship between GAA delegates in Inishowen and the County Board did little to help the promotion of Gaelic football in the region, and soccer organisers undoubtedly benefited from this hesitancy. Association football competitions were also organised in Buncrana (1926 and 1929) while the Inishowen league was staged in 1927 and 1928.[124] In 1932 and 1933 the Donagh Cup took place and competitions for parish teams were held in Culdaff in 1933 and 1934.[125] Soccer cups were also organised in Newtowncunningham in the early 1930s.[126] In this way, soccer organisers in North Donegal were doing in the 1920s what had been done in England in the late nineteenth century to assist the spread of association football. Although it must be noted that cups in Inishowen were arranged on a more ad hoc basis than the annual county championships and cups offered by the GAA, a complete lack of organisation of Gaelic football competitions in Inishowen after 1924 meant that the playing of soccer had little opposition in the form of Gaelic football matches there.

This growing interest in league and cup competitions in Inishowen had a knock-on effect in other areas in the north of the county and the number of soccer cup competitions increased in North-east Donegal in the period from 1926 to 1934. The organisation of cups afforded regular matches over a number of months and were usually run by cup councils and committees with affiliation fees necessary to gain entry. They also offered the incentive of a cup and medals for the winners while the runners-up were usually guaranteed medals. In a concentrated region west of Lough Swilly, these localised cup competitions became more popular at this time and the GAA struggled to get a foothold there. This organisation of soccer competitions outside Inishowen was dependent on a network of clubs, all relatively close to one another, such as Kilmacrennan, Rathmullan, Cranford, Kerrykeel, Loughkeel Celtic, Ramelton Ramblers and

Milford Celtic. Significantly, local organisers appear to have lacked sufficient interest in Gaelic football to make the changeover. Given the culture of soccer in this area, the re-organisation of the County Board in 1919 had little impact. There was no major organinsation of GAA clubs in these areas, unlike in regions such as East Donegal, the south and south-west in these early years of the new County Board. An attempt in July 1923, which saw visits planned to Milford and Rathmullan as part as a move to organise Gaelic games in the north-west, gained little long-term support.[127] Traditional soccer competitions, held over one or two days, were unaffected. A Kerrykeel tournament that same month had attracted eleven local soccer clubs while association football was also played at the Cranford Sports in August of that year.[128]

A strong tradition of soccer existed in Kerrykeel and Cranford by the 1920s and the first County Donegal FA in 1894 had drawn on a number of clubs from this north-east area. Cup competitions were hosted by Rathmullan in 1926 and 1927.[129] The revival of competitive soccer in this area brought a renewed rivalry and local pride in these competitions. One writer felt that with the organisation of the Rathmullan (Swilly) Cup in July 1926, 'not since the days of the old Donegal Shield has there been such keen rivalry amongst local teams . . . the committee were very lucky in securing for the season the field in which the final for the Donegal Shield was played, and I am sure a good many of the grandfathers will remember it'.[130] As Russell has stated in his study of soccer and rugby in Lancashire and Yorkshire in the late nineteenth century, 'through cup achievements, sports were embedded in local tradition'.[131] He has also noted how the success of clubs in areas where local rivalries were strong could lead to a strengthening in the permanency of that sport, with neighbouring teams increasing their efforts to match the success of their rivals.[132]

These competitions generally attracted good support from clubs in this North-east Donegal district. A five-a-side competition organised by Portsalon in May 1932 brought together eighteen clubs while the Milford Cup attracted sixteen clubs later that year.[133] Cup competitions were generally popular in their localities, and reports, although perhaps estimates, give some illustration of the level of support for them. The Kerrykeel Cup final between Cranford and Kerrykeel in October 1932 and the Milford Cup final between Creeslough and Cranford United in 1933 both drew crowds of around 1,000 spectators.[134] A similar attendance figure was noted at the Diamond Cup final of 1934, between the same clubs, with a special bus run from Creeslough to Milford.[135] The replay was held before 'one of the largest gatherings at a game seen in the locality'.[136] These games were generally well received locally. In September 1932 it was reported that the Milford Cup was being supported by local residents and merchants, who had 'promised the committee in charge of the soccer cup their support, financially and otherwise'.[137] The following month, the club's victory over Newtowncunningham in a challenge game for a silver cup 'was the cause of much jubilation amongst the townspeople' and a victory dance was held that evening.[138]

Despite the interest generated by these relatively localised competitions, only one soccer tournament was arranged to amalgamate the north and south of the county. Organising the entire county was to prove impossible. Unlike the GAA, soccer in Donegal lacked a central promoter or group of men willing to take on the responsibility of arranging an administrative structure for all the clubs in the county, until 1930. In April of that year, the County Donegal Perpetual Cup was organised by Ballybofey Wanderers. Its initiation meant that, technically, clubs isolated from the heart of soccer activity – such as Killybegs Emeralds and Ballyshannon – could compete with North Donegal-based clubs. However, this idea was not embraced by the majority of clubs and therefore the name of the trophy was somewhat misleading. As can be seen in Appendix 14, there were at least forty-two teams in the county that year. Only ten clubs participated in the cup's inaugural year and the county was divided into two divisions, with the league winners in each area meeting in the final. Evidently distance, transport and lack of enthusiasm were still a problem, as there were no clubs affiliated from Inishowen, West Donegal or the north-west of the county, with the exception of Creeslough Stars.[139]

The development of the cup was hindered by the failure of clubs to put individual problems behind them and work together. The following year five clubs had withdrawn with only two new participants, Loughkeel Celtic and Letterkenny Mental Hospital, affiliating along with the initial teams. The withdrawal of Milford Celtic, one of the county's leading soccer clubs, was certainly a blow.[140] This meant that only seven clubs out of the overall total of sixty-two teams in the county that year registered for the competition. Even if factors such as expense and the awkwardness of travel are taken into account, this is still a poor return. By the beginning of May it was noted that 'the withdrawal of local soccer teams from the northern section of the Donegal cup competition had proved detrimental' to the progress of the Loughkeel Celtic team 'in consequence of the poor standard of play shown in friendly games as compared with league contests'.[141] The cup competition did not take place in 1932. This illustrates a lack of the commitment which was necessary for the development of an overall county structure but would also indicate problems with travel and finance. It also highlights the superior administrative structure (though not immune to these difficulties) which the GAA had in place at the time. Competitive soccer in Donegal struggled to develop without regular league and cup competitions and many clubs, such as those in the west of the county, failed to think in terms of developing relationships with those in other areas, such as the north-east.

It was in the mid-1920s that competitive soccer in the north of the county began to receive more attention in the press and from clubs in Derry and, in turn, became more efficiently organised. The organisation of adequate transport was fundamental to this development. The rail network was a significant factor in the organisation of the Ballyliffin Cup in 1925–27 and again in 1931 and 1932. In August 1931 it was recorded that 'the two trains from Derry, Bridge End, Buncrana and Clonmany brought over three hundred persons, and a great number travelled from Carndonagh', to witness the two matches held on the first Sunday of the month.[142] Travel to this seaside village in the north-east of the Inishowen peninsula was therefore more convenient than that offered to areas in Donegal that lacked a railway line or tourist attractions. Timetables were published in the press after favourable rates had been secured with the manager of the Londonderry and Lough Swilly Railway. The cup committee offered competing teams free journeys in May 1932 as an incentive to participate.[143] This meant that Derry clubs of a higher standard could compete and the vast majority of competitions held in Inishowen were open to Derry as well as Donegal clubs, which added greatly to the standard of play and interest in soccer in this region. At a Ballyliffin Development committee meeting in June 1927, vice-president Patrick Quigley expressed his thanks to the Derry and District Football Association for their input 'as it raised the Ballyliffin Summer league to a status above any of its rivals'.[144] Donegal clubs such as Buncrana Celtic were also supported off the playing field and in October 1931 their dance attracted a large crowd from Derry.[145] The influence of Derry clubs in the development of competitive soccer could also be seen, to a lesser extent, in areas outside of Inishowen. Eleven competitions were held in the north-east of the county, excluding the Inishowen peninsula, between 1926 and 1934. The Swilly, Portsalon and Mitchell cups and the Lifford and District League all drew outside entries.[146] Donegal clubs generally managed to hold their own against these external clubs and their participation undoubtedly helped the development of soccer in these areas.

Soccer, rather than Gaelic football, also appealed to visitors, such as those from Scotland. The visits of junior teams from Scotland and of professionals such as Neil Mochan, Tommy Gallagher and Bobby Bogan to the north-west was fundamental to the popularity of the code in Donegal.[147] In England after the First World War, a shift occurred in attitudes to bathing and outdoor activities and the provision of a park for sports and recreation was an important development in Blackpool in 1926.[148] The presence of Scottish holidaymakers in the 1920s and 1930s did not go unnoticed by the organisers of the Ballyliffin Cup in their match previews and reports.[149] A number of Donegal clubs were able to attract interest from these tourists. Soccer matches, which would have been more familiar and more understandable to these visitors than those under GAA rules, were organised to accommodate Scottish players, while connections with those involved with Scottish clubs were at times mentioned to attract interest in previews. The Swilly Cup committee in 1926 was said to contain ex-Glasgow Celtic player Patsy Gallagher, who was born in a Donegal workhouse, and it was he who kicked off the Kerrykeel versus Cranford first-round match.[150] Buncrana Celtic were assisted by English and Scottish first division players on holiday in the town in their match against Fulton Rovers in 1928.[151] Milford Celtic were beaten by a team made up of Scottish drifters in May 1930 while a Scottish selection won the Ramelton Ramblers' five-a-side competition in July 1931.[152] Occasionally these visitors also became patrons; Joseph Lyons of Glasgow donated a set of medals for a match between Carndonagh United and Oakwood in November 1931.[153]

While these visits may have only been of a seasonal nature, they did help keep the game going and prolonged the tradition of soccer in a number of areas. One newspaper claimed in July 1929, perhaps rather fancifully, that 10,000 Scotch visitors arrived in Derry city over the course of a week and 'most of these went to all parts of the north-west', while a Scottish Fair was also held in Letterkenny that month.[154] This annual influx of Scottish visitors appears to have generally been to the north of the county and there is no evidence that the south of Donegal experienced this. This can be explained by the fact that traditional, seasonal migration to Scotland generally did not take place from this area and Scottish links were more prominent in the north and west of the county as a result of this earlier tradition. This adds greatly to R.V. Comerford's contention that 'in Donegal, strong links with Scotland meant that soccer was a widely popular sport'.[155]

The nature of the spread and reach of the Derry city hinterland was of huge significance in heightening interest in soccer in Inishowen and the north-east. The foundation of the professional club Derry City FC in 1928 added to this interest.[156] The Derry and District FA and the North-west FA were also firmly established by the end of this decade and this senior club attracted much attention from those in Inishowen and North-west Donegal in their Irish League matches. They were also able to secure enticing fixtures against British opponents such as Manchester City, Corinthians and Motherwell.[157] Some local talent in the north-east were also motivated by the prospect of securing a trial with the Derry club and a career in professional soccer. Those who did make the first team, such as Moville goalkeeper Packie Mahon in 1931, drew supporters who travelled from his home town.[158] One Milford Celtic correspondent stated that same year that 'the opportunities presented to youth where genius is apparent by the recent offer of Derry City to give local talent a try are manifold'.[159] The appeal of Derry City was a source of concern to some Donegal GAA writers. This relatively nearby attraction, which held a higher standard of soccer than that offered locally, was noted by one GAA writer in 1933 who felt that too much interest was being shown by 'large numbers of East Donegal people, some of them, I am sorry to say, Gaels'.[160] Another stated the following year that 'here in the east, the maiden city, and its horde of soccer fans, is the attraction'.[161] It was therefore in the late 1920s and early 1930s that the popularity of soccer was really cemented in the north-east and in Inishowen.

Variations in attitudes to the playing of Gaelic football and soccer within towns and villages in Donegal were also caused because certain areas were socially dislocated and struggled to unite under the banner of the GAA, or indeed to form an overall governing body for soccer in the county, due to a number of cultural and geographical factors. However, it must be added that in the 1920s, GAA organisers were able to unite the county more effectively than their soccer counterparts and this is reflected in their consistently organised, annual competitions. The impact of Derry city on Inishowen has been assessed in Chapter 1 and as noted, the Derryveagh and Blue Stack mountains also created dividing lines between the north-east and the south-west and south. East Donegal, in particular the towns of Letterkenny, Ballybofey and Lifford, lie in the Laggan Valley area, where customs and traditions associated with unionist East Ulster were stronger. This partially accounts for interest in soccer in these areas, although it appears that many players and administrators were Roman Catholic and Protestant influence was probably not as overtly strong in soccer clubs in Donegal as it may have been in some areas within Northern Ireland.

Given the majority Roman Catholic population in the county this is perhaps not surprising and there is little evidence that sectarianism led to the organisation of soccer clubs with strict religious divides in the county. It is clear that officials involved in the soccer clubs of Letterkenny, Ballybofey and Lifford in the late 1920s and early 1930s were overwhelmingly Roman Catholic.[162] Further north, Roman Catholic officials were also involved in other prominent Donegal soccer clubs, such as Loughkeel Celtic in 1931 and Milford Celtic the following year.[163] Certainly, the East Donegal area differed culturally from the south and south-west of the county, where the strength of Gaelic football lay by the end of the 1920s.

Another area which differed culturally from the south and south-west was along the west coast, where links with Scotland were stronger. There is no doubt that soccer remained very popular there and a number of references in the press highlight this. As previously mentioned, returning migrants from Scotland had been influential in the development of clubs and there is evidence that this interest continued well into the 1920s.[164] Newspaper references to the presence of seven teams in the area in 1927 illustrate the continued popularity of soccer over Gaelic football at this point but these appear again to have been friendly matches.[165] However, the number of Gaelic football teams in the area in this decade was low and this problem was discussed on a number of occasions at meetings of the Ulster Council and Donegal County Board. At a meeting of the Ulster GAA Council in Belfast in 1929, the difficulties of spreading Gaelic games into the west coast of Donegal were discussed. It was stated that 'people in the Irish-speaking districts went across to Scotland and came back with their heads full of soccer. Down in the islands off the Donegal coast, where there was very little communication with the mainland, they played nothing but soccer.'[166] By 1932, a change of sorts from soccer to Gaelic football was underway with clubs in operation in Falcarragh, Gweedore and Dungloe.[167] Local seven-a-sides were being held under Gaelic football rules, such as that in Keadue in July 1934.[168] A junior GAA club was reorganised in Dunfanaghy in October 1933 with former soccer player Dr Coll named president.[169] Some areas were hard to change, however. By the early 1930s soccer was well established in Creeslough and the hosting of the 1933 Gaelic football minor county final there in November did not attract sufficient interest for a club to be created, as promoted in the press.[170] It seems apparent that in many small villages, with a low population and only a small number of men controlling the organisation of sport, getting them to change their attitude and transfer to a different code was a difficult process, particularly after the nationalist fervour of the early 1920s had died down.

At a national level, encouragement of soccer in Donegal was poor and the GAA probably benefited from this in the 1920s, despite suffering from its own problems. The majority of clubs and organising committees in Donegal appear to have taken on the responsibility of arranging cup competitions and exhibitions and the general promotion of soccer without much help from either the Irish Football Association or the Football Association of Ireland for much of the period covered in this chapter. While clubs competing in the County Donegal FA in the 1890s were affiliated to the IFA from 1894 to 1898, there is little in their records to suggest that any major attempt was made to promote the game in the county by the latter organisation after this decline.[171] The FAI was formed in

Dublin on 2 September 1921 after relations between a number of Dublin clubs and the IFA in Belfast deteriorated; it was renamed the Football Association of the Irish Free State (FAIFS) in September 1923.[172] Donegal's geographical position meant that it did not fit into any of the areas under its regional Football Associations. This was because the FAI did not, at least initially, have a committee for Ulster clubs located in the Free State. By March 1922 there were 'upwards of two hundred affiliated clubs' in the FAI with regional bodies consisting of the Leinster Football Association, the Belfast and District Football Association, the Athlone and District Football Association and the Munster Football Association.[173]

While Donegal's GAA clubs of course remained within the area governed by the Ulster Council, and nationally the Central Council of the GAA (after 1922), the county's soccer teams were still rather isolated and a number of these in the north-east of the county continued to enter competitions provided by the Derry and District FA such as St Mary's, Carndonagh and Buncrana Celtic in 1929.[174] The views of the Free State's soccer organisation on the relationship between Donegal's soccer clubs and those in Northern Ireland are unclear. As previously noted, matches between Donegal clubs and those in Derry and Tyrone were quite common but drew little condemnation from either the FAIFS or the IFA, an indication of the lack of attention given to soccer in Donegal from these governing bodies.

An enthusiasm for participation in national competitions was lacking amongst Donegal soccer clubs for much of the 1920s. There is little evidence that any of these affiliated to the FAIFS, until at least 1928, with the entry of Ballybofey Wanderers and Ballyshannon in the Free State Junior Cup at the end of that year. These teams were grouped with Sligo as the competition was initially regionalised to limit travelling expenses.[175] In the period from 1929 until 1934 only a small number of Donegal clubs entered, with Buncrana Rangers, Creeslough, Lifford, Killybegs and Milford Celtic also involved.[176] Given that affiliation fees, travel expenses and referees' expenses all had to be paid, these matches would have been costly for these clubs without proper enclosures. It is difficult to establish exactly how much support the FAIFS gave to Donegal clubs, financially and in the promotion of the game. What is clear is that clubs needed to affiliate in order to get any financial aid.[177]

This was understandable and organising committees were meeting in Dublin to discuss the promotion of soccer throughout the country by at least November 1928. A reference in that month's minutes was the only mention of developing the game in Donegal found in the FAI's archives throughout this period. It indicates that the committee was awaiting 'replies before taking any step' towards the game in Donegal. Without previous or further reference to this, it is difficult to establish which areas were under consideration or who had been contacted. While it does show that efforts were being made at this stage and communications were taking place, this was rather late in comparison to the efforts made in Leinster and further south.[178] This lack of correspondence goes some way to prove that the organisation of soccer in Donegal was neglected and soccer clubs in the county were very much left isolated. Whereas the GAA had provincial structures where delegates from county boards met on a monthly basis to discuss progress and rectify problems, the organisation of soccer nationally appears to differ in that attempts to organise areas seem to have been initiated through correspondence from regional soccer administrators.

Provincial organisations were certainly in place, but county structures are more difficult to trace. Developmental patterns appear rather scattered as not every county had a league committee in operation. Local soccer councils did meet of course, but these meetings and competitions lacked the fixed and generally consistent nature of those held by the GAA in the 1920s and 1930s. An examination of correspondence indicates that the FAIFS' organising committee appeared to focus on urban areas in their attempts to promote the game and relied on local organisers to report on the state of clubs and competitions. Correspondence with organisers in Limerick, Kilkenny, Athlone, Monaghan, Mullingar, Wexford and Kildare in 1932 and 1933 illustrate attempts to monitor district leagues and assess progress.[179] This also illustrates the urban-based nature of soccer clubs as opposed to the rural strength of the GAA. However, like the GAA, the FAIFS provided assistance with cups and medals and the organisation of exhibition matches and leagues.

Finance was clearly a problem for both associations. FAIFS Secretary, J.A. Ryder felt in 1932 that 'the decision of the government to impose a tax on the game . . . must seriously hamper junior clubs, all of which have the utmost difficulty in finding funds to meet their commitments'.[180] This appears to be an accurate summary of the financial state of many soccer teams. In November 1932 £15 was granted 'to defray the cost of medals to the winners of the Connaught Cup in past seasons'.[181] Financial assistance was also given to clubs needing help with rental of grounds, which appears to have been a problem for a number of clubs; Kilkenny FC's application for a loan of £5 was passed in February 1933, 'towards payment of outstanding ground rent'.[182] While exhibition matches such as those in Limerick and Monaghan in 1932 and 1933 were encouraged, there is little evidence of any attempts to organise counter attractions to Gaelic games.[183] Attempts to promote soccer in Donegal saw exhibition matches against Derry and Fermanagh selections in 1926 and a Sligo selection in 1928, but these were organised locally.[184] Unlike the reports of the Donegal County Board and Ulster Council meetings, where the conflict with soccer was openly discussed, the minutes of committee meetings contain little of the views of soccer officials on the GAA. Disappointment was expressed in the FAIFS secretary's report of 1932 that the GAA was deemed exempt from government tax while soccer was not given this concession.[185] However, a scarcity of references to Gaelic games in their archives suggests that soccer officials did not worry about rival attractions, in contrast to those involved in organising the GAA.

The social background of Donegal's soccer players and administrators

As can be seen in Table 6.1, a total of 286 soccer players named in the local press were positively identified from the period 1891 to 1915.[186] The majority of soccer players identified were found to be from the industrial category (44 per cent). Tom Hunt has concluded from his study of seventy-five participants in soccer in Westmeath between 1900 and 1904 that urban teams were generally made up of skilled workers such as tradesmen, shop assistants and clerks or 'social class c' as he has termed it. This class made up 67 per cent of all players in Westmeath. The majority of involvement from this section of society correlates with Tranter's study of soccer players in Central Scotland and Ian Nannestead's work on Lincolnshire.[187]

The overwhelming involvement of these workers was also particularly the case in some towns in County Donegal. Association football clubs in Ardara, Killybegs and Donegal town in the opening decades of the twentieth century were generally made up of those working and living in their respective towns. For example, the Donegal Celtic team which won the Woods Cup in 1911 consisted mainly of those categorised as part of the industrial sector. It contained a railway shunter, a draper's assistant, a general labourer, two boot and shoemakers, a message boy, a shop assistant, a merchant, a miller, a solicitor's general clerk and a farm worker. Only 30 per cent of soccer players were found to be working in the agricultural sector and 11 per cent were in the professional category. Just over 8 per cent were from the commercial sector, with less than 4 per cent of the overall total categorised as belonging to the indefinite and non-productive classes, while the figure for the domestic class was also relatively low (3 per cent).

TABLE 6.1
Occupational categories of soccer players in County Donegal, 1891–1915

Category	*Number of players*	*% of total*
1: Professional	32	11.19
2: Domestic	8	2.80
3: Commercial	23	8.04
4: Agricultural	85	29.72
5: Industrial	127	44.41
6: Indefinite and non-productive	11	3.84
Total	286	100

SOURCES: *DJ, DP and DN, DV, DI* (1891–1915) and 'Census of Ireland 1901 and 1911; retrieved from http://www.census.nationalarchives.ie/ [Accessed 28 September 2012]

Table 6.2 illustrates the age groups of those playing association football in Donegal between 1891 and 1915. The majority of soccer players in Donegal (36 per cent) were drawn from the 16–20 age category and the average age of a soccer player in Donegal was found to be 23.01 years. Hunt has shown in his study of those playing in Westmeath that the average age of a soccer player was 22.6 years and therefore Donegal players were slightly older. This figure was also higher than the average age of professional footballers analysed by Neal Garnham, which was 22.7 years.[188]

TABLE 6.2

Ages of soccer players in County Donegal, 1891–1915

Age	*Number of players*	*% of total*
15 and under	15	5.24
16–20	104	36.36
21–25	75	26.22
26–30	42	14.69
31–35	16	5.59
36–40	9	3.14
41–45	8	2.80
46–50	5	1.75
Unknown	12	4.20
Total	286	100

SOURCES: *DJ, DP and DN, DV, DI* (1891–1915) and 'Census of Ireland 1901 and 1911; retrieved from http://www.census.nationalarchives.ie/ [Accessed 28 September 2012]

Garnham has stated that 'with regard to religion, association football seems to have drawn a mixed following'.[189] He has looked briefly at the role of Catholic educational establishments and the clergy in the spread of soccer in Dublin and Derry in the late nineteenth century and has shown that the majority of schools involved in the Irish Football Association's Schools' Cup in 1883 were Protestant institutions.[190] His analysis of professional footballers in Belfast at the beginning of the twentieth century has shown that the majority (34 per cent) were Presbyterian with Episcopalian Protestants making up 30 per cent while Roman Catholics (24 per cent) were also significantly represented. Methodists formed 6 per cent of the overall total along with other unnamed denominations (6 per cent).[191] The relationship between players, their teams and the local communities was 'often a distinct one in terms of religion' and 'professional footballers reflected the society from which they came, and which they eventually came to represent'.[192] By

1912, Linfield and Belfast Celtic were being seen in the English media as Protestant and Catholic teams respectively.[193]

TABLE 6.3
Religious denominations of soccer players in County Donegal, 1891–1915

Religious denomination	*Number of players*	*% of total*
Roman Catholic	244	85
Church of Ireland	9	3
Presbyterian	16	6
Reformed Presbyterian	4	1
Episcopalian	6	2
Church of England	1	0.35
Old Church of Ireland	8	0.35
Unknown	52	2
Total	286	100

SOURCES: *DJ, DP and DN, DV, DI* (1891–1915) and 'Census of Ireland 1901 and 1911; retrieved from http://www.census.nationalarchives.ie/ [Accessed 28 September 2012]

Table 6.3 illustrates the religious denominations of those playing soccer in Donegal between 1891 and 1915. Roman Catholics accounted for 85 per cent of soccer players. Protestants formed a total of 13 per cent, while 2 per cent of the overall total was unidentified. This differed from Westmeath where Hunt found that all seventy-five players sampled were Roman Catholics, as 'members of the Church of Ireland were of a higher social status and found sporting fulfilment in the more elitist recreational activities such as lawn tennis, croquet and golf'.[194] This was not the case in Donegal, where these sports failed to gain any widespread support at this time. There is no evidence that any Donegal soccer teams operated on a policy of exclusion of players on the grounds of religion and most clubs and teams seem to have been run on a cross-community basis, although in areas such as Ardara and Killybegs, which were predominantly Roman Catholic, there is little evidence that players from other religious denominations became involved. In contrast, clubs such as Ballyshannon Swifts were at times made up of a mix of religious denominations, but there is nothing in the press to suggest that any clubs came into conflict because of this or that any players were discriminated against. It also illustrates that many Catholics were keen to play soccer and did not see it as a British game or as something that undermined their nationality.

The dominant role of the industrial class in soccer in Donegal differed from the findings on those playing Gaelic games between 1905 and 1907, where the majority were employed in the agricultural sector. In contrast, fewer GAA players were employed in industrial work, while lesser numbers of soccer players were found to be working in the agricultural sector. This may be a result of the rural location of a number of GAA clubs, as opposed to the existence of many soccer clubs in urban areas. Soccer also attracted the interest of more professional men than Gaelic games in Donegal, while there was more involvement of those from the commercial classes in Gaelic football and camán/hurling than in soccer. The degree of involvement of those in the domestic categories was similar, with soccer attracting slightly more from this sector. Soccer appears to have attracted fewer students than Gaelic games in Donegal, as figures for those categorised in the indefinite and non-productive class were higher in the GAA data assessed. The majority of soccer players in Donegal were drawn from a younger age category (16–20 years old) than Gaelic games, where most players came from the 21–25 age category. The average age of a soccer player was slightly younger than those playing Gaelic games. Figures for the marital status of soccer players were quite similar to those of GAA players with 81 per cent of association football players falling into the single category.

Given the GAA's nationalist ethos, it was to be expected that there would be more involvement of non-Roman Catholics in association football. As shown, while 97 per cent of Gaelic players identified in the county were Catholics, only 85 per cent of soccer players came from this denomination. This divergence in involvement may therefore have strengthened soccer's popularity in the county as non-Catholic attitudes to Gaelic games clearly varied, with other religious denominations more likely to take part in soccer.

In examining the social backgrounds of those involved in the 1894 Athlone Association Football Club, Hunt noted the participation of a large number of those 'associated with the town's business community'.[195] Donegal's urban clubs appear to have been no different in this respect. Those responsible for organising the Woods Cup in Ballyshannon in 1909 were all based in the town and included a solicitor's general clerk, a coach maker, a spirit merchant, a gas works owner and a writing clerk. An examination of the local press for information on those with some involvement in the running of soccer clubs and competitions in Donegal between 1891 and 1915 resulted in the positive identification of 195 men for the purpose of this study.[196] The majority of involvement came from those in the industrial category (34 per cent), while 29 per cent of soccer organisers were identified as professionals. Those involved in the agricultural sector failed to play a major role in the organisation of soccer in Donegal with only 19 per cent coming from this category, while involvement of the commercial category was found to be smaller (14 per cent). Unsurprisingly, the organisational influence of those in the domestic class and students was minimal, with less than 4 per cent of these classes involved as organisers.

TABLE 6.4

Occupational categories of soccer administrators in County Donegal, 1891–1915

Category	*Number of administrators*	*% of total*
1: Professional	56	29
2: Domestic	3	2
3: Commercial	28	14
4: Agricultural	37	19
5: Industrial	67	34
6: Indefinite and non-productive	4	2
Total	195	100

SOURCES: *DJ, DP and DN, DV, DI* (1891–1915) and 'Census of Ireland 1901 and 1911; retrieved from http://www.census.nationalarchives.ie/ [Accessed 28 September 2012]

The organisers of soccer in Donegal differed from those in Gaelic games, in that the majority of involvement came from the industrial category as opposed to the professional category. This contrast can be partially explained by a lack of involvement in soccer from the clergy and national school teachers. Of those organising the GAA in Donegal between 1905 and 1907, 12 per cent were clergy of the Roman Catholic Church, while only 1 per cent of those involved as club presidents, vice-presidents, secretaries, treasurers, captains, vice-captains and delegates of soccer clubs were found to be members of the clergy. Similarly, national school teachers' involvement in Gaelic games was greater than in soccer in the periods compared here. Only 5 per cent of soccer administrators were registered as teachers while 14 per cent of the GAA administrators had experience of national school teaching. In contrast, some well-to-do members of society, such as doctors, did not get involved in the GAA in the 1905–07 period. The County Donegal FA could boast of the involvement of professional individuals such as doctors Patterson, Carre, McFadden and Loughnan at various times during the 1890s; there is no evidence that any medical doctors became involved in the GAA as organisers between 1905 and 1907.

Conclusion

A key finding in this chapter has been that nationalism in Donegal was less of a factor in the decision to take up Gaelic football, rather than continue with soccer, than has previously been assumed on the basis of national studies. Of critical importance in the spread of sport in Donegal was the ability to organise competitive structures and publicise these in the local press. The impact of physical geography and cultural boundaries on the development of sport has also been illustrated. Outside influences were fundamental to the choice of codes in the north-east while tradition also played a part in the decision to continue with association football. While transfer of personnel and parish identity were key factors in the decision to adhere to Gaelic football, there were clear geographical boundaries that the GAA was unable to penetrate. Soccer showed a resilience in these regions, illustrating the importance of how, in many cases, the development of sport is affected by which sport is first introduced into society. The fluidity of sporting choice must also be noted and in a number of areas, both codes were played. This was particularly notable in the east of the county where population levels were higher in such towns as Letterkenny and Ballybofey than in more rural villages such as Ardara. The lack of sporting unity and the significance of individual organisers in the development of sport has again been highlighted as, in the case of soccer, Donegal continued to be ignored by central administrative agencies. Soccer in Donegal was generally organised by those involved in the industrial sector while the majority of players were also categorised as coming from this class.

7

THE CONFLICT BETWEEN THE GAA AND ASSOCIATION FOOTBALL IN DONEGAL, 1905–1935

Introduction

There is no evidence that any of the county's first Gaelic football teams were in conflict with association football clubs, but in 1905 the GAA in Donegal certainly became more politicised. The presence of the soccer code undoubtedly affected interest levels in Gaelic football, although Donegal was not unique in this respect provincially. As Neal Garnham has noted, 'by 1905 in some areas of the province [Ulster], association football provided an entrenched opposition to a resurgent and rejuvenated GAA'.[1] In addition, the GAA's slow development in Ulster meant that by 1905 soccer was more firmly established there.[2] Certainly this was the case in Donegal at this point. It was the organisation of Gaelic games, and in particular Gaelic football, that was to first challenge soccer as the county's most popular game and this conflict was to divide public opinion, generally amongst those who claimed that soccer was a foreign sport and that Irish pastimes and games should be promoted, and those who felt that there was no reason why they should not participate in or attend association football matches. The presence of the GAA's ban on 'foreign games' and its nationalist ethos was instrumental in portraying soccer as a British and unionist game, and also led to its marginalisation throughout Ireland.[3]

The origins of the conflict and the role of the press

Although earlier bans on athletes and RIC men had been lifted, at the GAA's annual convention in January 1905, a motion was passed that those playing soccer, hockey, cricket, rugby 'or any imported games' would be banned from the organisation for two years 'from the date of playing such games', beginning on 1 February of that year.[4] According to Paul Rouse, 'initially, the Ban was introduced for organisational and administrative purposes; it later acquired a political dimension; but it was only in the decades after independence that it attained extreme ideological importance'.[5] Opinion was divided between those who thought it was a crucial part of the GAA's identity and history, and others who felt that the only thing it resulted in was the encouragement of hypocritical and deceitful behaviour by members of the organisation itself.[6] Mike Cronin has stated that the Ban was implemented to develop the GAA into a successful organisation and came as a result of the political spirit in Ireland at that time, but it was not issued as a manifesto.[7] As the twentieth century wore on, there were many who felt that it was becoming increasingly unnecessary, and many who ignored it, as Gaelic games became more firmly established within Irish society, although it was not removed from the GAA's constitution until 1971.[8]

It is clear that supporters of the GAA in Donegal, particularly in the 1920s and 1930s, were eager to stress a nationalist ideology and dedication to the cause while knowing that those interested in organising soccer could not claim this sense of devotion. While some contemporary Donegal soccer clubs expressed their nationalism through their naming policies, taking on titles such as Celtic, Harps, Hibernians and Shamrocks, they made few other efforts to illustrate their patriotism.[9] Unlike the founders of the GAA, which was clearly established to preserve what its organisers saw as being Ireland's national games and culture, soccer administrators in Ireland made no claims to being anything other than a sporting body. Although soccer was initially seen as a non-political game, by the early twentieth century it was being viewed within some sections of Irish society as having British connotations and a strong linkage with the military.[10] Problems also included a struggle between the Belfast-based IFA and the Football Association of Ireland for control of the sport. Soccer in the Free State did not receive enough support from the Catholic Church or the new government (after 1922), being viewed as a foreign game. The failure to take on a professional structure also hindered its development.[11] Added to this, the FAIFS struggled to create a functioning identity for itself at international level.

Although the FAIFS became recognised by FIFA in August 1923, the 'Home Nations' refused to acknowledge its status and it was not until 1946 that the Free State team played England. Therefore, initially, club friendlies were played against French opposition to spread interest and the first international fixture organised by the FAIFS was not played until 1926, against Italy.[12] The poor standard of the domestic game and the lack of success of the Free State and subsequent Republic of Ireland teams until the late 1980s and 1990s meant that it was difficult for Irish people to embrace the game before such success arrived.[13] This meant that Gaelic games remained the most popular sport in the twenty-six counties for much of the twentieth century although, as noted, in some areas (such as parts of north Donegal) soccer did manage to hold its own and the GAA struggled to penetrate these regions.

The foundation of the first Donegal GAA County Board in October 1905 came as part of the nationwide Gaelic Revival at the beginning of the twentieth century. It was also a reaction to the popularity of soccer in the county, the absence of an administrative structure to promote the playing of Gaelic games, and indeed the lack of interest in hurling and Gaelic football in most areas in Donegal. The proposal to run the Evans Cup for association football in Ardara in January of that year was met with strong opposition from GAA County Board founder Seumas MacManus. He felt that the competition should be played under the rules of Gaelic football as he saw association football as a 'foreign' sport and expressed his discontent in a series of letters published in the local press. Prior to this, the playing of association football within Donegal society was unchallenged and MacManus' call to have soccer clubs replaced by those of the GAA appears to be a unique attempt within Irish society at this time.

With the decline of Gaelic games in Donegal by 1908, soccer was again relatively unhindered until the County Board was reorganised in 1919. It was not until the 1920s that the GAA began to gain a foothold within Donegal. However, this was a difficult struggle for Donegal's GAA organisers and while they benefited from the lack of competitive soccer in the county in the first half of this decade, the growth in the number of soccer competitions organised in the years after 1925 further hampered the spread of Gaelic games. This was not well received by some GAA supporters.

The conflict between organisers of these codes in Donegal was most publicly expressed through the local press. At times both soccer and GAA organisers were in dispute over the perceived origins of Gaelic games and soccer. Many GAA supporters, while claiming that Gaelic games were Irish sports which had patriotic ties, felt that involvement in soccer was an illustration of West Britonism. Throughout the 1920s, GAA members continually expressed pride in, and at times appear to have been preoccupied with, their organisation's perceived struggle against those organising soccer in Donegal. At the Donegal GAA Convention in January 1929, chairman Seán Ó Caiside claimed that 'a most determined effort had been made during the past twelve months to torpedo the Gaelic movement in Donegal'.[14] This was a clear reference to the organisation of soccer and as will be seen, reflected the continuous rhetoric of those within the County Board with regard to their struggle to gain a monopoly on sport in the county.

Soccer organisers generally took on a more pacifist approach against this attitude but occasionally some felt compelled to defend their efforts. In a letter to the editor of the *Derry Journal* published in October 1928, Henry McGowan, the secretary of Ballybofey Wanderers AFC, claimed that 'for the past year the people who control the GAA in Donegal have been carrying on a campaign of abuse against those interested in Association football in this county'.[15] There can be no doubt that a campaign of this nature was underway at that time. There is evidence that County Board members were directly involved in the writing of GAA news, particularly in the 1920s and 1930s. GAA reporters such as John Tuohy of Dungloe, writing as 'Banner County', and Brother Cassin, under the penname of 'Assaroe', were later identified.[16] One County Board delegate, in a letter to Seán Ó Caiside in 1933, illustrated his views on using propaganda when he wrote: 'that's a great idea about the journalism . . . Yes I'm powerful with the pen. Feel like Kickham or Davis when I start on the GAA spirit stunt.'[17] The fact that GAA columns were generally written using pennames perhaps made it easier for these writers to criticise, given the rural nature of Donegal and its small population where those involved in sport tended to be well known locally. This fact did not go unnoticed by McGowan, who called on those criticising soccer to reveal themselves.[18]

In examining the conflict between rugby and soccer organisers in Northern England in the late nineteenth century, Tony Collins has noted the support given by some rugby union officials to soccer and the transferral of teams such as Manningham to the latter game, in addition to growing popular support for association football, as having a demoralising effect on rugby in the area in the late nineteenth and early twentieth centuries. The formation of the Northern Rugby League in 1901 was intended to prevent the spread of soccer, although this competition did not have any great success.[19] In addition to earlier measures undertaken by the GAA to counteract the spread of soccer, reports of GAA meetings in the 1920s illustrate an aggressive attitude towards the playing of soccer in Donegal.[20] Counteracting 'foreign games' through the organisation of clashing fixtures had in fact been recommended by the Central Council of the GAA at a special meeting on 17 August 1924 in Dublin, along with the appointing of vigilance committees to report members involved in banned sports.[21] As will be seen later, crossover from GAA to soccer was a big problem for GAA organisers. Provincially, the Ulster Council was also less than happy with having to compete with association football. At a reorganisation meeting in Clones on 22 October 1921, the founding of the FAI did not go unnoticed. It was moved 'that counties are hereby warned against countenancing any activity of the Football Association of Ireland'. This was felt necessary as the FAI was deemed to be 'as much antagonistic to [the] GAA if not more so than [the] IFA'.[22]

Nationally, the playing of soccer was defended in newspapers such as *Football Sports Weekly*, which ran for a brief period in the 1920s, while the *Gaelic Athlete* in turn was eager to attack association football while promoting Gaelic games. Initially the greater part of GAA coverage in Donegal was limited to sporadic match reports with no fixed sports page or columns (an exception being the *Derry People and Donegal News* front-page column in 1905), but by the 1920s an increase in GAA activity in the county meant that fixed columns composed by GAA writers began to appear more regularly in the local press. Although the GAA's hierarchy were said to be unhappy with the amount of coverage given at national level, until a change took place in the early 1930s with the publication of *The Irish Press*, Gaelic games in Donegal appear to have been reasonably well covered at a local level.[23] There were five local newspapers circulating in Donegal in 1905 and it was through the medium of the press that arguments for the promotion of the GAA were most publicly expressed. This was done by raising awareness of the state of these and other sports through the publishing of match reports, results and related letters and the writing of propagandist articles. Advertising of cup competitions, matches and social events was also helpful in bringing these sports to the public's attention.

The *Derry Journal* was first published in 1792 and the soccer–Gaelic football debate started by Seumas MacManus in 1905 was disseminated through this newspaper. However, its stance on politics was perhaps moderate-nationalist and other sports such as soccer and cricket continued to be covered in a neutral manner. This led to MacManus complaining about the lack of GAA coverage in the newspaper in September 1905; he labelled it 'a posing nationalist organ' after it gave only a quarter of a column to the Tyrone–Donegal Ulster hurling championship semi-final while giving a full column to soccer news.[24] The *Derry People and Donegal News* was first published in 1902 and initially provided reports on soccer competitions such as the Tyrone and Donegal Football Cup. However, by 1905 the newspaper had become a strong advocate of the Irish-Ireland movement and encouraged the spread of Gaelic games, the Irish language and Irish industry, while condemning the playing of association football in Donegal. The policy of this newspaper was illustrated when its editor stated that he hoped that the Grand Camán Parade 'would capture all that is good in the young Irish manhood of the North, and leave only the dross to mate with "Mr Thomas Atkins" on the Association football field'.[25]

The *Londonderry Sentinel*, a unionist paper founded in 1829, at times provided a forum for the criticism of Gaelic games through the publication of reports and letters.[26] The *Donegal Vindicator* was organised by a number of those involved in the Land League and went into circulation on 4 February 1889, apparently to counter the *Donegal Independent* which had focused on attracting the readership of the Ascendancy in Ballyshannon where both papers were published.[27] Both these Donegal newspapers covered Gaelic games and soccer although with varying degrees of enthusiasm. The *Donegal Democrat* was not published until 16 June 1919.[28] While originally claiming to be 'a non-political newspaper in a world of politics' but rather contradictorily expressing a desire to 'uphold anything that will further the national and local interests', the newspaper quickly developed a 'fairly militant nationalist policy'.[29] Raids on its premises during the War of Independence by police and British soldiers further stiffened its resolve. With the development of the GAA County Board through the 1920s, the newspaper became the organ of this sporting body in South Donegal and at times seemed almost too eager to criticise the playing of soccer in the area while generally refusing to publish results of local matches or do anything positive to contribute to its development. Another local paper, the *Donegal People's Press*, was first published in Lifford in 1931 and appears to have had a fairly neutral policy on the GAA and soccer, with reports on games reasonably free of partisanship. By September 1932 it claimed to have 'the largest circulation of any paper published in Donegal', although it is unclear if this was actually the case at the time.[30]

As noted, two of these newspapers were published in the south of the county in Ballyshannon and unsurprisingly had a tendency to focus on events in this area. These were the *Donegal Vindicator* and the *Donegal Independent*, which were weeklies. The three others were based outside the county in Derry city; the *Derry Journal* was published thrice weekly while the *Derry People and Donegal News*, like the Ballyshannon newspapers, left the printers at the weekend. The *Londonderry Sentinel*, which also covered events in Derry and Donegal, was circulated three times a week. Dublin weekly, *Sport*, also included reports on sporting events in Donegal, but these were published more sporadically and were often based on locally published reports as the newspaper did not comprehensively cover regional events.

The period from 1893 until 1905 saw little activity in the promotion of Gaelic games in Donegal despite the sporadic publishing of GAA results. The lack of Gaelic games in the county was also beginning to come under scrutiny in the local newspapers in the late 1890s and early years of the twentieth century when isolated attempts were made to propagate the playing of Gaelic games through the local press. These articles merely questioned the lack of interest in these sports in the county and failed to have any major impact on the choice of sport in Donegal.[31] Efforts to organise the Evans Cup in 1905 were met by what one correspondent called 'a campaign of impudent abuse' in south-west Donegal.[32] This was a reference to attempts begun by Seumas MacManus in March 1905 to promote Gaelic games at the expense of association football. In doing this he tried to portray soccer as a foreign game and those involved as West Britons. This debate was facilitated in the *Derry Journal* and the *Derry People and Donegal News* throughout 1905 and 1906.

Gaelic football and hurling on a codified basis had not been introduced to the south of the county prior to 1905. These games soon became a vehicle for MacManus to rally the youth of the area into becoming more involved in the playing of Irish sports, the use of the Irish language and in the promotion of Irish industries and pastimes. Mike Cronin has stated that 'cultural nationalists recognised that to fully mobilise opinions behind their goals, indeed to achieve those goals, all elements of British rule had to be removed from Ireland. This included British habits, customs, language and their sports.'[33] MacManus began his press campaign by using the nationalist card and claiming that Donegal, despite being 'one of the most Gaelic counties in Ireland', was not doing its duty in continuing 'games introduced by the foreigner'.[34] He also, rather provocatively, called for a meeting of the Donegal soccer clubs to take place in Letterkenny when the season was over and for those present to 'resolve to introduce the Gaelic game throughout the county, and to open next season patriotically'. This, he felt, would see 'the conclusion of the Association regime'.[35] He ended his letter by appealing to Ardara Emeralds FC to donate the Evans Cup to Gaelic football in South-west Donegal. This appeal was met with apathy by the majority of soccer clubs in the county. It was only in the district where MacManus resided that any real effort to change was made. Even then, only two clubs promised to make the changeover. These were the Donegal Celtic and Mountcharles Hibernians clubs, but it quickly became apparent that the former club was eager to continue playing soccer.[36] The failure of MacManus to immediately offer any alternative form of football no doubt hindered these plans.

The Ardara club's response was rather timid but they refused to give in to MacManus and chose largely to ignore him. They were undoubtedly sensitive to the political situation at the time but it is clear that the majority of soccer players and administrators there still saw themselves as being nationalist despite his pressure. In November 1905 they held a debate to decide which code was best and the majority decided they were more familiar with the rules of association football.[37] Criticism in the press did not stop the Evans Cup tournament going ahead under association rules in the spring of 1906 and the Ardara Emeralds were eager to illustrate their patriotism despite it being played under soccer rules. In a preview of the final they listed a number of prominent members whom they claimed 'may be relied upon to take, without precipitate and fanatical action, every necessary chance to further the national cause'.[38]

Mike Cronin believes that due to soccer's association in Ireland as a foreign game, and the conflict between the FAIFS and the IFA over international recognition, FAIFS organisers had to 'work twice as hard as the GAA to prove its nationalist credentials'.[39] Defining nationalism in the early 1900s was problematic and usually it was the playing of soccer which received the most criticism in the newspapers mentioned above. It is clear that there were a number of approaches to what constituted nationalism. Despite the pressure in the local press, many members of association football teams in Donegal in the early years of the twentieth century were also involved in the national revival and prior to MacManus' press appeal, there was little pressure exerted on these clubs to switch to Gaelic games. Irish was spoken at the post-match entertainment after the fixture between Erne FC and Bundoran in 1901 and traditional Irish songs were sung.[40] A number of the Evans Cup committee had subscribed to and been involved in the hosting of the Ardara Gaelic League festival in 1902.[41] Many soccer players were eager to continue with the game and saw no reason to change despite having their nationalist identity challenged in the press. They also came under pressure at meetings.

Meetings of clubs and organisations were also used to raise interest in switching to Gaelic football. MacManus had continued his appeal for soccer to end at a meeting of the district council of the Gaelic League, which was held in Donegal town on 8 April 1905. It was at this gathering that resolutions were made 'to discard the English Association football'.[42] On 16 April 1905, Donegal Celtic held a meeting where members were said to have promised to do this and two delegates, John McBrearty and John McGinty, were appointed to travel to Ardara to encourage 'the general adoption of the Gaelic games throughout South-west Donegal'.[43] There is no evidence that these men undertook this journey or that the Donegal town soccer club ceased its activities. In fact, they continued the following season and managed to retain McBrearty and McGinty, who turned out in the Irish Junior Cup against Erne FC at the end of October 1905.[44] In any case, Gaelic football in the town was slow to get organised and the Balldearg GAA club was not formed there until that same month.[45] Even so, adhering to Gaelic games proved difficult for members and they were later condemned for this in the press on a number of occasions.[46] Clearly, members of local nationalist groups were not immune to the lure of soccer. At the Evans Cup match between Donegal Celtic and Killybegs Emeralds, on 10 March 1907, it was reported that 'out and out Gaelic Leaguers so dubbed' were present and 'cheered vociferously for the Celtic team, indicative most certainly that they were in full accord that day with foreign imitations'.[47] At the end of July 1908 cricket was being played in Donegal town, and a number of former Balldearg camán players were also involved in cricket in 1910.[48]

The condemnation of 'English sports' was not uncommon in Westmeath around this time, although the playing of cricket appears to have received most of the criticism in the local press there.[49] The standard of play in the latter sport was also ridiculed there while MacManus' attack appears similar to T.F. O'Sullivan's press campaign against rugby in County Kerry in the early 1900s.[50] This approach of mocking sports perceived as unpatriotic was used in the Donegal papers too. For example, the clubs of Donegal Celtic and Mountcharles Hibernians apparently enjoyed refreshments 'in the shape of tobacco chews' after their match in October 1905.[51] A common tactic used by cultural nationalists was to blame soccer organisers for trying to poach or entice players through bribery around this time. Seumas MacManus felt it necessary to mock the low level of entries in the Evans Cup competition in 1906 and sarcastically claimed that 'medals were to be pelted at them whether they won or lost'.[52] However, this criticism did not lead to the demise of soccer in Donegal, largely due to a lack of public support for Gaelic football and the greater appeal of association football.

While at least fourteen GAA clubs fielded Gaelic football teams from 1905 to 1907, these were not sufficiently numerous to mount any serious challenge to association football. Part of the problem for the GAA in Donegal was that soccer was considered a better game than Gaelic football at that time, and its rules were more commonly understood. Neal Garnham believes that 'in short, when compared to its rivals, association football was a simple, cheap, exciting and safe sport that offered a measure of satisfaction to those who partook in it with only a minimal risk'.[53] Association football was defended in the Donegal press by a small number of men who highlighted its strengths. 'Inniskeel' felt that the advocates of Gaelic games had made a 'tactical mistake' in forcing their sports upon the people when they 'should have been taught gently and gradually'.[54] Soccer, he claimed, was simply a better game and was more commonly understood than Gaelic football, which he considered 'a mongrel game'.[55] After the foundation of the County Board in October 1905, Killybegs Emeralds manager Thomas Ward wrote to the organisers to say that 'he and his Killybegs boys, having considered the matter, found that the Irish game was inferior, and that they, consequently, would be sticking to the association football which they had been playing'.[56] Others were well aware that the image of the two codes was being unfairly manipulated in the press by MacManus and refused to be intimidated. Barnesmore man Alfred C. Ward also wrote to the GAA to say that 'the people of his district were not willing to take up the Irish games so long as "certain individuals" were at the head of the propaganda in this county'.[57]

It is apparent that the rules of soccer were simply more clearly understood in Donegal at this point and the game was very enjoyable for many, while Gaelic football in the county was a rather unknown quantity. There was generally little criticism of soccer in the north of the county, although there were one or two exceptions. The proposed annual soccer match at the 1906 Cranford Sports led to complaints from 'Gael' in the *Derry Journal* about prizes being given to 'foreign sports'.[58] In their defence, the committee said it was too late to cancel this but would be glad to see an exhibition of Gaelic football being given and offered 'a substantial prize' for the winners.[59] There is no evidence that this took place; the soccer match went ahead anyway.[60] In a number of cases such as this and the Evans Cup, the organisers firstly attempted to appease those applying the pressure by agreeing to have Gaelic football organised but then went ahead with soccer as there was more interest in this code. There were problems with the dissemination of Gaelic football within Donegal at the time and there is little evidence of the organising of any exhibition matches or planned instruction, in schools or at public events, being undertaken to promote the game. While the progress of the GAA after 1906 declined with MacManus' absence, it could be argued that he triggered an anti-soccer attitude among those who otherwise may have been neutral through his appeal in the press and also, in raising the profile of the GAA within the county, began to draw attention to a matter which up until that time had been relatively conflict-free.

With the lack of activity in the Donegal GAA between 1908 and 1919, there was a decline in criticism of soccer in the local press, although it continued to be condemned in the *Derry People and Donegal News.* The playing of soccer, rather than Gaelic football, in Donegal town drew attention in 1913 and 1914 but these criticisms were rather isolated.[61] Generally these years were relatively quiet, in comparison with the 1905–08 period and with the years after 1919, as the GAA suffered from lack of interest in most areas. By the 1920s, with the GAA beginning to get a foothold in County Donegal, its organisers felt threatened by soccer and some were determined to keep it out now they had got their clubs and competitions up and running. Gaelic football had gradually become more accepted within Donegal society in the 1920s and its rules more commonly known. This gave administrators more clout, and condemnation was frequently expressed when soccer was played or plans to hold competitions under association football rules were unveiled. GAA writers attempted to promote Gaelic games not only through their criticism of soccer but also through floating ideas in local newspapers. Generally this was done in the hope that by questioning the lack of GAA activity, or the growth of soccer in certain districts, some locals would take note and make an attempt to get clubs up and running. 'Searchlight' feared that a rise in the playing of soccer in Ballyliffin, Buncrana and Bundoran in 1926 would 'mean that Gaelic in Tír Conaill was becoming obsolete'.[62] Others felt these matters could be remedied. One GAA writer lamented the absence of entries for the *Democrat* Cup in 1928 from the areas of Ramelton, Milford, Kerrykeel, Creeslough and Kilmacrennan and felt that 'all that is wanted is some energetic person to take up the matter'.[63]

Intimidation was also used by overzealous writers. The Kilmacrennan soccer club were labelled 'shoneens' in 1923 and readers were assured that 'before long, Gaelic games will be played on a firm footing in the locality'.[64] Those in Kilmacrennan, Creeslough and Dunfanaghy who had shown no interest in forming

GAA clubs by 1933 were told that the GAA had 'a claim' on them in an attempt to get clubs organised.[65] At this point it was becoming clear that soccer was the most popular pastime in these three villages and this was thus an over-simplification of the challenge facing the GAA in developing their games there. This type of writing was generally designed to undermine the efforts of soccer promoters in the hope that the public would view Gaelic games as being more worthy of participation than those banned under GAA rules. However, there is little to suggest that anything was done in the immediate aftermath of this targeting. Others felt that advantage should be taken of a lull in soccer activity in order to get the GAA up and running in areas where its codes were weak. In 1931 a correspondent stated that 'soccer has disappeared around the Lifford district, so the time is ripe to affiliate a Gaelic club and keep the red flag down'.[66] An examination of County Board correspondence also highlights a number of delegates' views on this conflict. The failure of the Buncrana soccer team to fulfil a fixture in April 1933 was thought by one GAA administrator to be a result of hurling and Gaelic football activity in the town while he also stated that 'it is a pity that Lifford and a few more are not finished up too'. This was because Gaelic games were said to be attracting limited support there.[67] Clearly, attempts to organise clubs were done with one eye on what was happening within soccer circles. One County Board delegate offered his congratulations in a letter to Ó Caiside in December 1933, when he stated that 'your re-organisation scheme has done more to kill foreign games than was done for the last ten years'.[68]

Those organising soccer in Ballyshannon, Letterkenny and Ballybofey were particularly targeted through the press. Certainly in these more urban areas, it would have been harder to monitor GAA players' activities, given the wider choice of sport available and the larger populations. In 1926, Letterkenny was the second largest town in Donegal with a population of 2,308 while there were 2,112 people residing in Ballyshannon. Ballybofey had a population of 802 while nearby Stranorlar, with 448 residents, also boosted the number of people in that area.[69] In October 1925 the Aodh Ruadh GAA club denied authorising a notice in a local newspaper which warned off soccer and rugby players from using their pitch in Ballyshannon, but at the same time claimed that 'none but members of the GAA are allowed to practice [sic] in the park'.[70] This club had the backing of the local *Donegal Democrat* while the South Donegal soccer league, staged the following year, received virtually no coverage in this newspaper and a small number of matches were harshly criticised in the *Derry People and Donegal News*.[71] A friendly between Donegal Celtic and Erne FC in February 1926 was described as 'a feeble attempt to revive the alien game in our midst'.[72] The former club's matches were said to be poorly attended and at times the theory that soccer was a more scientific sport was ridiculed, with references to injuries on the playing field.[73] This tactic was also used after a match in Ballybofey in 1928 in which a player had suffered a fractured leg,[74] in an effort to disprove 'the contention that soccer is a scientific game'.[75] Certain newspapers also attempted to prove that it was violent and uncivilised. Headlines such as 'Wild scenes at soccer game' were undoubtedly an attempt to circulate this notion.[76]

This criticism was not unique to Donegal and appears to have been a national pattern, being encouraged by the GAA both locally and nationally. In 1912 the *Gaelic Athlete* claimed that foul play was frequent in soccer while professionalism was also condemned.[77] Soccer in Connacht was targeted in 1913 with a preview of a manufactured fixture, which implied that a game between 'United and Athletic' in County Mayo was organised purely for money-making purposes.[78] Less than six months into the First World War, the newspaper gleefully announced that 'soccer football in Great Britain and Ireland seems to be going to pieces', while Armagh was said in the following year to have been 'added to the long list of towns in the "Black north" where soccer is dead, never to be resurrected'.[79] As Tadhg Ó hAnnracháin has stated, 'soccer was not only associated in the eyes of many GAA observers with the British army and the British economic system, but its marriage of professionalism and sport was cordially despised'.[80]

References to the playing of soccer in Bundoran by Free State soldiers in one paper in April 1926 were denied by a *Donegal Democrat* writer who claimed that 'there has not been a game of soccer played in Bundoran for the past twenty years', while the *Gaelic Athlete* claimed that Bundoran United was 'in reality a few soldiers from Finner Camp, not a Bundoran footballer being among the number'.[81] While Gaelic games were portrayed as being Irish, attempts to tie soccer with the British military were not uncommon. In May 1926 an effort to undermine the constitution of the local soccer league was made by Ulster GAA Council delegate J.J. Woods, who stated that in Donegal, soccer 'was being played by ex-soldiers and Republicans and Specials from across the Border who did not support their game'.[82] This tone continued, with ex-army men blamed for organising soccer in the county in April 1930.[83] A County Board delegate claimed in April 1932 that 'they had squashed the soccer in Donegal town', but the continuation of association football in Ballyshannon was said to be due to the local branch of the British Legion.[84]

Those employed by the government in the Letterkenny Mental Hospital who stuck with soccer were criticised in the press in 1927 and a number of GAA writers advocated the philosophy that they had a duty to play Gaelic games.[85] County Board chairman Seán Ó Caiside stated in 1928 that customs officials in Lifford were not doing enough to promote the GAA there and that 'these people should be asked to do their duty towards the national games'.[86] Crossover of players, and sometimes officials, was quite common in the Letterkenny area, and this also led to public criticism. In July of 1927, Letterkenny GAA delegate Eunan Coyle, the secretary of the County Board, resigned his post having become disillusioned with the lack of GAA activity at that time.[87] Apparently he became the secretary of the newly formed Letterkenny Rovers FC and a number of GAA players who joined him were also condemned.[88] A failure to succeed at Gaelic football was given as a reason for the defection of players at this time.

Crossover of players had been a problem in Ballybofey in 1923 and in 1927 it was claimed in the *Derry People and Tír Conaill News* that the local GAA club's failure to field a team against Letterkenny Rovers GFC was 'all the more unreasonable in view of the fact that a soccer team from that town travelled to Letterkenny and played a game in the Mental Hospital grounds'.[89] This conflict came to a head in 1928 with the local soccer club's efforts to raise the profile of the game there. The Ballybofey Wanderers AFC, in their participation in the Lifford and District League, and organisation of exhibition matches and a five-a-side competition, heightened fears amongst GAA organisers that soccer was becoming too popular in their area. A match between Sligo and Derry soccer selections had been held in Ballybofey on 3 June with a parade to the field beforehand.[90] Plans for a cup competition for all teams in the north-west were unveiled at a later meeting of the local soccer club and the hosting of a juvenile league was also discussed, while it was revealed that gate receipts from the above fixture were 'a record gate for any match played at Ballybofey'.[91]

The Sarsfields GFC of Stranorlar attempted to counter this progress in June by declaring that they 'were determined to make every effort to induce the youth of the locality to play the native games and resist the soccer invasion'.[92] Action was taken a few weeks later when they began a seven-a-side juvenile league.[93] The St Vincent de Paul Charity Cup was also organised under Gaelic football rules by the local Erin's Hope GAA club, in November of that year.[94] This organisation of cups was advocated at meetings of the Ulster Council and at those of the Donegal County Board. A Cavan delegate to the former organisation recommended league matches in the summer, 'so as to keep the players from going to soccer' in Donegal in 1924.[95] The secretary, P. McFadden, felt that medals should be given 'in order to hold the teams together and give encouragement' as this had been a successful enterprise in Tyrone.[96] Permission was given by McFadden, the chairman of the Ulster Council in October 1925, for the formation of town leagues in Armagh, Monaghan, and Donegal. This, it was felt, would cater for 'the wants of people who might be on the look-out for sport of another kind'.[97] J.J. Woods felt the collecting of medals for the *Democrat* Cup in May 1926 was necessary, as competitive soccer was again being organised in his area at the time.[98]

Anger was aroused within Donegal GAA circles by a report on the growing popularity of the association code and the advertisement of another representative exhibition match, between County Donegal and Sligo selections, scheduled for 12 August 1928, in Ballybofey.[99] Soccer organisers advertised their match with the rather provocative request to patrons to 'come and see football as it should be played'.[100] The GAA attempted to counter the organisation of the exhibition match by arranging a challenge Gaelic football match, also in Ballybofey, between that year's two county finalists, for the same day and scheduled to begin at the same time.[101] This was clearly arranged after the soccer plans were announced, with the excuse given that the Ardara team had been too busy to take up the offer of a challenge match against Killygordon until then.[102]

The day passed without any major standoff. Both games, 'played in close proximity to each other and started simultaneously', were run off peacefully and despite supporters carrying banners and being accompanied by bands, meeting on the way to the game, 'beyond some cheering and shouting, there were no untoward incidents'.[103] According to the *Derry Journal* reporter present, the soccer match was attended by approximately 1,500 spectators while the Gaelic football fixture was watched by an estimated 500 supporters.[104] Both games certainly received much publicity. While instances of clashes in fixtures appear to be scarce in other areas in the county, in 1931 the Milford GAA club complained in the press that 'another game was arranged', with free admission, as a 'counter attraction' to one of their matches in May of that year.[105] Naturally, this criticism of rival codes was not one-sided, with some newspapers, such as *Football Sports Weekly*, drawing comparisons with soccer's progress at the expense of GAA in areas such as Drogheda in 1927.[106]

Given the difficulty in mustering enough enthusiasm to form and maintain clubs, the planning of exhibition and important matches was thought to be a way of encouraging Gaelic games at the expense of soccer, although these were not organised frequently enough to have any major impact. One Falcarragh GAA man claimed, in May 1929, that in his district there were 'about 20 soccer clubs . . . with the result that they were up against big odds', and requested the County Board to organise a challenge match so as to assist them in re-establishing a club there.[107] This request was granted and the match took place 'before a magnificent crowd' the following month. The club was subsequently reformed but appears to have been an exception in this regard that year;[108] by 1931 soccer was again being given priority there, which illustrates the difficulty in transition experienced in some areas.[109] Other members hoped to see important competitive matches held in their areas to assist the promotion of Gaelic games. A request by Sergeant M.J. Cullen to Seán Ó Caiside, in October 1933, that the Gaelic football minor county final be held in Churchill along with a challenge match on the same day to attract further interest, was unsuccessful.[110] This general failure to hold exhibition matches characterised the GAA in Donegal for much of the period in this chapter, as the handful of attempts noted illustrates.

A second clash of fixtures in Ballybofey in 1928 did not receive as much press coverage and the conflict appears to have lessened after this, as no notices of any other matches being staged simultaneously in the town were recorded in the press.[111] A letter from 'Uadharan' stated that 'while the GAA would further in its way as far as it can that individualism which we term nationality, the other [soccer organisers] would crush out nationality, restore the foreign connexion and set up the British as master again'.[112] Ballybofey AFC were strongly defended in the press by secretary Henry McGowan. He claimed that, unlike himself, no County Board members had been involved in Ireland's fight for independence. He declared his distaste for the recent abuse and stated that 'we, who are carrying on the Association football game here, do not want the British back, and have sense enough to know that Association football would be as useless a weapon in bringing them back as Gaelic football was in putting them away'.[113] The playing of soccer nationally had been defended in *Football Sports Weekly* and in particular in February of that year by Oscar Traynor, a TD who had been heavily involved in the struggle for Ireland's independence. In an article under the heading 'The crime of playing soccer', he stated that 'some of the highest executive officers of the Republican movement, from 1916 onwards, played the despised foreign games, and I never heard any of them apologising for doing so'.[114] As previously noted, the participation in Donegal County Board administration by those involved in the War of Independence had declined as the decade wore on and clearly those organising the GAA in Donegal by 1928 relied more on rhetoric than any major previous military involvement. The end result was that despite the controversy, soccer, cricket and Gaelic football continued to be played in Ballybofey and problems with the illegal crossover of players to soccer there were still being noted by the Eastern GAA Board in 1934.[115]

Donegal was not unique in respect of this soccer–GAA conflict. At an Ulster Council meeting at the end of September 1928, one delegate applied for an intercounty match to be held in Clones, to 'fight the soccer element', and wished to see a declaration that clubs would have nothing to do with soccer. Permission was given for this match to take place on 21 October without any reference to the declaration.[116] Although the early years of the reorganised County Board saw some GAA clubs instituted in areas where soccer had previously been played, this was reduced as the 1920s wore on. It must be stated that while GAA writers attempted to influence readers in their choice of sport, the actual effect of this is hard to establish, aside from drawing attention to these matches. Many of those interested in soccer appeared to simply ignore the GAA's criticism and there was no widespread decline of clubs or loss of support as a result of the press campaign. Continuous attempts by the GAA to counteract their own members' involvement in association football through implementation of GAA rules, such as the Ban, had a stronger impact on reducing interest in soccer, although attitudes towards its implementation varied and actions against offenders were marked by inconsistency.

The impact of the 'Ban'

The Donegal GAA County Board had set out its attitude to banned sports reasonably soon after its re-establishment. At a meeting in June 1919, clubs were warned that any involvement of members 'in sports programmes which include foreign games' would be punished with a six-month suspension.[117] This was initially difficult to monitor and not always rigidly implemented. Red Hugh's of Killygordon protested that St Patrick's of Bundoran's 1919 county final victory was illegal, as the winning team contained a player who had participated in a soccer match during the previous six months.[118] This was not a successful appeal and it must have been almost impossible to field teams which did not contain soccer players around this time given the low population in rural areas and the number of players available in the 18–35 age group.

Measures to monitor the involvement of GAA members in banned sports in Donegal do not appear to have been put in place until 1924, with the introduction of vigilance committees by the Central Council. The Donegal GAA County Board voted to retain the Ban in March and at the end of the year they established their first vigilance committee, whose duty was 'to report where foreign games are being played, and the attendance of members of the GAA as players or spectators at such functions'.[119] Although this was supposed to be a covert group, a variance in decisions against offenders taken at County Board meetings would suggest its duties were not carried out consistently in this decade. This work was hindered by the fact that in 1925 not all clubs and County Board delegates were in favour of retaining the Ban. A vote at a Donegal County Board meeting in

March 1925 to decide whether or not to retain this rule was only decided when president Seán Ó Caiside voted in favour of keeping the rule.[120] In general, suspension of players in the period immediately after 1924 seems to have been infrequent at times and the fear of losing team members and an inconsistent monitoring of players' other sporting activities appears to have been the reason for this.

The exact rules of the Ban were initially a source of confusion for clubs' administrators and players, and indiscretions were sometimes brought to the public's attention through the press. The inconsistent nature of the Ban was compounded by clubs and county selectors allowing soccer players to participate, despite uncertainty about or indeed definite knowledge of their soccer activities in some cases. At times these matters were only clarified by correspondence in the press. After the Donegal team was defeated by Derry in the Ulster Gaelic football championship in June 1923, one enraged correspondent exposed the fact that the Derry team contained a number of soccer players.[121] In particular, there seemed to be a lack of clarity over how long a player who took part in an association football match had to wait until he was deemed eligible to play Gaelic games, although this was supposed to be a six-month period. At the end of 1925, Cavan issued a protest against Donegal Gaelic football goalkeeper Bob Black, who had appeared against them in a league match. Black later claimed, in an open letter to the press, that the secretary of the Aodh Ruadh club had given him the all-clear to play, despite his attendance at a soccer match. The length of his suspension for this infringement was unclear to him.[122] Donegal were given the benefit of the doubt at an Ulster Council meeting in December, when General O'Duffy stated that 'he presumed that Donegal at the last moment selected the player and had no time to go into his legality'.[123] They retained the points and Black was reinstated in February 1926, having given an undertaking he would not commit a similar offence and on the recommendation of the County Board, which, it seems, placed too high a value on his talents to omit him.[124]

Others accused alleged they had been given the go-ahead by those involved in GAA administration. In March 1929 accusations by 'Upright' in the local press, that the Raphoe Gaelic football team which had defeated Dungloe in the semi-final of the Charity Cup had fielded a well-known soccer player, led to his suspension.[125] The player in question, Jim Harte, replied to 'Upright' and claimed that he had been given permission by his club and had 'ample proof' that he was registered.[126] Clearly the fact that players had participated in soccer was known to those attending matches. Reporters seemed well aware, so it is highly likely that so too did clubs. It is also likely that this exposing of players was done to deter members from straying to other codes. GAA members' attendance at soccer matches was also noted in the press. In February 1929, one press correspondent claimed that 'there were many Gaelic games enthusiasts from Donegal in the throng' at the Rock Cup final in Derry city and that 'talk of a ban is all nonsense. There is no attempt to enforce it.'[127] Again this seems to have been a national trend, with the *Gaelic Athlete* particularly scathing about the failure of vigilance committees in Dublin in 1925 to enforce the rules of the GAA, stating that 'unfortunately what was known here in Dublin was equally true in other places'. The editor also claimed he would rather see 'the GAA smashed in defence of an honest principle than see it existing as a fraud and farce'.[128]

More discreetly, letters were sometimes sent to the Donegal GAA county chairman informing him of offenders, but at times even the Donegal County Board was uncertain how to deal with these. In June 1933 county chairman Seán Ó Caiside received a letter reporting three Ardara GAA players who had attended a soccer match in Killybegs the day after they helped defeat Carrick Gaelic football team. A protest was entered by the Carrick club claiming the points as a result of the Ardara players' indiscretion.[129] Clearly the chairman was unsure of what to do as it appears he wrote to the offices of the Leinster GAA seeking instruction and was later notified that Ardara should lose the points.[130] This seems to have been an exceptional case in Donegal GAA at this time, but illustrates the problems of dealing with offenders. As can be seen, correspondence to the County Board and newspaper reports provided accounts of players' non-adherence to rules in playing and attending so-called foreign games, and therefore indirectly helped the administration of the GAA.

As the case of Bob Black demonstrates, GAA teams in Donegal simply could not afford to lose players and were willing to show leniency in dealing with them. This was not uncommon within Ulster GAA circles. In March 1917, a number of Derry players were reinstated to the GAA; even though 'none of them' had waited 'the recognised period from soccer', it was felt by the Ulster Council that this would help the GAA movement in Derry.[131] Tyrone GAA officials 'handed in a long list for reinstatement including some who had already been reinstated', at an Ulster Council meeting in June 1924.[132] In 1927 there were applications from at least thirty-three Donegal footballers and in July 1928, the names of thirteen Donegal players seeking readmission were noted at an Ulster Council meeting.[133] Players were also sometimes pardoned locally without being brought to the Ulster Council's attention. In March 1926, Aodh Ruadh GAA club readmitted players who were supposed to have played soccer, having decided there was not enough evidence to suspend them.[134] This approach did not always prove successful. A number of St Eunan's Gaelic football players who had switched to the local soccer club in the late 1920s were pardoned and readmitted by the County Board 'on the strength of undertakings regarding their future conduct'.[135] This was not sufficient to deter them, however. One writer noted that 'for a while there was constancy to the old standards, but eventually the soccer craze again overwhelmed a considerable portion of players'.[136] Attitudes to soccer amongst GAA members varied in Letterkenny for much of the 1920s and into the next decade. The Letterkenny GAA club proposed the removal of the Ban in 1927 and 1928.[137] GAA clubs in Letterkenny at times certainly advocated a policy of leniency towards the playing of soccer and the Ban was a source of frustration to many of their members, who often chose to play soccer instead. Teams were severely weakened because of suspensions in March 1932 and July 1934.[138] By 1934 there was no significant shift in favour of the Ban within the St Eunan's GAA club and some members made an attempt to have it removed completely.[139] Generally the idea did not receive enough support at the highest levels of GAA administration, either in Donegal or nationally, at this time.[140]

Some offending GAA members were punished more severely than others. At a meeting of the County Board in June 1931, a Ballyshannon player was given the all-clear after he had satisfactorily explained his attendance at a 'banned game'. Other players did not get off so lightly, as some players from the Ballybofey and Letterkenny areas were 'suspended for the full period'. This also suggests that the GAA was keen to keep those it knew would be loyal, while getting rid of those who would probably return to soccer. It is also clear that not every area had a vigilance committee in operation at this time.[141] 'Gael' claimed in July 1931 that 'officers might be more active in certain districts', as 'in some districts players are being allowed to attend and in some cases, even to take part in foreign games'.[142] The appointing of 'vigilance men' seems to have still been poorly organised in the early 1930s judging by the number of requests to the chairman in 1933, Seán Ó Caiside, to sanction delegates for this type of work at short notice.[143]

In January 1934, Eastern Board delegate Leo McCarron called for a stricter policy to be shown in that division with regard to the sanctioning of officers and for only 'good, genuine, vigilance men [to] be appointed'.[144] Opinions clearly varied in that area. A plea for leniency was called for at an Eastern Board meeting in July 1934, when a number of delegates felt that some offending players were only 'pauns' [sic] in 'a sinister move to try and destroy Gaelic football'.[145] It was the view of the secretary, Patrick O'Donnell, that 'this rule should be drastically dealt with'.[146] One Eastern Board delegate also stated that 'vigilance men were far too strict' and 'they should exercise discretion, and a little intelligence and common sense in carrying out their duties'.[147] Eventually the matter was adjourned with the chairman given authority to take whatever action he felt was necessary.

This inconsistency was not unique to Donegal. Opinions were divided on dealing with players in Monaghan in 1925 with a Mr Murphy of Clones and General O'Duffy rejecting an attempt to have fifteen soccer players reinstated after they had given their word to stick to Gaelic games.[148] A Louth County Board delegate claimed in August 1927 that 'most of those who were clamouring for the suspension of soccer players were regular attendants at Association football'.[149] Strong action was, however, sometimes taken against players in order to set an example to other clubs. A number of Rapparees and Ardee players were suspended in 1927 for their involvement in soccer by the Louth County Board; the secretary stated that 'they would have to make a start somewhere' in their actions against players' involvement in banned codes.[150] There was great difficulty in adhering to the Ban when many GAA members were clearly interested in maintaining their support for other codes and activities banned by the GAA.

Conclusion

As Ó hAnnracháin has stated, 'the premises on which the leadership of the GAA trumpeted the cultural significance of sport in general and Gaelic games in particular were deeply flawed and imbued with many of the same notions that helped to vitiate contemporary governmental attempts at linguistic and cultural revival'.[151] While this chapter has shown how rivalry between sporting organisers can be exacerbated in the press, the GAA in Donegal failed in its attempt to turn public opinion against soccer by portraying it as a 'foreign' game, and measures to counteract the playing of this code were generally unsuccessful. Methods of dealing with offending players were marked by inconsistency, while efforts to organise Gaelic football exhibitions in areas where this code was weak did not receive sufficient attention from the County Board. The GAA relied more on rhetoric, generally expressed through the press, than on actual physical efforts to counteract soccer. Liam O'Callaghan has illustrated in his study of Munster rugby that 'the Ban mentality was a contested concept' and overlaps between rugby and Gaelic football were evident.[152] Opinions on the Ban clearly varied in Donegal where a tradition of soccer, low population levels and the threat of emigration meant that many teams could not afford to lose players, no matter what their sporting preferences were.

Conclusion

This book is centred around three key themes. Firstly, it has shown how sports develop in a geographically peripheral area. The development of the GAA in Donegal was neglected by provincial and national governing bodies for much of the period covered here and its eventual success relied on the agency of a small group of local men for administration. There were no other sports which managed to sustain an administrative structure to cover the entire county in the period covered here. Secondly, it illustrates the incompleteness of the Irish sporting 'revolution'. It is clear that sport in Donegal simply could not develop at the same rates of growth as in many parts of England and in some areas of Ireland. Thirdly, and also of key significance to this book, is that the development of the GAA was of a rather mundane nature and had less to do with political identity than has been presumed previously by a number of GAA historians and writers. This new understanding of how the GAA worked in a rural setting challenges the macro-argument of politics and identity made by Mandle and De Burca, and illustrates that nationalist politics was only a minimal aspect of the GAA's development in Donegal.[1] Richard Holt's assertion that 'the formation and early history of the GAA is arguably the most striking instance of politics shaping sport in modern history' may also be challenged in regard to its development at a micro level in Donegal.[2] Local conditions varied and this should be taken into consideration in any study of how the GAA spread throughout the country, rather than its development being seen as a uniform movement which was accepted in all counties and at the same rates of growth.

Given the lack of political involvement in the development of the GAA in Donegal, one would also have to ask the question: despite

Catholics replacing Protestants as the dominant social force in the early twentieth century, just how politically nationalist was Donegal society? Although definitions of nationalism can vary, certainly its location meant that it was somewhat removed from events in more southern areas which were central to Ireland's struggle for independence. As noted earlier, Desmond Murphy has stated that low levels of political consciousness existed in Donegal until the Truce.[3] While election results illustrate a large amount of support for nationalist parties, for long periods the GAA in Donegal lacked the involvement of, or a crossover with, politicians, and the participation of those in political parties such as Sinn Féin was sporadic and varied.[4] This contrasts with Kerry, where key events in the rise of nationalist support, such as the Cultural Revival, boosted the GAA's development.[5]

The GAA in Donegal could not be considered to have played any major role in Ireland's struggle for independence and the Association there was not 'drenched in blood', unlike other counties, such as Kerry. McElligott has stated that 'the evolving political situation in Ireland significantly impacted on the Kerry GAA' and during the War of Independence, 'dozens of its local membership took an active and prominent part in the fighting, ensuring that as an organisation the Kerry GAA significantly shaped the conflict'.[6] In Waterford, Cronin, Duncan and Rouse have claimed that 'when the fighting ended and society was once again calm, the impulses that drove Irish nationalism did not dissipate; from the 1920s onwards, they found alternative expression in, amongst other things, the politics of culture and sport.'[7] The case of Cork illustrates how men who had been prominent in the Civil War were later to command major positions of administration in the Irish Free State and the GAA.[8]

Donegal remained on the periphery of the Irish Revolution and the GAA there later lacked this raw, emotional 'nationalist' connection, despite the participation of some of its members and an effort in the local press to overstate its involvement in the fight for independence. While it would be naive to assume that participation in sport in Donegal was not influenced by nationalism at the time, without this overt physical military involvement of its members, and any sense that the conflict was being fought in the county, the ideological development of the GAA was hindered there to some extent. Donegal was not the only county where the GAA was relatively unaffected by this conflict, as the case of Kildare, where the GAA was 'anything but a hotbed of radical nationalism', illustrates.[9] However, by the early 1930s, the Donegal GAA County Board was unique amongst sports organisers in the county, in that it had managed to, at least partially, develop a 'county identity' through its Gaelic football intercounty team; it is clear that the media, particularly the local press, was one of the tools which the GAA in Donegal used in the construction of its own version of events to bolster national identity. The *Donegal Democrat*, in particular, in its policy of ignoring local soccer, undoubtedly attempted to portray Gaelic games as the most popular sports in the area.

Given the cultural boundaries already mentioned in Donegal, it would be incorrect to say that the entire county was united behind the Donegal GAA intercounty Gaelic football or hurling teams, at any point in the years discussed in this book. While the religious make-up in the county contrasted with Mayo and Kerry, and was probably sufficient reason to ensure that there were sections of Donegal society that remained at a distance from GAA events, within the organisation of the Donegal GAA itself there was a failure to unite.[10] While progress had been made in the construction of a 'county identity' through the Donegal team in the late 1920s, as late as 1933 there were still problems in attracting support in all areas throughout the county. Although Donegal's appearance in a national final undoubtedly raised interest levels and helped to popularise this code, not every area was affected, and some sections of society remained unconcerned.[11] In particular, the Protestant population in East Donegal remained very much part of unionist East Ulster in outlook. Their efforts to foster cricket and hockey as part of their culture were efforts to replicate wider trends associated with what Michael Cusack saw as the attempted Anglicisation of Ireland.

While the early 1930s have been noted as 'an era of remarkable expansion for the GAA', the organisation's development in Donegal did not run parallel to more centralised developments.[12] However, it must be stated that by 1934, the Donegal GAA County Board, with its intercounty Gaelic football team and parish set-up, as well as its league and championship structures, had produced a form of an 'identifiable' Donegal. Certainly, structures for sport were evident in Donegal to a limited extent in the Victorian era, but there was nothing that provided people with a sense of belonging to the county. The GAA could undoubtedly claim to have made more progress in fostering this county identity than the organisers of other sports within Donegal society. In general, Donegal's GAA clubs, as well as engaging in what were deemed to be more 'nationalist' sports than their soccer, rugby, hockey or cricket counterparts, helped in fostering national identity through their organisation of céilís, although the organisation of Irish language classes was not something most clubs were concerned with. Whether their members were any more nationalist than the Milford rugby players who sang 'The Soldier's Song' at the end of their annual dance in December 1932 is, however, questionable.[13]

Soccer remained unable to construct any type of county identity within Donegal. The lack of a county-based structure, unlike that offered by the GAA, was undoubtedly a problem but, as seen in the lack of progress after divisional matches in the late 1920s and the collapse of the County Donegal Cup after only two seasons, initial interest in forging together regional areas could not be maintained without regular fixtures and the participation of all clubs in the county. Due largely to soccer organisers' inability to form a structure for all clubs in Donegal, they could not hope to gain enough interest in all areas and gather sufficient popular support throughout the county. The lack of a sense of regional identification with a top club in the south and south-west was particularly evident, while the parish structure of the GAA generally outweighed anything local soccer organisers could consistently offer. Regional successes, such as Killybegs Emeralds' Connacht Cup victory in 1934, undoubtedly meant a lot to those in their local area, but there was no widescale attempt to get behind them throughout the county.[14] Sporting identification in the north-east was undoubtedly influenced by soccer in Derry and Scotland, while some clubs, such as Kilmacrennan Celtic (in their naming of their grounds as Hampden Park), were eager to display the latter connection.[15] Certainly soccer clubs, such as Ramelton FC, who organised an excursion to Portrush at the end of August 1933, were eager to foster a local identity, but these teams generally refrained from explicitly associating themselves with the Irish language, music and céilís.[16]

Rugby, hockey and cricket remained minority sports, with cricket generally restricted to the east of the county by the late 1920s, and rugby clubs appearing sporadically around the Letterkenny area at the beginning of the following decade. Clearly the lack of involvement of a county cricket, hockey, rugby or soccer selection in any national competitions, through a general failure of their national governing bodies to follow the example of the GAA in its national infrastructure, meant that sporting identification with these codes remained localised and regional and failed to be developed into something which all the people of Donegal could support. An assessment of earlier cricket players within the county has illustrated the strong presence of Protestants within the sport, both as players and administrators, highlighting the religious diversity of Donegal; at a more localised level, Ballyshannon provided a strong example of a town where sport played an important part in cross-community relations, and hockey and rugby were still being played there, albeit sporadically, in the 1930s. Other voluntary clubs with strong Protestant links were established, but Roman Catholics were also welcome in their sports clubs. The efforts of James Sproule Myles were essential to the development of these sports in this town. In general, there was little evidence of any sectarianism within sports clubs in Donegal in the period covered here. In addition to this, as Mike Cronin has stated, 'in the Free State, and later in the Republic, the GAA stood as a movement projecting unblemished nationalist credentials'.[17] None of the other sports mentioned above could claim this sense of nationalism, and this undoubtedly had an impact on the public's identification with them, not just in Donegal, but throughout the country.

While the 1919 County Board did have political backing, this lessened in the early 1920s and the administrative success of the GAA in Donegal depended largely on a strong network of national school teachers who were dedicated to Gaelic football. Donegal's GAA players were primarily involved in agricultural work and the majority of administrators were professionals. This contrasted with soccer, where the majority of players were based in industrial work, and indicates that GAA players in Donegal were more rural than urban based. Donegal's soccer organisers also differed in that most of these men also came from the industrial category. Similarly, the majority of cricket players came from the industrial sector while the game's administrators were mainly drawn from the professional class. The presence of what Hunt has termed 'industrial paternalism' can be seen at a lower level in the case of the Convoy Cricket Club, although the formation of workplace teams was not a significant factor in the development of sports clubs in Donegal.[18] Military involvement was significant within the nineteenth century, particularly in cricket, but this declined in the opening decades of the twentieth century.

In highlighting the difficulties of uniting Donegal for sporting purposes, this book adds to the work of Bale, Metcalfe, Huggins, Russell and Collins on the geography of sports and builds upon the recent work of Hunt, McAnallen and McElligott on local dimensions of Gaelic games, while providing a comparison point for future studies on the spread of the GAA nationally and its relationship with other sports.[19] Richard McElligott has posed a significant question relating to Donegal in his own work. In accounting for the GAA's success in Kerry, he asks if the lack of tradition and key organisers were factors in the failure of the Association to develop to the same extent in other rural areas of a similar geographical structure such as Galway, Mayo and Donegal.[20] There can be no doubt that organisers of Gaelic football in Donegal did not enjoy the same monopoly on sport as they did in Kerry. Certainly an absence of significant organisers and the early failure to develop a tradition of Gaelic football played a huge part in Donegal's slow development. A lack of success also meant that public interest in Gaelic football remained lower than in Kerry, where success in the 1903 All-Ireland Gaelic football final, played in 1905, boosted levels of interest in this sport.[21] Donegal's first All-Ireland championship final victory did not come until 1992; Kerry had won thirty of these titles by then.[22] Provincially, Donegal did not win an Ulster senior Gaelic football championship until 1972 and this again highlights the slow development of the GAA in the county.[23] Kerry's win in the 2014 All-Ireland championship final over Donegal was their thirty-seventh victory at senior level while Donegal have won only two of these titles.

Problems with transport and finance also affected the GAA in Kerry, but it could be argued that in many areas of Donegal the GAA never became as active a force in society and culture as it did in Kerry. Regional variations between sports possibly existed in more Irish counties than has been assumed and this requires further study. Localised factors that encouraged the diffusion of soccer in Donegal were absent in Kerry. Kerry lacked the external influences of areas like Derry and Scotland, which were fundamental to the growth of soccer in Donegal, while the south-west county similarly did not have a planted area such as in Donegal, where traditions associated with unionist East Ulster were strong. Clearly Donegal had a set of factors which meant that a tradition of Gaelic football was much slower to develop, while soccer benefited. Just how peculiar Donegal was in regard to its sporting preferences in comparison with others counties is unclear. Urban areas such as Longford town and Sligo have enjoyed traditional support for soccer.[24] Although these are towns and the strength of the GAA has often been said to be rural, until a history of soccer in Ireland is written – similar to *The GAA: County by County* in its geographical spread – it is difficult to assess how individual Donegal was in its choice of sports. Support for soccer was not always centred in Donegal's urban areas and with regard to the Ban, support and participation in both football codes throughout Ireland was fluid and not always restricted to one form of football. Similarly, until more in-depth research is undertaken on sports such as hockey, cricket and rugby throughout Ireland, it is difficult to offer an authoritative comparison.

This book has, however, attempted to locate the study of sport in Donegal within wider debates in sports history and Irish history. It is clear that Donegal society in the late nineteenth century lacked the necessary preconditions for the rapid development of organised sport. Despite the distinct differences between the east and west of the county, factors associated with the development of sport – such as an increasing population, high levels of industry and an efficient education system – were absent from Donegal society. The key differences between Donegal and Westmeath appear to have been that the latter county was more prosperous and its gentry were at the centre of sporting activity; its central location and more efficient transport system also meant that a number of sports were sustained through strong social networks. In contrast, Donegal, with its scattered rural population, particularly in the west of the county, remained somewhat disjointed in attempts to organise sport; this was not helped by a number of cultural and physical boundaries, which existed largely because of the awkward geology of the county and its sheer size in comparison to the majority of Irish counties.

Sports in Donegal could not progress without sufficient financial backing and transport links. Without these, early attempts to run competitive structures lasted only briefly. As Cronin and Higgins have noted, 'a sport simply existing is not enough for it to be successful, and to become popular'.[25] Tony Collins has stated that 'the reason why Britain developed these sports was it was the first nation to become an industrial, capitalist economy where people had disposable income'.[26] This was crucial, he believes, as 'there was the wealth to generate both an interest in sports and also markets for sports'.[27] As has been illustrated throughout, this lack of wealth, which came with an absence of industry in Donegal, was a major factor in the failure of sport to take off there in the late nineteenth century. Sport was not a big business in Donegal and was never going to develop from a simple pastime to something capable of providing a living for the ordinary working man at this time. Clubs were never going to attract shareholders and businessmen seeking a profitable investment like those in England, and the population simply did not exist for games to develop into forms of mass entertainment.[28]

An important theme in this book has been the diffusion of sport through outside influences. This was particularly evident in the north-east; the spread of both soccer and Gaelic football were initially helped by those in Derry city, where both structures for the administration of soccer and GAA clubs were in existence by the late 1880s. The development of cricket was also quicker in the East Donegal Laggan valley area where connections with Tyrone and the presence of the Finn Valley railway boosted this sport. However, it would be incorrect to assume that a sporting 'revolution' took place in the Laggan Valley. Hockey and rugby clubs were generally forced to link up with those outside of Donegal for competitive action, and the East Donegal Cricket Union failed to attract support from other areas in the county. This type of administrative networking continued despite the partition of Ireland in 1922.

The eventual success of the GAA in Donegal was due to the enthusiasm of small groups of local individuals. It is clear that until the 1920s, Donegal was primarily a soccer county and the GAA was always going to struggle to establish itself after this lengthy delay in organising. That it did so was a credit to its organisers who showed more awareness of the value of the media and the importance of creating divisional league and cup structures than their soccer counterparts. Their ability to put in place an administrative structure, while perhaps not so influential in some areas such as Inishowen, was crucial to the GAA's development and regular meetings were fundamental to this organisation. As Mason has stated in his major publication on soccer, 'clubs, like most other voluntary organisations, depend for their success on people doing things. When they stop, the club stops.'[29] This was as much the case in Donegal's GAA clubs as in soccer clubs in England. The 1920s in Ireland was an era in which a number of improvements in administration benefited the GAA. A type of social engineering was possible with the movement of Garda Síochána strengthening the GAA in the Free State. National school teachers also placed more emphasis on participating in Gaelic games than soccer and these men had steady jobs with fixed hours and free time. Experience of paperwork also meant they could organise matches effectively and build strong networks as can be seen in the dominance of teachers at County Board level in Donegal in the period 1919–34. They were also amongst the pillars of society and were much less likely to emigrate, and could use their influence in the classroom and local society to promote Gaelic games (although a lack of school facilities such as playing fields was a problem). Hurling, in particular, suffered from a lack of equipment and Gaelic football was much easier to demonstrate and learn, which meant that the diffusion of hurling suffered.

By the early 1930s there were clear boundaries between Gaelic football and soccer zones and despite the presence of the Ban and a smear campaign in the local press, the GAA was unsuccessful in the drive to eradicate soccer from Donegal society. At this time it was clear that the south and south-west of Donegal was where the strength of Gaelic football lay; this code was rather weak further north. Movement between codes in parts of Donegal, such as the east and north-west, was more fluid and both forms of football were played there. Gaelic football was strengthened through the organisation of parish leagues and local competitions and the arranging of divisional structures improved administration. South and south-west Donegal continued to dominate Gaelic football for the rest of the twentieth century and into the new millennium. By 2014, eleven out of seventeen clubs which had won the Donegal Senior Gaelic football club championship were from the south and south-west areas. Only five clubs from East Donegal have won it, and only one from the north-west has lifted the trophy. Inishowen still awaits its first winning club.[30] While Donegal's All-Ireland victory in 1992 gave the county a massive boost, success at a national level has been limited, although the intercounty team enjoyed a revival from 2010 to 2014 with Jim McGuinness as manager.[31]

The popularity of soccer in Donegal has certainly had an effect on interest in the GAA. In addition to a national comparative study of the rivalry between Gaelic football and soccer administrators, more research needs to be undertaken on the links between seasonal migration and the importation of soccer as an alternative driver of sporting diffusion. While it is difficult to be precise on the advent of scouting by British clubs in Ireland, this cross-channel involvement has been going on since the early part of the twentieth century in Donegal and links with Scotland undoubtedly provided opportunities for talented players to break into professional soccer. More recently, Donegal's strong tradition of soccer can also be seen in the cases of English Premier League players Shay Given, Seamus Coleman and, a little further back, Gary Doherty; and in Scotland, Glasgow Celtic's Packie Bonner.[32] All these players hail from strong soccer areas – Bonner from the West Donegal fishing village of Burtonport, Given from the border town of Lifford, Doherty from Carndonagh (Inishowen) and Coleman from Killybegs. While this trend requires further investigation, it seems that there is no other peripheral Irish county which has produced as many professional soccer players who have played at a top level in Britain in recent times.[33] Due to his success as manager of the Donegal Gaelic football intercounty team, in 2012 Jim McGuinness secured a contract with Glasgow Celtic to work as a Sports Performance consultant – illustrating both the lure of professional football and Donegal's strong cultural connections with Scotland – although he was able to continue to manage and coach Donegal until he resigned in 2014.[34] As was seen in the 1930s, this prospect of a career in professional soccer has undoubtedly influenced many young Donegal players to pursue an interest in association rather than Gaelic football and this has continued to the present day.[35] While speculative, this pattern may previously have had a negative effect on the development of Gaelic football, with levels of interest in both codes varying, but it offers another understanding of how the competition between sports within Donegal society has affected the dominance of any single code throughout the county.

Bibliography

Primary Sources

Archival Sources

CARDINAL Ó FIAICH LIBRARY

Ulster GAA Council Archives, 1917–39

Volume 1: March 1917–October 1927

Volume 2: January 1928–September 1934

Volume 3: October 1934–July 1939

COUNTY DONEGAL ARCHIVES

Donegal GAA Archives, 1927–34

GAA/1/4/1(1–12)

GAA/1/4/2 (1–2)

CROKE PARK ARCHIVES

Central Council GAA Archives, 1899–1934

Central Council Minute Books, 1899–1911, GAA/CC/01/01

Central Council Minute Books, 1911–25, GAA/CC/01/02

Central Council Minute Books, 1925–29, GAA/CC/01/03

Central Council Minute Books, 1929–32, GAA/CC/01/04

Central Council Minute Books, 1932–34, GAA/CC/01/05

Annual Reports Volume 1, Congress Minutes 1911–28

Annual Reports Volume 2, Congress Minutes 1928–38

GRAND LODGE OF FREEMASONS

Masonic Lodge Membership Registers, 1882–1935, numbers 129 and 287

NATIONAL ARCHIVES OF IRELAND

Royal Irish Constabulary Monthly reports, 1887–1919, CO 904

Crime Branch Special: DICS Reports Box No. 6: Monthly Secret Report of the Northern Division, 4 November 1887, 261/6939

Crime Branch Special: DICS Reports Box No. 6: Monthly Secret Report of the Northern Division, 4 March 1888, 521/7556

Crime Branch Special: DICS Reports Box No. 6: Monthly Secret Report of the Northern Division, 4 May 1888, 521/7931

Crime Branch Special: DICS Reports Box No. 6: Monthly Secret Report of the Northern Division, December 1888, 4 January 1889, 1/10297

Crime Branch Special: DICS Reports Box No. 6: Monthly Secret Report of the Northern Division, 6 February 1889, 522/9501

Crime Branch Special: DICS Reports Box No. 6: Monthly Secret Report of the Northern Division, 4 March 1889, 522/9501

Crime Branch Special: DICS Reports Box No. 6: Monthly Secret Report of the Northern Division, April 1889, 5 May 1889, 521/9835

Crime Branch Special: DICS Reports Box No. 6: Monthly Secret Report of the Northern Division, 2 June 1889, 521/9983

Crime Department Special Branch GAA: Approximate Strength under Clerical and Fenian Control, by Divisions, 5 May 1890, 296/S

Crime Department Special Branch Report on the GAA in the Northern Division: Progress Made During the Year Ended 31 December 1890, 10 February 1891, 2701/S

Crime Branch Special Northern Division, District Inspector's Monthly Report for Donegal, July 1892, 520S/9248

Crime Branch Special Northern Division, District Inspector's Monthly Report for Donegal, January 1892, 520S/8058 and February 1893, 520S/10368

Crime Branch Special Northern Division, District Inspector's Monthly Report for Donegal, January 1894, 520S/12012

Crime Branch Special, Inspector General and Chief Inspector's Monthly Report for Donegal, October 1905, 379/S

Crime Branch Special, Inspector General and Chief Inspector's Monthly Report for Donegal, May 1906, 821/S

Crime Branch: Returns of Political Organisations in Donegal on 30 September 1919. Letterkenny, 1 October 1919, CO904/110

National Library of Ireland

Seumas MacManus Papers, 1898–1960, MS 32, 629 /A-D; MS33, 669 /A-Q

Public Record Office of Northern Ireland

Papers of the Irish Football Association, 1880–1927

D/4196/A/1 IFA Minute Book, 1898–1902

D/4196/A/2 IFA Minute Book, 1903–9

D/4196/A/3 IFA Minute Book, 1909–28

D/4196/G/1 Junior Committee Minutes, 1909–27

D/4196/S/1 Cash Book of the IFA, 1880–97

University College Dublin

Ó hEochaidh, Seán, Creideann in Inis Bo Finne. MS917. Folklore Commission, 1943, pp. 48–52

—, Christmas Day traditions in Cloughaneely. MS932. Folklore Commission, 1943, pp. 455–62

Papers of the Football Association of Ireland, 1921–34

P137/1 International Recognition of the Football Association of the Irish Free State, 1922–56

P137/11 Finance Committee, 1921–31

P137/12 Finance Committee, 1931–48

P137/25 Junior Committee Minutes, 1923–38

P137/26 Junior Committee Minutes, 1928–40

P137/35 Rules, Ratification and Referees Committees, 1924–29

P137/38 Consultative Committee Minutes, 1924–34

NEWSPAPERS

Anglo-Celt, 1904–05

Ballyshannon Herald and North-Western Advertiser, 1880–83

Derry People and Donegal News, 1902–25

Derry People and Tír Conaill News, 1925–34

Derry Journal, 1860–1934

Derry Standard, 1888–99

Donegal Democrat, 1919–34

Donegal Independent, 1884–1927

Donegal People's Press, 1931–34

Donegal Post, 2008

Donegal Vindicator, 1889–1934

Fermanagh Herald, 1903–14

Football and Sports Weekly, 1925–28

Gaelic Athlete, 1912–16, 1925–26

Impartial Reporter, 1880–1900

Irish Press, 1931–34

Leitrim Observer, 1911

Londonderry Sentinel, 1884–1906

Nation, 1884

Sport, 1880–1934

Ulster Herald, 1901–14

DIRECTORIES AND WORKS OF REFERENCE

Lawrence, John, *Handbook of Cricket in Ireland, Number Six, 1870–1* (Dublin: John Lawrence, 1871)

—, *Handbook of Cricket in Ireland, Number Seven, 1871–2* (Dublin: John Lawrence, 1872)

—, *Handbook of Cricket in Ireland, Number Eight, 1872–3* (Dublin: John Lawrence, 1873)

—, *Handbook of Cricket in Ireland, Number Nine, 1873–4* (Dublin: John Lawrence, 1874)

—, *Handbook of Cricket in Ireland, Number Twelve, 1876–7* (Dublin: John Lawrence, 1877)

—, *Handbook of Cricket in Ireland, Number Thirteen, 1877–8* (Dublin: John Lawrence, 1878)

Slater's Directory 1894 (London: Slater's Directory Co., 1894)

Thom's Official Directory of the United Kingdom of Great Britain and Ireland for the year 1883 (Dublin: Alexander Thom, 1883)

Thom's Official Directory of the Kingdom of Great Britain and Ireland for the year 1884 (Dublin: Alexander Thom, 1884)

Thom's Official Directory of Ireland for the year 1930 (Dublin: Alexander Thom, 1930)

Thom's Irish Almanac and Official Directory 1931 (Dublin: Alexander Thom, 1931)

CONTEMPORARY WORKS

Shaw Mason, William, *A Statistical Account, or Parochial Study of Ireland, drawn up from the communications of the clergy, volume 2* (Dublin: Graisberry & Campbell, 1816)

The Donegal's Own Journal: a monthly journal of the 5th Battalion Royal Inniskilling Fusiliers, 1901–1904

The Gaelic Athlete Annual and County Directory for 1907–8 (Dublin: Sealy, Bryers & Walker, 1907)

O'Sullivan, T.F., *The Story of the GAA* (Dublin: Unknown Publisher, 1916)

ONLINE SOURCES

'Census of Ireland for the year 1881. Religious professions of the people. Table XXVIII. Religious professions and sexes of the inhabitants, and number of families, in each parish in the county of Donegal', pp. 451–2, retrieved from http://parlipapers.chadwyck.co.uk.jproxy.nuim.ie/fulltext/readview.do?area=hcpp&id=1882-058905&source=&pagenum=452&resultNum=34&entries=187&queryId=..%2Fsession%2F1406552477_8061&backto=FULLREC&fromSearchHistory=&searchWithin=county+of+donegal&showall=&enlarge=Y [Accessed 28 July 2014]

'Census of Ireland for the year 1881. Religious professions of the people. Table XXIX. Religious professions and sexes of the parliamentary and municipal boroughs and principal towns in the county of Donegal, and the number of families in each', p. 452, retrieved from http://parlipapers.chadwyck.co.uk.jproxy.nuim.ie/fulltext/readview.do?area=hcpp&id=1882-058905&source=&pagenum=452&resultNum=34&entries=187&queryId=..%2Fsession%2F1406552477_8061&backto=FULLREC&fromSearchHistory=&searchWithin=county+of+donegal&showall=&enlarge=Y [Accessed 28 July 2014]

'Census of Ireland for the year 1881. Religious professions of the people. Table XXVIII. Religious professions and sexes of the inhabitants, and number of families, in each parish in the county of Mayo', p. 400, retrieved from http://parlipapers.chadwyck.co.uk.jproxy.nuim.ie/fulltext/fulltext.do?area=hcpp&id=1882-058906&pagenum=1&backto=FULLREC [Accessed 2 August 2014]

'Census of Ireland for the year 1881. Religious professions of the people. Table XXVIII. Religious professions and sexes of the inhabitants, and number of families, in each parish in the county of Kerry', pp. 515–16, retrieved from http://parlipapers.chadwyck.co.uk.jproxy.nuim.ie/full-text/fulltext.do?area=hcpp&id=1882-058904&pagenum=1&backto=FULLREC [Accessed 11 July 2010]

Census of Ireland 1901 and 1911, retrieved from http://www.census.nationalarchives.ie/ [Accessed 10 December 2011]

'The Gaelic Athletic Association through History and Documents, 1870–1920: Teachers' resource pack. Letter from Michael Cusack to Maurice Davin, 26 August 1884', retrieved from http://www.crokepark.ie/getmedia/e35fa6c0-37od-4d68-831c-85df0f874a0d/web1.pdf [Accessed 11 July 2010]

Secondary Sources

Books and Articles

Bairner, Alan (ed.), *Sport and the Irish: Histories, Identities, Issues* (Dublin: University College Dublin Press, 2005)

Bale, John, 'Sport and National Identity: A Geographical View', *British Journal of Sports History*, vol. 3, no. 1 (1986), pp. 18–41

—, *Sports Geography* (London/New York: E. & F.N. Spon, 1989)

Bardon, Jonathan, *A History of Ulster* [Updated edition] (Belfast: Blackstaff Press, 2001)

Beattie, Seán, 'Folklore and Customs in North-west Donegal', *Donegal Annual: Journal of the County Donegal Historical Society*, no. 53 (Letterkenny: Browne Printers, 2001), pp. 44–49

—, 'Cottage Industries: Arts and Crafts in Donegal 1880–1920', *Donegal Annual, 2008*, no. 60 (Letterkenny: Browne Printers, 2008), pp. 59–81

—, 'Freemasonry in Donegal, 1757–1953', *Donegal Annual*, 2010, no. 62 (Letterkenny: Browne Printers, 2008), pp. 30–9

—, *Donegal in Transition: The Impact of the Congested Districts Board* (Sallins: Merrion, 2013)

Begley, Anthony, '*The Liberator*, 1839: A Forgotten Ballyshannon Newspaper', *Donegal Annual, 2003,* no. 55 (Letterkenny: Browne Printers, 2003), pp. 54–69

—, *Ballyshannon and Surrounding Areas: History, Heritage and Folklore* (Ballyshannon: Carrickboy Publishing, 2009)

Begley, Joe, Bell, Dave, Flanders, Steve and White, David, *The County Donegal Railway: A Visitor's Guide* (Leicester: The County Donegal Railway Restoration Society, 1996)

Bell, Dave and Flanders, Steve, *The Londonderry and Lough Swilly Railway: A Visitor's Guide* (Donegal: The County Donegal Railway Restoration Society, 1995)

Bolger, Pat, 'The Congested Districts Board and the Co-ops in Donegal', in William Nolan, Liam Ronayne and Mairead Dunlevy (eds), *Donegal History and Society: Interdisciplinary Essays on the History of an Irish County* (Dublin: Geography Publications, 1995), pp. 649–71

Bonagee United Football Club: 40 Years of Football 1970–2010 (Letterkenny: Bonagee United FC, 2010)

Bourke, Marcus, 'The Early GAA in South Ulster', *The Clogher Record*, vol. 7, no. 1 (1969), pp. 5–26

Boylan, Henry, *A Dictionary of Irish Biography* (Dublin: Gill & Macmillan, 1978)

Boyle, Seán, 'History of the GAA in Letterkenny and St Eunan's Club', *The Donegal GAA Yearbook* 1982 (Ballyshannon: Donegal Democrat, 1982), pp. 89–90

Bracken, Patrick, *'Foreign and Fantastic Field Sports': Cricket in County Tipperary* (Thurles: Liskiveen Books, 2004)

Bradley, Joseph M., 'Football in Scotland: A History of Political and Ethnic Identity', *International Journal of the History of Sport*, vol. 12, no. 1 (1995), pp. 81–98

—, 'Integration or Assimilation? Scottish Society, Football and Irish Immigrants', *International Journal of the History of Sport*, vol. 13, no. 2 (1996), pp. 61–79

—, *The Gaelic Athletic Association and Irishness in Scotland* (Argyll: Argyll Publishing, 2007)

Campbell, Donal, Dowds, Damian and Mullan, Damian, *Against the Grain: A History of Burt, its People and the GAA* (Burt: Burt GAA Club, 2000)

Cashman, Richard and McKernan, Michael (eds), *Sport in History* (Brisbane: University of Queensland Press, 1979)

Clerkin, C.A., 'History of Public Transport in Donegal', *Donegal Annual, 1952,* vol. 2, no. 2 (Ballyshannon: Donegal Democrat, 1952), pp. 405–17

Collins, Tony, *Rugby's Great Split: The Culture and Origins of Rugby League Football* (London: Frank Cass, 1998)

Comerford, R.V. , *Ireland: Inventing the Nation* (London: Bloomsbury Academic, 2003)

Conaghan, Pat, *Bygones: New Horizons on the History of Killybegs* (Killybegs: Bygones Enterprise, 1989)

—, *The Zulu Fishermen: Forgotten Pioneers of Donegal's First Fishing Industry* (Killybegs: Bygones Enterprise, 2003)

Corry, Eoghan, *Oakboys: Derry's Football Dream Come True* (Dublin: Poolbeg Press, 1993)

—, 'The Mass Media and the Popularisation of Gaelic Games, 1884–1934', in Dónal McAnallen, David Hassan and Roddy Hegarty (eds), *The Evolution of the GAA: Ulaidh, Éire agus Eile* (Armagh: Ulster Historical Foundation, 2009), pp. 100–11

Crampsie, Arlene, 'Relieving the Destitute Poor: A History of Milford Workhouse', *Donegal Annual, 2004,* no. 56 (Letterkenny: Browne Printers, 2004), pp. 68–87

Crawford, Joe and McCool, Dan (eds) *Golden Memories: A History of Gaelic Games around the Twin Towns,1916–1966* (Ballybofey: Seán MacCuamhaills GAA Club, 1999)

Cronin, Mike, *Sport and Nationalism in Ireland: Gaelic Games, Soccer and Irish Identity since 1884* (Dublin: Four Courts Press, 1999)

—, 'Enshrined in Blood: The Naming of Gaelic Athletic Association Clubs and the English Influence on Irish Sport', *The Sports Historian*, vol. 17, no. 2 (1998), pp. 90–104

—, 'Fighting for Ireland, Playing for England? The Nationalist History of the Gaelic Athletic Association and the English Influence on Irish Sport', *International Journal of the History of Sport,* vol. 15, no. 3 (1998), pp. 35–56

Cronin, Mike and Higgins, Roisín, *Places We Play: Ireland's Sporting Heritage* (Cork: The Collins Press, 2011)

Cronin, Mike, Murphy, William and Rouse, Paul (eds), *The Gaelic Athletic Association, 1884–2009* (Dublin: Irish Academic Press, 2009).

Cronin, Mike, Duncan, Mark and Rouse, Paul, *The GAA: A People's History* (Cork: The Collins Press, 2009)

—, *The GAA: County by County* (Cork: The Collins Press, 2011)

Crump, Jeremy and Mason, Tony, 'Hostile and Improper Demonstrations: Football Violence, 1880–1980', *The Bulletin of the Society for the Study of Labour History,* no. 50 (1985), pp. 11–12

Cunningham, John B., 'The Port of Ballyshannon', *Donegal Annual 2000,* no. 52 (Letterkenny: Browne Printers, 2000), pp. 7–37

Curran, Conor, 'Cricket in Donegal, 1864–1914', *Donegal Annual 2011: Journal of the County Donegal Historical Society,* no. 63 (Letterkenny: Browne Printers, 2011), pp. 64–70

—, *Sport in Donegal: A History* (Dublin: The History Press, 2010)

—, 'Leisure in Ballyshannon in the Late Nineteenth Century'. Paper given at the Society for the Study of Nineteenth-Century Ireland, Eighteenth Annual Conference, 28 June 2012

Daly, Mary E. (ed.), *County and Town: One Hundred Years of Local Government in Ireland* (Dublin: Institute of Public Administration, 2001)

Day, Angelique and Patrick McWilliams (eds), *Ordnance Survey Memoirs: Parishes of Donegal I, 1833–5: North-east Donegal* (Belfast: Institute of Irish Studies in association with the Royal Irish Academy, 1997)

De Blaghd, Earnán, 'Organising the IRB in Donegal', *Donegal Annual 1966,* vol. 7, no. 1 (Donegal: Donegal Democrat, 1966), pp. 41–4

De Burca, Marcus, *The GAA: A History* [Second edition] (Dublin: Gill & Macmillan Ltd, 2000)

Deery, Leo and O'Kane, Danny (eds), *Doire: A History of the GAA in Derry 1884–1984* (Coleraine: CLCG Doire, 1984)

Deignan, Pádraig, 'The importance of fraternities and social clubs for the Protestant community in Sligo from 1914 to 1949', in Jennifer Kelly and R.V. Comerford (eds), *Associational Culture in Ireland and Abroad* (Dublin: Irish Academic Press, 2010), pp. 191–213

Devlin, P.J., *Our Native Games* (Dublin: MH Gill & Son Ltd, 1935)

Duffy, Dick, 'The Growth of Soccer in Letterkenny', *Letterkenny and District Christmas Annual 2011* (Letterkenny: Browne Printers, 2011), pp. 42–4

Duncan, Tom, *The 1608 Royal Schools Celebrate 400 Years of History, 1608–2008* (Armagh: Premier Print and Design Ltd, 2007)

Dunning, Eric, Maguire, J.A., Murphy, Patrick and Williams, John, 'The Social Roots of Football Violence', *Leisure Studies*, vol. 1, no. 2 (1982), pp. 139–56

Ferriter, Diarmaid, *The Transformation of Ireland, 1900–2000* (London: Profile Books, 2004)

Fitzpatrick, David, 'The Geography of Irish Nationalism, 1910–1921', *Past and Present*, no. 78 (1978), pp. 113–44

Fitzgerald, Patrick, 'Emigration from Donegal and the Irish Emigration Database Project' *Donegal Annual, 2000*, no. 52 (Letterkenny: Browne Printers, 2000), pp. 57–62

Fleming, Sam, *Letterkenny Past and Present* (Ballyshannon: Donegal Democrat, 1979)

Foster, Roy, *Modern Ireland, 1600–1972* (London: Penguin, 1988).

Garnham, Neal, *Association Football and Society in Pre-partition Ireland* (Belfast: Ulster Historical Foundation, 2004)

—, (ed.), *The Origins and Development of Sport in Ireland. Being a Reprint of R.M. Peter's Irish Football Annual of 1880* (Belfast: Ulster Historical Foundation, 1999)

—, 'Accounting for the Early Success of the Gaelic Athletic Association', *Irish Historical Studies*, vol. xxxiv, no. 133 (2004), pp. 65–78

—, 'Sport and the State in Ireland: An Overview', *Leidschrift. Brood en spelen. Sports als kracht in de samenleving*, vol. 3, no. 3 (2008), pp. 99–117

—, 'The Roles of Cricket in Victorian and Edwardian Ireland', *Sporting Traditions*, vol. 19, no. 2 (2003), pp. 27–48

—, 'Football and Identity in Pre-Great War Ireland', *Irish Economic and Social History*, no. 28 (2001), pp. 13–31

Garvin, Tom, *The Evolution of Irish Nationalist Politics* [Second edition] (Dublin: Gill & Macmillan, 2005)

Gavin, Robert, 'Social and Economic Links Between Derry and Donegal in the Eighteenth and Early Nineteenth Centuries', in Jim MacLaughlin and Seán Beattie (eds), *An Historical, Environmental and Cultural Atlas of County Donegal* (Cork: Cork University Press, 2013), pp. 188–98

Gillespie, Simon and Hegarty, Roddy, 'Camán and Crozier: The Catholic Church and the GAA, 1884–1902', in McAnallen, Hassan and Hegarty, *The Evolution of the GAA*, pp. 112–22

Gorman, Trevor, *Kilmacrennan FC: An Illustrated History: A Nostalgic Look at a Century of Football* (Letterkenny: Greenlight Media, 2012)

Hart, Peter, 'The Geography of Revolution in Ireland, 1917–1923', *Past and Present*, vol. 155, no. 1 (1997), pp. 142–76

Harvey, Adrian, *The Beginnings of a Commercial Sporting Culture in Britain, 1793–1850* (Aldershot: Ashgate, 2004)

Hassan, David, 'Rugby Union, Irish Nationalism and Nationality in Northern Ireland', *Football Studies,* vol. 6, no. 1 (2003), pp. 5–18

—, 'The GAA in Ulster', in Cronin, Murphy and Rouse (eds), *The Gaelic Athletic Association, 1884–2009*, pp. 77–91

Holt, Richard, *Sport and Society in Modern France* (London: Palgrave Macmillan, 1981)

—, *Sport and the British: A Modern History* (Oxford: Clarendon Press, 1989)

—, 'Ireland and the Birth of Modern Sport', in Cronin, Murphy and Rouse (eds), *The Gaelic Athletic Association, 1884–2009,* pp. 33–46

Hornby, Hugh, *Uppies and Downies: The Extraordinary Football Games of Britain* (Swindon: English Heritage, 2008)

Huggins, Mike, 'The Spread of Association Football in North-east England, 1876–90: The Pattern of Diffusion', *International Journal of the History of Sport,* vol. 6, no. 3 (1989), pp. 299–318

Huggins, Mike and Tolson, John, 'The Railways and Sport in Victorian Britain: A Critical Reassessment', *Journal of Transport History,* vol. 22, no. 2 (2001), pp. 99–114

Hunt, Tom, *Sport and Society in Victorian Ireland: The Case of Westmeath* (Cork: Cork University Press, 2007)

—, 'The GAA: Social Structure and Associated Clubs', in Cronin, Murphy and Rouse (eds), *The Gaelic Athletic Association 1884–2009*, pp. 183–202

—, 'Parish Factions, Parading Bands and Sumptuous Repasts: The Diverse Origins and Activities of Early GAA Clubs', in McAnallen, Hassan and Hegarty, *The Evolution of the GAA,* pp. 86–99

Hutchinson, John, 'Some Aspects of Football Crowds Before 1914'. Paper presented to the Society for the Study of Labour History, University of Sussex, 1975

Jackson, Alvin, *Ireland 1798–1998* (Oxford: Blackwell Publishing, 1999)

Kelly, James, 'Horse Racing in Eighteenth-Century Ireland'. Paper given at the Sixth Annual Conference of Sports History Ireland, 25 September 2010

Kelly, Jennifer and Comerford, R.V. (eds), *Associational Culture in Ireland and Abroad* (Dublin: Irish Academic Press, 2010)

King, Seamus, *A History of Hurling* (Dublin: Gill & Macmillan, 1996)

Kinsella, Eoin, 'Riotous Proceedings and the Cricket of Savages: Football and Hurling in Early Modern Ireland', in Cronin, Murphy and Rouse (eds), *The Gaelic Athletic Association, 1884–2009*, pp. 15–31

Lecky, Reverend Alexander G., *In the Days of the Laggan Presbytery* (Belfast: Davidson & McCormack, 1908)

Lee, J.J., *Ireland, 1912–1985: Politics and Society* (Cambridge: Cambridge University Press, 1989)

Legg, Mary-Louise, *The Irish Provincial Press, 1850–1892* (Dublin: Four Courts Press, 1999)

Lennon, Joe, 'An Overview of the Playing Rules of Gaelic Football and Hurling, 1884–2010', in McAnallen, Hassan and Hegarty, *The Evolution of the GAA*, pp. 164–74

Leydon, Michael, *Dunmore MacHales: A History of Football in Dunmore Parish* (Dunmore: the author, 1983)

Mac a' Ghoill, Pádraig S., 'Cross-country Hurling in Ardara', *CLCG Ard a' Ratha* (Ardara: CLGC Ard a' Ratha, 1980), pp. 53–7

—, 'So We Began', *CLCG Ard a' Ratha* (Ardara: CLGC Ard a' Ratha, 1980), pp. 2–3

—, '100 Years of the GAA in Donegal', *Donegal Annual, 1984*, no. 36 (Ballyshannon: Donegal Democrat, 1984), pp. 89–94

Mac Conaill, Seán (ed.), *Idir Peil agus Pobal: A History of the GAA in the Parish of Ardara, 1921–2003* (Ardara: Blacklion Books, 2004)

MacDonagh, Oliver, Mandle W.F. and Travers, Pauric (eds), *Irish Culture and Nationalism 1750–1950* (London: Macmillan in association with Humanities Research Centre, Australian National University, 1983)

MacLaughlin, Jim and Beattie, Seán (eds), *An Historical, Environmental and Cultural Atlas of County Donegal* (Cork: Cork University Press, 2013)

MacLaughlin, Jim (ed.), *Donegal: The Making of a Northern County* (Dublin: Four Courts Press, 2007)

—, 'The Politics of Nation-building in Post-Famine Donegal', in Nolan, Ronayne and Dunlevy (eds), *Donegal History and Society*, pp. 583–623

—, 'Towns and Villages in Donegal', in MacLaughlin and Beattie (eds), *An Historical, Environmental and Cultural Atlas of County Donegal*, pp. 376–89

MacManus, Seumas, *The Story of the Irish Race: A Popular History of Ireland* (New York: Irish Publishing Co., 1921)

Malcolm, Elizabeth, 'Popular Recreation in Nineteenth-century Ireland', in MacDonagh, Mandle and Travers, *Irish Culture and Nationalism 1750–1950*, pp. 40–55

Mallon, Moira, 'Killybegs Emeralds', in *Dearcadh: The Ardara View, 1996–7* (Letterkenny: The Donegal Stationery Company, 1996), pp. 52–3

Mandle, W.F., *The Gaelic Athletic Association and Irish Nationalist Politics, 1884–1924* (London: Christopher Helm Publishers, 1987)

—, 'The Gaelic Athletic Association and Popular Culture', in MacDonagh, Mandle and Travers (eds), *Irish Culture and Nationalism, 1750–1950*, pp. 104–55

—, 'Sport as Politics: The Gaelic Athletic Association 1884–1916' in Cashman and McKernan (eds), *Sport in History*, pp. 99–123

Martin, Joseph, *The GAA in Tyrone: The Long Road to Glory* [Second edition] (Omagh: Tyrone GAA County Board, 2003)

Mason, Tony, *Association Football and English Society, 1863–1915* (Brighton: Harvester Press, 1980)

McAnallen, Dónal, Hassan, David and Hegarty, Roddy (eds), *The Evolution of the GAA: Ulaidh, Éire agus Eile* (Armagh: Ulster Historical Foundation, 2009)

McAnallen, Dónal, 'Cén Fáth a Raibh Cúige Uladh Chomh Lag Chomh Fada Sin? Deacrachtaí CLG ó Thuaidh, 1884–1945' (Why was the province of Ulster so weak for so long? Difficulties of the GAA in the North, 1884–1945), in McAnallen, Hassan and Hegarty, *The Evolution of the GAA*, pp. 138–151

McCaul, Very Reverend Liam, 'From Thurles to Ardara, 1884–1921', *Donegal Annual, 1985,* no. 37 (Ballyshannon: Donegal Democrat, 1985), pp. 67–73

McConville, Kieran and McAnallen, Dónal, 'The Search for John McKay' in McAnallen, Hassan and Hegarty, *The Evolution of the GAA*, pp. 240–53

McGettigan, Darren, *The Donegal Plantation and the Tír Chonaill Irish, 1610–1710* (Dublin: Four Courts Press, 2010)

McElligott, Richard, 'Degenerating, From Sterling Irishmen into Contemptible West Britons: The GAA and Rugby Football in Kerry, 1885–1905'. Paper delivered at the Sixth Annual Conference of Sports History Ireland, 25 September 2010

McLaughlin, Michael, *Inishowen's Senior Soccer Players* (Letterkenny: Browne Printers, 2004)

McMahon, Timothy G., *Grand Opportunity: The Gaelic Revival and Irish Society* (New York: Syracuse University Press, 2008)

McNiffe, Liam, *A History of the Garda Síochána: A Social History of the Force, 1922–52, With an Overview of the Years 1952–97* (Dublin: Merlin, 1997)

Meehan, Helen, *Inver Parish in History* (Mountcharles: the author, 2005)

—,'The MacManus Brothers', *Donegal Annual, 1994,* no. 46 (Ballyshannon: Donegal Democrat, 1994) pp. 5–19

—, and Godfrey H. Duffy, *Tracing Your Donegal Ancestors* [Second edition] (Dublin: Flyleaf Press, 2008)

Mehigan, P.D., *Gaelic Football* (Dublin: Gaelic Publicity Services, 1941)

—, *Hurling: Ireland's National Game* (Dublin: Gaelic Publicity Services, 1942)

Metcalfe, Alan, 'Football in the Mining Communities of East Northumberland, 1882–1914', *International Journal of the History of Sport,* vol. 5, no. 3 (1988), pp. 269–91

—,'The Control of Space and the Development of Twenty-two Sports in the Mining Communities of East Northumberland, 1880–1914', *The Sports Historian,* no. 15 (1995), pp. 23–33

Milne, Ida, 'The Quiet Corner-back: Rural Protestants and the GAA in the 26 Counties'. Paper delivered at Ninth Annual Sports History Ireland Conference, Magee College, Derry, 14 September 2013

Monaghan, Eamonn, *Remembering Our Founders* (Donegal: Donegal GAA County Board, 1997)

Murphy, Desmond, 'The Land War in Donegal, 1879–1891', *Donegal Annual, 1980*, no. 32 (Ballyshannon: Donegal Democrat, 1980), pp. 476–86

—, *Derry, Donegal and Modern Ulster, 1790–1921* (Derry: Aileach Press, 1981)

Murphy, William, 'The GAA during the Irish Revolution', in Cronin, Murphy and Rouse (eds), *The Gaelic Athletic, 1884–2009*, pp. 61–76

Murrin, Gary (ed.), *St Catherine's FC: A Celebration of 100 Years of Soccer in Killybegs* (Ballyshannon: Donegal Democrat, 1997)

Nolan, William, Ronayne, Liam and Dunlevy, Mairead (eds), *Donegal History and Society: Interdisciplinary Essays on the History of an Irish County* (Dublin: Geography Publications, 1995)

Nolan, Willliam (ed.), *The Gaelic Athletic Association in Dublin ,1884–2000* (Dublin: Geography Publications, 2005)

Oriard, Michael, *Reading Football: How the Popular Press Created an American Spectacle* (Chapel Hill: The University of North Carolina Press, 1993)

Ó Baoighill, Pádraig, *Cardinal Patrick O'Donnell, 1856–1927* (Fintown: Chró na mBothán, 2008)

Ó Baoill, Seán (ed.), *Donegal GAA Yearbook, 1982: CLCG Dhún na nGall* (Ballyshannon: Donegal Democrat, 1982)

Ó Caithnia, Liam P., *Scéal na hIomána* (Dublin: An Chlóchomhar Tta, 1980)

—, *Báirí Cos in Éirinn: Roimh Bhunú na gCumann Eagraithe* (Dublin: An Chlóchomhar Tta, 1984)

Ó Caiside, Seán, 'It Was the Gaelic Leaguers Who Rallied Donegal', *The Irish Press GAA Golden Jubilee Supplement, 1934*

O'Callaghan, Liam, *Rugby in Munster: A Social and Cultural History* (Cork: Cork University Press, 2011)

O'Connell, Aiden, 'The Ulster Covenant in Donegal, 1912', in Seán Beattie (ed.), *Donegal Annual: Journal of County Donegal Historical Society, 2011*, no. 63 (Letterkenny: Browne Printers, 2011), pp. 45–58

Ó Domhnaill, Micheál (ed.), *CLG Cill Chartha, 1924–1984* (Donegal: CLG Cill Chartha, 1984)

O'Donnell, Ben, *The Story of the Rosses* (Lifford: Caoran Publishing, 1999)

O'Dowd, Anne, 'Seasonal Migration to the Lagan and Scotland', in Nolan, Ronayne and Dunlevy (eds), *Donegal History and Society*, pp. 625–48

Ó Duibhir, Liam, *The Donegal Awakening: Donegal and the War of Independence* (Cork: Mercier Press, 2009)

—, *Donegal and the Civil War: The Untold Story* (Cork: Mercier Press, 2011)

Ó Gallchóir, An t-Ath Seán, *The Raidió na Gaeltachta Book of Donegal GAA Facts* [Third Edition] (Letterkenny: Raidió na Gaeltachta, 1996)

Ó hAnnracháin, Tadhg, 'The Heroic Importance of Sport: The GAA in the 1930s', *International Journal of the History of Sport,* vol. 25, no. 10 (2008), pp. 1326–37

Ó Maolfabhail, Art, *Camán: 2,000 Years of Hurling in Ireland: An Attempt to Trace the History and Development of the Stick-and-Ball Game in Ireland During the Past 2,000 Years* (Dundalk: Dundalgan Press, 1973)

—, Hegarty, Roddy and McAnallen, Dónal 'From Cú Chulainn to Cusack: Ball-playing, Camán, Shinny and Hurling in Ulster before the GAA', in McAnallen, Hassan and Hegarty, *The Evolution of the GAA,* pp. 62–78

Platt, William, *History of St Johnston Cricket Club, 1939–2000* (Coleraine: the author, 2001)

—, *North-west of Ireland Hockey: 1895–1968* (Coleraine: the author, 2006)

Porter, Liam, 'Donegal's Regular Player at Croke Park' *Dún na nGall GAA Yearbook 2008* (Donegal: Donegal GAA County Board, 2008), pp. 58–61

Potter, Matthew, '"Geographical Loyalty"? Counties, Palatinates, Boroughs and Ridings' *History Ireland,* vol. 20, no. 5 (2012), pp. 24–7

Reid, Seán, 'The Place of Irish Cricket in the Nineteenth-Century British Empire of Cricket'. Paper delivered at the Sixth Annual Conference of Sports History Ireland, 25 September 2010.

Rouse, Paul, 'The Politics of Culture and Sport in Ireland: A History of the GAA Ban on Foreign Games,1884–1971. Part One: 1884–1921', *International Journal of the History of Sport,* vol. 10, no. 3 (London, 1993), pp. 333–60

—, 'Sport and the Offaly Tradition: The Gaelic Athletic Association', in William Nolan and Timothy P. O'Neill (eds), *Offaly History and Society: Interdisciplinary Essays on the History of an Irish County* (Dublin: Geography Publications, 1998), pp. 889–928

—, 'Sport and Ireland in 1881', in Bairner (ed.), *Sport and the Irish: Histories, Identities, Issues,* pp. 7–21

—, 'Why the GAA was Founded', in Dónal McAnallen, David Hassan and Roddy Hegarty, *The Evolution of the GAA,* pp. 79–85

—, 'The Hand of Power', in 'Celebrating 125 Years of the GAA' in *The Irish Times,* 29 January 2009, pp. 51–3

Russell, David, 'Sporadic and Curious: The Emergence of Rugby and Soccer Zones in Yorkshire and Lancashire, c. 1860–1914', *International Journal of the History of Sport,* vol. 5, no. 2 (1988), pp. 185–205

Ryan, Liam, 'The GAA: Part of What We Are', *The Furrow* (Maynooth: St Patrick's College, 1984), pp. 752–64

Saorstat na hÉireann: Irish Free State Statistical Abstract 1931, Compiled By the Department of Industry and Commerce (Dublin: Department of Industry and Commerce, 1931)

Short, Con, *The Ulster GAA Story* (Rossan: Comhairle Uladh, 1984)

Siggins, Gerard, *Green Days: Cricket in Ireland, 1792–2005* (Gloucestershire: The History Press, 2005)

Strain, Hugh, *In Kilmacrennan Long Ago* (Kilmacrennan: the author, 1997)
'St Catherine's FC Profile' *Donegal Post*, 5 March 2008
Sugden, John and Bairner, Alan, *Sport, Sectarianism and Society in a Divided Ireland* (Leicester: Leicester University Press, 1993)
Sweeney, Frank, *The Murder of Conell Boyle, County Donegal, 1898* (Dublin: Four Courts Press, 2002)
Swilly Rovers FC: Team of '62 (Letterkenny: Swilly Rovers FC, 2002)
Taylor, Matthew, *The Association Game: A History of British Football* (Harlow: Pearson Education Ltd, 2008)
The Donegal GAA Yearbook, 1978 (Ballyshannon: Donegal Democrat, 1978)
Thompson, Kelly, 'Tattie Hokers and the IRA: The Impact of Migration to Scotland on the IRA in Donegal During the War of Independence', in Seán Beattie (ed.), *Donegal Annual, 2009*, no. 61 (Letterkenny: Browne Printers, 2009), pp. 52–9
Tranter, Neil, *Sport, Economy and Society in Britain, 1750–1914* (Cambridge: Cambridge University Press, 1998)
—, 'The Patronage of Organized Sport in Central Scotland, 1820–1900', *Journal of Sports History*, vol. 16, no. 3 (1989), pp. 227–47
—,'The Chronology of Organized Sport in Nineteenth-century Scotland: A Regional Study, I – Patterns' *International Journal of the History of Sport*, vol. 7, no. 2 (1990), pp. 188–203
—, 'The Chronology of Organized Sport in Nineteenth-century Scotland: A Regional Study, II – Causes', *International Journal of the History of Sport*, vol. 7, no. 3 (1990), pp. 365–87
—, 'The Cappielow Riot and the Composition and Behaviour of Soccer Crowds in Late Victorian Scotland', *International Journal of the History of Sport*, vol. 12, no. 3 (1995), pp. 124–40
Tunney, John, 'The Marquis, the Reverend, the Grandmaster and the Major: Protestant Politics in Donegal, 1868–1933', in Nolan, Ronayne and Dunlevy (eds), *Donegal History and Society*, pp. 675–94
Unknown, 'History of Glenties GAA Club', *Donegal GAA Yearbook, 1978* (Ballyshannon: Donegal Democrat, 1978), pp. 23–4
Vamplew, Wray, 'Sports Crowd Disorder in Britain, 1870–1914: Causes and Controls', *Journal of Sport History*, vol. 7, no. 1 (1980), pp. 5–20
Van Esbeck, Edmund, *One Hundred Years of Irish Rugby: The Official History of the Irish Rugby Football Union* (Dublin: Gill & Macmillan, 1974)
Walker, Andrew, 'Reporting Play: The Local Newspaper and Sports Journalism, c. 1870–1914', *Journalism Studies*, vol. 6, no. 2 (2006), pp. 452–62
Walker, B.M. (ed.), *Parliamentary Election Results in Ireland, 1801–1922* (Dublin: Royal Irish Academy, 1978)
—, *Parliamentary Election Results in Ireland, 1918–92: Irish Elections to Parliaments and Parliamentary Assemblies at Westminster, Belfast, Dublin, Strasbourg* (Dublin: Royal Irish Academy, 1992)

Walton, John K., *The British Seaside: Holidays and Resorts in the Twentieth Century* (Manchester: Manchester University Press, 2000)

Walvin, James, *The Only Game: Football in our Times* (Harlow: Longman, 2001)

Wright, Jonathan, 'Britain's Love of Sport', *BBC History,* vol. 13, no. 2 (Bristol: Immediate Media Co., 2012), pp. 78–9

Published and Unpublished Theses

Doherty, Derek, 'The History of the Gaelic Athletic Association in Donegal', unpublished MA thesis, National University of Ireland, Maynooth, 1998

McAnallen, Dónal, 'Playing on the Fourth Green State: The Gaelic Athletic Association and the Northern Ireland State, 1921–1968', unpublished PhD thesis, National University of Ireland, Galway, 2010

McElligott, Richard, 'Forging a Kingdom: The Establishment and Development of the Gaelic Athletic Association in Kerry, 1884–1924', PhD thesis, University College Dublin, 2011. Published by The Collins Press, 2013 as *Forging A Kingdom: The GAA in Kerry, 1884–1934.*

Online Sources

'About the GAA – rolls of honour – All Ireland senior football championship', retrieved from http://www.gaa.ie/about-the-gaa/gaa-history/rolls-of-honour/ [Accessed 9 February 2012]

'Achill Rovers History – The early years', retrieved from http://achill-rovers.com/achill_rovers_history_early_years_dooiver_swifts_htm [Accessed 2 September 2012]

'Census of England, 1881', retrieved from www.findmypast.co.uk/censushousehold search for 6, Knutsford Street, Kings Norton, Worcestershire. Census of England 1881. Public Record Office, RG 11/2950 [Accessed 29 July 2011]

'Census of England and Wales, 1911', retrieved from www.findmypast.co.uk/censushousehold search for 136 Salisbury Road, Moseley, Birmingham [Accessed 29 July 2011]

'Census of Ireland for the year 1881. Part 1. Area, Houses and Population: also the ages, civil or conjugal condition, occupations, birthplaces, religion and education of the people. Vol. III. Province of Ulster', retrieved from http://parlipapers.chadwyck.co.uk.jproxy.nuim.ie/fulltext/readview.do?area=hcpp&id=1882-058905&source=&pagenum=452&resultNum=34&entries=187&queryId=..%2Fsession%2F1406552477_8061&backto=FULLREC&fromSearchHistory=&searchWithin=county+of+donegal&showall=&enlarge=Y [Accessed 28 July 2014]

'Dáil Éireann Members Database: Major James Sproule Myles', retrieved from http://www.oireachtas.ie/members-hist/default.asp?housetype=

0&HouseNum=4&MemberID=806&ConstID=47 [Accessed 23 July 2014]

'Donegal Democrat – Democrat History', retrieved from http://www.donegaldemocrat.ie/CustomPages/CustomPage.aspx?PageID=56736 [Accessed 30 October 2010]

'Donegal GAA Boss Jim McGuinness Accepts Celtic Role', retrieved from http://www.bbc.co.uk/sport/0/northern-ireland/20254492 [Accessed 4 December 2012]

'FAI history: The early years', retrieved from http://www.fai.ie/fai/history/the-early-years.html [Accessed 17 October 2011]

'Football Association of Ireland – Ireland's international players', retrieved from http://www.fai.ie/international/senior-men/irelands-international-players.html [Accessed 9 February 2012]

Garnham, Neal, 'A sporting challenge', review of Tom Hunt, *Sport and Society in Victorian Ireland: The Case of Westmeath*, pp. 1–2, p. 2, retrieved from http://www.abdn.ac.uk/riiss/Reviews/Garnham_A%20sporting%20challenge.pdf [Accessed 8 December 2011]

Gray, Lisa, 'Shay Given interested in Celtic switch', retrieved from http://www.independent.co.uk/sport/football/premier-league/shay-given-interested-in-celtic-switch-2288798.html [Accessed 9 February 2012]

'Herdman's Mill in Sion Mills sold to lottery winner Margaret Loughrey', retrieved from http://www.bbc.com/news/uk-northern-ireland-foyle-west-28398820 [Accessed 23 July 2014]

'History: 1900–1910', retrieved from http://www.cavangaa.ie/1900_to_1910.html [Accessed 24 May 2013]

'History of Ballina Town', retrieved from http://www.ballinatc.ie/AboutBallina/HistoryofBallinaTown/ [Accessed 28 October 2012]

'HNAG Database of Irish Historical Statistics', British Parliamentary Papers, Accounts and papers, Session 16, January 1902–18 December 1902, Volume CXXIX, available at Jason Begley, Frank Geary and Kevin H. O'Rourke (eds), retrieved from http://www.tcd.ie/iiis/HNAG/HNAG_database_population_page_1.htm [Accessed 20 December 2011]

Hoban, Brian, 'Muriel Gahan (1897–1995)', retrieved from http://towns.mayo-ireland.ie/WebX?14@213.BPtFe4YwNNr.0@.ee7a78d [Accessed 25 August 2009]

Johnes, Martin, 'Historiography of Sport in Modern Britain', pp. 1–21, p. 8, retrieved from http://www.academia.edu/197884/Historiography_of_Sport_in_Britain [Accessed 27 October 2012]

'Irish Genealogy Toolkit', retrieved from http://www.irish-genealogy-toolkit.com/County-map-of-Ireland.html [Accessed 30 October 2011]

'IRFU History', retrieved from http://www.irishrugby.ie/300_285.php [Accessed 25 August 2009]

'Irish War Memorials', retrieved from http://www.irishwarmemorials.ie/html/showMemorial.php?show=338 [Accessed 15 October 2011]

'Launch of historical golf book', retrieved from http://www.donegaldemocrat.ie/lifestyle/launch_of_historical_golf_book_1_3177016 [Accessed 2 November 2011]

'Londonderry and Lough Swilly Railway', retrieved from http://www.irishrailwayana.com/pa206.htm [Accessed 19 October 2011]

McGeady, Simon, 'Greencastle Regatta website goes live in May', retrieved from http://www.inishowennews.com/08GreenMemorable.htm [Accessed 24 September 2009]

'Munster GAA-Senior football-number of titles', retrieved from http://munster.gaa.ie/history/sf_teams/ [Accessed 9 February 2012]

Ó Riordan, Tomás, 'Hanna Sheehy Skeffington', retrieved from http://multitext.ucc.ie/d/Hanna_Sheehy-Skeffington [Accessed 4 February 2012]

'Red Hugh's GAA Club/CLG Aodh Rua, Cúil na gCúirrdín', retrieved from http://www.redhughsgaa.com/n_history.htm [Accessed 1 June 2011]

'Rosapenna Hotel & Golf Resort', retrieved from http://www.rosapenna.ie/history.php [Accessed 2 November 2011]

'Sport and the British – The dawn of professional football', retrieved from http://www.bbc.co.uk/podcasts/series/sportbrit#playepisode3 [Accessed 13 February 2012]

'The plantation of the Laggan, County Donegal', retrieved from http://www.askaboutireland.ie/reading-room/history-heritage/history-of-ireland/the-ulster-plantation/the-plantation-of-the-lag/ [Accessed 20 October 2011]

Ward, John, 'Pa McAdam – The Grandfather I Never Knew', retrieved from http://www.vindicator.ca/history/vinStory/vinStory1.html [Accessed 31 October 2010]

—, 'Of the centre and its extremities', retrieved from http://www.vindicator.ca/kindly/chapterThree.html [Accessed 23 July 2014]

Whelan, Kevin, 'The Geography of hurling', retrieved from http://www.askaboutIreland.ie/show_narrative_page.do?page_id=2352 [Accessed 13 February 2008]

APPENDIX 1

Religious breakdown per parish of Donegal in 1881, including percentage of Protestant population per parish

Parish (1881) and corresponding-no. on map	Overall Total	Roman Catholic	Protestant Episco-palians	Presby-terians	Meth-odists	All others	Total Protestant population per parish
Aghanunshin (1)	674	284	118	269	1	2	57.56%
All Saints (2)	2365	1041	352	963	7	2	55.89%
Aughnish (3)	2959	1653	485	765	10	46	42.58%
Barr of Inch or Mintiaghs (4)	297	296	0	1	0	0	33.00%
Burt (5)	2153	1143	195	807	3	3	46.67%
Clonca (6)	5066	4225	243	586	10	0	16.60%
Clondahorky (7)	4914	3547	1190	162	1	11	7.53%
Clondavaddog (8)	6253	5357	637	250	4	3	14.24%
Clonleigh (9)	3050	1745	541	738	14	12	42.39%
Clonmany (10)	5037	5015	9	13	0	0	0.43%
Convoy (11)	3332	2135	350	782	0	55	33.97%
Conwal (12)	8753	6073	1082	1491	5	99	30.58%
Culdaff (13)	4221	3717	239	130	48	0	9.87%
Desertegny (14)	1356	1259	89	8	0	0	7.15%
Donagh (15)	4306	3719	292	265	30	0	13.63%
Donaghmore (16)	7503	4961	918	1473	18	133	31.99%
Donegal (17)	4767	3301	953	315	174	21	29.83%
Drumhome (18)	6135	3283	2502	73	227	0	45.67%
Fahan Lower (19)	4195	3837	401	228	3	23	15.06%
Fahan Upper (20)	2000	1277	292	430	0	1	38.60%
Gartan (21)	1213	1005	134	72	0	2	16.98%
Glencolumb-kille (22)	4139	3887	223	24	0	5	5.96%
Inch (33)	533	366	54	113	0	0	31.33%
Iniskeel (34)	9902	9158	508	6	163	7	6.83%
Inishmacsaint (35)	3593	3136	374	58	24	1	12.69%
Inver (36)	8415	7148	1100	19	147	1	0.15%
Kilbarron (23)	5667	4578	859	139	89	2	19.18%
Kilcar (24)	3319	3201	115	0	0	0	3.46%
Killaghtee (25)	3330	2154	779	4	393	0	35.31%
Killea (26)	615	224	177	214	0	0	63.50%

Appendix 1 (cont.)

Religious breakdown per parish of Donegal in 1881, including percentage of Protestant population per parish

Parish 1881 and corresponding-no. on map	Overall Total	Roman Catholic	Protestant Episco-palians	Presby-terians	Meth-odists	All others	Total Protestant population per parish
Killybegs Lower (27)	2582	2271	227	1	83	0	12.04%
Killybegs Upper (28)	3127	2549	461	23	88	3	18.29%
Killygarvan (29)	2121	1687	257	173	0	4	20.27%
Killymard (30)	2962	1958	895	71	38	0	33.89%
Kilmacrennan (31)	5795	4389	431	890	1	81	22.81%
Kilteevoge (32)	4495	3821	618	38	0	18	14.59%
Leck (37)	2013	1231	230	563	0	16	39.39%
Lettermacaward (38)	2547	2421	121	5	0	0	4.94%
Mevagh (39)	4191	3683	341	155	11	1	12.09%
Moville Lower (40)	4716	3677	672	309	56	2	21.98%
Moville Upper (41)	3775	2717	486	500	69	3	27.94%
Muff (42)	2523	1196	307	1015	0	5	52.39%
Raphoe (43)	3399	1388	553	1433	0	25	58.42%
Raymoghy (44)	3134	1390	376	1365	0	3	55.26%
Raymunterdoney (45)	1853	1630	183	35	1	4	3.93%
Stranorlar (46)	4109	2922	737	367	4	79	26.96%
Taughboyne (47)	3494	1354	461	1022	0	57	59.61%
Templecarn (48)	2803	1556	851	181	216	0	44.52%
Templecrone (49)	11525	11137	361	14	12	1	1.11%
Tullaghobegley (50)	9636	9392	225	16	3	0	2.53%
Tullyfern (51)	3709	1854	305	1420	3	127	46.58%
Urney (52)	1141	651	292	187	9	2	42.75%

Sources: 'Census of Ireland for the year 1881. Religious professions of the people. Table XXVIII. Religious professions and sexes of the inhabitants, and number of families, in each parish in the county of Donegal', pp. 451–2, retrieved from http://parlipapers.chadwyck.co.uk.jproxy.nuim.ie/fulltext/readview.do?area=hcpp&id=1882-058905&source=&pagenum=452&resultNum=34&entries=187&queryId=..%2Fsession%2F1406552477_8061&backto=FULLREC&fromSearchHistory=&searchWithin=county+of+donegal&showall=&enlarge=Y [Accessed 28 July 2014]. Map adapted from 'Ulster Historical Foundation: Civil parishes of Donegal', retrieved from http://www.ancestryireland.com/civil-parish-maps-for-ulster/civil-parishes-of-county-donegal/ [Accessed 3 August 2014]

APPENDIX 2

Number of matches involving Donegal GAA clubs/teams recorded in the local and national press, 1888–92

Year	Name	Number of Hurling Matches recorded	Number of Gaelic football matched recorded
1888	Burt Hibernians	3	0
	Cahir O's Buncrana	1 unspecified	0
1889	Burt Hibernians	2	0
	Portlough Harps	1	0
	Killea Hibernians	3	3
	Cahir O's	7	6
	Bundoran Irish Hearts	0	1
	Finner	0	1
1890	Burt Hibernians	4	3
	Cahir O's	3	2
	Portlough Harps	2	2
	Killea Hibernians	3	3
	Buncrana Emmets	1	2
	Newtowncunningham Harps	4	3
1891	Burt Hibernians	2	0
	Newtowncunningham Harps	2	0
	The Joys	0	1
	Green Volunteers	0	1
	Moville Harps	0	1
	Ballynelly Pioneers	0	1
1892	Burt Hibernians	2	0
	Newtowncunningham Harps	1	0

SOURCES: Sport, *DV*, *DI* and *DJ* (1888–92)
Abandoned matches have also been included.

Appendix 3
Political background of competitive GAA clubs, 1905–07

Name	Date founded	Origins of club name	Founder(s)	Political involvement
Lámh Dearg, Mountcharles	c. Feb. 1905	Red Hand, motto of O'Neill clan	Seumas Macmanus	Cumann na Gaedheal
Ethna Carberry's, Croagh	1905	Wife of Seumas MacManus, Gaelic League activist	John McGrath	Cumann na nGaedheal
Ardaghey Old Celts	1905	Irish allegiance	James Maguire	Unknown
Thomas Davis, Dunkineely	14 May 1905	Nineteenth-century Irish political figure	Seamus McHugh	Cumann na nGaedheal
Balldearg, Donegal town	20 Oct. 1905	Birthmark peculiar to O'Donnell clan	P.M. Gallagher, R.C. Bonner	Gaelic League
Clann Conaill, Brackey	c. Aug. 1905	Family of son of , Irish High King, Conall Gulban	Charles McGill	Unknown
Inver	c. Feb. 1906	Unknown	Unknown	Unknown
Killybegs	c. April 1906	Unspecified	Joseph Rowan, John O'Friel	Unknown
Sinn Féin, Bundoran	c. Oct. 1906	Political organisation	Edward Daly	Gaelic League
Rory Ógs, Ballybofey	14 May 1906	1st Earl of Tyrconnell, Rory O'Donnell	Unknown	Unknown
Burt Hibernians	5 Feb. 1888	Irish allegiance	Unknown but GAA introduced to parish by Derry club, St Patrick's	Unknown
Newtown-cunningham Harps	c. 1889 refounded 1905	Irish allegiance	Unknown 1889 but 1905 founded by Daniel McConville	Unknown
Lámh Dearg, Letterkenny	18 Sept. 1905	Red Hand, motto of O'Neill clan	James Peoples	Irish National Federation, United Irish League
St Mura's, Fahan	c. 1899	Irish saint	Unknown	Unknown
Gweedore Old Celts	5 Nov. 1905	Irish allegiance	Neil J. Ferry	Unknown
St Columba's, Churchill	1906	Irish saint	Unknown	Unknown
Creeslough	9 Nov. 1905	Unspecified	Michael Harkin, Patrick McCarry	Ancient Order of Hibernians
Inch Emeralds	1906	Irish allegiance	Unknown	Unknown

Sources: *DJ*, *DP* and *DN*, *DI* and *DV* (1905–07)

Appendix 4

Political background of non-competitive GAA clubs, 1905–07

Name	Date founded	Origins of club name	Founder(s)	Political involvement
Doorin Young Irelanders	c. July 1905	Nineteenth-century Irish political movement	Unknown	Unknown
Naomh Conaill, Kilraine	28 July 1905	Irish saint	Neal McNelis, D. McDwyer	Cumann na nGaedheal
True Gaels, Meenabradden	22 Oct. 1905	Irish allegiance	Unknown	Cumann na nGaedheal
Tír Conaill, Fintown	c. Nov. 1905	Kingdom formerly belonging to Conall Gulban	Rev. Charles Kennedy	Unknown
Glenfin	c. Oct. 1905	Unspecified	Rev. Burns	Gaelic League, AOH
Colmcille club, Lettermore	c. 1905	Irish saint	Unknown	Unknown
Killygordon	6 Jan. 1906	Unspecified	P.A. Maguire, James McGranaghan	Unknown
Ardara	15 April 1906	Unspecified	P. Molloy	Unknown
Glenswilly	Unknown	Unspecified	Unknown	Unknown
Drumkeelin	Unknown	Unspecified	Unknown	Unknown
Frosses	Unknown	Unspecified	Unknown	Unknown

Sources: As Appendix 3

Appendix 5
Gaelic football teams in Donegal, 1919–34

Year	1919	1920	1921	1922	1923	1924	1925	1926	1927	1928	1929
South	6	5	4	4	2	8	4	4	4	4	4
West	3	0	4	4	4	3	2	2	2	1	2
East	7	7	13	7	8	8	7	12	7	11	7
South-west	1	0	3	4	3	5	3	4	5	4	3
Inishowen	1	5	1	1	2	6	0	0	0	0	2
Overall Total	**18**	**17**	**25**	**20**	**19**	**30**	**16**	**22**	**18**	**20**	**18**

Year	1930	1931	1932	1933	1934
South	7	8	12	12	10
West	4	3	3	9	14
East	16	20	19	16	25
South-west	10	14	10	17	17
Inishowen	2	3	1	1	1
Overall Total	**39**	**48**	**45**	**55**	**67**

Sources: *DJ, DV, DI, DP and DN, DP and TN, DPP* (1919–34)

Appendix 6

Gaelic football teams in South Donegal, 1919–34

Club	1919	1920	1921	1922	1923	1924	1925	1926	1927	1928	1929
Aodh Ruadh, Ballyshannon	✓	✓	✓	✓	✓	✓	✓	✓	✓	–	✓
Assaroe	–	–	–	–	–	✓	–	–	–	–	–
Ballintra Emeralds	✓	–	–	–	–	✓	–	–	–	–	–
Belleek (Fermanagh)	–	✓	–	✓	–	–	–	–	–	–	–
Cashelard	–	–	–	–	–	–	–	–	✓	–	✓
Corlea (Fermanagh)	–	–	–	–	–	–	–	–	–	✓	–
Drimarone	✓	–	–	–	–	–	–	–	–	–	–
Eire Óg	–	–	–	–	–	✓	–	–	–	–	–
Finner Camp	–	–	–	–	–	✓	–	✓	✓	–	–
Four Masters, Donegal Town	✓	✓	✓	–	–	–	–	–	–	–	–
Killymard	–	✓	–	–	–	–	✓	–	–	–	–
Kinlough (Leitrim)	✓	–	–	–	–	–	–	–	–	–	–
Mountcharles	–	–	–	✓	–	✓	✓	–	✓	–	–
St Patrick's, Bundoran	✓	✓	✓	✓	✓	✓	–	✓	–	✓	✓
Pettigo	–	–	✓	–	–	–	–	–	–	✓	✓
Tanatallon (Mountcharles)	–	–	–	–	–	–	–	–	–	✓	–
Young Tír Conaills	–	–	–	–	–	✓	✓	✓	–	–	–
Total	**6**	**5**	**4**	**4**	**2**	**8**	**4**	**4**	**4**	**4**	**4**

Club	1930	1931	1932	1933	1934
Aodh Ruadh, Ballyshannon	✓	✓	✓	✓**	✓**
Ballintra	–	✓	✓	–	–
Barnes	✓	–	–	–	–
Cashelard	✓	✓	✓	✓*	✓
Clyhore (Fermanagh)	–	–	–	✓*	–
Corlea (Fermanagh)	–	–	–	✓*	✓*
Croagh	–	–	–	✓	–
Donegal Town	✓	✓	✓	✓**	✓
Drimarone	–	–	–	✓	–
Driminin	–	–	✓	–	–
Drumbar	–	✓	–	–	–
Drumholm, Ballintra	–	✓	–	–	–
Frosses	–	–	✓	–	–
Finner Camp	✓	–	–	–	–
Killymard	–	–	✓	✓	✓
Lough Eske	–	–	✓	–	–
Meenagran	–	–	✓	–	–
Mountcharles	✓	–	✓	–	–
Star of the Sea, Bundoran	✓	✓	✓	✓	✓
St Ernan's, Ballintra	–	–	–	–	✓
St Patrick's, Bundoran	–	–	–	–	–
Pettigo	–	–	–	✓	✓*
Tanatallon (Mountcharles)	–	✓	–	✓*	✓
Townawilly	–	–	✓	✓*	✓*
Total	**7**	**8**	**12**	**12**	**10**

* Denotes junior team
** Denotes junior and senior team

Sources: As Appendix 5

APPENDIX 7

Gaelic football teams in East Donegal, 1919–34

Club	1919	1920	1921	1922	1923	1924	1925	1926	1927	1928	1929
Belalt (Tyrone)	–	✓*	✓	–	–	–	–	–	–	–	–
Ballybofey Kickhams	–	–	–	–	–	–	–	–	–	✓	–
Carrigans	–	–	–	–	–	✓	–	✓	✓	–	–
Carrigart	–	–	–	–	✓	✓	✓	✓	–	–	–
Castlefin Emmets	–	–	✓	✓	–	–	–	✓	–	–	–
Churchill	–	–	–	–	–	✓	–	–	–	–	–
Clonleigh	–	–	–	–	–	✓	–	✓	–	–	–
Con Colbert's, Castlefin	✓	✓*	✓	–	✓	–	–	–	–	–	–
Convoy	–	–	–	–	–	–	–	–	–	–	✓
Creeslough	✓	–	–	–	✓	✓	–	✓	–	–	–
Crossroads (Ballybofey)	–	–	–	–	–	–	–	–	–	✓	–
Downings	✓	–	–	–	–	–	–	–	–	–	–
Éire Óg, Ballybofey	–	✓*	✓	–	–	–	✓	✓	✓	–	–
Erin's Hope (Ballybofey and Stranorlar Utd)	–	–	–	–	–	–	–	–	–	✓	✓
Geraldines, Letterkenny	–	–	–	–	–	–	✓	✓	✓	–	–
Goland	–	–	–	–	–	–	–	–	–	✓	–
Kevin Barry's, Stranorlar	–	✓*	✓	✓	–	–	–	–	–	–	✓
Lifford	–	–	–	–	✓	✓	–	–	–	–	–
Liscooley	–	–	–	–	–	–	–	–	–	✓	–
Milford	–	–	–	–	✓	✓	–	–	–	–	–
Letterkenny Faugh a Ballaghs	✓	✓	✓	–	–	–	–	–	–	–	–
Letterkenny Rovers	–	–	–	–	–	–	✓	✓	✓	–	–
O'Toole's, Raphoe	–	–	✓	✓	–	–	–	–	–	–	–
Rabstown (Tyrone)	✓	–	–	–	–	–	–	–	–	–	–
Raphoe	–	–	–	–	✓	–	✓	✓	–	✓	✓
Rathmullan Rovers	–	–	–	–	–	✓	–	–	–	–	–
Red Hugh's, Killygordon	✓	✓**	✓	–	–	–	–	–	✓	✓	✓
Red Hugh's, Letterkenny	–	–	–	–	✓	–	–	–	–	–	–
Sarsfields, Stranorlar	–	–	–	–	–	–	✓	✓	–	✓	
St Eunan's, Letterkenny	–	–	–	–	–	–	–	–	✓	✓	–
St Eunan's College, Letterkenny	–	–	–	–	–	–	–	–	–	–	–
St Mary's, Castlefin	–	–	✓	✓	–	–	–	✓	✓	✓	✓
St Pat's, Derry	–	–	–	–	–	–	–	✓	–	–	–
Swilly Rovers, Churchill	–	–	–	–	–	–	–	–	–	–	–
The Mental Hospital, Letterkenny	–	–	–	–	–	–	✓	–	–	–	✓
Tír Conaill Harps, Murlog	–	–	✓	✓	–	–	–	–	–	–	–
Trusk	–	–	–	–	–	–	–	–	–	✓	–
William Pearse's, Clady (Tyrone)	✓	✓	✓	–	–	–	–	–	–	–	–
Young McCartan's, Ballybofey	–	–	✓	✓	–	–	–	–	–	–	–
Young McCarron's, Ballybofey	–	–	✓	✓	✓	–	–	–	–	–	–
Total	7	7	13	7	8	8	7	12	7	11	7

APPENDIX 7 (cont.)
Gaelic football teams in East Donegal, 1919–34

Club	1930	1931	1932	1933	1934
Ballinamore	–	–	–	–	✓
Ballyheerin	✓	–	✓	✓	✓
Ballyhuirke	–	–	✓	✓	–
Ballywhoriskey	–	–	✓	–	–
Carrigart	✓	–	–	–	–
Carry Rovers	–	–	✓	–	–
Cashel (Fanad)	–	–	–	✓	–
Churchill	–	✓	–	–	–
Cloghan	✓	–	✓	✓	✓*
Cloghan Invincibles	–	–	–	–	✓*
Convoy	✓	✓	✓	✓	✓
Crossroads (Ballybofey)	–	–	–	–	✓
Crossroad Rangers (Fanad)	–	–	✓	–	–
Downings	✓	–	–	–	–
Erin's Hope (Ballybofey and Stranorlar Utd)	✓	✓	✓	✓	–
Fanad Creeve Roes	–	✓	✓	✓	✓
Finn Rovers (Ballybofey)	–	–	–	–	✓
Fintown	✓	–	–	✓	✓*
Gartan	–	✓	–	–	✓
Glenfin Rangers	–	–	–	–	✓*
Glenswilly	✓	✓	–	–	–
Glendoan	–	–	–	✓	–
Glenvar	–	–	–	✓	–
Goland	–	–	✓	–	–
Gortnatra	–	–	–	✓	–
Kilmacrennan	–	–	✓	–	–
Kingarrow	–	–	–	–	✓
Knock Sarsfields	–	–	–	–	✓
Lennon Swifts	–	✓	–	–	–
Lifford	–	✓	–	–	–
Main Street, Ballybofey	–	–	–	–	✓
Milford	✓	✓	✓	–	✓
Murlog	–	✓	–	–	–
Meenlaharry	–	–	–	–	✓
Letterkenny Rovers	–	–	–	–	✓*
Porthall	–	✓	✓	✓	✓
Portsalon Gaels	✓	–	–	–	–
Raphoe	✓	✓	✓	✓	✓*
Red Hugh's, Killygordon	✓	✓	–	–	✓
Rossgier	–	✓	–	–	–
St Eunan's, Letterkenny	✓	✓	✓**	✓	✓
St Eunan's College, Letterkenny	✓	✓	✓	–	–
St Mary's, Castlefin	✓	✓	✓	–	✓
St Mary's, Rossgier	✓	✓	–	–	✓
St Pat's, Derry	–	–	–	–	–
Swilly Rovers, Churchill	–	✓	✓	✓	✓
The Pat's, Letterkenny	–	✓	✓	–	–
Toame	–	–	–	✓	–
42nd Street, Ballybofey	–	–	–	–	✓
Total	**16**	**20**	**19**	**16**	**25**

SOURCES: As Appendix 5

Appendix 8
Gaelic football teams in West Donegal, 1919–34

Club	1919	1920	1921	1922	1923	1924	1925	1926	1927	1928	1929
Annagry	–	–	–	–	–	–	–	–	–	–	–
Burtonport	✓	–	–	–	✓	–	–	–	–	–	–
Derrybeg Emmets	–	–	✓	✓	–	–	–	–	–	–	–
Dunfanaghy	–	–	–	–	✓	✓	✓	–	–	–	–
Dungloe	–	–	–	–	–	✓	✓	✓	✓	✓	✓
Falcarragh	–	–	✓	✓	–	–	–	–	✓	–	✓
Fontenoy's, Rosses	✓	–	–	–	–	–	–	–	–	–	–
Gortahork	✓	–	–	–	✓	–	–	–	–	–	–
Gweedore	–	–	✓	✓	–	–	–	–	–	–	–
Kincasslagh Rovers	–	–	✓	✓	–	✓	–	–	–	–	–
Maghery	–	–	–	–	✓	–	–	✓	–	–	–
Marameelin	–	–	–	–	–	–	–	–	–	–	–
Mullaghduff	–	–	–	–	–	–	–	–	–	–	–
Rannafast	–	–	–	–	–	–	–	–	–	–	–
Rosses Rovers	–	–	–	–	–	–	–	–	–	–	–
Total	3	0	4	4	4	3	2	2	2	1	2

Club	1930	1931	1932	1933	1934
Annagry	✓*	–	–	✓*	–
Ballinacarrick	–	–	–	–	✓*
Doochary	–	–	–	–	✓*
Dooey	–	–	–	–	✓
Dunfanaghy	–	–	–	✓*	–
Dungloe	✓	✓	✓	✓**	✓*
Falcarragh	✓	✓	✓	✓	✓*
Gweebarra	–	–	–	–	✓*
Gweedore	✓	✓	✓	✓*	✓*
Kincasslagh Rovers	–	–	–	✓	–
Maas	–	–	–	–	✓
Marameelin	–	–	–	✓*	✓*
Meendernasole Rovers	–	–	–	–	✓*
Meenmore	–	–	–	–	✓
Mullaghduff	–	–	–	✓*	–
Rannafast	–	–	–	✓*	–
Roddy's Rovers	–	–	–	–	✓*
Rosses Celtic	–	–	–	–	✓*
Rosses Rovers	–	–	–	–	✓*
Total	4	3	3	9	14

*Despite their north-western location, Creeslough, Downings and Carrigart were grouped in the eastern area by the County Board for Gaelic football purposes and have been included in the Eastern table.

Sources: As Appendix 5

APPENDIX 9

Gaelic football teams in South-west Donegal, 1919–34

Club	1919	1920	1921	1922	1923	1924	1925	1926	1927	1928	1929
Ardara	–	–	✓	✓	✓	✓	✓	✓	✓	✓	✓
Bruckless	–	–	–	–	–	–	–	✓	–	–	–
Carrick	–	–	–	–	–	✓	–	–	–	–	–
Dunkineely	–	–	–	–	–	–	–	✓	✓	✓	–
Glenties	–	–	✓	✓	✓	✓	✓	✓	✓	–	–
Glenties Utd	–	–	–	–	–	–	–	–	–	✓	✓
Kilcar	–	–	–	✓	–	✓	✓	–	✓	–	–
Killaghtee	–	–	–	–	–	–	–	–	–	✓	✓
Killybegs	✓	–	✓	✓	✓	✓	–	–	✓	–	–
Total	**1**	**0**	**3**	**4**	**3**	**5**	**3**	**4**	**5**	**4**	**3**

Club	1930	1931	1932	1933	1934
Ardara	✓	✓**	✓	✓**	✓**
Ballydhu	✓	✓	–	–	–
Bruckless	–	✓	✓	✓	–
Carrick	✓	✓	✓	✓	✓
Cashel	–	–	–	–	✓
Commons	–	–	✓	✓	✓
Croagh	–	✓	✓	✓	–
Downstrands	–	✓	–	–	–
Dunkineely	–	–	✓	✓	✓
Fintown	✓	–	–	–	✓*
Fintra	–	✓	–	✓	✓
Glencolumbkille	–	–	–	✓	✓**
Glenties	–	–	–	–	–
Glenties Utd	✓	✓	✓*	✓	–
Kilcar	✓	✓	✓	✓	✓
Killaghtee	–	–	–	✓*	✓*
Killybegs	–	–	–	–	–
Killybegs Niall Mors	✓	✓	✓	✓	✓
Maghera	–	–	✓	–	–
Malinmore	✓	✓	–	–	–
Meenacross	✓	✓	–	✓	✓
Meenaneary	–	–	–	✓	✓
Straleel	✓	✓	–	✓	✓
St John's Point	–	–	–	✓	✓*
Teelin	–	–	–	–	✓
Tullycleave	–	✓	–	–	–
Owentocker (Glenties)	–	–	–	✓*	✓
Total	10	14	10	17	17

SOURCES: As Appendix 5

Appendix 10
Gaelic football teams in Inishowen, 1919–34

Club	**1919**	**1920**	**1921**	**1922**	**1923**	**1924**	**1925**	**1926**	**1927**	**1928**	**1929**
Burnfoot Kevin Barry's	–	–	–	–	–	✓	–	–	–	–	–
Burt	–	–	–	–	–	–	–	–	–	–	✓
Burt Éire Óg	–	–	–	–	–	✓	–	–	–	–	–
Burt Hibernians*	–	–	–	–	–	–	–	–	–	–	✓
Cahir O's, Buncrana	✓	✓	–	✓	✓	✓	–	–	–	–	–
Carndonagh	–	✓	–	–	–	–	–	–	–	–	–
Clonmany	–	–	–	–	✓	–	–	–	–	–	–
Maginns	–	✓	–	–	–	–	–	–	–	–	–
Newtowncunningham	–	✓	–	–	–	✓	–	–	–	–	–
St Mary's, Clonmany	–	–	–	–	–	✓	–	–	–	–	–
St Mura's, Fahan	–	–	✓	–	–	✓	–	–	–	–	–
St Patrick's, Buncrana	–	✓	–	–	–	–	–	–	–	–	–
Total	1	5	1	1	2	6	0	0	0	0	2

Club	**1930**	**1931**	**1932**	**1933**	**1934**
Burnfoot Kevin Barry's	–	–	–	–	–
Burt	✓	✓	–	✓	–
Inch	–	✓	–	–	–
Umricam	–	–	✓	–	✓
United Services, Buncrana	✓	✓	–	–	–
Total	**2**	**3**	**1**	**1**	**1**

*Burt Hibernians had taken the name Éire Óg by the summer of 1924

Sources: As Appendix 5

APPENDIX 11
Hurling teams in Donegal, 1919–34

Club	1919	1920	1921	1922	1923	1924	1925	1926	1927	1928	1929
Aodh Ruadh, Ballyshannon	✓	–	–	–	✓	✓	✓	–	✓	✓	✓
Ballybofey	–	–	–	–	–	–	–	–	✓	–	–
Ballyshannon Harps	–	–	–	–	–	–	✓	✓	–	–	–
Buncrana Military Garrison	–	–	–	–	–	–	✓	✓	–	–	–
Bundoran	–	–	–	–	–	–	–	–	–	✓	✓
Burt	–	–	–	–	–	–	–	–	–	–	✓
Burt Hibernians	–	–	–	–	✓	✓	✓	✓	–	–	–
Cahir Os, Buncrana	–	–	–	–	✓	✓	–	–	–	–	–
Carndonagh Cuchulainns	–	✓	✓	✓	✓	✓	✓	–	–	–	–
Cashelard	–	–	–	–	–	✓	–	–	–	–	–
Cloneen	–	–	–	–	–	–	–	✓	–	–	–
Derry	–	–	–	–	–	–	–	–	–	✓	–
Éire Óg, Moville	–	✓	✓	–	–	–	–	–	–	–	–
Geraldines	–	–	–	–	–	–	–	✓	✓	–	–
Kevin Barry's, Quigley's Point	–	–	✓	✓	–	–	–	–	✓	–	–
Kinlough (Leitrim)	–		–	–	–	–	✓	✓	–	–	–
Inch Emeralds	–	–	✓	✓	✓	–	✓	–	–	–	✓
Raphoe	–	–	–	–	✓	–	–	–	–	–	–
Red Hugh's, Moville	–	–	–	–	✓	✓	✓	✓	✓	–	✓
St Comgall's, Carrowmore	–	–	✓	✓	✓	✓	✓	–	✓	–	–
St Eunan's, Letterkenny	–	–	–	–	–	–	–	–	–	✓	–
St Finian's, Moville	–	–	–	–	–	–	–	✓	✓	✓	✓
St Mura's, Fahan	–	–	✓	–	–	–	–	–	–	–	–
Letterkenny	–	–	–	–	✓	✓	–	–	✓	–	✓
Letterkenny Mental Hospital	–	–	–	–	–	–	–	–	✓	–	–
Lifford	–	–	–	–	✓	–	–	✓	–	–	–
Manorhamilton	–	–	–	–	–	–	✓	✓	–	–	–
National Army, Finner	–	–	–	–	✓	–	✓	✓	✓	–	–
National Army, Finner B team	–	–	–	–	–	–	–	–	✓	–	–
Newtowncunningham Red Hughs	–	✓	✓	–	–	✓	✓	✓	✓	✓	✓
Stranorlar	–	–	–	–	–	–	–	–	–	✓	–
Young Irelands (Ballyshannon)	–	–	–	–	–	–	✓	✓	–	–	–
Total	1	3	7	4	11	9	13	13	12	7	8

APPENDIX 11 (cont.)
Hurling teams in Donegal, 1919–34

Club	1930	1931	1932	1933	1934
Aodh Ruadh, Ballyshannon	✓	✓	✓	✓	✓
Bundoran	–	–	✓	–	–
Burt	✓	✓		✓	✓
Carndonagh Cuchulainns	–	–	–	✓	✓**
Carndonagh Cuchulainns B team	–	–	–	✓	–
Four Masters, Donegal Town	–	–	–	–	✓*
Inch Emeralds	✓	✓		✓	✓
St Comgall's, Carrowmore	–	–	–	✓	✓
St Eunan's, Letterkenny	✓	✓		✓	✓**
St Eunan's College, Letterkenny	–	–	–	–	✓
St Finian's, Moville	–	–	–	–	–
St Mary's, Buncrana	–	–	–	✓	✓*
Red Hugh's, Moville	–	–	–	–	✓*
Milford	–	✓	–	–	–
United Services, Buncrana	✓	–	–	–	–
Total	**5**	**5**	**2**	**8**	**10**

SOURCES: As Appendix 5

Appendix 12

Number of association football clubs in Donegal by area, 1905–14

Areas	1905	1906	1907	1908	1909	1910	1911	1912	1913	1914
South-west	2	2	3	0	3	1	3	4	2	4
South	9	6	3	3	5	4	7	2	9	3
West/North-west	4	0	2	0	5	3	3	4	7	6
East/North-east	14	11	3	5	9	11	13	11	11	5
Inishowen	3	0	2	0	5	4	3	1	0	0
Total	**32**	**19**	**13**	**8**	**27**	**23**	**29**	**22**	**29**	**18**

Sources: *DJ*, *DV*, *DI*, *DP* and *DN* (1905–14)

Appendix 13

Number of association football clubs in Donegal by area, 1915–24

Areas	1915	1916	1917	1918	1919	1920	1921	1922	1923	1924
South-west	5	4	1	1	0	0	0	0	0	0
South	2	7	5	2	0	0	2	0	0	0
West/North-west	1	11	5	1	0	0	1	0	1	0
East/North-east	3	2	11	7	13	10	13	0	9	0
Inishowen	0	0	0	0	0	2	0	0	9	0
Total	**11**	**24**	**13**	**11**	**13**	**12**	**16**	**0**	**19**	**0**

Sources: *DJ*, *DV*, *DI*, *DP*

Appendix 14

Number of association football clubs in Donegal by area, 1925–34

Areas	1925	1926	1927	1928	1929	1930	1931	1932	1933	1934
South-west	0	0	0	1	1	1	1	1	3	1
South	2	5	2	2	1	2	2	1	2	2
West/North-west	0	4	8	3	2	2	6	6	4	2
East/North-east	0	19	13	7	14	34	36	50	56	66
Inishowen	9	17	19	13	5	3	17	36	36	32
Total	**11**	**45**	**42**	**26**	**23**	**42**	**62**	**94**	**101**	**103**

Sources: As Appendix 12 (1925–34) and *DPP* (1931–1934)

Appendix 15
Association football leagues, cups and patrons in Donegal, 1906–34

No.	Competition and Patron	Years	No.	Competition and Patron	Years
1	Evans Cup, Robert E.L. Evans, bedstead manufacturer	1906, 1907	18	Buncrana Foresters Cup, Unknown	1929
2	Woods Cup, J.J. Woods, publican	1909–10, 1910–1911, 1911–1912, 1912–13	19	County Donegal Perpetual Cup, William Holmes	1930, 1931
3	Charity Cup, Edward Rogers, shop assistant and publican	1913	20	Newtown-cunningham Cup, James Devenney	1931, 1932, 1934
4	St Vincent De Paul Cup, unknown	1913	21	Donagh Cup, P.R. Doherty	1932, 1933–34 1934
5	Britton Cup, William Britton, watchmaker and jeweller	1913–14, 1914–15	22	Kerrykeel Cup Unknown	1932, 1933
6	Ballyliffin Cup, Ballyliffin Development Committee	1925, 1931, 1932	23	Milford Cup, Unknown	1932–33, 1934–35
7	Ballyliffin Open & Confined Cups, Ballyliffin Development Committee	1926, 1927	24	Culdaff Parish League, Culdaff Parish Association Football Committee	1933, 1934
8	South Donegal League, Frank cinema manager	1926	25	Culdaff Parish Cup, Culdaff Parish Association Football Committee	1933
9	Swilly Cup, Swilly Cup Committee	1926, 1927	26	Portsalon Cup, Portsalon Cup Committee	1933, 1934
10	Buncrana Summer League, Buncrana FA	1926	27	Mitchell Cup, Carol Mitchell, wholesale bottler	1933, 1934
11	Burnfoot FA Cup, J.P. McIvor, County Councillor	1927	28	Donagh Charity Cup, Unknown	1933
12	Inishowen League, Laurence Nash, senior stevedore	1927, 1928	29	Illistrin Cup, Unknown	1933
13	Inishowen Summer League, Laurence Nash, senior stevedore	1928	30	Diamond Cup, Mr Diamond	1933–34
14	Manorcunningham Cup, Unknown	1928	31	St Johnston Summer League, Unknown	1934
15	Burt Summer League, Unknown	1928	32	Cranford Cup, Cranford Cup Committee	1934
16	Lifford and District League, Unknown	1926, 1927, 1928, 1929, 1931–32, 1934	33	Ballindrait League, Unknown	1934
17	Buncrana Central Cup, Unknown	1929	34	Nash Cup, Laurence Nash, senior stevedore	1934

Sources: *DJ, DP and DN, DP and TN, DV, DI, DPP* (1906–34)

Notes and References

Introduction

1 Mike Cronin, Mark Duncan and Paul Rouse, *The GAA: A People's History* (Cork: The Collins Press, 2009), pp. 10–13. For an alternative view of the sporting 'revolution' see Adrian Harvey, *The Beginnings of a Commercial Sporting Culture in Britain, 1793–1850* (Aldershot: Ashgate, 2004). Harvey argues that by the middle of the nineteenth century, sports events in Britain were more firmly established than has been accepted by many sports historians.

2 John Bale, 'Sport and National Identity: A Geographical View', *British Journal of Sports History*, vol. 3, no. 1 (1986), pp. 18–41, 32–4.

3 Neil Tranter, *Sport, Economy and Society in Britain, 1750–1914* (Cambridge: Cambridge University Press, 1998), p. 24.

4 Ibid., pp. 24–6.

5 Ibid., p. 15.

6 Ibid., p. 96.

7 Mike Cronin, *Sport and Nationalism in Ireland: Gaelic Games, Soccer and Irish Identity Since 1884* (Dublin: Four Courts Press, 1999), p. 103.

8 Paul Rouse, 'Sport and Ireland in 1881', in Alan Bairner (ed.), *Sport and the Irish: Histories, Identities, Issues* (Dublin: University College Dublin Press, 2005), pp. 7–21, 8.

9 See, for example, *Derry People and Donegal News*, 18 October 1902 (hereafter referred to as *DP and DN*). The Tyrone and Donegal Football League provides a strong illustration of this.

10 See Appendices 5 and 14.

11 David Fitzpatrick, 'The Geography of Irish Nationalism, 1910–1921', *Past and Present*, no. 78 (1978), pp. 113–44, 113.

12 See Tom Hunt, *Sport and Society in Victorian Ireland: The Case of Westmeath* (Cork: Cork University Press, 2007); Liam O'Callaghan, *Rugby in Munster: A Social and Cultural History* (Cork: Cork University Press, 2011); Dónal McAnallen, 'Playing on the Fourth Green State: The Gaelic Athletic Association and the Northern Ireland State, 1921–1968', PhD thesis, National University of Ireland, Galway, 2010; Richard McElligott, 'Forging a Kingdom: The Establishment and Development of the Gaelic Athletic Association in Kerry, 1884–1924', PhD thesis, University College Dublin, 2011. (McElligott's thesis was published as *Forging A Kingdom: The GAA in Kerry, 1884–1934* by The Collins Press in 2013.)

13 See William Nolan (ed.), *The Gaelic Athletic Association in Dublin, 1884–2000* (Dublin: Geography Publications, 2005) and Patrick Bracken, *'Foreign and Fantastic Field Sports': Cricket in County Tipperary* (Thurles: Liskiveen Books, 2004).

14 See, for example, Roy Foster, *Modern Ireland, 1600–1972* (London: Penguin, 1988) and J.J. Lee, *Ireland, 1912–1985: Politics and Society* (Cambridge: Cambridge University Press, 1989). For twentieth-century specialist histories of the GAA see T.F. O'Sullivan, *The Story of the GAA* (Dublin: Unknown Publisher, 1916); P.J. Devlin, *Our Native Games* (Dublin: MH Gill & Son Ltd, 1935); P.D. Mehigan, *Gaelic Football* (Dublin: Gaelic Publicity Services, 1941) and *Hurling: Ireland's National Game* (Dublin: Gaelic Publicity Services, 1942); Marcus De Burca, *The GAA: A History* [Second edition] (Dublin: Gill & Macmillan Ltd, 2000) and W.F. Mandle, *The Gaelic Athletic Association and Irish Nationalist Politics* (London: Christopher Helm Publishers, 1987).

15 Diarmaid Ferriter, *The Transformation of Ireland, 1900–2000* (London: Profile Books, 2004), p. 101. See also R.V. Comerford, *Ireland: Inventing the Nation* (London: Bloomsbury Academic, 2003) for an examination of the growth of sport in Ireland.

16 For an assessment of the origins of the Irish Republican Brotherhood see Tom Garvin, *The Evolution of Irish Nationalist Politics* [Second edition] (Dublin: Gill & Macmillan Ltd, 2005), pp. 67–8. Founded in 1858, the IRB was a secret oath-bound society which advocated the removal of British rule in Ireland by militaristic means. For an explanation of the Ban see Cronin, *Sport and Nationalism*, p. 84. By the end of February 1905, three significant bans had been introduced by the GAA. Under the first of these, introduced in 1885, athletes who participated in non-GAA events were prohibited from taking part in GAA competitions. Two years later, members of the Royal Irish Constabulary were excluded from membership. Although both of those lasted only briefly, early in 1905 a new ban was implemented which stated that those who participated in 'rugby, soccer, hockey, cricket or any imported games shall be suspended for two years from date of playing such games, and this rule to take effect from 1 February 1905'. Members of the police and army were also denied membership of the GAA under this ban.

17 Mike Cronin, 'Fighting for Ireland, Playing for England? The Nationalist History of the Gaelic Athletic Association and the English Influence on Irish Sport', *International Journal of the History of Sport*, vol. 15, no. 3 (1988), pp. 36–56, 36.

18 See, for example, Dónal McAnallen, David Hassan and Roddy Hegarty, *The Evolution of the GAA: Ulaidh, Éire agus Eile* (Armagh: Ulster Historical Foundation, 2009); Mike Cronin, William Murphy and Paul Rouse (eds), *The Gaelic Athletic Association, 1884–2009* (Dublin: Irish Academic Press, 2009); Cronin, Duncan and Rouse, *The GAA: A People's History* and *The GAA: County by County* (Cork: The Collins Press, 2011).

19 W.F. Mandle, 'Sport as Politics: The Gaelic Athletic Association 1884–1916', in Richard Cashman and Michael McKernan (eds), *Sport as History* (St Lucia: University of Queensland Press, 1979), pp. 99–123, p. 108.

20 See Mehigan, *Gaelic Football*, p. 100.

21 See, for example, Jim MacLaughlin and Seán Beattie (eds), *An Historical, Environmental and Cultural Atlas of County Donegal* (Cork: Cork University

Press, 2013); William Nolan, Liam Ronayne and Mairead Dunlevy (eds), *Donegal History and Society: Interdisciplinary Essays on the History of an Irish County* (Dublin: Geography Publications, 1995) and Jim MacLaughlin (ed.), *Donegal: The Making of a Northern County* (Dublin: Four Courts Press, 2007). For GAA see P.S. Mac a' Ghoill, '100 years of the GAA in Donegal', *Donegal Annual, 1984,* no. 36 (Ballyshannon: Donegal Democrat Printers, 1984), pp. 89–94; Very Reverend Liam McCaul, 'From Thurles to Ardara, 1884–1921' in the *Donegal Annual, 1985*, no. 37 (Ballyshannon: Donegal Democrat, 1985), pp. 67–73; Cronin, Duncan and Rouse, *The GAA: County by County*, pp. 105–17.

22 See Donal Campbell, Damian Dowds and Damian Mullan (eds), *Against the Grain: A History of Burt, its People and the GAA* (Burt: Burt GAA Club, 2000); Seán Mac Conaill (ed.), *Idir Peil agus Pobal: A History of the GAA in the Parish of Ardara, 1921–2003* (Ardara: Black Lion Books, 2004) Micheál Ó Domhnaill (ed.), *CLG Cill Chartha, 1924–1884* (Donegal: CLG Cill Chartha, 1984) and Joe Crawford and Dan McCool, *Golden Memories: A History of Gaelic Games around the Twin Towns, 1916–1966* (Ballybofey: Seán MacCuamhaills GAA Club, 1999).

23 Conor Curran, 'The Social Importance of Gaelic Games and Association Football, 1884–1914', MA thesis, St Patrick's College, Dublin, 2007. This thesis was published in 2010 as *Sport in Donegal: A History* (Dublin: The History Press Ireland, 2010).

24 Neal Garnham, *Association Football and Society in Pre-Partition Ireland* (Belfast: Ulster Historical Foundation, 2004); John Sugden and Alan Bairner, *Sport, Sectarianism and Society in a Divided Ireland* (Leicester: Leicester University Press, 1993); *Bonagee United Football Club: 40 Years of Football, 1970–2010* (Letterkenny: Bonagee Utd FC, 2010); *Swilly Rovers FC: Team of '62* (Letterkenny: Swilly Rovers FC, 2002). See also Trevor Gorman, *Kilmacrennan FC – An Illustrated History: A Nostalgic Look at a Century of Football* (Letterkenny: Greenlight Media, 2012) and Gary Murrin (ed.), *St Catherine's FC: A Celebration of 100 Years of Soccer in Killybegs* (Ballyshannon: Donegal Democrat, 1997).

25 Dónal McAnallen, 'Cén Fáth a Raibh Cúige Uladh Chomh Lag Chomh Fada Sin? Deacrachtaí CLG ó Thuaidh, 1884–1945', in McAnallen, Hassan and Hegarty, *The Evolution of the GAA*, pp. 138–51.

26 Garnham, *Association Football and Society.*

27 Hunt, *Sport and Society*, p. 194.

28 Nolan (ed.), *The Gaelic Athletic Association in Dublin, 1884–2000.*

29 O'Callaghan, *Rugby in Munster: A Social and Cultural History*, p. 52 and pp. 141–69.

30 Michael Oriard, *Reading Football: How the Popular Press Created an American Spectacle* (Chapel Hill: The University of North Carolina Press, 1993).

31 Andrew Walker, 'Reporting Play: The Local Newspaper and Sports Journalism, c. 1870–1914', *Journalism Studies,* vol. 6, no. 2 (2006), pp. 452–62.

32 Eoghan Corry, 'The Mass Media and the Popularisation of Gaelic Games, 1884–1934', in McAnallen, Hassan and Hegarty (eds), *The Evolution of the GAA*, pp. 100–11, p. 108.

33 Cronin, Duncan and Rouse, *The GAA: A People's History*, pp. 179–207.

34 David Russell, 'Sporadic and Curious: The Emergence of Rugby and Soccer

Zones in Yorkshire and Lancashire, c. 1860–1914', *International Journal of the History of Sport*, vol. 5, no. 2 (1988), pp. 185–205, p. 185.

35 See, for example, Bale, 'Sport and National Identity', pp. 18–41, Russell, 'Sporadic and Curious', pp. 185–205, Alan Metcalfe, 'Football in the Mining Communities of East Northumberland, 1882–1914', *International Journal of the History of Sport*, vol. 5, no. 3 (1988), pp. 269–91; Alan Metcalfe, 'The Control of Space and the Development of Twenty-two Sports in the Mining Communities of East Northumberland, 1880–1914', *The Sports Historian*, no. 15 (1995), pp 23–33; Mike Huggins, 'The Spread of Association Football in North-east England, 1876–90: The Pattern of Diffusion', *International Journal of the History of Sport*, vol. 6, no. 3 (1989), pp. 299–318 and Tony Collins, *Rugby's Great Split: Class, Culture and the Origins of Rugby League Football* (London: Frank Cass, 1998).

36 Neal Garnham, 'A Sporting Challenge', review of Tom Hunt, *Sport and Society in Victorian Ireland: The Case of Westmeath*, pp. 1–2, 2. Retrieved from http://www.abdn.ac.uk/riiss/Reviews/Garnham_A%20sporting%20challenge.pdf [Accessed 8 December 2011].

37 See *Derry Journal*, 19 February 1934 and Mac Conaill (ed.), *Idir Peil agus Pobal*, pp. 68–70.

1. Donegal: the social context

1 For a wider discussion of Ireland's sporting development in the nineteenth century see Mike Cronin and Roisín Higgins, *Places We Play: Ireland's Sporting Heritage* (Cork: The Collins Press, 2011), pp. 29–42.

2 *Thom's Official Directory of the Kingdom of Great Britain and Ireland for the Year 1884* (Dublin: Alexander Thom, 1884), p. 1057.

3 Jim MacLaughlin, 'Introduction: The Making of a Northern County', in MacLaughlin (ed.), *Donegal: The Making of a Northern County*, pp. 1–21, p. 6.

4 Patrick Fitzgerald, 'Emigration from Donegal and the Irish Emigration Database Project', *Donegal Annual, 2000*, no. 52 (Letterkenny: Browne Printers, 2000), pp. 57–62, p. 52.

5 Alvin Jackson, *Ireland, 1798–1998* (Oxford: Blackwell Publishing, 1999), p. 81.

6 Jonathan Bardon, *A History of Ulster* [Updated edition] (Belfast: Blackstaff Press, 2001), p. 307.

7 Ibid., pp. 307–8.

8 Ibid., p. 308.

9 Arlene Crampsie, 'Relieving the Destitute Poor: A History of Milford Workhouse', *Donegal Annual, 2004*, no. 56 (Letterkenny: Browne Printers, 2004), pp. 68–87, p. 68.

10 *DJ*, 3 December 1883.

11 *Thom's Official Directory of the United Kingdom of Great Britain and Ireland for the Year 1883* (Dublin: Alexander Thom, 1883), p. 1023 and *Thom's Directory, 1884*, p. 1057.

12 *Thom's Official Directory, 1884*, p. 1057.

13 Russell, 'Sporadic and Curious', p. 195.

14 Ibid., p. 196.

15 *Thom's Official Directory of Ireland for the Year 1930* (Dublin: Alexander Thom, 1930), p. 1007.

16 Frank Sweeney, *The Murder of Conell Boyle* (Dublin: Four Courts Press, 2002), p. 57.

17 Ibid., p. 9.
18 'Census of Ireland for the year 1881. Religious professions of the people. Table XXVIII. Religious professions and sexes of the inhabitants, and number of families, in each parish in the county of Donegal'. pp. 451–2. Retrieved from http://parlipapers.chadwyck.co.uk.jproxy.nuim.ie/fulltext/readview.do?area=hcpp&id=1882-058905&source=&pagenum=452&resultNum=34&entries=187&queryId=..%2Fsession%2F1406552477_8061&backto=FULLREC&fromSearchHistory=&searchWithin=county+of+donegal&showall=&enlarge=Y [Accessed 28 July 2014].
19 Reverend Alexander G. Lecky, *In the Days of the Laggan Presbytery* (Belfast: Davidson & McCormack, 1908), p. 1.
20 Anne O'Dowd, 'Seasonal Migration to the Lagan and Scotland', in Nolan, Ronayne and Dunlevy (eds), *Donegal History and Society*, pp. 625–48, p. 632.
21 Lecky, *In the Days of the Laggan Presbytery*, p. 1.
22 Retrieved from http://www.askaboutireland.ie/reading-room/history-heritage/history-of-ireland/the-ulster-plantation/the-plantation-of-the-lag/ [Accessed 20 October 2011]
23 Darren McGettigan, *The Donegal Plantation and the Tír Chonaill Irish, 1610–1710* (Dublin: Four Courts Press, 2010), p. 58.
24 Jim MacLaughlin, 'The Politics of Nation-building in Post-Famine Donegal', in Nolan, Ronayne and Dunlevy (eds), *Donegal History and Society*, pp. 583–623, p. 587.
25 Ibid.
26 Ibid.
27 MacLaughlin, 'Introduction: The Making of a Northern County', p. 3.
28 Ibid., p. 2.
29 Ibid.
30 Bardon, *A History of Ulster*, pp. 400, 402.
31 McGettigan, *The Donegal Plantation*, p. 59.
32 Ibid.
33 *Thom's Official Directory, 1884*, p. 1057.
34 'Census of Ireland for the year 1881. Religious professions of the people. Table XXIX. Religious professions and sexes of the parliamentary and municipal boroughs and principal towns in the county of Donegal, and the number of families in each', p. 452. Retrieved from http://parlipapers.chadwyck.co.uk.jproxy.nuim.ie/fulltext/readview.do?area=hcpp&id=1882-058905&source=&pagenum=452&resultNum=34&entries=187&queryId=..%2Fsession%2F1406552477_8061&backto=FULLREC&fromSearchHistory=&searchWithin=county+of+donegal&showall=&enlarge=Y [Accessed 28 July 2014]. There was just one person belonging to an unclassified religious denomination listed in that year's census for the town.
35 *Impartial Reporter*, 21 September 1882 (hereafter referred to as *IR*).
36 Mary E. Daly (ed.), *County and Town: One Hundred Years of Local Government in Ireland* (Dublin: Institute of Public Administration, 2001), p. 9.
37 'Census of Ireland for the year 1881. Religious professions of the people. Table XXVIII. Religious professions and sexes of the inhabitants, and number of families, in each parish in the county of Mayo', p. 400. Retrieved from http://parlipapers.chadwyck.co.uk.jproxy.nuim.ie/fulltext/fulltext.do?area=hcpp&id=1882-058906&pagenum=1&backto=FULLREC [Accessed 2 August 2014].

38 'Census of Ireland for the year 1881. Religious professions of the people. Table XXVIII. Religious professions and sexes of the inhabitants, and number of families, in each parish in the county of Donegal', pp. 451–2. Retrieved from http://parlipapers.chadwyck.co.uk.jproxy.nuim.ie/fulltext/readview.do?area=hcpp&id=1882-058905&source=&pagenum=452&resultNum=34&entries=187&queryId=..%2Fsession%2F1406552477_8061&backto=FULLREC&fromSearchHistory=&searchWithin=county+of+donegal&showall=&enlarge=Y [Accessed 28 July 2014].

39 'Census of Ireland for the year 1881. Religious professions of the people. Table XXVIII. Religious professions and sexes of the inhabitants, and number of families, in each parish in the county of Kerry', pp. 515–16. Retrieved from http://parlipapers.chadwyck.co.uk.jproxy.nuim.ie/fulltext/fulltext.do?area=hcpp&id=1882-058904&pagenum=1&backto=FULLREC [Accessed 28 July 2014].

40 Cronin, Duncan and Rouse, *The GAA: A People's History*, p. 256.

41 Ida Milne, 'The Quiet Corner-back: Rural Protestants and the GAA in the 26 Counties'. Paper given at Ninth Annual Sports History Ireland Conference, Magee College, Derry, 14 September 2013. I am grateful to Ida for granting me access to her paper.

42 *Thom's Official Directory, 1884*, p. 1057.

43 Robert Gavin, 'Social and Economic Links Between Derry and Donegal in the Eighteenth and Early Nineteenth Centuries', in MacLaughlin and Beattie (eds), *An Historical, Environmental and Cultural Atlas of County Donegal*, pp. 188–98, pp. 194–9.

44 Ibid., p. 198.

45 Bardon, *A History of Ulster*, pp. 395–6.

46 Campbell, Dowds and Mullan, *Against the Grain*, p. 121.

47 Tranter, *Sport, Economy and Society in Britain, 1750–1914*, p. 29. An exception to this trend would be North Tipperary, a poorly industrialised area which had a large concentration of GAA clubs in the late nineteenth century.

48 Desmond Murphy, 'The Land War in Donegal, 1879–1891', *Donegal Annual, 1980*, no. 32 (Ballyshannon: Donegal Democrat Printers, 1980), pp. 476–86, p. 477.

49 Pádraig S. Ó Baoighill, *Cardinal Patrick O'Donnell, 1856–1927* (Fintown: Chró na mBothán, 2008), p. 28.

50 Bardon, *A History of Ulster*, pp. 362–4.

51 Ibid., p. 363.

52 *DJ*, 4 July 1884.

53 Garnham, *Association Football and Society*, p. 11.

54 Cronin, *Sport and Nationalism in Ireland*, p. 104.

55 *Londonderry Sentinel* (hereafter referred to as *LS*), 3 May 1906.

56 Ibid.

57 Ibid., 8 May 1906.

58 See, for example, *Derry Standard* (hereafter referred to as *DS*), 16 October 1894 and 29 November 1895 for Co. Donegal FA fixtures and ibid., 14 June, 1, 3 and 17 July 1895 for matches in the Co. Donegal Cricket League.

59 *Thom's Official Directory, 1884*, p. 1057 and John Tunney, 'The Marquis, the Reverend, the Grandmaster and the Major: Protestant Politics in Donegal, 1868–1933', in Nolan, Ronayne and Dunlevy (eds), *Donegal History and Society*, pp. 675–95, p. 685.

60 MacLaughlin, 'Introduction: The Making of a Northern County', p. 12.
61 Jim MacLaughlin, 'Social Class Impact of the Famine in Donegal', in MacLaughlin (ed.), *The Making of a Northern County,* pp. 192–8, p. 194.
62 Ibid.
63 Pat Conaghan, *The Zulu Fishermen: Forgotten Pioneers of Donegal's First Fishing Industry* (Killybegs: Bygones Enterprise, 2003), pp. 31–5 and p. 297.
64 Seán Beattie, *Donegal in Transition: The Impact of the Congested Districts Board* (Sallins: Merrion, 2013), p. 224.
65 MacLaughlin, 'Conclusion', in MacLaughlin (ed.), *Donegal: The Making of a Northern County,* pp. 358–70, p. 364.
66 Ibid., p. 363.
67 *Thom's Official Directory, 1884,* p. 1057.
68 Ibid.
69 O'Dowd, 'Seasonal Migration to the Lagan and Scotland', p. 643.
70 Ibid., p. 631.
71 Ibid., p. 629.
72 Pat Bolger, 'The Congested Districts Board and the Co-Ops in Donegal', in Nolan, Ronayne and Dunlevy (eds), *Donegal History and Society,* pp. 649–71, p. 649.
73 O'Dowd, 'Seasonal Migration to the Lagan and Scotland', p. 643.
74 Ibid., p. 630.
75 Desmond Murphy, *Derry, Donegal and Modern Ulster, 1790–1921* (Derry: Aileach Press, 1981), p. 223.
76 Ibid., p. 228.
77 Ibid.
78 Rouse, 'Sport and Ireland in 1881', in Bairner (ed.), *Sport and the Irish,* pp. 7–21, pp. 20–1.
79 *Thom's Official Directory, 1884,* p. 1057.
80 Murphy, *Derry, Donegal and Modern Ulster,* pp. 227–9 and Sweeney, *The Murder of Conell Boyle,* pp. 17–19. The Gaeltacht is an Irish-speaking region, mainly containing parts of counties Donegal, Mayo, Galway, Kerry, Cork and Waterford and, further inland, areas of County Meath.
81 Murphy, *Derry, Donegal and Modern Ulster,* p. 229.
82 Mary-Louise Legg, *Newspapers and Nationalism: The Irish Provincial Press, 1850–1892* (Dublin: Four Courts Press, 1999), p. 175.
83 See, for example, Tranter, *Sport, Economy and Society in Britain,* p. 29 and Cronin, Duncan and Rouse, *The GAA: A People's History,* p. 13.
84 MacLaughlin, 'Introduction: The Making of a Northern County', p. 12.
85 Helen Meehan and Godfrey H. Duffy, *Tracing Your Donegal Ancestors* [Second edition] (Dublin: Flyleaf Press, 2008), pp. 93–9.
86 See 'Census of Ireland for the year 1881. Religious professions and education of the people. Table XXIX. Summary of Educational Establishments for the County of Donegal', p. 464. Retrieved from http://parlipapers.chadwyck.co.uk.jproxy.nuim.ie/fulltext/readview.do?area=hcpp&id=1882-058905&source=&pagenum=452&resultNum=34&entries=187&queryId=..%2Fsession%2F1406552477_8061&backto=FULLREC&fromSearchHistory=&searchWithin=county+of+donegal&showall=&enlarge=Y [Accessed 28 July 2014]. There were eight 'superior' schools in the county by 1881, with three Endowed Schools, three Private, one Ecclesiastical and one Convent

recorded, although only the Royal School Raphoe, two Prior Schools and the Diocesan Seminary are noted.

87 Ó Baoighill, *Cardinal Patrick O'Donnell*, p. 181 and p. 289.
88 *DJ*, 14 October 1896.
89 Ó Baoighill, *Cardinal Patrick O'Donnell*, p. 215.
90 Ibid., p. 217.
91 Ibid.
92 Ibid., p. 219.
93 See Hunt, *Sport and Society in Victorian Ireland,* pp. 171–4.
94 *Thom's Official Directory ,1884*, p. 1057.
95 *DJ*, 4 July 1884.
96 Ibid., 8 October 1886.
97 MacLaughlin, 'Introduction: The Making of a Northern County', p. 11.
98 *DS*, 2 October 1893. See also *DJ*, 2 March 1894.
99 Cronin and Higgins, *Places We Play*, p. 44.
100 Ibid.
101 Bardon, *A History of Ulster*, p. 318.
102 See Hunt, *Sport and Society*, pp. 8–9 and Bracken, '*Foreign and Fantastic Field Sports*', p. 18.
103 Hunt, *Sport and Society*, p. 9.
104 Joe Begley, Dave Bell, Steve Flanders and Dave White (eds), *The County Donegal Railway: A Visitor's Guide* (Donegal: The County Donegal Railway Restoration Society, 1996), p. 4.
105 Dave Bell and Steve Flanders, *The Londonderry and Lough Swilly Railway: A Visitor's Guide* (Donegal: County Donegal Railway Restoration Society, 1995), p. 5.
106 C.A. Clerkin, 'History of Public Transport in Donegal', *Donegal Annual, 1952,* vol. 2, no. 2 (Ballyshannon: Donegal Democrat Printers, 1952), pp. 405–17, p. 407.
107 Ibid., p. 407.
108 Bell and Flanders (eds), *The Londonderry and Lough Swilly Railway*, p. 7.
109 Anthony Begley, *Ballyshannon and Surrounding Areas: History, Heritage and Folklore* (Ballyshannon: Carrickboy Publishing, 2009), p. 299.
110 Begley, Bell, Flanders and White (eds), *The County Donegal Railway*, p. 4.
111 Ibid.
112 Ibid.
113 Ibid.
114 'Londonderry and Lough Swilly Railway', retrieved from http://www.irishrailwayana.com/pa206.htm [Accessed 19 October 2011].
115 Bell and Flanders (eds), *The Londonderry and Lough Swilly Railway*, p. 57.
116 Ibid., p. 4.
117 Ibid.
118 John Tunney, 'The Marquis, the Reverend, the Grandmaster and the Major: Protestant Politics in Donegal, 1868–1933', in Nolan, Ronayne and Dunlevy (eds), *Donegal History and Society*, pp. 675–94, p. 675.
119 Ibid.
120 Ibid., p. 677.
121 Murphy, *Derry, Donegal and Modern Ulster*, p. 148.
122 Murphy, 'The Land War in Donegal, 1879–1891', p. 476.
123 Jackson, *Ireland, 1798–1998*, p. 134.

124 Ó Baoighill, *Cardinal Patrick O'Donnell*, p. 42.
125 Jackson, *Ireland, 1798–1998*, pp. 446–7.
126 Ibid., pp. 444–7 and Ó Baoighill, *Cardinal Patrick O'Donnell*, p. 29.
127 Tunney, 'The Marquis, the Reverend, the Grandmaster and the Major', p. 683.
128 Ferriter, *The Transformation of Ireland*, pp. 38–9.
129 Tunney, 'The Marquis, the Reverend, the Grandmaster and the Major', p. 684.
130 Aiden O'Connell, 'The Ulster Covenant in Donegal, 1912', in Seán Beattie (ed.), *Donegal Annual: Journal of County Donegal Historical Society, 2011*, no. 63 (Letterkenny: Browne Printers, 2011), pp. 45–58, p. 46.
131 MacLaughlin, 'Conclusion', p. 364.
132 Daly (ed.), *County and Town*, pp. 7–8.
133 Ibid., p. x.
134 Ibid., p.7.
135 Ibid., p. 8.
136 Ibid., p. 9.
137 Bardon, *A History of Ulster*, p. 467.
138 *DJ*, 20 October 1922.
139 Ibid.
140 *Saorstát na hÉireann: Irish Free State Statistical Abstract 1931, Compiled by the Department of Industry and Commerce* (Dublin: Department of Industry and Commerce, 1931), p. 158.
141 See, for example, *DJ*, 15 July 1927 and *DP and TN*, 10 March 1934.
142 Bardon, *A History of Ulster*, p. 588.
143 Ibid.
144 Jim MacLaughlin, 'Towns and Villages in Donegal', in MacLaughlin and Beattie (eds), *An Historical, Environmental and Cultural Atlas of County Donegal*, pp. 376–89, p. 383.
145 Beattie, *Donegal in Transition*, p. 224.
146 MacLaughlin, 'Conclusion', p. 364.
147 Tranter, *Sport, Economy and Society*, p. 34.

2. Pre-codified and 'minority' sports in Donegal

1 Richard Holt, *Sport and the British: A Modern History* (Oxford: Clarendon Press, 1989), p. 70.
2 Campbell, Dowds and Mullan, *Against the Grain*, p. 70.
3 Eoin Kinsella, 'Riotous Proceedings and the Cricket of Savages: Football and Hurling in Early Modern Ireland', in Mike Cronin, William Murphy and Paul Rouse (eds), *The Gaelic Athletic Association, 1884–2009* (Dublin: Irish Academic Press, 2009), pp. 15–31, p. 19.
4 Ibid., p.16.
5 Ibid.
6 Seán Beattie, 'Folklore and Customs in North-west Donegal', *Donegal Annual, 2001,* no. 53 (Letterkenny: Browne Printers, 2001), pp. 44–9, p. 45.
7 Liam P. Ó Caithnia, *Scéal na hIomána* (Baile Átha Cliath: An Chlóchomhar Tta, 1980), p. 644.
8 See *DJ*, 1 January 1897 and 29 December 1899, *Donegal Vindicator* (hereafter referred to as *DV*), 14 February 1902, *DP and DN*, 23 May 1903, 8 July 1905 and 27 January 1906. A report on the Fanad Sports of 1897 mentioned 'the good old days of twenty golden years ago when hurling or

camán play was in vogue' but failed to state why this ended. In 1899 it was stated that camán's decline in Newtowncunningham may have been due to 'the depopulation of the country or to the shooting proclivities of the young men of the district' who had formed a rifle club. One Carrigart correspondent claimed in 1902 that 'hurling and other old fashioned games, so dear to the lad of twenty years ago' were long gone. The decline of camán was lamented by a Glenties writer in January 1906 who stated that 'about twenty years ago all the men in our townland would repair either to the strand or some level field' to play this game, although no reasons for its decline were given.

9 William Shaw Mason, *A Statistical Account, or Parochial Study of Ireland, Drawn up from the Communications of the Clergy, volume 2* (Dublin: Graisberry and Campbell, 1816), p. 160.

10 Angelique Day and Patrick McWilliams (eds), *Ordnance Survey Memoirs: Parishes of Donegal I, 1833–5: North-east Donegal* (Belfast: Institute of Irish Studies in association with the Royal Irish Academy, 1997), p. 17.

11 Ibid., p. 43 and p. 60.

12 Ó Caithnia, *Scéal na hIomána*, p. 644.

13 Ibid., p. 437.

14 Ibid.

15 Ibid., p. 279.

16 Ibid., p. 644.

17 Ibid., p. 316.

18 Ibid., p. 312.

19 Ibid., p. 330.

20 Art Ó Maolfabhail, *Camán: 2,000 Years of Hurling in Ireland: An Attempt to Trace the History and Development of the Stick-and-Ball Game in Ireland During the Past 2,000 Years* (Dundalk: Dundalgan Press, 1973), p. 96 and Figure IV.

21 Ó Caithnia, *Scéal na hIomána*, p. 226 and Seamus J. King, *A History of Hurling* (Dublin: Gill & Macmillan, 1996), p. 221.

22 Ó Caithnia, *Scéal na hIomána*, p. 437.

23 Ibid.

24 Ibid., p. 279.

25 Campbell, Dowds and Mullan, *Against the Grain*, p. 74 and Ó Caithnia, *Scéal na hIomána*, p. 25.

26 Seán Ó hEochaidh, Christmas Day Traditions in Cloughaneely, MS932, Folklore Commission, 1943, pp. 455–62.

27 Ó Caithnia, *Scéal na hIomána*, p. 410.

28 Hugh Hornby, *Uppies and Downies: The Extraordinary Football Games of Britain* (Swindon: English Heritage, 2008).

29 Ibid., pp. 8–17.

30 Neal Garnham, 'Sport and the State in Ireland: An Overview', *Leidschrift. Brood en spelen. Sports als kracht in de samenleving*, vol. 3, no. 3 (2008), pp. 99–117, p. 100.

31 Ó Caithnia, *Scéal na hIomána*, pp. 411–12.

32 Elizabeth Malcolm, 'Popular Recreation in Nineteenth-century Ireland', in Oliver MacDonagh, W.F. Mandle and Pauric Travers, *Irish Culture and Nationalism, 1750–1950* (London: Macmillan in association with Humanities Research Centre, Australian National University, 1983), pp. 40–55, pp. 46–7.

33 Ibid., p. 45.
34 Jackson, *Ireland, 1798–1998*, p. 81.
35 Ó Caithnia, *Scéal na hIomána*, p. 563.
36 Ibid.
37 Hunt, *Sport and Society*, p. 217.
38 Ibid., pp. 217–18.
39 Art Ó Maolfabhail, Roddy Hegarty and Dónal McAnallen, 'From Cú Chulainn to Cusack: Ball-Playing, Caman, Shinny and Hurling in Ulster before the GAA', in McAnallen, Hassan and Hegarty, *The Evolution of the GAA*, pp. 62–78, p. 73.
40 Pádraig S. Mac a' Ghoill, 'Cross-country Hurling in Ardara', *CLCG Ard a' Ratha* (Ardara: CLGC Ard a' Ratha, 1980), p. 53.
41 See, for example, *DJ*, 28 December 1888 and 28 January 1889.
42 Ibid., 8 February 1888.
43 Ibid.
44 Matthew Taylor, *The Association Game: A History of British Football* (Harlow: Pearson Education Limited, 2008), p. 29 and Tony Mason, *Association Football and English Society, 1863–1915* (Brighton: Harvester Press, 1980), p. 16.
45 *DJ*, 8 February 1888.
46 Ibid., 29 December 1899.
47 Ó Maolfabhail, Hegarty and McAnallen, 'From Cú Chulainn to Cusack', p. 78.
48 Campbell, Dowds and Mullan, *Against the Grain*, p. 87 and p. 165 and *DP and DN*, 5 May 1906. Burt continued to use the camán in their play until the 1950s.
49 King, *A History of Hurling*, p. 219.
50 Ibid.
51 Simon McGeady, 'Greencastle Regatta Website Goes Live in May', retrieved from http://www.inishowennews.com/08GreenMemorable.htm [Accessed 24 September 2009].
52 *DJ*, 3 September 1862 and 17 September 1862.
53 Ibid., 24 September 1862.
54 Ibid.
55 Ibid., 17 September 1862.
56 Ibid., 24 September 1862.
57 Ibid., 3 June 1871.
58 Ibid., 5 July 1880.
59 Ibid., 24 July 1876.
60 Ibid., 18 August 1879.
61 Ibid., 31 July 1882.
62 Ibid.
63 Ibid., 16 August 1878.
64 Ibid., 15, 22 and 24 August 1883.
65 Hunt, *Sport and Society*, p. 219; *LS*, 29 December 1908 and *Fermanagh Herald*, 28 August 1909 (hereafter referred to as *FH*).
66 *DV*, 19 August 1922.
67 Ibid., 9 August 1924.
68 *DJ*, 9 August 1929.
69 Cronin, Duncan and Rouse, *The GAA: A People's History*, pp. 16–19.
70 See, for example, *DJ*, 24 June 1871, 10 April 1889, *DS*, 20 May 1893.

71 *DS*, 20 May 1893.
72 Ibid.
73 Ibid., 15 January 1904.
74 Ibid., 8 February 1904.
75 Ibid.
76 Ibid., 30 December 1895.
77 Ibid., 26 June 1893.
78 *DJ*, 19 September 1866.
79 *DS*, 20 September 1893.
80 Ibid., 12 August 1895.
81 Ibid., 30 December 1895.
82 *IR*, 31 December 1896.
83 *DV*, 31 July 1891.
84 *DJ*, 5 July 1909.
85 Ibid.
86 *Donegal People's Press*, 27 June 1931 (hereafter referred to as *DPP*).
87 *DV*, 20 July 1929.
88 See, for example, *DJ*, 15 July 1927. Twenty soccer teams took part in a competition as part of the Portsalon Athletic Sports on the Killavee grounds that month.
89 *Donegal Democrat*, 7 June and 5 July 1930 (hereafter referred to as *DD*).
90 Ibid., 5 July 1930.
91 Ibid., 12 July 1930.
92 'IRFU history', retrieved from http://www.irishrugby.ie/300_285.php [Accessed 25 August 2009].
93 *DJ*, 22 September 1893. See also Brian Hoban, 'Muriel Gahan (1897–1995), retrieved from http://towns.mayo-ireland.ie/WebX?14@213.BPtFe4YwNNr.0@.ee7a78d [Accessed 25 August 2009] and 'Residents of a house 1 in Knockacroghery (Castlebar Urban, Mayo)', retrieved from http://www.census.nationalarchives.ie/pages/1901/Mayo/Castlebar_Urban/Knockacroghery/1584321/ [Accessed 25 August 2009]
94 *DS*, 4 and 18 March 1892.
95 *Donegal Independent*, 2 February 1889 (hereafter referred to as *DI*).
96 Ibid., 30 March 1889.
97 Ibid., 18 January and 29 March 1890 and *DJ*, 21 March 1890.
98 *DV*, 2 November 1889 and 28 October 1898.
99 *DV*, 28 October and 18 November 1898.
100 *FH*, 25 February 1956.
101 Ibid., and 'Dáil Éireann Members Database: Major James Sproule Myles', retrieved from http://www.oireachtas.ie/members-hist/default.asp?housetype=0&HouseNum=4&MemberID=806&ConstID=47 [Accessed 23 July 2014].
102 *FH,* 25 February 1956.
103 John Ward, 'Of the centre and its extremities', retrieved from http://www.vindicator.ca/kindly/chapterThree.html [Accessed 23 July 2014].
104 David Hassan, 'Rugby Union, Irish Nationalism and Nationality in Northern Ireland', *Football Studies*, vol. 6, no. 1 (2003), pp. 5–18, p. 15. Donegal's rugby clubs are currently located in Letterkenny, Ballyshannon, Donegal town, Carrickfinn, Carndonagh and Stranorlar.
105 Ibid., pp. 10–11.

106 Ibid., p. 11.
107 Hunt, *Sport and Society*, pp. 174–6.
108 *DS*, 22 November 1895.
109 Hassan, 'Rugby Union', p. 10.
110 *DS*, 18, 25 November, 18 December 1895 and 2 March 1896.
111 *LS*, 1 January 1898.
112 Cronin, Duncan and Rouse, *The GAA: A People's History*, p. 13.
113 O'Callaghan, *Rugby in Munster*, p. 28.
114 *DV*, 3 October 1925.
115 Ibid., 13 February and 27 March 1926.
116 Ibid., 3 November 1928.
117 *FH*, 10 August 1929 and 3 March 1934.
118 Ibid., 3 March 1934.
119 *DV*, 7 January 1933.
120 *DPP*, 29 April 1933.
121 Ibid., 22 April 1933.
122 *DJ*, 3 March 1930.
123 Ibid.
124 Ibid., 11 March 1932.
125 Ibid.
126 Ibid., 25 March and 6 April 1932.
127 Ibid., 22 April 1932.
128 Ibid., 2 September 1932.
129 Ibid., 8 and 15 April 1932; *DPP*, 29 April 1933.
130 Ibid., 4 and 23 November, 2 December 1932, 17 February, 10 March, 3 November 1933 and 2 March 1934.
131 *DPP*, 4 February 1933 and *DJ*, 27 October 1933.
132 Ibid., 29 April 1932 and 29 September 1933.
133 Ibid., 8 October 1932.
134 Ibid., 8 April 1933.
135 Ibid.
136 *DJ*, 15 and 22 April 1932.
137 See, for example, *DPP*, 22 April 1933.
138 *DP and DN*, 16 April 1932.
139 Ibid.
140 Ibid.
141 *DJ*, 13 April 1932.
142 Ibid.
143 Neal Garnham, 'The Roles of Cricket in Victorian and Edwardian Ireland', *Sporting Traditions,* vol. 19, no. 2 (2009), pp. 27–48, p. 28.
144 Ibid.
145 Ibid., pp. 28–9.
146 *DS*, 22 June 1892.
147 Gerard Siggins, *Green Days: Cricket in Ireland, 1792–2005* (Gloucestershire: The History Press, 2005), p. 36.
148 Begley, Bell, Flanders and White, *The County Donegal Railway*, p. 4. See *DJ*, 10 May, 5 August and 2 September 1865 for references to these teams.
149 Neil Tranter, 'The Chronology of Organized Sport in Nineteenth-century Scotland: A Regional Study II – Causes', *International Journal of the History of Sport*, vol. 7, no. 3 (1990), pp. 365–87, p. 384.

150 See, for example, Swilly CC in *John Lawrence's Handbook of Cricket in Ireland, Number Seven, 1871–2* (Dublin: John Lawrence, 1872), p. 150; Falcarragh CC in *John Lawrence's Handbook of Cricket in Ireland, Number Eight, 1872–3* (Dublin: John Lawrence, 1873), pp. 133–4 and Co. Donegal CC in *John Lawrence's Handbook of Cricket in Ireland, Number Twelve, 1876–7* (Dublin: John Lawrence, 1877), p. 100 and *DJ*, 25 July, 1890.

151 See, for example, *DJ*, 19 and 29 May, 2 June, 5 and 17 July, 14 and 30 August 1882. Ballyshannon CC took part in matches against H Company Royal Inniskilling Fusiliers, Enniskillen CC, Donegal CC, Mountcharles CC and North Leitrim CC that year.

152 Meehan and Duffy, *Tracing Your Donegal Ancestors*, pp. 99–100.

153 In 1870 these teams were all noted in the *DJ*.

154 See *DJ*, 4 October 1870 and *John Lawrence's Handbook of Cricket in Ireland, Number Six, 1870–1* (Dublin: John Lawrence, 1871), p. 137.

155 *DJ*, 12 August 1871.

156 Ibid., 26 August 1871.

157 Garnham, 'The Roles of Cricket in Victorian and Edwardian Ireland', pp. 29–30. There were no Donegal entries in Lawrence's publications until 1871 and only a small number of Donegal clubs sent their returns in that decade, these being the Co. Donegal CC, Swilly and Falcarragh, and after the 1875 edition, the Co. Donegal CC was the only one which decided to correspond.

158 Ibid., 23 May 1881.

159 Ibid., 7 September 1881.

160 Ibid., 24 April 1882.

161 See ibid., 24 April and 10 July 1885 for references to Burtonport, Dungloe and Rosses CC. See *DI*, 9 October 1891 for Ardara CC.

162 *John Lawrence's Handbook of Cricket in Ireland, Number Nine, 1873–4* (Dublin: John Lawrence, 1874), p. 122.

163 Ibid.

164 *John Lawrence's Handbook of Cricket in Ireland, Number Thirteen, 1877–8* (Dublin: John Lawrence, 1878), p. 105.

165 Ibid., and *IR*, 20 November 1884.

166 *Lawrence's Handbook of Cricket in Ireland, Number Seven*, p. 150.

167 See *DS*, 27 May 1892 and *DJ*, 20 March 1908 and 20 May 1912. In March 1908, the club appealed to supporters for help in securing grounds.

168 See, for example, *DJ*, 26 July 1890.

169 See Hunt, *Sport and Society*, pp. 113–40 and Bracken, 'Foreign and Fantastic Field Sports', pp. 35–105.

170 *DJ*, 29 April 1891.

171 Ibid., 2 October 1895.

172 *DS*, 11 September 1891.

173 *DJ*, 22 June, 27 July and 15 August 1892.

174 Ibid., 12 June 1895.

175 Ibid., 2 October 1895.

176 Ibid., 5 May 1897 and *LS*, 1 January 1898.

177 Ibid., 12 May 1890.

178 Ibid., 21 April 1890 and 22 April 1901.

179 Ibid., 18 February 1895 and 27 April 1892.

180 Ibid., 2 September 1865.

181 Ibid. See also Hunt, *Sport and Society*, pp. 131–5.

182 *DJ*, 25 July 1890.
183 *DV*, 28 August 1891.
184 *DJ*, 2 October 1895.
185 Ibid., 28 September 1910.
186 *IR*, 1 June 1882 and 25 September 1884.
187 *DV*, 25 September 1891.
188 *DJ*, 28 May 1893.
189 *DS*, 3 March 1893.
190 *LS*, 31 May 1892.
191 Sean Beattie, 'Cottage Industries: Arts and Crafts in Donegal, 1880–1920', *Donegal Annual, 2008*, no. 60 (Letterkenny: Browne Printers, 2008), pp. 59–81, p. 65.
192 'Herdman's Mill in Sion Mills sold to lottery winner Margaret Loughrey', retrieved from http://www.bbc.com/news/uk-northern-ireland-foyle-west-28398820 [Accessed 23 July 2014].
193 The following clubs noted in the *DV*, *DI*, *LS*, *DJ* and *DS* were analysed: Malin, Culdaff, Mountcharles, Ballyshannon, Ballyshannon Wanderers, Glenfin, Donegal town, Raphoe, Manorcunningham, Letterkenny, Convoy, Carrigans, Lifford, Ballybofey, Buncrana, St Johnston, Moville, Burt, Bundoran Visitors and Clonleigh.
194 Hunt, *Sport and Society*, pp. 135–6.
195 *DJ*, 30 August 1882.
196 Ibid., 29 November 1895 and 11 January 1901.
197 *Hunt, Sport and Society*, p. 6 and p. 135.
198 Ibid., pp. 135–6.
199 Nolan (ed.), *The Gaelic Athletic Association in Dublin, Vol. 1, 1884–1959*, p. 58.
200 *DP and DN*, 4 October 1902.
201 *DJ*, 8 April 1882.
202 Ibid., 24 April 1882.
203 Ibid., 19 January 1883.
204 *DV*, 26 April 1930.
205 *DJ*, 19 and 29 May, 2 June, 17 July, 7, 14 and 30 August 1882.
206 *DI*, 20 July 1889.
207 Ibid., 28 March and 23 May 1884, *DV*, 5 April 1890 and 15 April 1892.
208 *DJ*, 29 May and 14 August 1882.
209 See, for example, *DI*, 2 June, 20 July and 10 August 1889.
210 Ibid., 14 August 1882.
211 Ibid.
212 Ibid., 16 March 1889.
213 *DV*, 30 November 1889 and 5 April 1890.
214 Ibid., 19 June 1896.
215 *DI*, 13 April 1900.
216 *DV*, 18 April 1902.
217 Ibid., 10 July 1903.
218 In 1900 the *DJ* noted teams in Inishowen at Buncrana, Malin, Culdaff and Moville; Carrigans, Clonleigh, Convoy, St Johnston, Letterkenny, Raphoe, Churchill and the Royal School in Raphoe in the east; and in the south at Mountcharles.
219 *DJ*, 31 July 1903.

220 Ibid., 1 July 1907 and 10 June 1914.
221 *DV*, 2 August 1895. See also *Sport*, 18 July 1896. Gwynn was said to have made over 1,000 runs for Trinity College in the 1896 season with an average of over fifty, while his ninety-six wickets were said to be 'the most ever taken for Trinity in a season'.
222 *DV*, 2 August 1895.
223 *DI*, 21 August 1908.
224 Mike Cronin and Roisín Higgins, *Places We Play: Ireland's Sporting Heritage* (Cork: The Collins Press, 2011), p. 35.
225 Seán Reid, 'The Place of Irish Cricket in the Nineteenth Century British Empire of Cricket'. Paper given at the Sixth Annual Conference of Sports History Ireland, 25 September 2011.
226 *DJ*, 1 February 1915.
227 Ibid., 25 July 1927.
228 Ibid., 27 April 1928.
229 Ibid., 3 August 1928.
230 Ibid., 3 October 1928 and 12 June 1929.
231 *DV*, 10 May 1930.
232 *LS*, 1 January 1898. Initial clubs which affiliated included Ballymena, Ballymoney, Coleraine, Route, Londonderry and Lacrosse.
233 *DS*, 22 April 1898.
234 Ibid.
235 *DJ*, 20 November 1899.
236 W.H.W. Platt, *North-west of Ireland Hockey, 1895–1968* (Coleraine: the author, 2006), pp. 39–43.
237 Ibid., p. 126 and p. 133.
238 Ibid., p. 143, p. 154, p. 170.
239 Ibid., p. 167 and p. 172.
240 *DS*, 5 January 1898.
241 *DV*, 4 February 1898.
242 Ibid., 15 and 29 March 1901.
243 Ibid., 22 March 1901.
244 Ibid., 20 September 1901.
245 Ibid., 6 November 1903.
246 Jennifer Kelly and R.V. Comerford, 'Introduction', in Jennifer Kelly and R.V. Comerford (eds), *Associational Culture in Ireland and Abroad* (Dublin: Irish Academic Press, 2010) pp. 1–10, p. 1.
247 Pádraig Deignan, 'The importance of fraternities and social clubs for the Protestant community in Sligo from 1914 to 1949', in Kelly and Comerford (eds), *Associational Culture in Ireland and Abroad*, pp. 191–213, p. 209.
248 *DV*, 31 December 1897.
249 *Sport*, 21 August 1897 and *FH*, 13 August 1904 and Masonic Lodge numbers 129 and 287, 1882–1935 (Grand Lodge of Freemasons, Dublin, Masonic Lodge membership registers, 1882–1935).
250 Robert T. Bashford, 'The History of Freemasonry in Donegal', retrieved from http://irishfreemasonry.com/Freemasonry%20in%20Donegal.pdf [Accessed 4 July 2013] and Seán Beattie, 'Freemasonry in Donegal, 1757–1953', *Donegal Annual, 2010*, no. 62 (Letterkenny: Browne Printers, 2008), pp. 30–9, p. 37.
251 Beattie, 'Freemasonry in Donegal', p. 37.

252 Masonic Lodge numbers 129 and 287, 1882–1935 (Grand Lodge of Freemasons, Dublin, Masonic Lodge membership registers).
253 *FH,* 8 February 1908.
254 Ibid., 1 February 1908.
255 Beattie, 'Freemasonry in Donegal', p. 37.
256 Masonic Lodge numbers 129 and 287, 1882–1935 (Grand Lodge of Freemasons, Dublin, Masonic Lodge membership registers).
257 Deignan, 'The Importance of Fraternities and Social Clubs', p. 209.
258 *FH*, 10 October 1925 and 23 April 1927.
259 Ibid., 23 April 1927.
260 *DD*, 23 June 1928 and *FH*, 15 December 1928 and 1 March 1930.
261 *DV*, 2 and 16 September 1933.
262 Ibid., 16 September 1933.
263 Ibid., 10 and 17 February 1934.
264 Platt, *North-west of Ireland Hockey, 1895–1968,* p. 190.
265 Ibid., p. 173 and p. 179.
266 *DV*, 29 November 1930.
267 Tranter, *Sport, Economy and Society,* p. 24.
268 Hunt, *Sport and Society,* pp. 75–86.

3. The early GAA in Donegal, 1884–1905

1 Paul Rouse, 'Why the GAA was Founded', in McAnallen, Hassan and Hegarty, *The Evolution of the GAA*, pp. 79–85, pp. 84–5.
2 Richard Holt, 'Ireland and the Birth of Modern Sport', in Cronin, Murphy and Rouse (eds), *The Gaelic Athletic Association, 1884–2009*, pp. 33–46, p. 33.
3 Foster, *Modern Ireland, 1600–1972*, p. 447.
4 Kieran McConville and Dónal McAnallen, 'The Search for John McKay', in McAnallen, Hassan and Hegarty, *The Evolution of the GAA*, pp. 240–53, p. 240.
5 *The Nation*, 8 November 1884. It was noted in the press that 'about sixty letters and telegrams', written by 'representative men both lay and clerical', were read at the meeting but only a small number were published at the time.
6 Paul Rouse, 'The Politics of Culture and Sport in Ireland: A History of the GAA Ban on Foreign Games, 1884–1971. Part One: 1884–1921', *International Journal of the History of Sport,* vol. 10, no. 3 (1993), pp. 333–60, p. 342 and p. 344.
7 Ibid.
8 Cronin, Duncan and Rouse, *The GAA: A People's History*, pp. 145–7.
9 'The Gaelic Athletic Association through History and Documents, 1870–1920', Teachers' resource pack. Letter from Michael Cusack to Maurice Davin, 26 August 1884 retrieved from http://www.crokepark.ie/getmedia/e35fa6c0-37od-4d68-831c-85df0f874a0d/web1.pdf [Accessed 11 July 2010].
10 Tom Garvin, *The Evolution of Irish Nationalist Politics* [Second edition] (Dublin: Gill & Macmillan, 2005), p. 12 and p. 74. The Ribbonmen were a secret Catholic agrarian organisation which had succeeded the Defenders in the early nineteenth century and who opposed the Orange Order.
11 McAnallen, 'Cén Fáth a Raibh Cúige Uladh Chomh Lag Chomh Fada Sin?', p. 138.
12 David Hassan, 'The GAA in Ulster', in Cronin, Murphy and Rouse (eds), *The Gaelic Athletic Association, 1884–2009*, pp. 77–91, p. 78.

13 Ibid.
14 Ibid.
15 *DJ*, 29 October 1888.
16 Ibid., 18 December 1889.
17 Con Short, *The Ulster GAA Story* (Rossan: Comhairle Uladh, 1984), p. 31.
18 *DD*, 26 April 1930.
19 Tom Hunt, 'Parish Factions, Parading Bands and Sumptuous Repasts: The Diverse Origins and Activities of Early GAA Clubs', in McAnallen, Hassan and Hegarty, *The Evolution of the GAA*, p. 86.
20 Taylor, *The Association Game*, pp. 32–4.
21 Hunt, 'Parish Factions, Parading Bands and Sumptuous Repasts', p. 87.
22 See, for example, *DJ*, 20 March 1889.
23 Ibid., 19 March 1890.
24 Leo Deery and Danny O'Kane (eds), *Doire: A History of the GAA in Derry, 1884–1984* (Coleraine: CLCG Doire, 1984), p. 10.
25 *Slater's Directory, 1894* (London: Slater's Directory Co., 1894).
26 Ibid.
27 See Begley, Bell, Flanders and White, *The County Donegal Railway: A Visitor's Guide*, p. 4 and p. 7 and Dave Bell and Steve Flanders, *The Londonderry and Lough Swilly Railway: A Visitor's Guide* (Donegal: The County Donegal Railway Restoration Society, 1995), p. 57.
28 *DI*, 20 April 1889, *DV*, 20 April 1889 and 4 January 1890.
29 *DS*, 14 April 1893.
30 See Hunt, *Sport and Society*, p. 166 and Neal Garnham (ed.), *The Origins and Development of Football in Ireland, Being a Reprint of R.M. Peter's Irish Football Annual of 1880. With an Introduction by Neal Garnham* (Belfast: Ulster Historical Foundation, 1999), p. 171.
31 Michael Leydon, *Dunmore MacHales: A History of Football in Dunmore Parish* (Dunmore: the author, 1983).
32 *DJ*, 18 December 1889.
33 *DV*, 13 November 1891.
34 *DJ*, 18 November 1891.
35 See, for example, Crime Branch Special Northern Division District Inspector's Monthly Report for Donegal, January 1892, 520S/8058 and February 1893, 520S/10368.
36 See Sam Fleming, *Letterkenny Past and Present* (Ballyshannon: Donegal Democrat Printers, 1979), pp. 78–9 and *DJ*, 8 January 1892.
37 Hunt, *Sport and Society*, p. 162.
38 *DJ*, 29 December 1886.
39 Ibid.
40 Huggins, 'The Spread of Association Football in North-east England', pp. 302–7.
41 *DJ*, 3 June 1896.
42 Crime Branch Special: DICS Reports Box 6. Monthly Secret Report of the Northern Division, 4 March 1889, 522/9501.
43 Garvin, *The Evolution of Irish Nationalist Politics*, p. 88.
44 In 1888 the *Derry Journal* provided regular reports on the activities of thirty-seven of these clubs.
45 National League clubs in South Derry were heavily linked to GAA clubs in the mid-1880s. I am grateful to Dónal McAnallen for this reference.

46 Cronin, Duncan and Rouse, *The GAA: A People's History*, pp. 3–4 and p. 142.
47 Crime Branch Special: DICS Reports Box 6. Monthly Secret Report of the Northern Division, 4 November 1887, 261/6939.
48 Ibid.
49 Murphy, *Derry, Donegal and Modern Ulster ,1790–1921*, pp. 135–6.
50 McElligott, 'Forging a Kingdom', p. 29 and p. 40.
51 Ibid., p. 22.
52 Cronin, Duncan and Rouse, *The GAA: A People's History*, p. 82.
53 McElligott, 'Forging a Kingdom', p. 37.
54 Ibid., p. 70.
55 Cronin, Duncan and Rouse, *The GAA: County by County*, p. 279.
56 De Burca, *The GAA: A History*, p. 68.
57 *Irish Press GAA Golden Jubilee Supplement, 1934*, p. 56 and 'History of Ballina Town', retrieved from http://www.ballinatc.ie/AboutBallina/HistoryofBallina Town/ [Accessed 28 October 2012].
58 For a breakdown of these matches see Appendix 2. While it is unclear if the Joys, Green Volunteers, Ballynelly Pioneers, Moville Harps, Finner and the Bundoran Irish Hearts were actually clubs, they have been included.
59 Hunt, *Sport and Society*, p. 155.
60 *DJ*, 19 November 1888.
61 Rouse, 'The Politics of Culture and Sport in Ireland', p. 341.
62 Cronin, Duncan and Rouse, *The GAA: A People's Story*, p. 37.
63 Joe Lennon, 'An Overview of the Playing Rules of Gaelic Football and Hurling, 1884–2010', in McAnallen, Hassan and Hegarty, *The Evolution of the GAA*, pp. 164–74, p. 167.
64 Ibid., pp. 166–7.
65 Rouse, 'The Politics of Culture and Sport in Ireland', p. 341.
66 *DJ*, 31 January 1890. See also ibid., 2 May 1890. A Gaelic football match between Young Irelands and Portlough Harps was reduced to 'two quarters' at the agreement of each captain, 'it getting well on the evening'.
67 Ibid., 31 December 1890.
68 Ibid., 30 July 1890.
69 Neal Garnham, 'Accounting for the Early Success of the Gaelic Athletic Association', *Irish Historical Studies*, vol. xxxiv, no. 133 (2004), pp. 65–78, p. 71.
70 Ibid., pp. 71–2.
71 *DJ*, 25 December 1889.
72 Garnham, 'Accounting for the Early Success of the Gaelic Athletic Association', p. 74.
73 *DJ*, 28 December 1888.
74 Ibid.
75 Ibid., 30 October 1889.
76 Ibid., 2 May 1890.
77 Ibid., 10 March 1890.
78 Ibid., 9 April 1890.
79 See *DJ*, 1889 and 1890.
80 See Figure 3.2 and Appendix 2.
81 *DJ*, 12 and 26 March 1890.
82 Hassan, 'The GAA in Ulster', p. 78.
83 W.F. Mandle, 'The Gaelic Athletic Association and Popular Culture', in

MacDonagh, Mandle and Travers (eds), *Irish Culture and Nationalism, 1750–1950*, pp. 104–21, pp. 111–12.

84 Hunt, 'Parish Factions, Parading Bands and Sumptuous Repasts: The Diverse Origins and Activities of Early GAA Clubs', in McAnallen, Hassan and Hegarty, *The Evolution of the GAA*, pp. 86–99.

85 See *DJ*, 8 February 1888 and Campbell, Dowds and Mullan, *Against the Grain*, p. 77.

86 *DJ*, 15 September and 17 September 1888.

87 Ibid., 19 November 1888.

88 Ibid., 18 November 1889 and 16 December 1889.

89 Ibid., 31 January 1890.

90 Ibid., 4 April 1890.

91 De Burca, *The GAA: A History*, pp. 41–2. Cavan had the most clubs in Ulster with thirty-seven out of Ulster's total of eighty-eight, with the initial national figure recorded that year at 875.

92 Hunt, *Sport and Society in Victorian Ireland*, p. 160.

93 Henry Boylan, *A Dictionary of Irish Biography* (Dublin: Gill & Macmillan, 1978), pp. 100–1 and p. 258. O'Doherty, Lord of Inishowen, was killed by Crown forces on 5 July 1608 having sacked and burned Derry city and Emmet was the leader of a rising against the British government in 1803 and was later hanged for treason.

94 *DJ*, 30 December 1889.

95 Garnham, *Association Football and Society*, pp. 134–5.

96 Crime Department Special Branch Report on the GAA in the Northern Division: Progress Made During the Year Ended 31 December 1890, 10 February 1891, 2701/S and Mike Cronin, 'Enshrined in Blood: The Naming of Gaelic Athletic Association Clubs and the English Influence on Irish Sport', *The Sports Historian*, vol. 17, no. 2 (1998) pp. 90–104, p. 96.

97 Nolan (ed.), *The Gaelic Athletic Association in Dublin, Vol. 1, 1884–1959*, p. 22.

98 Crime Department Special Branch Report on the GAA in the Northern Division: Progress Made During the Year Ended 31 December 1890. 10 February 1891. 2701/S.

99 Garvin, *The Evolution of Irish Nationalist Politics*, p. 106.

100 Crime Department Special Branch Report on the GAA in the Northern Division: Progress Made During the Year Ended 31 December 1890. 10 February 1891. 2701/S.

101 De Burca, *The GAA: A History*, pp. 40–1.

102 *DJ*, 1888–1892 and 'Census of Ireland 1901 and 1911', retrieved from http://census.nationalarchives.ie [Accessed 10 December 2011].

103 Neil Tranter, 'The Patronage of Organized Sport in Central Scotland, 1820–1900', *Journal of Sports History*, vol. 16, no. 3 (1989), pp. 227–47, p. 229.

104 *DJ*, 28 October 1891 and 29 February 1892. See also ibid., 1 January 1892. The Letterkenny club also received financial aid from their president Major H.A. Doyne, JP, and W.H. Boyd, JP at the end of 1891.

105 Ibid., 4 March, 21 September and 28 September 1892.

106 See, for example, *DV*, 6 July 1889, 25 September 1891 and *DJ*, 27 May 1892.

107 Campbell, Dowds and Mullen (eds), *Against the Grain*, p. 80.

108 *DJ*, 28 December 1888.

109 Ibid., 21 April 1890.

110 See also ibid., 24 December 1888. The use of subscriptions for the running of the Cahir O's GAA club was noted at their meeting in December 1888.
111 Hunt, *Sport and Society*, p. 218. See Garnham, *Association Football and Society*, pp. 115–17; Neil Tranter, 'The Cappielow Riot and the Composition and Behaviour of Soccer Crowds in Late Victorian Scotland', *International Journal of the History of Sport*, vol. 12, no. 3 (1995), pp. 124–40, p. 130 and Tony Mason, *Association Football and English Society, 1863–1915* (Brighton: Harvester Press, 1980) pp. 155–7.
112 Tranter, 'The Cappielow Riot', p. 130. See Wray Vamplew, 'Sports Crowd Disorder in Britain, 1870–1914: Causes and Controls', *Journal of Sport History*, vol. 7, no. 1 (1980), pp. 5–20; John Hutchinson, 'Some Aspects of Football Crowds before 1914', paper presented to the Society for the Study of Labour History, University of Sussex, 1975; Eric Dunning, J.A. Maguire, Patrick Murphy and John Williams, 'The Social Roots of Football Violence', *Leisure Studies*, vol. 1, no. 2 (1982), pp. 139–56; Jeremy Crump and Tony Mason, 'Hostile and Improper Demonstrations: Football Violence, 1880–1980', *Bulletin of the Society for the Study of Labour History*, no. 50 (1985), pp. 11–12.
113 Garnham, *Association Football and Society*, p. 129.
114 Hunt, 'Parish Factions, Parading Bands and Sumptuous Repasts', pp. 95–6.
115 Short, *The Ulster GAA Story*, p. 31.
116 Cronin, *Sport and Nationalism*, p. 109.
117 *DJ*, 28 January 1889.
118 Ibid., 20 March 1889.
119 *Sport*, 4 January 1890.
120 *DJ*, 9 April 1890.
121 Ibid., 5 November 1890.
122 Ibid.
123 Ibid., 28 December 1888.
124 Ibid., 2 January 1893.
125 Ibid., 10 April 1893.
126 Deery and O'Kane (eds), *Doire: A History of the GAA in Derry*, p. 13 and Nolan, *The Gaelic Athletic Association in Dublin, Vol. 1, 1884–1959*, p. 59.
127 *DJ*, 20 March 1889.
128 Hunt, 'Parish Factions, Parading Bands and Sumptuous Repasts', p. 95.
129 See, for example, *DJ*, 23 June 1888.
130 Ibid., 8 February 1888 and 2 January 1893.
131 Garnham, 'Accounting for the Early Success of the Gaelic Athletic Association', p. 73.
132 *DJ*, 27 October 1890.
133 Nolan (ed.), *The Gaelic Athletic Association in Dublin: Vol. 1, 1884–1959*, p. 59.
134 Crime Branch Special: DICS Reports Box 6. Monthly Secret Report of the Northern Division, 6 February 1889, 522/9501 and 2 June 1889, 521/9983.
135 De Burca, *The GAA: A History*, p. 64.
136 Simon Gillespie and Roddy Hegarty, 'Camán and Crozier: The Catholic Church and the GAA, 1884–1902', in McAnallen, Hassan and Hegarty, *The Evolution of the GAA: Ulaidh, Éire agus Eile*, pp. 112–22, p. 122.
137 Paul Rouse, 'The Hand of Power', in *Celebrating 125 years of the GAA* in *The Irish Times*, 29 January 2009, pp. 51–3, p. 52.
138 Short, *The Ulster GAA Story*, p. 31.

139 McAnallen, 'Cén Fáth a Raibh Cúige Uladh Chomh Lag Chomh Fada Sin?' in McAnallen, Hassan and Hegarty, *The Evolution of the GAA*, pp. 138–9.
140 Ibid., p. 139 and Marcus Bourke, 'The Early GAA in South Ulster', *The Clogher Record,* vol. VII, no. 1 (1969), pp. 5–26, pp. 10–11.
141 Hunt, *Sport and Society,* p. 142 and Paul Rouse, 'The Hand of Power', *The Irish Times*, 29 January 2009. 'Celebrating 125 years of the GAA', pp. 51–3, p. 51.
142 Deery and O'Kane (eds), *Doire: A History of the GAA in Derry*, pp. 12–13.
143 *DJ*, 3 October 1890.
144 Ibid., 14 May and 27 October 1890.
145 *Sport,* 5 July 1890.
146 *DJ*, 18 and 27 August 1890.
147 See, for example, Crime Department Branch Special, Northern Division, Monthly Secret Report for December 1888, 4 January 1889, 1/10297 and Crime Department Branch Special, Northern Division, Monthly Secret Report for April 1889, 5 May 1889, 1/11144.
148 *Sport*, 11 October 1890.
149 Ibid.
150 Murphy, *Derry, Donegal and Modern Ulster*, pp. 171–2.
151 Ibid.
152 *DJ,* 16 May 1890. Portlough Harps played only four matches in 1890 and received less attention in the local press than other clubs. In May 1890 their delegate to the Derry county committee, Bernard McElhinney, withdrew from this organisation which was showing signs of difficulties. This appears to have been the end of the club's short-lived participation in the GAA.
153 Killea Hibernians had performed fairly regularly over a five-month period from December 1889 until April 1890, participating in six Gaelic football and six hurling matches.
154 Hunt, 'Parish Factions, Parading Bands and Sumptuous Repasts', pp. 88–9.
155 See *DJ* and *Sport*, 1888–92.
156 *DJ*, 30 December 1895 and 29 December 1899.
157 Campbell, Dowds and Mullan, *Against the Grain*, p. 80.
158 Ibid.
159 *DJ*, 13 July 1892.
160 Ibid., 12 August 1892.
161 Ibid., 15 August 1892.
162 Ibid., 28 September 1892.
163 Ibid., 12 October 1892.
164 McAnallen, 'Cén Fáth a Raibh Cúige Uladh Chomh Lag Chomh Fada Sin?', p. 141.
165 Crime Department Special Branch Report on the GAA in the Northern Division: Progress Made During the Year Ended 31 December 1890, 10 February 1891, 2701/S.
166 *Sport*, 3 January 1891.
167 Ibid.
168 McAnallen, 'Cén Fáth a Raibh Cúige Uladh Chomh Lag Chomh Fada Sin?', p. 141.
169 Rouse, 'The Politics of Culture and Sport in Ireland', p. 344.
170 Ibid.
171 *DJ*, 2 April 1902 and 29 May, 18 July, 1 August and 5 December 1903.

172 *DP and DN*, 9 April, 7 May 1904 and *DV*, 22 April 1904.
173 Garnham, 'Accounting for the Early Success of the GAA', pp. 69–78.
174 Mike Huggins and John Tolson, 'The Railways and Sport in Victorian Britain: A Critical Reassessment', *The Journal of Transport History*, vol. 22, no. 2 (2001), pp. 99–115, p. 113.

4. The failure of the GAA in Donegal, 1905–1919

1 Huggins, 'The Spread of Association football in North-east England', p. 299.
2 Cronin, Duncan and Rouse, *The GAA: A People's History*, p. 147.
3 Ferriter, *The Transformation of Ireland*, p. 101.
4 Dónal McAnallen, 'Cén Fáth a Raibh Cúige Uladh Chomh Lag Chomh Fada Sin?', p. 143.
5 *DJ*, 25 October 1905.
6 Ibid., 17 November 1905.
7 Ibid., 9 October 1905.
8 *DP and DN*, 12 May 1906.
9 Ibid., 7 February, 6 April 1906, *DP and DN*, 19 May 1906 and *DI*, 6 April, 28 November 1906.
10 *DP and DN*, 5 May 1906.
11 See *DJ, DI, DV* and *DP and DN*, 1905–6.
12 Hunt, *Sport and Society*, p. 190.
13 Ibid., p. 191.
14 Garvin, *The Evolution of Irish Nationalist Politics*, p. 111 and p. 113.
15 Ibid., pp. 111–12.
16 Ibid., p. 112.
17 Helen Meehan, *Inver Parish in History* (Mountcharles: the author, 2005), p. 234 and pp. 419–20 and 'The MacManus Brothers', *Donegal Annual, 1994* (Letterkenny: Donegal Democrat Printers, 1994), pp. 5–18, p. 7.
18 Meehan, *Inver Parish in History*, p. 235. MacManus, born in 1868 in Mountcharles, and having become a national school teacher, was forced to resign his post as principal of Glencoagh NS in 1897 after expressing his nationalist views. He became a prominent author and lecturer.
19 Ferriter, *The Transformation of Ireland*, p. 36.
20 *DP and DN*, 26 September 1903.
21 Ibid., and *DJ*, 25 October 1905.
22 *DP and DN*, 26 September 1903.
23 Foster, *Modern Ireland, 1600–1972*, p. 457
24 Ferriter, *The Transformation of Ireland*, p. 81.
25 Meehan, *Inver Parish in History*, p. 239. Anna Johnston's pen name was Ethna Carberry and she played a significant role in the Gaelic Revival in Belfast.
26 *DJ*, 27 February 1905.
27 *DP and DN*, 20 May 1905.
28 See, for example, Crime Branch Special, Inspector General and Chief Inspector's Monthly Report, October 1905, 379/S, 4 November 1905 and May 1906, 821/S, 4 June 1906. The RIC noted the presence of only four Cumann na nGaedheal clubs in October 1905 and they were said to be 'mostly in the Ballyshannon district'. By May 1906 this figure had not changed and these clubs were said to be 'not very active'.
29 Murphy, *Derry, Donegal and Modern Ulster, 1790–1921*, p. 195.

30 B.M. Walker (ed.), *Parliamentary Election Results in Ireland, 1801–1922* (Dublin: Royal Irish Academy, 1978), pp. 339–41.
31 Murphy, *Derry, Donegal and Modern Ulster*, p. 195.
32 Nolan (ed.), *The Gaelic Athletic Association in Dublin: Vol. 1, 1884–1959*, p. 69.
33 Tom Hunt, 'The GAA: Social Structure and Associated Clubs', in Cronin, Murphy and Rouse (eds), *The Gaelic Athletic Association, 1884–2009*, pp. 200–1 and David Hassan, 'The GAA in Ulster', in Cronin, Murphy and Rouse (eds), *The Gaelic Athletic Association, 1884–2009*, pp. 77–91, p. 81.
34 Hassan, 'The GAA in Ulster', p. 81.
35 *DJ*, 27 October 1905.
36 *DV*, 27 October 1905.
37 *DP and DN*, 18 November 1905 and 31 March 1906. A Glenfin team which played Glenswilly in March 1906 was said to have been started in connection with the local Gaelic league branch but failed to join the county board.
38 Jackson, *Ireland, 1798–1998*, p. 180.
39 *DD*, 28 July 1934. This was an Irish name for Donegal.
40 *DJ*, 20 September 1905.
41 *DP and DN*, 14 October 1905.
42 Ibid., 20 January 1906.
43 Ibid., 9 September 1905.
44 *DJ*, 12 January 1906 and *DI*, 18 May 1906.
45 *DP and DN*, 10 June 1905.
46 *DJ*, 17 July 1905.
47 Foster, *Modern Ireland, 1600–1972*, p. 359.
48 Timothy G. McMahon, *Grand Opportunity: The Gaelic Revival and Irish Society* (New York: Syracuse University Press, 2008), p. 156. See also *DP and DN*, 29 July 1905. MacGiolla Iosa discussed the 'folly of emigration' and the shame of joining the British army or the RIC at another series of camán matches at the end of July.
49 *DJ*, 8 September 1905. At a céilí held at Croagh in September, chairman James Molloy illustrated the nationalist rhetoric when he claimed that they did not want to hear about English songs, dances or games being organised.
50 Ibid., 18 July 1906.
51 Campbell, Dowds and Mullan, *Against the Grain*, p. 87.
52 See *DP and DN*, 8 and 29 July 1905. For an overview of these traditional rules see Mac a' Ghoill, 'Cross-country Hurling in Ardara', pp. 53–7.
53 Gaelic football teams assessed included Lámh Dearg (Letterkenny), Lámh Dearg (Mountcharles), Killybegs, Dunkineely, Balldearg, Gweedore Old Celts and St Columba's of Churchill. The camán teams of Balldearg, Letterkenny and Mountcharles GAA clubs, Sinn Féin (Bundoran), Burt Hibernians, St Mura's of Fahan and Newtowncunningham Harps were also used.
54 McElligott, 'Forging a Kingdom', p. 119.
55 Ibid., p. 128 and Hunt, 'The GAA: Social Structure', p. 192.
56 Hunt, 'The GAA: Social Structure', p. 192.
57 McElligott, 'Forging a Kingdom', p. 129.
58 Hunt, 'The GAA: Social Structure', p. 192 and McElligott, 'Forging a Kingdom', p. 127.
59 Ibid.

60 See Table 4.2. These included county board officials and those from the clubs of Balldearg, Lámh Dearg (Mountcharles), Clann Conaill (Brackey), Ardara, Killybegs, Lámh Dearg (Letterkenny), Gweedore Old Celts, True Gaels (Meenabradan), Ethna Carberry (Croagh), Killygordon, Glenfin, Naomh Conaill (Kilraine), Dunkineely, Newtowncunningham Harps, St Mura's (Fahan) and Creeslough.
61 See *DJ*, 25 October 1905 and *DP and DN*, 18 November 1905.
62 McElligott, 'Forging a Kingdom', p. 126.
63 See *DJ*, 7 June and 11 August 1905.
64 Murphy, *Derry, Donegal and Modern Ulster*, p. 195.
65 Jim MacLaughlin, 'The Age of Transition', in MacLaughlin (ed.), *Donegal: The Making of a Northern County*, pp. 283–91, p. 288.
66 *DJ*, 4 October 1905.
67 Ibid., 9 October 1905.
68 *DP and DN*, 14 October 1905.
69 *DJ*, 9 October 1905.
70 Ibid.
71 Ibid.
72 Ibid., 25 October 1905.
73 Meehan, *Inver Parish in History*, p. 241.
74 *DJ*, 25 October 1905.
75 Ibid.
76 Ibid., 15 November 1905.
77 Ibid.
78 Ibid., 18 April and 18 July 1906.
79 *Sport*, 31 August 1907.
80 *DJ*, 26 April 1907.
81 Ibid., 25 October, 17 November 1905 and 7 February 1906.
82 Ibid., 26 January 1906.
83 *DI*, 18 May 1906.
84 *DJ*, 22 January 1906.
85 *DP and DN*, 23 December 1905, *DJ*, 22 January 1906 and *DI*, 9 March 1906.
86 *DP and DN*, 25 November 1905.
87 *DI*, 9 March 1906.
88 *DV*, 7 December 1906.
89 Ibid., 1 March 1907.
90 *DV*, 15 February 1907.
91 *DP and DN*, 5 May 1906.
92 Ibid., 27 July 1907.
93 *The Gaelic Athletic Annual and County Directory for 1907–8* (Dublin: Sealy, Bryers & Walker, 1907), p. 33.
94 See *DJ*, *DI*, *DV* and *DP and DN*, 1907.
95 De Burca, *The GAA: A History*, p. 73.
96 Ibid.
97 McAnallen, 'Cén Fáth a Raibh Cúige Uladh Chomh Lag Chomh Fada Sin?', pp. 143–6.
98 See *LS*, 17 May 1906.
99 *DP and DN*, 30 December 1905.
100 Ibid., 3 February 1906 and *DJ*, 12 February 1906. This progress was said to be even worse in the eastern division at this time.

101 See *DP and DN*, 21 April and 5 May 1906.
102 *DP and DN*, 12 May 1906. See also *DJ*, 27 April 1906. The previous month Lámh Dearg of Letterkenny could only get thirteen players to make the journey to Gweedore for their Gaelic football match.
103 *DJ*, 29 December 1905.
104 Ibid., 14 March 1906. It was reported at the Western Board meeting at the beginning of March that nearly all the clubs that had been asked to select their best players 'could not see their way to send any members, as they had been engaged all the time to the camán, and had given no time to Gaelic football. The Gweedore team was a notable exception.' See also ibid., 19 March 1906. The Donegal team heavily beaten by Derry was hastily made up of players from clubs in Gweedore, Fahan, Newtowncunningham (East Division) and Mountcharles and Bundoran (West Division), which illustrates the lack of development in the county of Gaelic football at this stage.
105 *DP and DN*, 2 June, 7 July and 9 November 1906. Both Killybegs and Bundoran appear to have withdrawn early in the competition and were replaced by teams from Dunkineely and Croagh.
106 See *DI*, 26 October and 21 December 1906.
107 Nolan (ed.), *The Gaelic Athletic Association in Dublin, Vol. 1, 1884–1959*, p. 54.
108 See, for example, *DJ*, 22 and 29 December 1905.
109 *DI*, 19 October 1906.
110 *DP and DN*, 12 May 1906.
111 Ibid., 19 May 1906.
112 *DI*, 19 October 1906.
113 *DJ*, 6 July 1906.
114 McAnallen, 'Cén Fáth a Raibh Cúige Uladh Chomh Lag Chomh Fada Sin?', p. 146.
115 *DP and DN*, 18 November 1905.
116 *DJ*, 6 April 1906.
117 Ibid., 9 December 1908.
118 *DI*, 3 May 1907.
119 McAnallen, 'Cén Fáth a Raibh Cúige Uladh Chomh Lag Chomh Fada Sin?', pp. 143–5.
120 *DI*, 19 October 1906.
121 *DJ*, 16 February 1934. This letter was published much later as part of a 'Gleanings by Spur' column. McDyer recommended the appointing of deputy delegates by clubs so that they would attend divisional meetings if chief delegates could not appear and that delegates would hold their positions for 'at least three years'. Protests were to be allowed to accumulate until quarterly meetings and witnesses from each club involved in these disputes were to be questioned.
122 *DV*, 26 July 1907.
123 *DJ*, 28 November 1906. An exception was a 'monster' tournament organised for 26 December in Newtowncunningham.
124 Ibid., 12 December 1906.
125 Campbell, Dowds and Mullan, *Against the Grain*, p. 93.
126 *DV*, 8 November 1907 and *DI*, 19 June and 7 August 1908.
127 See *DI*, 19 October 1906 and *DJ*, 20 November 1908. MacManus' absence from the West Division meeting was noted in October 1906. He was by then

engaged in lectures in the United States and by November 1908 had been made a professor of literature at Notre Dame University.

128 *DJ*, 14 June 1906.
129 McElligott, 'Forging a Kingdom', pp. 130–2, p. 160 and p. 163.
130 McAnallen, 'Cén Fáth a Raibh Cúige Uladh Chomh Lag Chomh Fada Sin?', p. 146.
131 *DJ*, 12 February 1915.
132 Ibid., 1 April 1910.
133 Ibid., 14 October 1910.
134 *DV*, 14 June 1911.
135 Ibid., 20 October 1911.
136 Ibid.
137 Ibid., 11 November 1911 and 24 February 1913 and *DP and DN*, 9 May 1914.
138 See, for example, *DV*, 26 March, 28 April and 20 August 1915.
139 Ibid., 1 June and 14 December 1917.
140 Jim MacLaughlin, 'Introduction: The Making of a Northern County', in MacLaughlin (ed.), *Donegal: The Making of a Northern County*, pp. 1–21, p. 5.
141 Cronin, Duncan and Rouse, *The GAA: A People's History*, p. 148.
142 Ferriter, *The Transformation of Ireland*, p. 141.
143 Ibid., p. 154.
144 *DJ*, 14 September 1923.
145 See *DJ*, 24 March, 5 July 1915 and *DI*, 3 April 1915. There were two teams located in Letterkenny, while Burt and Fahan also fielded Gaelic football selections in 1915. See *DP and DN*, 18 March 1916 and *DJ*, 14 April, 26 July, 2 August, 27 October 1916 and 3 January 1917 and Crawford and McCool (eds), *Golden Memories*, pp 2–4. Teams were located in Letterkenny, Burt, Killea, Newtowncunningham, Buncrana, Bridgend, Ballybofey, Stranorlar, Ballyshannon and Ballintra in 1916. See *DJ*, 23 February, 2 and 16 March, 6 April 1917; *DI*, 21 April 1917 and *DV*, 25 May 1917. In 1917 there were teams noted in Killea, Buncrana, Burt, Newtowncunningham, Ballybofey, Stranorlar and Ballyshannon. In April 1917 Burt and Newtowncunnningham Harps withdrew from the Derry Gaelic football league 'as they intended to confine themselves solely to hurling' while Ballintra returned to soccer having played only one Gaelic football match in 1916 and were said to have played their eleventh soccer game of the season by May 1917.
146 William Murphy, 'The GAA during the Irish Revolution', in Cronin, Murphy and Rouse (eds), *The Gaelic Athletic Association, 1884–2009*, pp. 61–76, p. 67.
147 Cronin, Duncan and Rouse, *The GAA: A People's History*, p. 151 and Nolan (ed.), *The Gaelic Athletic Association in Dublin*, p. 126.
148 Earnán de Blaghd, 'Organising the IRB in Donegal', *Donegal Annual, 1966*, vol. 3, no. 1 (Donegal: Donegal Democrat Printers, 1966), pp. 41–4, p. 44.
149 Ibid., p. 41.
150 Liam Ó Duibhir, *The Donegal Awakening: Donegal and the War of Independence* (Cork: Mercier Press, 2009), pp. 39–40.
151 De Burca, *The GAA: A History*, p. 111.
152 *DV*, 26 July 1918.
153 *DP and DN*, 13 July 1918.
154 *DI*, 3 August 1918.
155 De Burca, *The GAA: A History*, p. 112.

156 Cronin, Duncan and Rouse, *The GAA: A People's History*, p. 152.
157 *DV*, 30 August 1918.
158 Ibid., 4 October 1918.
159 Nolan (ed.), *The Gaelic Athletic Association in Dublin, Vol. 1, 1884–1959*, p. 81.

5. The Growth of the GAA in Donegal, 1919–1935

1 Ulster GAA Council Minutes, Volume 1, Ulster GAA Convention 1919 Minutes, 16 March 1919.
2 Ibid., Secretary's Report to the Ulster GAA Provincial Council, 16 March 1919.
3 Ibid., Ulster GAA Council Meeting Minutes, 12 April 1919.
4 *DJ*, 11 April 1919.
5 Ibid.
6 *DD*, 25 March 1923.
7 Ibid., 22 June 1923.
8 *DP and DN*, 10 May 1919.
9 *DJ*, 2 May 1919.
10 Ibid. After the second meeting in Ballybofey at the end of April, it was reported that the 'poor attendance of club delegates rendered the business of the meeting of a routine character'.
11 *DP and DN*, 10 May 1919. These were South Donegal, which contained the areas of Bundoran, Ballyshannon, Frosses, Ballintra and Donegal town while Kinlough (Leitrim) and Belleek (Fermanagh) were also included. The South-west district covered Kilcar, Glencolumbkille, Carrick, Rosbeg, Killybegs, Ardara, Glenties and Lettermacaward. The West Donegal district included Burtonport, Annagry, Gweedore, Gortahork and Falcarragh. Further north, the North-west area was comprised of Creeslough, Termon, Carrigart, Glen, Rossnakill, Kerrykeel, Ramelton, Milford and Rathmullan. North Donegal (or Inishowen) contained Burt, Fahan, Buncrana, Clonmany, Malin, Carndonagh and Culdaff. Areas such as Letterkenny, Castlefin and Killygordon were named in the Eastern division.
12 See *DV*, 23 May, 8 August 1919 and *DD*, 4 July 1919.
13 See *DJ*, 18 June and 29 August 1919.
14 *DI*, 8 March 1919.
15 *DP and DN*, 19 January 1918.
16 *DJ*, 29 October 1909.
17 Ó Duibhir, *The Donegal Awakening: Donegal and the War of Independence*, p. 57.
18 See, for example, *DJ*, 24 February and 13 September 1913, 24 March 1915 and 5 April 1916, 29 March 1919 and *DP and DN*, 8 November 1913.
19 'Red Hugh's GAA Club/CLG Aodh Rua, Cúil na gCúirrdín', retrieved from http://www.redhughsgaa.com/n_history.htm [Accessed 1 June 2011].
20 Murphy, 'The GAA during the Irish Revolution', in Cronin, Murphy and Rouse (eds), *The Gaelic Athletic Association, 1884–2009*, p. 68.
21 Ibid.
22 Murphy, *Derry, Donegal and Modern Ulster*, p. 246.
23 Ibid., p. 247.
24 Crime Branch. Returns of Political Organisations in Donegal on 30 September 1919, 1 October 1919. CO904/110.
25 See *DD*, 4 July 1919 and *DJ*, 29 August 1919.

26 *DP and DN*, 13 July 1918 and *DJ*, 23 June 1919.
27 Peter Hart, 'The Geography of Revolution in Ireland, 1917–1923', *Past and Present*, vol. 155, no. 1 (1997), pp. 142–76, p. 142.
28 Murphy, *Derry, Donegal and Modern Ulster, 1790–1921*, p. 258.
29 Ibid., pp. 258–9.
30 Hart, 'The Geography of Revolution in Ireland', pp. 157–60. Hart has stated that 'local initiative and organisation were the deciding factor, not guns'.
31 Garvin, *The Evolution of Irish Nationalist Politics*, pp. 138–9.
32 Ibid., p.136.
33 Murphy, *Derry, Donegal and Modern Ulster*, pp. 261–2.
34 Ulster GAA Council Minutes, Vol. 1, Ulster Council Reorganising Meeting Minutes, 22 October 1921.
35 Ibid. GAA activity in counties Monaghan and Armagh had stalled but this was not deemed a problem as it was felt that they could quickly be reorganised. Tyrone was also said to be inactive but in Derry, Fermanagh, Cavan and Down, championships were going ahead and the Council ordered that the 1921 Gaelic football championships be played at once.
36 Murphy, 'The GAA during the Irish Revolution', p. 74.
37 Ó Duibhir, *The Donegal Awakening*, pp. 126–7.
38 *DP and DN*, 10 April 1920.
39 See *DD*, 25 January 1925 and 15 December 1934.
40 *DJ*, 21 May 1920.
41 Ibid., 16 September 1921 and 11 November 1921. The White Cross fund was organised to raise money for families of Volunteers involved in the War of Independence. Tómás O'Riordan, 'Hanna Sheehy Skeffington', retrieved from http://multitext.ucc.ie/d/Hanna_Sheehy-Skeffington [Accessed 4 February 2012].
42 *DJ*, 25 November 1921.
43 Murphy, 'The GAA during the Irish Revolution', p. 70.
44 *DP and DN*, 25 June 1921.
45 *DD*, 16 September 1921.
46 See *DJ*, 15 and 29 July, 5, 12 and 19 August, 9, 16 and 30 September 1921.
47 Hunt, *Sport and Society*, p. 199.
48 *DJ*, 3 March 1922.
49 Ibid., 20 January, 17 March and 19 May 1922.
50 'History of Glenties GAA Club', *Donegal GAA Yearbook, 1978* (Ballyshannon: Donegal Democrat Printers, 1978), pp. 23–4, p. 24.
51 Ibid., p. 23 and Seán MacConaill (ed.), *Idir Peil agus Pobal: A History of the GAA in the Parish of Ardara* (Ardara: Black Lion Books, 2004), p. 10.
52 P.S. Mac a' Ghoill, 'So We Began', *CLG Ard a' Ratha* (Ardara: CLCG Ard a' Ratha, 1980), pp. 2–3, p. 3 and 'History of Glenties GAA Club', p. 23.
53 Mac Conaill (ed.), *Idir Peil agus Pobal*, p. 24.
54 *DD*, 11 November 1921.
55 Ibid., 2 December 1921.
56 Ferriter, *The Transformation of Ireland*, pp. 254–5.
57 See *DD*, 13 April 1923 for a report of the 1922–3 Gaelic football county final between Ardara and Ballybofey.
58 Cronin, Duncan and Rouse, *The GAA: A People's History*, p. 154.
59 Ibid., p. 154.
60 *DD*, 1 June 1923.

61 Liam Ó Duibhir, *Donegal and the Civil War: The Untold Story* (Cork: Mercier Press, 2011), p. 48.
62 *DD*, 21 April 1922.
63 Ibid., 2 June 1922.
64 Cronin, Duncan and Rouse, *The GAA: A People's History*, p. 154.
65 See Appendices 5–10 for a breakdown of Gaelic football teams by area.
66 Neil Tranter, 'The Chronology of Organized Sport in Nineteenth-century Scotland: A Regional Study I – Patterns', *International Journal of the History of Sport*, vol. 7, no. 2 (1990), pp. 188–203, p. 200.
67 *DD*, 15 November 1930.
68 *DI*, 8 March 1919.
69 *DP and DN*, 18 August 1934.
70 Ibid., 19 November 1932.
71 Ibid., 9 December 1933 and 17 March 1934.
72 *DJ*, 5 June 1925. The Castlefin club, which won the county championship in 1922 failed to affiliate for the next two years' competitions. A dispute with the County Board over a failure to produce winners' medals and expenses for the semi-final and final appears to have been the cause of this. See also ibid., 1 April 1927. This poor relationship continued after a club had been reorganised under a new name in the area. In April 1927 St Mary's voted unanimously for their withdrawal from the County Board, their delegate listing a number of grievances against the Association that they felt had developed. These included the turning down of a player for intercounty selection and frustration with treatment of their protests.
73 *DD*, 8 February 1930.
74 *The Irish Press*, 23 February 1934.
75 *Thom's Irish Almanac and Official Directory, 1931* (Dublin: Alexander Thom, 1931), pp. 1007–8.
76 *DP and DN*, 8 May 1926.
77 *DJ*, 24 December 1926 and 20 July 1927 and *Gaelic Athlete* (hereafter referred to as *GA*), 3 April 1926.
78 These had been organised in Dunfanaghy, Annagry, Kincasslagh, Marameelin and Mullaghduff by the end of 1933 while senior clubs such as Dungloe and Gweedore also fielded reserve teams to strengthen competition there.
79 *DJ*, 27 July 1928.
80 Pat Conaghan, *Bygones: New Horizons on the History of Killybegs* (Killybegs: Bygones Enterprise, 1989), p. 294.
81 See *DD*, 25 February 1928 and *DJ*, 31 October 1930.
82 *DJ*, 7 November 1930.
83 See *DD*, 23 October 1933 and 21 November 1933.
84 *DJ*, 21 November 1930.
85 Ibid., 20 November 1931.
86 Ibid., 24 March 1933. Glencolumbkille, Kilcar and Killaghtee entered the senior championship along with Ardara. Ardara were also represented in the junior competition along with Killaghtee and Owentocker.
87 Ibid., 21 January 1924.
88 Ibid., 25 January 1924.
89 See *DP and DN*, *DJ* and *DPP*, 1934 for references to these teams.
90 De Burca, *The GAA: A History*, p. 161.
91 Ibid.

92 Kevin Whelan, 'The Geography of Hurling', retrieved from http://www.askaboutIreland.ie/show_narrative_page.do?page_id=2352 [Accessed 13 February 2008].
93 Ibid.
94 *DJ*, 11 April 1919.
95 Ibid., 3 December 1924.
96 Hunt, *Sport and Society in Victorian Ireland*, pp. 197–8.
97 See *DJ*, 2 January 1924 and *DD*, 14 November 1924.
98 *DP and DN*, 13 October 1928.
99 See, for example, *DJ*, 10 December 1920 and 18 May 1923.
100 Ibid., 31 August 1923. Exhibition matches in both Gaelic football and hurling were organised at Pollan Greens, Ballyliffin, 'to raise interest' on 23 September with special train services to be run, while Mr Fay agreed to present medals for the league winners. Inch Emeralds, Cahir O's, Carndonagh, Carrowmore, Burt Hibernians, Carrowkeel and Moville joined this hurling league.
101 Ibid., 2 January 1924 and 4 April 1924. Burt Hibernians won the hurling title on 26 December 1923. See also ibid., 28 September 1923. A league was also said to have been set up in 1923 by the County Board with three teams in the east affiliating but there is no evidence that this was finished. Lifford, Letterkenny and Raphoe were all said to be involved in this but there was little recorded of their progress.
102 Ibid., 28 September 1923.
103 *DD*, 26 December 1924.
104 Ibid., 9 January 1925.
105 Ibid., 13 August 1926. Burt Hibernians, Newtowncunningham Red Hughs, Buncrana Military and Lifford were all named as participants.
106 Ibid., 15 January, 26 March 1927 and 19 May 1928. Only three teams, all from the Ballyshannon area, were included in the draw in 1927 but the following year, six teams had entered with Inishowen clubs Moville and Newtowncunningham becoming involved. Derry Gaels and Letterkenny joined these two teams in the northern section while in the south, Ballyshannon and Bundoran also entered.
107 Ibid., 27 April 1923.
108 Ibid.
109 *DV*, 15 March, 10, 17 May and 7 June 1924 and *DD*, 5 December 1924.
110 *DV*, 4 April 1925 and *DD*, 2 October 1925.
111 *DD*, 4 February 1933.
112 *DJ*, 5 May 1933. Guard Walsh was particularly scathing of the lack of effort shown by the County Board and claimed that they were in operation only to promote Gaelic football. He felt that his club, St Eunan's, had 'done all it could to further hurling but it found the county board lacking'.
113 Ibid.
114 Ibid., 22 May 1933.
115 *DD*, 23 December 1934.
116 Ibid. A competition for under sixteens had also been played, with Buncrana, Burt, Letterkenny and Carndonagh playing for the Toal Cup, donated by the Ballyshannon club.
117 *DJ*, 10 December 1934. Inishowen teams Burt, Inch, St Mary's (Buncrana), Carndonagh Cuchulainns, St Comgall's of Carrowmore and

Moville took part along with St Eunan's of Letterkenny and Donegal town.
118 *DD*, 21 August 1926 and *DV*, 22 August 1931.
119 *DP and DN*, 20 January 1934.
120 Ibid.
121 Ibid.
122 Ulster GAA Council Minutes, Vol. 1, Annual Convention, 13 March 1926.
123 *DP and DN*, 31 August 1918 and 22 March 1919 and *DI*, 5 October 1918.
124 *DP and DN*, 31 July and 28 August 1920.
125 Ibid., 31 August 1921.
126 *DJ*, 8 August and 12 September 1923 and 20 August 1924.
127 *DD*, 20 February 1920.
128 Ibid., 3 July 1922. The National Athletics and Cycling Association took over the responsibility from the GAA of organising athletics that year. See Cronin, Duncan and Rouse, *The GAA: A People's History*, p. 50.
129 *DJ*, 7 September 1923. With the low number of clubs in the south and south-west, the decision was taken to combine these divisions for the 1923–4 season, as only six clubs from Ardara, Killybegs, Glenties, Bundoran, Ballyshannon and Donegal town had affiliated in these areas.
130 *DD*, 7 November 1924.
131 Ibid., 28 February 1928. This all-county league was deemed a failure with a number of teams withdrawing before Christmas. See also *DJ*, 27 November 1925 and *DD*, 29 May 1926.
132 *DJ*, 27 July and 9 November 1928.
133 *DJ*, 5 November 1926. Apart from 1926–7, the county championship was played on a divisional league basis with a knockout system coming into play at the semi-final stage.
134 See, for example, *DP and TN*, 13 May 1933.
135 Ibid.
136 *DD*, 15 March 1930.
137 See, for example, Ulster GAA Council Minutes, Vol. 1, Meeting of Council, 1 July 1922.
138 *DD*, 7 April 1928.
139 Ibid., 2 April 1926.
140 Ibid., 12 April 1930.
141 An tAth. Seán Ó Gallachóir, *The Raidio na Gaeltachta Book of Donegal GAA Facts* [Third edition] (Letterkenny: Raidió na Gaeltachta, 1996), p. 97.
142 *DD*, 25 May 1923.
143 De Burca, *The GAA: A History*, p. 131.
144 *The Irish Press GAA Golden Jubilee Supplement, 1934*, p. 26.
145 An extensive trawl of information on soccer clubs and organising committees in the press revealed few references to the involvement of national school teachers in the 1920s and early 1930s. These men were usually denoted with an 'NT' in GAA news. One exception was J. O'Boyce, who presented medals after a Portsalon soccer tournament in May 1932 (see *DJ*, 20 May 1932).
146 *DD*, 6 February 1925.
147 McAnallen, 'Cén Fáth a Raibh Cúige Uladh Chomh Lag Chomh Fada Sin?', pp. 138–51, p. 148.
148 Liam McNiffe, *A History of the Garda Síochána: A Social History of the Force*

1922–52, With An Overview of the Years 1952–97 (Dublin: Merlin, 1997), p. 113.

149 Ibid.

150 See, for example, *DJ*, 22 December 1922 and 11 April 1924.

151 *DJ*, 22 December 1922 and 2 November 1923 and *DD*, 8 February 1924. This Donegal town team went on to win the county championship that year.

152 *DJ*, 23 November 1923.

153 Ibid., 3 December 1932.

154 *DD*, 8 February 1930 and *DJ*, 13 November 1931.

155 *DJ*, 30 June 1924.

156 Ibid., 6 October 1930.

157 Ibid., 11 March 1932.

158 McNiffe, *A History of the Garda Síochána*, p. 116.

159 *DJ*, 17 February 1928.

160 Ibid., 13 January 1928.

161 De Burca, *The GAA: A History*, p. 145.

162 *DP and DN*, 28 February 1931.

163 *DD*, 10 October 1931.

164 Ibid., 13 January 1934.

165 Ibid.

166 Ibid., 9 September 1933.

167 See Ó Gallchóir, *The Raidio na Gaeltachta Book of Donegal GAA Facts*, pp. 24–5 and Donegal GAA Archives. GAA /1/4/1 (7) (1–16) and GAA /1/4/1 (8) (1–16).

168 Donegal GAA Archives, Letter from Seán Collins to Seán Ó Caiside, 31 August 1933. GAA/1/4/1 (6) (28).

169 Donegal GAA Archives, Undated letter from Seán Ó Caiside to each member of Donegal team before the All-Ireland junior Gaelic football semi–final, 1933. GAA/1/4/1 (11) (1).

170 *DD*, 13 January 1934.

171 Donegal GAA Archives. Letter from Seán Ó Caiside to Brother Lucien, 13 November 1933. GAA /1/4/1/ (9) (6).

172 Ibid., 8 February 1924.

173 *DD*, 6 February 1932.

174 Donegal GAA Archives, Telegram from Micheál Óg McFadden to Seán Ó Caiside, 29 September 1933. GAA/1/4/1 (7) (16).

175 De Burca, *The GAA: A History*, p. 138.

176 McAnallen, 'Cén Fáth a Raibh Cúige Uladh Chomh Lag Chomh Fada Sin?', p. 149.

177 *DP and TN*, 29 May 1926.

178 *DJ*, 17 February 1928.

179 *DD*, 25 January 1930.

180 Ibid., 3 January 1931.

181 Ibid., 27 May 1933.

182 Ibid., 30 June 1934.

183 Ibid., 28 March 1924.

184 Ibid.

185 Ibid., 16 April and 21 August 1926.

186 Ibid., 2 April 1926.

187 *FH*, 6 June 1903. Belturbet United won the Jackson Cup, a competition for soccer clubs in South Ulster, in 1903.
188 *DP and TN*, 9 February 1929.
189 See, for example, *DP and DN*, 26 April, 1924, *DD*, 13 February and 10 October 1925.
190 *DD*, 25 November 1921 and *DJ*, 24 November 1922.
191 *DJ*, 24 November 1921.
192 *DD*, 5 March and 2 April 1932.
193 *DP and DN*, 3 September 1921.
194 *DD*, 21 August 1926.
195 *DJ*, 21 December 1931 and 18 November 1932.
196 *DV*, 7 March 1931.
197 *DD*, 1 August 1931.
198 See Cronin, Duncan and Rouse, *The GAA: A People's History*, p. 281. While the encouragement of Irish music, songs and the language are part of the GAA's *Official Guide*, it was not until 1969 that Scór was founded to promote cultural competitions and its levels of success have varied with some counties showing greater interest than others.
199 Tadhg Ó hAnnracháin, 'The Heroic Importance of Sport: The GAA in the 1930s', *International Journal of the History of Sport*, vol. 25, no. 10 (2008), pp. 1326–37, p. 1334.
200 *DD*, 20 March 1925.
201 Ibid., 22 October 1927.
202 *DV*, 2 June 1928.
203 Ibid., 16 June 1928. The meeting was addressed by A.J. Cassidy, TD, and a provisional committee was formed.
204 *DD*, 16 January 1932.
205 *DJ*, 10 August 1934.
206 Ibid., 13 October 1928.
207 Ibid., 19 March 1920.
208 Ibid., 13 April 1923.
209 Ibid., 13 June 1924.
210 Ibid., 12 May 1928.
211 Ibid.
212 Cronin, Rouse and Duncan, *The GAA: A People's History*, pp. 77–106.
213 *DD*, 15 May 1926.
214 Ibid., 12 March and 19 March 1926.
215 Ibid., 14 May 1927.
216 Cronin, Duncan and Rouse, *The GAA: A People's History*, p. 50.
217 *DV*, 16 June 1928.
218 De Burca, *The GAA: A History*, p. 135.
219 *DJ*, 3 July 1925.
220 *DD*, 12 October 1929.
221 Ibid., 29 October 1929,
222 Ibid., 2 August 1930.
223 *DV*, 24 May 1924.
224 *DJ*, 17 June 1925.
225 Ibid., 23 February 1934.
226 Ibid., 19 January 1934.
227 Ibid.

228 Ibid., and *DD*, 3 February 1934.
229 *DD*, 3 February 1934.
230 *DJ*, 7 December 1934.
231 Ibid.
232 Ibid.
233 Ibid., 15 January 1934.
234 *DD*, 3 February 1934.
235 Ibid.
236 Ibid.
237 Donegal GAA Archives, Letter from Seán Bonner to Seán Ó Caiside, 4 October 1933. GAA/1/4/1/(8) (3).
238 See *DJ*, 6 March 1925 and GAA Archives, Letter from A. Delap to Seán Ó Caiside, 4 Jan 1934. GAA/1/4/1 (12) (1).
239 Donegal GAA Archives, Letter from F.J. Murphy to Seán Ó Caiside, 7 July 1933. GAA 1/4/1/(5) (2). 'Weans' is a Scottish, North-east England and Donegal word for children.
240 *DD*, 11 January 1930.
241 Donegal GAA Archives. Letter from F.J. Murphy to Seán Ó Caiside, 31 August 1933. GAA 1/4/1/ (6) (31).
242 De Burca, *The GAA: A History*, p. 151.
243 Hart, 'The Geography of Revolution in Ireland', p. 169.
244 Cronin, Duncan and Rouse, *The GAA: A People's History*, p. 50.

6. The development of association football in County Donegal, 1881–1935

1 Garnham, *Association Football and Society*, pp. 4–5.
2 Taylor, *The Association Game*, pp. 30–1.
3 Ibid., p. 28. The Sheffield Football Club appears to have been the first of these in 1855.
4 *DV*, 30 March 1894.
5 Mason, *Association Football and English Society*, p. 1.
6 Dick Duffy, 'The Growth of Soccer in Letterkenny', *Letterkenny and District Christmas Annual, 2011* (Letterkenny: Browne Printers, 2011), pp. 42–4, p. 42.
7 *DJ*, 25 July 1881. This appears to be the first reference to the playing of 'association football' in the county.
8 Ibid.
9 Ibid., 23 February 1885.
10 Tranter, 'The Patronage of Organised Sport in Central Scotland', p. 227.
11 *DJ*, 30 January 1882. See also 9 and 11 August 1882.
12 Ibid., 12 June 1885.
13 *Sport*, 2 May and 24 October 1885.
14 *DJ*, 1 February 1882.
15 James Walvin, *The Only Game: Football in our Times* (Harlow: Longman, 2001), p. 33.
16 Hunt, *Sport and Society*, p. 183 and *DJ*, 24 April 1882. See also *DS*, 22 May and 14 October 1895.
17 In 1891 the *DV* and *DJ* contained a number of references to three clubs in Rathmullan and two each in Castlefin, Letterkenny and Bundoran. Buncrana, Kerrykeel, Milford, Ramelton, Cranford, Ballyshannon, Ardara and Nairn

were all able to field teams that year. Clubs recorded the following year included Castlefin, Doohan, Letterkenny FC, Kerrykeel FC, Carradoan, Golan, Milford Harps, Milford Swifts, Boylagh Champion Kilclooney AFC, Castlefin Wanderers, Castlefin Young Stars, Ramelton FC, Ramelton Sunbursts, Cranford Athletics FC, The Rivals (Letterkenny), Volunteers (Letterkenny), Ray Shamrocks, Tyrconnell Swifts, Buncrana FC, Sea View, Carrick, Glenree, Rathmullan, Craig, Carradoan Fr Matthew FC, Dungloe FC, Kincasslagh Shamrocks, Dungloe Swifts, Millview, Ramelton United, Bridge End Celtic, Moville FC, Kilraine Grand Rapids FC, Manorcunningham FC and St Adaman's Swifts.

18 *DJ*, 7 April 1890.

19 See ibid., 26 September 1890, 21 October 1891, 4 March 1892 and 28 April 1893.

20 Ibid., 17 October 1890 and *DS*, 30 November 1891.

21 *DJ*, 9 March 1894.

22 Ibid., 3 October and 29 October 1894 and 16 March 1898.

23 Ibid., 30 March 1894.

24 Ibid., 19 September 1894.

25 Ibid., 9 March 1894.

26 Ibid., 14 and 16 March 1894.

27 Ibid., 31 May 1895.

28 Ibid., 6 March 1896.

29 See, for example, ibid., 25 March, 22 November 1895 and 3 June 1896.

30 Ibid., 3 June 1896 and Metcalfe, 'Football in the Mining Communities of East Northumberland', p. 279.

31 Taylor, *The Association Game*, p. 39. The Sheffield FA was founded in 1867.

32 Garnham, *Association Football and Society*, p. 5.

33 Ibid., pp. 5–6 and *Anglo-Celt*, 12 November 1904.

34 *Leitrim Observer*, 9 December 1911.

35 McElligott, 'Forging a Kingdom', p. 89. Soccer was not introduced into Kerry until 1894 and only six matches involving Kerry teams were played in the 1890s. McElligott also states that the game was largely restricted to foreign employees and the military within the county in the late nineteenth and early twentieth centuries.

36 Irish Football Association Minute Book 1903–1909, Council Meeting, Belfast, 9 October 1906. D/4196/A/2. p. 165

37 Taylor, *The Association Game*, p. 39.

38 See Appendix 12.

39 Garnham, *Association Football and Society*, p. 45.

40 *IR*, 10 January 1889; *DI*, 24 April 1896 and *DV*, 17 and 24 April 1896.

41 *DV*, 1 May and 4 September 1891. See Moira Mallon, 'Killybegs Emeralds', *Dearcadh: The Ardara View, 1996–7* (Letterkenny: The Donegal Stationary Co., 1996), pp. 52–3, p. 52 and 'St Catherine's FC Profile', *Donegal Post*, 5 March 2008. Railway workers from Derry are said to have brought soccer to Killybegs a few years prior to this foundation.

42 *DV*, 1 May 1890.

43 'St Catherine's FC Profile', *Donegal Post*, 5 March 2008.

44 *DI*, 26 April and 31 May 1890.

45 *DJ*, 5 February and 24 August 1892.

46 Ibid., 21 March 1892.

47 Ibid., 9 August 1882, 21 March 1890 and 31 May 1895.
48 *FH,* 28 March and 25 April 1908.
49 *DJ,* 7 February and 24 March 1899.
50 Ibid., 20 March 1895 and 14 October 1896.
51 See, for example, Hunt, 'Parish Factions, Parading Bands and Sumptuous Repasts', p. 90 and Garnham, *Association Football and Society*, pp. 47–9.
52 *IR*, 22 January 1891 and 3 March 1892.
53 *DJ,* 11 February 1898.
54 *Sport*, 22 January 1887.
55 For an assessment of the impact of soccer and Glasgow Celtic on Irish immigrants in Scotland see Joseph M. Bradley, 'Football in Scotland: A History of Political and Ethnic Identity', *International Journal of the History of Sport*, vol. 12, no. 1 (1995), pp. 81–98 and 'Integration or Assimilation? Scottish Society, Football and Irish Immigrants', *International Journal of the History of Sport*, vol. 13, no. 2 (1996), pp. 61–79.
56 Joseph M. Bradley, *The Gaelic Athletic Association and Irishness in Scotland* (Argyll: Argyll Publishing, 2007), p. 50.
57 *DJ,* 15 June 1892. Dungloe Swifts and Kincasslagh Shamrocks met in a return match at Cruit Island on 21 August 1892. This appears to be the first reference in the local press to a match in the West Donegal area.
58 Derek Doherty, 'The History of the Gaelic Athletic Association in Donegal', unpublished MA thesis, National University of Ireland, Maynooth, 1998, p. 27.
59 See Ben O'Donnell, *The Story of the Rosses* (Lifford: Caoran Publishing, 1999), p. 382. He states that the Keadue team participated in matches against other local sides such as Cruit, Kincasslagh, Braide, Annagry, Mullaghduff, Maghery, Marameelan, Arranmore, Gweedore and Kincasslagh Shamrocks around this time.
60 'History: 1900–1910', retrieved from http://www.cavangaa.ie/1900_to_1910. html [Accessed 24 May 2013].
61 'Achill Rovers History: The Early Years', retrieved from http://achillrovers.com/achill_rovers_history_early_years_dooiver_swifts_htm [Accessed 2 September 2012].
62 Bracken, *'Foreign and Fantastic Field Sports'*, p. 115.
63 *DV*, 19 February 1897. Other teams noted in the *DV* in the Ballyshannon area that year included Ballyshannon Swifts, Coolmore, Kilbarron, Bright Stars, Lisahully, Cashelard, Cashel Heroes and Doobally.
64 Ibid.
65 Mason, *Association Football and English Society*, p. 31.
66 Conor Curran, 'Leisure in Ballyshannon in the Late Nineteenth Century'. Paper given at the Society for the Study of Nineteenth-Century Ireland Eighteenth Annual Conference, 28 June 2012.
67 *FH,* 23 December 1905.
68 Ibid., 6 October 1906.
69 Irish Football Association Minute Book 1903–1909, Council Meeting, Belfast, 9 October 1906. D/4196/A/2. p. 165.
70 See Appendix 12.
71 Tables have been compiled using information found in the *Derry Journal*, *Donegal Democrat*, *Donegal Vindicator*, *Donegal Independent*, *Derry People and Donegal News*, *Derry People and Tir Conaill News* and *Donegal People's Press* newspapers.

72 See Mac Conaill (ed.), *Idir Peil agus Pobal*, pp. 9–10; Micheál Ó Domhnaill (ed.), *CLG Cill Chartha, 1924–1884* (Donegal: CLG Cill Chartha, 1984), p. 10 and 'History of Glenties GAA Club', p. 23.
73 See Mac a' Ghoill, 'So We Began', p. 2 and *DP and DN*, 9 December 1916 for the last newspaper reference to Ardara Emeralds. Mac a' Ghoill has suggested that this decline in soccer in Ardara was in place as early as 1910 but this is at odds with newspaper reports.
74 *DJ*, 26 February 1915. Ardara Emeralds were beaten 5–0 at home to Killybegs Emeralds the previous week and do not appear to have won any trophies in the period from their foundation in 1891 until 1916.
75 *DV*, 25 May 1917.
76 *DP and DN*, 20 January 1917.
77 See Collins, *Rugby's Great Split*, pp. 180–8; Richard Holt, *Sport and Society in Modern France* (London: Palgrave Macmillan, 1981); Russell, 'Sporadic and Curious', p. 189 and Hunt, *Sport and Society in Victorian Ireland*, p. 166.
78 *DP and DN*, 20 January 1917.
79 Ó Domhnaill (ed.), *CLG Cill Cartha*, p. 10.
80 See *DI*, 28 February 1896 and *DV*, 17 December 1909. In 1896 Nyhan was a founder member of Erne FC while Woods donated a cup for soccer competition in 1909.
81 See *DP and DN*, 8 November 1924 and 14 February 1925.
82 *DV*, 18 August 1928.
83 See, for example, *DJ*, 2 July 1909 and *DJ*, 13 Feb 1911. While the annual soccer competition in connection with the Cranford Sports, first staged in the 1880s, and other sporadically held events such as an 'Inishowen Football Tournament', organised in 1911 as part of Clonmany Church Bazaar, did take place, it should be noted that these were usually held over a day or a few days and lacked a weekly knockout structure or league basis over which competitions were later staged. The football competition in aid of Clonmany Church was held for a set of silver medals with four teams involved in February 1911.
84 *DJ*, 19 January 1917.
85 Metcalfe, 'Football in the Mining Communities of East Northumberland', p. 273.
86 See *DJ*, 7 March 1906, 31 January 1912, 19 December 1913; *DV*, 7 January 1910; *DI*, 14 February 1914.
87 *Ulster Herald*, 10 January 1903 and 23 December 1905.
88 See *DJ*, 23 February 1906 and 16 January 1907; *DI*, 4 May 1906; *DV*, 17 December 1909, 7 January 1910, 31 January 1912, 17 January, 7 March 1913 and *DI*, 11 April 1913 and 14 February 1914.
89 See, for example, Tranter, 'The Patronage of Organised Sport in Central Scotland', pp. 227–47 and Hunt, *Sport and Society*, p. 164.
90 Retrieved from www.findmypast.co.uk/censushousehold search for 6, Knutsford Street, Kings Norton, Worcestershire. Census of England 1881. Public Record Office, RG 11/2950. [Accessed 29 July 2011]
91 Ibid., Census of England and Wales, 1911. Transcription details for 136 Salisbury Road, Moseley, Birmingham. [Accessed 29 July 2011].
92 See, for example, *DJ*, 30 January 1905.
93 See *DI*, 15 May 1915 and *DD*, 17 February 1956. Killybegs Emeralds' player Patrick Murrin was killed in action at Neuve Chapelle on Easter Monday,

1915. Ballyshannon Swifts founder James Sproule Myles was wounded at the Battle of the Somme and later decorated. See also *DV*, 28 January and 24 March 1916. A letter from Corporal Schoales, a native of Letterkenny, to the local press, requesting footballs to be sent to their base in Salonika, indicates the presence of soccer players from the Rosses and Letterkenny in a team he had selected. Two footballs were sent on 25 January by St Eunan's Sewing Guild for Soldiers' Comforts and were gratefully accepted by the corporal, as shown in a second letter. Corporal Schoales was 'one of three brothers serving at the front' and had worked for the Lough Swilly Railway Company prior to enlisting. He was wounded in action at the Dardanelles.

94 'Irish war memorials', retrieved from http://www.irishwarmemorials.ie/html/showMemorial.php?show=338 [Accessed 15 October 2011] and Cronin and Higgins, *Places We Play*, p. 90.

95 Garnham, *Association Football and Society*, pp. 167–74.

96 Irish Football Association Papers, Minute Book of IFA 1909–1928. D/4196 A/3 Report of Commission, 20 June 1919, p. 269.

97 *DJ*, 27 June 1919 and 7 July 1920.

98 Ibid., 25 July 1921.

99 *DV*, 13 February 1926.

100 Metcalfe, 'Football in the Mining Communities of East Northumberland', p. 277.

101 *DV*, 22 May and 23 October 1926 and *DJ*, 8 October 1926.

102 *DV*, 22 May and 23 October 1926.

103 *DJ*, 8 October 1926.

104 See, for example, *DV*, 20 February, 24 April and 29 May 1926.

105 *DV*, 13 February 1926.

106 See, for example, ibid., 6 March, 27 March and 3 April 1926.

107 Ibid., 10 December 1927.

108 *DV*, 10 April, 5 and 12 June 1926.

109 Liam Ryan, 'The GAA: Part of What We Are', *The Furrow* (Maynooth: St Patrick's College, 1984), pp. 752–64, p. 757.

110 *DJ*, 7 November and 12 December 1894 and *DI*, 17 January and 28 March 1913. In 1894, clubs from Buncrana and Letterkenny were criticised in the local press for fielding non-locals in friendlies and competitive matches respectively and it was also a problem in the Woods and Charity cups in Ballyshannon in 1913.

111 *DPP*, 26 March 1932 and 23 September 1933.

112 See, for example, *DV*, 31 August 1929, 15 February, 19 April and 7 June 1930; *DP and DN*, 8 and 15 April 1933 and *DJ*, 18 December 1931.

113 See *DJ*, 3 April 1932 and 2 March 1934 and FAI Junior Committee Minutes, September 1928–April 1932. P137/26. The Connacht Cup win by Killybegs was actually the delayed final for the previous season. While generally a competition for Connacht clubs, which was first organised after the trophy was donated by a Mr Travers in 1927, a number of more ambitious Donegal clubs such as Killybegs, Ballyshannon, Lifford United and Buncrana Rangers were in the draw in 1932.

114 *DPP*, 1 September 1934. See also *DJ*, 10 July 1931.This arrangement led to local GAA organisers boycotting the event in 1931.

115 For a discussion of this theory, see Campbell, Dowds and Mullan, *Against the Grain*, p. 142. The fact that Lough Swilly was heavily militarised by the

British until 1938 was thought to be the primary factor in the spread of soccer in this peninsula.

116 See *DJ*, 10 and 22 May 1929, 12 August 1932, 14 July 1933, 13 July and 14 September 1934. Teams representing the British Garrison at Fort Leenan appeared in 1929 and 1934. Dunree Rovers were in operation in 1932, 1933 and 1934 and competed in the Portsalon Cup in 1933 and 1934 and in the Kerrykeel Cup in 1933.

117 Ibid., 8 December 1934.

118 Ibid., 12 March 1923 and 12 June 1925.

119 Ibid., 29 August 1924.

120 Ibid., 19 September 1924.

121 Ibid., 21 January, 1 and 15 February 1924.

122 *DP and DN*, 29 November 1924.

123 *DJ*, 10 August 1934.

124 Ibid., 26 May 1926, 2 January 1927, 3 August 1928 and 31 May 1929.

125 Ibid., 27 May 1932, 18 August 1933 and 11 May 1934.

126 See *DPP*, 8 and 29 October 1932.

127 *DD*, 20 July 1923.

128 *DJ*, 16 July and 31 August 1923.

129 Ibid., 6 August 1926 and 6 July 1927.

130 *DJ*, 16 July 1926.

131 Russell, 'Sporadic and Curious', p. 195.

132 Ibid.

133 *DPP*, 21 May and 1 October 1932.

134 Ibid., 14 October 1932 and 7 April 1933.

135 *DJ*, 9 March 1934 and *DP and DN*, 10 March 1934.

136 *DJ*, 23 March 1934.

137 Ibid., 9 September 1932.

138 *DPP*, 29 October 1932.

139 *DJ*, 11 April 1930. The Northern section was instead made up of the clubs of Milford Celtic, Kerrykeel, Creeslough Stars, Ramelton and Portsalon Celtic while the southern section consisted of Erne FC, Killybegs, Ballybofey Wanderers, Ballybofey Rangers and Drumoghill.

140 Ibid., 23 March 1931.

141 Ibid., 1 May 1931.

142 Ibid., 7 August 1931.

143 Ibid., 13 May 1932.

144 Ibid., 6 June 1927.

145 Ibid., 30 October 1931.

146 Ibid., 6 August 1926, 4 and 19 May 1933, 11 May 1934 and *DV*, 5 June 1926.

147 Derek Doherty, 'The History of the Gaelic Athletic Association in Donegal', unpublished MA thesis, National University of Ireland, Maynooth, 1998, pp. 28–9.

148 John K. Walton, *The British Seaside: Holidays and Resorts in the Twentieth Century* (Manchester: Manchester University Press, 2000), p. 97 and p. 103.

149 *DJ*, 3 July 1925, 23 July 1926 and 8 July 1932.

150 Ibid., 16 and 21 July 1926. A number of other Donegal players born in the north-east went on to play professionally in Britain. These included Charlie O'Hagan, who played for Everton and Tottenham Hotspur and a number of

Scottish clubs and Billy Gillespie, who captained Sheffield United to FA Cup Final victory in 1925. News of these players' progress appeared only sporadically in the local press, however.

151 Ibid., 25 July 1928.
152 Ibid., 28 May 1930 and 24 July 1931.
153 *DP and TN*, 27 November 1931.
154 Ibid., 27 July 1929.
155 Comerford, *Ireland: Inventing the Nation*, p. 226.
156 Campbell, Dowds and Mullan, *Against the Grain*, p. 120.
157 *DPP*, 2 May 1931 and 26 March 1932.
158 Ibid., 15 and 22 August 1931. See also Michael McLaughlin, *Inishowen's Senior Soccer Players* (Letterkenny: Browne Printers, 2004), p. 36. Mahon played one game in the Irish League which was a 1–0 victory against Bangor.
159 *DPP*, 15 August 1931.
160 *DP and TN*, 28 January 1933.
161 Ibid., 3 February 1934.
162 For Letterkenny Rovers 1927 organisers see *DP and DN*, 24 September 1927. For Ballybofey Wanderers administrators see, for example, *DJ*, 4 June, 5 October 1928, 4 April 1930 and 2 October 1931. For Lifford United see *DJ*, 18, 22 March 1929 and 4 December 1931.
163 See *DJ*, 1 May 1931 and 21 October 1932. The majority of Loughkeel Celtic and Milford Cup officials identified were Roman Catholics.
164 See, for example, *DP and TN*, 9 July, 23 July and 20 August 1927 for references to matches involving clubs representing Gweedore, the Rosses and Kincasslagh.
165 Ibid., 18 June, 9 July, 23 July, 6 and 20 August 1927.
166 *DD*, 19 January 1929.
167 *DPP*, 18 July 1931.
168 Ibid., 30 June 1934.
169 *DJ*, 27 October 1933.
170 *DP and TN*, 2 December 1933.
171 Irish Football Association Papers, Cash Book of the IFA, 1880–1897. D/4196 S/1.
172 Garnham, *Association Football and Society*, p. 178 and p. 181.
173 FAI Archives, International Recognition of the Football Association of the Irish Free State, 1922–1956, 17 March 1922. P137/1.
174 *DJ*, 1 April 1929 and *DP and TN*, 5 October 1929.
175 FAI Archives, Junior Committee Minutes, September 1928–March 1940, Meeting of organising committee, 17 September 1928. P137/26.
176 FAI Archives, Junior Committee Minutes, September 1928–March 1940. P137/26. For FAI junior cup draws see 14 December 1928, 20 December 1929, 12 December 1930, 11 December 1931, 8 January 1932, 1 December 1932, 1 December 1933 and 30 November 1934. Not all of these Donegal clubs entered each year and there were no Donegal entries in the draws for the 1930–1 and 1933–4 seasons.
177 FAI Archives, Consultative Committee Minutes, 1924–34, 30 November 1932 and 3 February 1933. P137/38.
178 Ibid., 29 November 1928. P137/38.
179 FAI Archives, Consultative Committee Minutes, 1924–34, 30 November 1932, 3 February and 31 March 1933. P137/38.

180 FAI Archives, Junior Committee Minutes, September 1928–March 1940, Ninth Annual Report, 7 June 1932. P137/26. See also De Burca, *The GAA: A History*, pp. 138–9. This was a reference to an entertainment tax imposed by de Valera's government in 1932 which exempted the GAA and NACA but included other sporting bodies such as the FAIFS.
181 FAI Archives, Consultative Committee Minutes 1924–1934, 30 November 1932. P137/38.
182 Ibid., 3 February 1933.
183 Ibid., 14 October and 30 November 1932.
184 *DV*, 10 April and 5 June, 1926 and *DJ*, 28 September 1928.
185 FAI Archives, Junior Committee Minutes, 1928–March 1940, Ninth Annual Report, 7 June 1932. P137/26.
186 The following clubs and teams were used for the purpose of this study: Ardara Emeralds, Donegal Celtic, Killybegs Emeralds, Ramelton, Letterkenny, Milford Swifts, Kerrykeel, Hunters (Milford), Harps (Milford), Letterkenny Rivals, Letterkenny Volunteers, Kerrykeel Wanderers, Milford Rovers, Buncrana FC, Rathmullan, Ramelton United, Bridgend Celtic, Greencastle, Carradoan, Cranford, Carrownaganonagh Shamrocks, Clonmany, Milltown Mills (Convoy), Gleneely, Killybegs Tyrconnells, Killybegs Shamrocks, Drimgorman Swifts, Raphoe Rangers, Gortmacall Gems, Loughkeel Celtic, Erne FC, Erne Stars, Ballintra, Ballyshannon Swifts, Cashelard, Doobally, Cashel Heroes, Ballintra Hibernians, Erne 98s, Glenties, Glenties Sunlights, Bundoran De Wets and Ballyshannon Blazers.
187 Hunt, *Sport and Society*, p. 186.
188 Ibid., p. 187.
189 Garnham, *Association Football and Society*, p. 66.
190 Ibid.
191 Ibid., p. 97.
192 Ibid., p. 99.
193 Ibid.
194 Hunt, *Sport and Society*, p. 188.
195 Ibid., p. 178.
196 These included members of the County Donegal FA, the Evans Cup committee, the Woods Cup committee, the Britton Cup committee, Donegal Celtic, Ballyshannon Blazers, Killybegs Emeralds, Erne FC, Ardara Emeralds, Ardara Sons of Tyrconnell, Kilclooney Boylagh Champion, Donegal Shamrocks, Convoy Celtic, Mountcharles Football & Cricket Club, Dungloe, Dungloe Rovers, Burnfoot FA, Milford, Ballybofey Hibernians, Rosses Rovers, Gweedore Celtic, Loughkeel Celtic, Ballybofey, Kerrykeel, Ramelton, Ramelton Sunbursts, Letterkenny, Cranford Athletics, The Vindicator FC (Rathmullan), Milford Swifts, Moville, Kilraine Grand Rapids, Manorcunningham, Glenties Hibernians, Downstrands Young Bloods and Castlefin.

7. The conflict between the GAA and association football in County Donegal, 1905–1935

1 Garnham, *Association Football and Society in Pre-partition Ireland*, p. 30.
2 Ibid.
3 Taylor, *The Association Game*, p. 105.
4 *Anglo-Celt*, 14 January 1905.
5 Rouse, 'The Politics of Culture and Sport in Ireland', p. 334.

6 Ibid.
7 Cronin, *Sport and Nationalism in Ireland*, p. 85.
8 Ferriter, *The Transformation of Ireland*, p. 427.
9 Examples include Gweedore Celtic, Gweedore Harps, Cashleenan Hibernians and Buncrana Shamrocks.
10 Cronin, *Sport and Nationalism*, p. 124.
11 Ibid., p. 125.
12 'FAI History: The Early Years', retrieved from http://www.fai.ie/fai/history/the-early-years.html [Accessed 17 October 2011].
13 Cronin, *Sport and Nationalism*, p. 129.
14 *DV*, 19 January 1929.
15 *DJ*, 5 October 1928.
16 Ibid., 3 December 1926 and 17 February 1928.
17 Donegal GAA Archives, Letter from S. Maguidir to Seán Ó Caiside, 15 March 1933. GAA/1/4/1(1) (8).
18 *DJ*, 5 October 1928.
19 Collins, *Rugby's Great Split*, pp. 180–8.
20 See, for example, *DJ*, 13 August 1928.
21 GAA Archives, Croke Park. Central Council Minute Book, 1911–1925. GAA/CC/01/02. Central Council Special Meeting, 24 August 1924, p. 748.
22 Ulster GAA Council Minutes, Vol. 1, Reorganising Meeting, 22 October 1921.
23 Cronin, Duncan and Rouse, *The GAA: A People's History*, p. 192.
24 *DP and DN*, 30 September 1905.
25 Ibid.
26 See, for example, *LS*, 21 November 1905, 3 and 17 May 1906.
27 John Ward, 'Pa McAdam: The Grandfather I Never Knew', retrieved from http://www.vindicator.ca/history/vinStory/vinStory1.html [Accessed 31 October 2010].
28 'Donegal Democrat: Democrat History', retrieved from http://www.donegaldemocrat.ie/CustomPages/CustomPage.aspx?PageID=56736'Donegal Democrat-Democrat History' [Accessed 30 October 2010].
29 Ibid.
30 *DPP*, 10 September 1932.
31 See *DV*, 7 May 1897 and 14 February 1902 and 10 February 1905; *DJ*, 30 November 1898 and *DI*, 7 October 1904.
32 *LS*, 17 August 1905.
33 Cronin, *Sport and Nationalism*, p. 78.
34 *DJ*, 1 March 1905.
35 Ibid.
36 Ibid., 19 May 1905 and 11 May 1906.
37 Ibid., 10 November 1905.
38 Ibid., 20 April 1906.
39 Cronin, *Sport and Nationalism*, p. 124.
40 *DI*, 15 November 1901.
41 *DJ*, 18 August 1902.
42 Ibid., 14 April 1905.
43 Ibid., 19 April 1905.
44 Ibid., 3 November 1905.

45 Ibid., 27 October 1905.
46 See, for example, *DP and DN*, 24 February and 26 October 1906 and *DI*, 8 February 1907.
47 *DI*, 15 March 1907.
48 Ibid., 7 August 1908 and *DP and DN*, 21 May 1910.
49 Hunt, *Sport and Society*, pp. 193–6.
50 McElligott, 'Forging a Kingdom', pp. 129–32.
51 *DI*, 27 October 1905.
52 *DP and DN*, 5 May 1906. See also *DV*, 5 December 1919. Ulster GAA Council secretary Eoin O'Duffy claimed in 1919 that an attempt had been made by 'an official of the Derry soccer council' to bribe the Donegal GAA county secretary John Curran with the offer of a cup, financial aid and the organisation of a soccer competition. It is difficult to prove whether or not this attempt was made but the organisation of soccer in Donegal did not improve at the time.
53 Garnham, *Association Football and Society*, p. 40.
54 *LS*, 17 August 1905.
55 Ibid.
56 *DJ*, 17 November 1905.
57 Ibid.
58 Ibid., 14 May 1906.
59 Ibid., 16 May 1906.
60 Ibid., 6 July 1906.
61 *DP and DN*, 18 October, 13 December 1913, 21 February, 7 March and 9 May 1914.
62 *DP and TN*, 12 April 1926.
63 Ibid., 12 May 1928.
64 *DD*, 20 July 1923. 'Shoneen' was a derogatory term used to describe an Irish person said to be imitating English conduct.
65 *DP and TN*, 27 May 1933.
66 Ibid., 7 February 1931.
67 Donegal GAA Archives, Letter from J. Hourihane to Seán Ó Caiside, 3 April 1933. GAA 1/4/1 (2) 1.
68 Ibid., Letter from A. Delap to Seán Ó Caiside, 27 December 1933. GAA /1/4/1 (10) (11).
69 *Thom's Irish Almanac and Official Directory, 1931* (Dublin: Alexander Thom, 1931), p. 1014.
70 *DD*, 23 October 1925.
71 See, for example, *DP and TN*, 23 February 1926.
72 *DP and TN*, 23 February 1926.
73 See, for example, ibid., 13 March, 3 July and 14 August 1926.
74 *DJ*, 13 August 1928.
75 Ibid.
76 *DP and TN*, 26 July 1930.
77 *GA*, 3 February 1912.
78 Ibid., 15 March 1913.
79 Ibid., 30 January 1915 and 4 March 1916.
80 Ó hAnnracháin, 'The Heroic Importance of Sport', p. 1332.
81 *DD*, 16 April 1926 and *GA*, 27 February 1926.
82 *DV*, 15 May 1926.

83 *DJ*, 9 April 1930.
84 *DP and TN*, 16 April 1932.
85 Ibid., 12 February 1927.
86 *DJ*, 17 February 1928.
87 Ibid., 15 July 1927.
88 Ibid., 30 September and 24 October 1927.
89 *DD*, 13 July 1923 and *DP and TN*, 5 February 1927.
90 *DJ*, 4 June 1928.
91 Ibid., 18 June 1928.
92 Ibid., 20 June 1928.
93 Ibid., 27 July 1928.
94 Ibid., 9 November 1928.
95 *DP and DN*, 5 January 1924.
96 Ibid.
97 *DP and TN*, 4 October 1925.
98 *DD*, 15 May 1926.
99 *DJ*, 27 July and 1 August 1928.
100 Ibid., 6 August 1928.
101 Ibid., 12 August 1928.
102 Ibid., 10 August 1928.
103 Ibid., 13 August 1928.
104 Ibid., 13 August and 17 August 1928.
105 *DP and TN*, 30 May 1931.
106 *Football Sports Weekly*, 5 February 1927. I am grateful to David Toms for drawing my attention to this newspaper (hereafter referred to as *FSW*).
107 *DD*, 25 May 1929.
108 *DJ*, 24 June 1929.
109 *DPP*, 18 July 1931.
110 Donegal GAA Archives, Letter from Sergeant Cullen to Seán Ó Caiside, 4 October 1933. GAA/1/4/1 (8) (2) and *DP and TN*, 2 December 1933.
111 *DJ*, 28 September 1928.
112 Ibid. This letter listed a county selection to play Killygordon in the second counter fixture although whether it was written by those within the county board is not clear. The writer also stated that 'we claim and have the right to get the support of the whole county for our games'. Although today it is spelt *Uachtarán*, meaning president, this word appears to have been written in old Irish in the 1928 letter.
113 *DJ*, 5 October 1928.
114 *FSW*, 11 February 1928. Traynor, a Republican leader in the Civil War, had played in goal for Belfast Celtic during the 1911–12 and 1912–13 seasons. See also ibid., 2 April 1927. Belfast club Alton Celtic, who won the FAIFS Cup in 1923, were said to have been 'practically all members' of the Northern Division of the IRA.
115 *DJ*, 20 July 1934.
116 *DP and TN*, 29 September 1928.
117 *DJ*, 18 June 1919.
118 *DD*, 14 May 1920.
119 Ibid., 28 March and 26 December 1924.
120 Ibid., 20 March 1925.
121 Ibid., 29 June 1923.

122 Ibid., 1 January 1926.
123 *DP and TN*, 19 December 1925.
124 Ibid., 23 February 1926.
125 *DJ*, 18 March 1929.
126 Ibid., 22 March 1929.
127 Ibid., 15 February 1929.
128 *GA*, 10 October 1925.
129 Donegal GAA Archives, Letter from Seán Ó Cinneide to Seán Ó Caiside, 19 June 1933. GAA /1/4/1 (4) (6) and letter from James Cunningham to Seán Ó Caiside, 19 June 1933. GAA /1/4/1(4) (7).
130 Ibid. Letter from Leinster GAA to Seán Ó Caiside, 28 June 1933. GAA /1/4/1 (4) (11).
131 Ulster GAA Council Minutes, Vol. 1, Annual Convention, 17 March 1917.
132 Ulster GAA Council Minutes, Vol. 1, Ulster Council Meeting, 4 June 1924.
133 Ulster GAA Council Minutes, Vol. 2, Ulster Council Meeting, 14 July 1928.
134 *DD*, 12 March 1926.
135 *DJ*, 20 September 1929.
136 Ibid.
137 Ibid., 7 January 1927 and 28 January 1928.
138 *DP and TN*, 5 March 1932 and *DJ*, 1 August 1934. In July 1934, St Eunan's could only name six regulars in their senior team and had to field nine minor players.
139 *DJ*, 7 December 1934.
140 Ibid., 21 January 1935.
141 See *DV*, 27 June 1931 and *DD*, 27 June 1931.
142 *DP and TN*, 25 July 1931.
143 See, for example, Donegal GAA Archives, Letter from J. Hourihan to Seán Ó Caiside, 3 April 1933. GAA /1/4/1 (2) (1) and letter from Brother Lucien to Seán Ó Caiside, 13 April 1933. GAA/1/4/1 (2) (5).
144 *DP and TN*, 27 January 1934.
145 Ibid., 3 August 1934.
146 Ibid.
147 Ibid., 4 August 1934.
148 *DJ*, 7 November 1925.
149 Ibid., 26 August 1927.
150 Ibid.
151 Ó hAnnracháin, 'The Heroic Importance of Sport', p. 1336.
152 O'Callaghan, *Rugby in Munster*, p. 177.

CONCLUSION

1 De Burca, *The GAA: A History* and Mandle, *The Gaelic Athletic Association and Irish Nationalist Politics.*
2 Holt, *Sport and the British: A Modern History*, p. 238.
3 Murphy, *Derry, Donegal and Modern Ulster*, pp. 261–2.
4 See B.M. Walker, *Parliamentary Election Results in Ireland, 1801–1922* (Dublin: Royal Irish Academy, 1978), pp. 339–87 and *Parliamentary Election Results in Ireland, 1918–92: Irish Elections to Parliaments and Parliamentary Assemblies at Westminister, Belfast, Dublin, Strasbourg* (Dublin: Royal Irish Academy, 1992), pp. 101–33.
5 McElligott, 'Forging a Kingdom', pp. 273–4.

6 Ibid., p. 274.
7 Cronin, Duncan and Rouse, *The GAA: County by County*, p. 389.
8 Ibid., p. 81.
9 Ibid., p. 189.
10 *DD*, 14 October 1933. This can be best seen in the controversy surrounding the comments of Donegal GAA County Board chairman Seán Ó Caiside prior to the 1933 All-Ireland junior final regarding the South and West Donegal areas where the players were centred, which he had noted was 'only half the county'. This left members of the Eastern divisional board feeling aggrieved, but internal conflict was not something new, having also been a problem for the organisation of the 1905–7 County Board.
11 Donegal GAA Archives. Letter from Henry Forbes to Seán Ó Caiside, 9 August 1933. GAA 1/4/1 (6) (2). This was evident in the lead-up to the semi-final clash with Cork, when it was stated by the manager of the County Donegal Railways at Stranorlar that, having made enquiries 'at all our stations', he found that 'there would be very few travelling, more particularly as there are excursions arranged on this day to Enniskillen'.
12 Ó hAnnracháin, 'The Heroic Importance of Sport', p. 1327.
13 *DP and TN*, 10 December 1932.
14 *DJ*, 2 March 1934.
15 *DP and TN*, 29 July 1933.
16 Ibid., 2 September 1933.
17 Cronin, *Sport and Nationalism in Ireland*, p. 91.
18 Hunt, *Sport and Society*, p. 177.
19 See Bale, 'Sport and National Identity' and *Sports Geography*; Russell, 'Sporadic and Curious', pp. 185–205; Metcalfe, 'Football in the Mining Communities of East Northumberland', pp. 269–91; Huggins, 'The Spread of Association Football in North-east England', pp. 299–318; Collins, *Rugby's Great Split*; Hunt, *Sport and Society*; McAnallen, 'Playing on the Fourth Green State', National University of Ireland, Galway, 2010 and McElligott, 'Forging a Kingdom'.
20 McElligott, 'Forging a Kingdom', p. 275.
21 Ibid., p. 154.
22 'About the GAA – Rolls of Honour – All-Ireland Senior Football Championship', retrieved from http://www.gaa.ie/about-the-gaa/gaa-history/rolls-of-honour/ [Accessed 9 February 2012].
23 Ó Gallachóir, *The Raidió na Gaeltachta Book of Donegal GAA Facts*, p. 20. Donegal's 2014 Ulster final victory was only their eight provincial senior Gaelic football championship. In contrast, Kerry have won seventy-six Munster senior Gaelic football titles. 'Munster GAA – Senior Football – Number of Titles', retrieved from http://munster.gaa.ie/history/sf_teams/ [Accessed 17 December 2012].
24 Cronin, Duncan and Rouse, *The GAA: County by County*, p. 255 and p. 348.
25 Cronin and Higgins, *Places We Play*, p. 43.
26 Tony Collins, cited in Jonathan Wright, 'Britain's Love of Sport', *BBC History*, vol. 13, no. 2 (2012) pp. 78–9, p. 78.
27 Ibid.
28 'Sport and the British: The Dawn of Professional Football', retrieved from http://www.bbc.co.uk/podcasts/series/sportbrit#playepisode3 [Accessed 13 February 2012].

29 Mason, *Association Football and English Society, 1863–1915*, p. 21.

30 Ó Gallchóir, *The Raidió na Gaeltachta Book of Donegal GAA Facts*, pp. 60–1. In 2012, Glenswilly became the seventeenth Donegal GAA club to win the Dr Maguire Cup.

31 In 1992 fourteen of Donegal's starting fifteen in the final against Dublin were from the south and south-west. Donegal failed to add to their fifth Ulster senior Gaelic football championship, won in 1992, until their 2011 triumph over Derry and in 2012 they defeated Down in the Ulster final. In 2014 they beat Monaghan in the Ulster final. In September 2012 they won their second All-Ireland senior Gaelic football championship. The county was also successful in the National League final of 2007.

32 'Football Association of Ireland – Ireland's International Players', retrieved from http://www.fai.ie/international/senior-men/irelands-international-players.html [Accessed 17 December 2014]. As of 19 November 2014 Given was the Republic of Ireland's second-highest-capped international with 127 caps. Doherty was born in Carndonagh in 1980 and played thirty times for his country between 2000 and 2005. Coleman has already played twenty-five times at international level while Bonner finished his career in 1996 with eighty international appearances. Born in 1986, Ramelton's Conrad Logan is now part of Leicester City's first team squad and has appeared in goal a number of times for his club. Although recently released, in 2010 Manchester United signed then sixteen-year-old goalkeeper Joe Coll, who is a native of Gortahork in the north-west. Coll also played Gaelic football for Donegal Under 21s. Shay Given has stated that experience of ball handling and punching gained while playing Gaelic football as a teenager undoubtedly benefited his development as a goalkeeper. See Liam Porter, 'Donegal's Regular Player at Croke Park', *Dún na nGall GAA Yearbook, 2008* (Donegal: Donegal GAA County Board, 2008), pp. 58–61, p. 59.

33 Lisa Gray, 'Shay Given Interested in Celtic Switch', retrieved from http://www.independent.co.uk/sport/football/premier-league/shay-given-interested-in-celtic-switch-2288798.html [Accessed 9 February 2012]. Bonner and Given both joined Glasgow Celtic as teenagers.

34 'Donegal GAA Boss Jim McGuinness Accepts Celtic Role', retrieved from http://www.bbc.co.uk/sport/0/northern-ireland/20254492 [Accessed 4 December 2012].

35 See, for example, the case of Declan Boyle of Killybegs. In 1993, nineteen-year-old Boyle, arguably one of the most gifted dual footballers Donegal has ever produced, made his debut for Donegal in the Ulster senior Gaelic football championship against Armagh. He later joined Glasgow Celtic and, having failed to obtain a regular first-team place, returned to play professionally in the League of Ireland and Irish League.

Index

Note: page numbers in bold indicate illustrations. References to the GAA as an organisation are listed under Gaelic Athletic Association (GAA), while references to GAA as a sport are listed under Gaelic Games. All references to Gaelic football and hurling are included under Gaelic Games, as well as in their own separate entries.